Conversations with Eudora Welty

18.00

Conversations
with Eudora Welty

Edited by
Peggy Whitman Prenshaw

University Press of Mississippi
Jackson

Books by Eudora Welty
A Curtain of Green. Garden City: Doubleday, Doran, 1941.
The Robber Bridegroom. Garden City: Doubleday, Doran, 1942.
The Wide Net and Other Stories. New York: Harcourt, Brace, 1943.
Delta Wedding. New York: Harcourt, Brace, 1946.
The Golden Apples. New York: Harcourt, Brace, 1949.
The Ponder Heart. New York: Harcourt, Brace, 1954.
The Bride of the Innisfallen and Other Stories. New York: Harcourt, Brace, 1955.
The Shoe Bird. New York: Harcourt, Brace and World, 1964. (Children's Book)
Losing Battles. New York: Random House, 1970.
One Time, One Place: Mississippi in the Depression: A Snapshot Album. New
   York: Random House, 1971.
The Optimist's Daughter. New York: Random House, 1972.
The Eye of the Story: Selected Essays and Reviews. New York: Random House,
   1978.
The Collected Stories of Eudora Welty. New York: Harcourt Brace Jovanovich,
   1980.
One Writer's Beginnings. Cambridge: Harvard University Press, 1984.
Photographs. Jackson, Mississippi: University Press of Mississippi, 1989.

Library of Congress Cataloging-in-Publication Data
Main entry under title:

Conversations with Eudora Welty.

   Includes index.
   1. Welty, Eudora, 1909–   —Interviews.   2. Authors,
American—20th century—Biography.   I. Prenshaw,
Peggy Whitman.
PS3545.E6Z464   1984   813'.52   83-21668
ISBN 0-87805-205-4
ISBN 0-87805-206-2 (pbk.)

British Library Cataloging-in-Publication Data available

Contents

Introduction

This collection of interviews spans forty years of Eudora Welty's literary career. From these conversations an image of Welty emerges that differs in some respects from the authorial presence one meets in Welty's essays. Although she discusses many of the same subjects she has written about with great insight and understanding—writers and writing, the play of the imagination, her experience of growing up and living in the South, the Southern literary tradition—her exchanges with interviewers reflect a broader range of personality and mood than one typically encounters in Welty's more formal and highly crafted essays.

By her own admission, Welty is often uncomfortable at the beginning of an interview (she speaks sometimes of being a shy person), but as an interview progresses, she typically warms to her subjects and to the interviewers, especially to those who show they have read her fiction and are interested chiefly in having her talk about it. One senses that Welty's acquiescence to being interviewed comes both from her professionalism and her generosity. She evidently feels a sense of responsibility to the literary world, indeed a sense of community with this world very much like that she shares with friends and neighbors in Jackson, Mississippi. And so she has granted interviews when her books have been published, when she has won a Pulitzer Prize, when young scholars have wanted to "feature" her in their college literary magazines, as well as when writers and literary scholars have sought her out. In a few instances, she is interviewed by good friends, and with them she is understandably more open and more at ease than she is with others. With friend or stranger, however, Welty clearly relishes good conversation. Whatever resistance or wariness she expresses to being interviewed seems more a reaction to the tape recorder or note pad than to the social exchange.

In the summer of 1978, Tom Royals and John Little, both members of a creative writing class that Welty taught in 1964–65 at Millsaps College in Jackson, began their conversation with her by asking her opinion of the usefulness of interviews, specifically as an aid to understanding a writer's work. What is clear about her answer is her ambivalence about interviews. "I've always been tenacious in my feeling that we don't need to know a writer's life in order to understand his work," she said, "and I have really felt opposed to a lot of biographies that have been written these days . . . it's good to know something about a writer's background, but only what pertains. I'm willing to tell you anything I can if I think it has that sort of value. You asked me what I thought the value [of interviews] was, and I'm just not sure."

Despite her occasional discomfort and her doubts about the value of interviews, Welty has talked openly and thoughtfully about a variety of subjects in the twenty-six interviews collected here. From the earliest interview, Robert Van Gelder's 1942 piece for the *New York Times Book Review,* Welty has most often discussed her writing, especially the enjoyment she takes in the act of writing itself, the active play of the imagination with experience, the transmuting of place and society into setting and character. She has frequently been asked to compare the varying techniques required in the writing of short stories and in novels. She has dutifully answered questions about her daily writing routine, her method of revising, her early attempts at writing, and her self-taught lessons in her craft (mainly through reading and trial and error). Occasionally subjects arise, even regarding writing, that touch a nerve—questions about symbolism in her work, or in fiction in general, for instance. But even these questions she entertains seriously and patiently.

Throughout these conversations Welty speaks repeatedly of her good fortune in having had mentors and friends in the publishing world who from the beginning have helped her—her agent, Diarmuid Russell, her editor, John Woodburn, the early *Southern Review* staff, Robert Penn Warren, Cleanth Brooks, Albert Erskine. She tells of acts of generosity from Ford Madox Ford, Katherine Anne Porter, and many others. In virtually every interview she also discusses the writers whose work she enjoys reading. In her essays she has frequently written of her lifelong love of reading, and so it is no surprise that she speaks readily and at length to her interviewers about fiction she admires. Many of the writers she speaks of are those she has written about in *The Eye of the Story*—Jane Austen, Chekhov, Willa Cather, Katherine Anne Porter, and Henry Green. In the interviews, as in her writings, she also mentions Elizabeth Bowen, Katherine Mansfield, E. M. Forster, and William Faulkner, among others, as writers whose work she admires.

Second to the subject of writers and writing, Welty is most often questioned about her Southern background and her relation to the Southern literary tradition. She talks to Linda Kuehl about the designation, "regional writer," and discusses with her and many other interviewers, including William F. Buckley, Jr., the storytelling tradition in the South, which in Welty's view has been a shaping force on the Southern literary imagination. To Bill Ferris, Jean Todd Freeman, and others, she describes her travels in Mississippi during the 1930s when she worked with the Works Progress Administration and tells of the influence of the experience on her writing. She answers questions about racial relationships in the South, particularly during the 1960s, in interviews with Don Lee Keith, Alice Walker, Royals and Little, and others.

Often Welty's conversations about the South arise from questions about her childhood and family, and about her school days in Jackson and early college years at Mississippi State College for Women. She speaks of these personal experiences in a number of interviews, but particularly in those conducted by Jacksonians. For example, she talks to Christine Wilson and a group of Jackson school children about her years at Davis Elementary School in Jackson. Some of her most detailed accounts of growing up in Jackson and of her parents and family occur in the interviews conducted by Jane Reid Petty and John Griffin Jones.

Since many of the conversations take place at Welty's home in Jackson, interviewers typically include descriptions of her house and gardens, either in introductory comments or—usually in greater detail—in the body of those interviews that are written up as newspaper or magazine articles. To her friend Charlotte Capers, formerly the director of the Mississippi Department of Archives and History, Welty speaks of a number of her friends of long standing, prompted to do so in recounting the guests who were invited to Jackson to a special event proclaimed by the governor of Mississippi to honor her. The interview, which took place shortly after the announcement of Welty's winning the Pulitzer Prize for Fiction in 1973, also includes Welty's reactions to winning the prize.

Although Welty quite clearly regards some aspects of a writer's private life as properly belonging to him or her, not to be offered up to anyone with a question and a tape recorder, she is characteristically gracious and surprisingly forthcoming in taking on questions that are personal as well as professional. (The word "gracious" occurs repeatedly in interviewers' descriptions of her.) From the earliest interviews Welty has routinely refused to discuss work in progress, with the exception of a few comments in the Royals-Little interview, but she has answered innumerable questions about her published short stories and novels. The 1970 publication of *Losing Battles* furnishes the occasion for the Frank Hains and Walter Clemons interviews, for example, and she discusses the novel freely with both of them. Questions about women's issues, and about being a female writer, do not especially interest Welty, but she answers them tactfully and in good faith. She responds in writing to Barbaralee Diamonstein's lengthy questionnaire, which includes many such questions, and she talks forthrightly to Martha van Noppen about some of her experiences as a woman making her living as a writer.

Other kinds of topics clearly draw more interest from Welty. Time after time one senses her pleasure in talking about favorite subjects—her love of the theatre, for example, and her treasured memories of the New York theatre season in the early 1930s when she was living in New York. She speaks to several interviewers of her enjoyment of various dramatizations and musical productions of her works, and of her interest in the special demands of playwriting and theatrical production, differing as they do in many ways from literary composition. Despite Welty's obvious enjoyment of the conversations with her interviewers, she acknowledges to Jean Todd Freeman and others the toll of time and energy that interviewing exacts. Nevertheless, she has through the years generously and agreeably given a number of interviews, many of which appear in this volume.

The interviews I have selected for this collection represent in my judgment the most informative, and thereby the most important, of the published interviews with Eudora Welty. I have also sought to reflect in my selection among existing interviews something of the variety one finds in subjects discussed, in the kinds of publications in which the interviews originally appeared, and in the backgrounds of the interviewers. I have aimed to include all published interviews of substantial length that have appeared in question-answer format. For the most part, these are edited transcriptions of tape recorded interviews. Two other comparable interviews, those by Charlotte Capers and by Christine Wilson and the Jackson school children, have not been previously published. I am grateful to Miss Welty, the interviewers, and the Mississippi Department of Archives and History for permission to publish these.

Included in the collection are seven newspaper and magazine articles based on interviews. Two of these appeared in the *New York Times Book Review,* and two are long features that ran in the *Washington Post* and the New Orleans *Times-Picayune.* Of the number of articles appearing in the Jackson *Clarion-Ledger/Jackson Daily News* and other local publications, I have selected the pieces by Frank Hains, Raad Cawthon and Jane Petty for inclusion. With the exception of the Buckley interview of Welty and Walker Percy for the *Firing Line* program, which was subsequently published, I have not included transcriptions of televised interviews. Video tape recordings of some of these, most of which are quite brief, are available at the Mississippi Department of Archives and History, the major depository for Welty's papers. I have also excluded a few feature length articles because of the necessary limits of space, but most interviews omitted are those that have appeared in newspapers and magazines in connection with Welty's travels and lectures across the country. These pieces rarely give much more than biographical information, a summary of Welty's published works and literary awards, and a few brief answers to general questions.

The interviews in the collection are arranged chronologically according to the dates they took place; I have cited these dates following the title and the name of the interviewer. If no date of interview is recorded by the interviewer, I have used the publication date and internal evidence for dating the interview. Full bibliographical information about original publication is given on the first page of each interview.

I am deeply grateful to the many persons whose respect for Eudora Welty's writing led initially to these interviews, as well as to the publishers whose permission to reprint them made the collection possible. I wish also to acknowledge my gratitude to Miss Welty, who has given us, in addition to so many excellent books, so much excellent conversation.

PWP
Hattiesburg, Mississippi
September 1983

Conversations with Eudora Welty

An Interview with Eudora Welty

Robert Van Gelder / 1942

From *The New York Times Book Review,* 14 June 1942; reprinted in *Writers and Writing,* ed. Robert Van Gelder (New York: Scribner's, 1946), 287–90. © 1942 by The New York Times Company. Reprinted by permission.

Eudora Welty, the short-story writer, said that when she was younger she was very much interested in herself and always projected herself into her stories.

"The stories were awful. I'm from Jackson, Miss., and never had been much of anywhere else, but the action in my stories took place in Paris. They were awful. I remember the first line in one of them: 'Monsieur Boule deposited a delicate dagger in Mademoiselle's left side and departed with a poised immediacy.' This, of course, makes no sense at all. I loved the 'poised immediacy' so much that I've remembered the whole sentence.

"When I wrote the stories about Paris I thought that I was very good. I think that you're likely to believe that something you write is good so long as it is about something of which you are totally ignorant. You project yourself into some situation of which you know nothing but that pleases you.

"Then I went home and started writing about what I knew. I was older and I guess had a little more sense, enough sense so that I could see the great rift between what I wrote and what was the real thing."

"Do you ever feel, in your stories, that you have closed the rift?"

"Sometimes in the middle of a story I have the illusion that I've closed it. But never for more than a minute. Your common sense tells you that you haven't done it. When you see yourself in proportion—as you're bound to do when you get some sense—then you see how much greater what is real is than anything you can put down."

She writes easily, perfectly naturally, enjoying the job and lost in it.

"I sort of hang stories in my mind and let them hang for a long time. As an example, I have just heard that a long short story or a short novel—I don't know which it is—that I have written is to be published. It's a wrong length and I guess no one will pay much attention to it, but I enjoyed doing it. It is about the Natchez Trace, and planters' beautiful daughters and Indians and bayonets and so on are in it—and a lifetime of fairy-tale reading. Everything in it is something I've liked as long as I can remember and have just now put down."

"You write for yourself entirely, don't you, without the reader in mind at all?"

"Oh, no, I certainly never think of who is going to read it. I don't see how any one could. I don't think of myself either—at least, I don't believe I do. I just think of what it is that I'm writing. That's enough to do.

"Anyway, so long a time elapsed between the original writing of most of my stories and their publication that I lost all sense of connection between writing and print. A lot of the stories that have been published lately were written five or six years ago.

"Yes, I changed them. I revised as I recopied. I think that as you learn more about writing you learn to be direct. When you start you don't say the thing that is behind the writing—maybe you're not sure enough of how it should be said, or maybe you yourself know it so well that you don't feel that the saying is necessary, or maybe you just don't realize what it is. So you write around it.

"In some of the stories, as I retyped, I simply put the kernel, the nut, in. Now that my stories are beginning to find a market—or rather, now that I have an agent who has drummed up a small market—I don't revise as much and the stories don't hang so long. It may be that in ten years I'll wish they had never seen the light of day."

Miss Welty has written some of the most memorable short stories to appear in print during the last few years. Each story is distinct, purely individual, born of its subject and a point of view that is so wide and deeply understanding that it is as though there were no brand of one mind upon the stories. Their outstanding similarity is formed of the intensity that went into their writing. They create moods as powerful as the moods developed by good poetry.

But Miss Welty obviously finds it difficult to talk about herself and not only difficult but not interesting. She is without a public attitude.

Born and brought up in Jackson, Miss., the daughter of the head of a Southern insurance company, she studied at the University of Wisconsin and then came to New York, where she attended Columbia's School of Business, specializing in advertising writing. "I quit advertising because it was too much like sticking pins into people to make them buy things that they didn't need or really much want. And then, too, advertising is so filled with taboos—you are scared to say this thing and that thing; scared to use this page and that kind of type, and so on. What's the use of learning fears?"

Returning to Jackson, she took a variety of jobs. "I used to write everything that was said over a small-town radio station—and to keep the job wrote myself a lot of fan letters each week. At the same time I was writing society for the *Commercial Appeal* at Memphis, and then I moved into a government publicity job that let me get about the State and gave me an honorable reason to talk to people in all sorts of jobs.

"One day I was on an assignment at a fair and talked to a man who was building a booth at the fair grounds. He told me the story that I used in 'Keela, the Outcast Indian Maiden'—about a little Negro man in a carnival who was made to eat live chickens. That's the only actual story I've used. I guess if you read it you must have known that it was true and not made up—it was too horrible to make up.

"When I decided just to go ahead and write stories, I no longer could meet as many people, but that doesn't seem to matter much. Why, just to write about what might happen along some little road like the Natchez Trace—which reaches so far into the past and has been the trail for so many kinds of people—is enough to keep you busy for life."

The Artist and the Critic

Millsaps College Symposium / 1 May 1960

From *Stylus* [Millsaps College, Jackson, MS], 9 (18 May 1960), 21–28. © 1960 by Millsaps Department of English. Reprinted by permission.

A discussion of the nature of the creative process and the relationship of criticism to it.

Members of the Symposium: Eudora Welty, Honored Guest; George W. Boyd, Professor of English; John Greenway, Millsaps junior; Mary Lee Stubblefield, Millsaps senior; Gail Garrison, Millsaps sophomore; Margaret Ann Rogers, Millsaps senior, Moderator.

The Symposium was sponsored by the Cultural and Educational Committee of the Millsaps Union, and was held in the Union Building on Sunday afternoon, May 1, 1960.

Preceding the Symposium, Miss Welty read parts of her essay, "How I Write," *Virginia Quarterly Review,* 31 (Spring 1955), 240–251, to an overflow audience, and some references to the essay appear in the discussion which follows.

Miss Welty graciously consented to a tape recording of the Symposium and the subsequent publication of it in *Stylus.* The staff of *Stylus* is deeply grateful.

Mr. Greenway: I've been sort of wondering about the term, regional writing. In your opinion do you think the regional writer, by confining his writing to a particular area, has difficulty communicating with people who have no idea about the area? For instance, Faulkner in his Yoknapatawpha County, to people who have no idea what goes on in the South—like people in Maine. Do you think he would have trouble communicating?

Miss Welty: No, I don't. I don't think so at all because any work of art, I think, has to be confined by something. If not by region, by some intention, or something like that. It has to be confined in order to—*squirt up!* I think that Faulkner may be better understood in Maine than in Mississippi.

Dr. Boyd: He may be more *read* in Maine.

Miss Garrison: How would you like for your stories to be read?

Miss Welty: I would like to feel they gave pleasure. I haven't read much analysis of my own stuff. I don't like to read those analyses. And I am speaking sort of off the top of my head, on the basis of my own case. It's very unnerving to read anything about yourself. But, and I don't know, if people—I'd like people to be moved, to feel that they have passed through some experience with me, and whatever anybody sees in my stories is fine with me. It's okay, but I don't feel that I'm responsible. I mean that after I've finished, I've done the best I can. I mean I have been most responsible. I've been as responsible as I know how. Once I've done that, one can't do any more. I once was asked to tell one of my stories in my own words.

Miss Stubblefield: I know that you've written poetry besides your short stories, and I want to know if you think it's difficult for a writer to change from one medium to another in that respect. Should a writer find his best medium and stay with it?

Miss Welty: Well, that's a mistake that I've written other things. I never have written a drama. I think I only wrote one little verse and that was just on a Christmas card. I feel that fiction is the only thing about which I can speak, but that happens to be me; I mean each person, when he writes, has different ways. There are plenty of people. Look, all the world of literature written in everything. I myself just have one direction that I feel at home in.

Dr. Boyd: Is it possible for us to talk about how the imagination gets at truth in fiction, Miss Welty?

Miss Welty: I think that's the most important thing in fiction, don't you?

Dr. Boyd: He does it first by being true to what he knows—is that what you said just now [while reading the essay "How I Write"]—to the place he knows?

Miss Welty: Yes, I suppose so. I don't know. When you talk about something like the imagination, don't you think of that as your only source, the only tool, I should say, to work with? But it's got to have something solid to work at.

Dr. Boyd: Which may be place, may be character?

Miss Welty: Yes, don't you think so?

Dr. Boyd: Yes.

Miss Welty: I'll try to answer better since it's carrying farther. Dr. Boyd asked what I think about the imagination and place, and all I think is that the imagination is the tool with which any fiction writer does his work, and he's got to have something solid at which to dig. That can be place, as Dr. Boyd said, place or character, or whatever it is that you reach your truth through. I and you can't just sit up and pull it out of the sky, at least—maybe you can!

Dr. Boyd: Perhaps William Blake could.

Miss Welty: Yes, poets can.

[Here Dr. Boyd mentioned Miss Welty's essay "Place in Fiction," quoting from it.]

Miss Welty: Yes, and I think that's true of the other things you mentioned. I mean human nature. Of course, fiction's whole world is human nature. That will never be changed either, I suppose. But the imagination is the only thing that can find out anything about it and the only way you can see.

Dr. Boyd: I wonder if we can go now to questions about your characters. Miss Welty, I think *The Ponder Heart* was an extremely funny book. I hope it was meant to be.

Miss Welty: Oh, I laughed.

Dr. Boyd: Edna Earle, I went to school with a girl named Edna Earle.

Miss Welty: I didn't think you were that old.

Dr. Boyd: To show you that I've done my homework on this symposium, I asked my wife . . . where in the world did Miss Welty get Edna Earle, and she said, "Don't you know?" And I don't—I haven't had a course in literature of the South. She said you got it from a novel by Saint—or is it called *Saint Elmo?*

Miss Welty: It's called *Saint Elmo.*

Dr. Boyd: Called *Saint Elmo?* Now that's before my time.

Miss Welty: It's before mine too. Well, I had so many letters from people all over the country whose names *were* Edna Earle, and they said where in the world did you get hold of my unusual name? And so I wrote some of them back and said you were named after Edna Earle in *Saint Elmo,* which I never read, but I know she's supposed to be the epitome of virtue, and a whole generation of people were named after her.

Miss Garrison: I'd like to know if you have any favorites among your characters.

Miss Welty: No, I don't feel that way. Whatever I happen to be working on, I'm fascinated by the people there, but I don't—well, I sort of still like *The Ponder Heart,* but that is the last thing I've written. I mean I feel closer to them. Yes, I loved all those people in that.

Miss Rogers: Do your characters come through your imagination, from things you have read, or from childhood experiences, or are they ever a conglomerate of types?

Miss Welty: I better, if I, if anyone, any writer ever knows where, exactly where, they come from. I mean you have ideas of human nature which gradually take form as a character probably from an observation of thousands of things mixed together.

Miss Rogers: And it is through the process of the imagination?

Miss Welty: Yes. As you write. Especially they take form with me. I'm sure that must be true of all writers, don't you think so, Dr. Boyd?

Dr. Boyd: I think so, indeed.

Miss Welty: I don't think you'd ever know the exact source. You couldn't write real life into a story, I know that.

Mr. Greenway: A few weeks ago in the *Saturday Review* John Ciardi made a statement about poetry that a poet doesn't choose the poems he will write, rather the poems choose him as they go. And it's his job to fix them. Do you feel that this is true of prose, or, in particular, your own stories? Do you feel that this is the way your stories come to you?

Miss Welty: I don't know. It's such an unself-conscious act when you write that I—*no,* I don't. I think that all the time things are inside you which gradually work to a point that you want to write them down. I don't feel that anything flies in the window and comes into your mind and you write it down. I think the final thing may fly in through the window, but only if you've received it by a constant brooding on something. I think it's a much longer process. I can only speak for myself, and I don't know anything about poetry.

Mr. Greenway: In your stories then, when you feel that the story's ready, do you consider—is each of your characters a separate entity? Do you find that you consider them each a separate person?

Miss Welty: Oh, sure, they're real people to me. Certainly. Their identities are the only things that you hang on to.

Mr. Greenway: I was sort of wondering about *The Ponder Heart.* You see them through the eyes of Edna Earle, but you consider each of the people as a separate entity? Then you follow them all through Edna Earle?

Miss Welty: No. I wrote it. It was the other way around. My story really was about her, and it was her vision of these people that I was writing about. So, I knew them through her. I did everything through her, including my own ideas, of course. I worked back and forth and made—oh, well, you know what I mean.

Miss Stubblefield: Do you ever feel that sometimes you have a character that you have to write a story for, or does the story come first, or do the characters come maybe just simultaneously?

Miss Welty: I don't know. I think in a short story things are more likely to be simultaneous. Of course, in a novel, which requires much development and change of character and growing of events and much more complicated things, it would probably be different. But in a short story it's more or less to me a simultaneous kind of thing, all playing back and forth on each other.

Mr. Greenway: The comment you made on the critic [in reading the essay previously]. What then do you feel is the critic's job? Is this a person sort of playing a game or writing for his own amusement in hopes—a sort of independent writer?

Miss Welty: No, I wouldn't see much point in that. No, I think criticism has a very high purpose. I didn't mean to be disparaging of criticism. I was just—what I said was I didn't think it was much help to a writer. Much immediate help about a definite thing. No, I think they have a very high function.

Mr. Greenway: By criticism, I meant the critic will tell you what you meant to write in the story, the critic who reads very detailed symbols into the writing. You made mention of that—hanging your story upside down [in the essay just now]. Do you feel that this has any help for the reader?

Miss Welty: I don't know. I don't know. To me it's devastating, but that's all I can say. I really am not very knowledgeable of it. I don't mean to sound—

Dr. Boyd: I think maybe we're just about at a good point to turn toward the problem of obscurity in modern art, perhaps. But may I ask a question before we turn, about theme. This word hasn't appeared—I have twenty-five freshmen who hate the word—theme in novel and story and plays. Miss Welty, do you worry about theme at all?

Miss Welty: I don't *worry* about it.

Dr. Boyd: I mean, well—

Miss Welty: I know what you mean. I don't know. I may not even know what you teach. Tell me what you say!

Dr. Boyd: I don't tell the freshmen; they're supposed to tell me in eighteen pages or less. I think I mean idea which the story in all of its elements embodies.

Miss Welty: I didn't know whether—as distinct from your subject? I mean, I don't really know the exact way you use it.

Dr. Boyd: Well, I don't know whether you can separate theme from subject.

Miss Welty: That's what I—well, I don't know.

Dr. Boyd: Well, then, you conceive of subject and place and character and action and don't worry about theme.

Miss Welty: Well, here's what I think. Now, this may not be right, may not be intelligible to anyone else. I think that people write on the same subject probably all their lives, I mean, you know. It's the kind of thing any writer thinks about all the time. He always writes about it in different ways, but he might use a different theme in that subject, a different thread running through that he follows for that particular work. *I just now thought of this:* I do think every now and then you read a novel, and you think this writer has talent, but he hasn't found what his subject is yet, you know; and by that, you think what he always will write about once he's found it. You think of Proust; I mean his subject.

Dr. Boyd: He found it.

Miss Welty: Yes, he found it. And he had a lot of themes.

Dr. Boyd: That's the best thing I've heard on theme in years. I wish I could say it Monday.

Miss Rogers: I think the discussion has taken the turn which we had hoped it would, and that is the consideration of, well, one, criticism of modern writing; the article by Shapiro to which we have referred in the *New York Times Book Review* in December. It is an attack against, one, T. S. Eliot, and, two, other modern writers in general whom the author feels are obscure. Now the title of the essay is "What's the Matter With Modern Poetry?" more or less, and Shapiro takes the stand that modern poetry is obscure, too obscure, for the modern reader, and he deals at some length with the criticism of the author's work. Now, we have asked Miss Welty to read this article, and would at this time like to turn the general questioning toward the development of some sort of discussion about this article.

Dr. Boyd: Do we all mean the same thing by obscurity, now? Is the question this: Is modern art—and let us mean poetry and short story and novel—let's broaden it. Is modern art deliberately obscure, and if so, why and what can we do about it? Is that the question? Do you think it's obscure, Miss Welty? The short story, the novel, or poetry?

Miss Welty: Poetry's obscure to me—the short story and the novel I don't find. Yes, I do think it's obscure, and a lot of abstract painting is obscure to me. So you think it's our fault?

Dr. Boyd: The artist's fault?

Miss Welty: No, the reader, the viewer, us.

Dr. Boyd: The audience?

Miss Welty: Yes.

Dr. Boyd: Mr. Shapiro is saying it's the poet's fault. He is deliberately cultivating obscurity; he's deliberately cultivating his little cult of people who are thinking as beautiful souls and know what he means, and that leaves the rest of us out. Is poetry the only [art] that does this, or is it also in the story and in the novel? I think that's the question now. Miss Welty says it's in poetry but not elsewhere.

Miss Stubblefield: Don't you think that it would depend? You can consider a poet as a person writing for the masses? Writing maybe for himself to express himself in some way?

Miss Welty: I refuse to consider that because I don't think you're right. I don't think you think for what you are writing. I mean the *masses!*

Miss Stubblefield: That's what I meant. He's not considering who he's writing for.

Miss Welty: Well, but who is he writing for?

Miss Stubblefield: That's what I want to know.

Miss Welty: I think he's doing a work of art—here it is. I don't mean to sound high-handed, but really people can take it or leave it, you know, and you can't tell people; I mean Mr. Shapiro aggravated me a little when he said that we've got to just tell people that they're not to take this kind of thing. You can't just say from now on it's going to be just like the desegregation bit. You can't just say from now on everybody's got to say down with T. S. Eliot, write so everybody can understand, etc.—any more than T. S. Eliot said from now on everybody write—you know. You can't tell people what to read or enjoy. Do you think so, now? And I mean in thinking of the masses or in thinking of a little cult, or thinking of anything. That isn't the way a work of art gets done. After all, I mean, you've got in the end, it's one person sitting down to the typewriter and writing something. It's between him and the page. What he does, and if he's doing the best he can, and it's obscure to us, I suppose we have to take it. And if we understand it we can enjoy it. But I don't see that you can make any kind of law about it. Do you?

Miss Stubblefield: That was my idea.

Miss Welty: I know what you mean. It's about responsibility. I don't know. Poets may have different feelings and responsibilities, do they?

Dr. Boyd: No, I don't think the good ones do.

Miss Welty: I shouldn't think so.

Dr. Boyd: Their responsibility is to make reality real. But the question is, when it's made real, will it then be communicable to an audience, I think. Mr. Shapiro, I may say in an aside, aggravated me no end with that essay and then the one that followed in the *Saturday Review,* called "The Death of Literary Judgment." Mr. Eliot's seventy-two, I think, but I wish they—they'd better watch out!

Miss Welty: Did he write that too, Mr. Shapiro?

Dr. Boyd: Yes.

Miss Welty: Well, I hate that popularity idea. Oh, it just plays into the hands of people who don't really want to understand anything. Now they don't have to. Now, they've been given permission. It's a recess, you know, going to play.

Dr. Boyd: They've been given permission by Mr. Karl Shapiro at the University of Nebraska to like only Whitman and Dylan Thomas, and, I guess, Shapiro.

Miss Welty: Yes, sure—and D. H. Lawrence.

Miss Garrison: In one of your essays that I read you mentioned that a fine story writer seems to be in a sense an obstructionist . . . in "Place in Fiction," I believe.

Miss Welty: Gee, I don't remember saying that. I don't know in what sense I said that. I really can't explain it. I really don't know— I'm not doubting you—but I must have meant something in context that I can't get my finger on. I'm sorry.

Mr. Greenway: Do you feel that if a poem written by one of the modern poets—that means to say one who is very obscure—do you feel that if a person reads this poem and it says absolutely nothing to him the first time, do you feel that it's worth the trouble to go down and try and understand it? I mean sit and pore over it.

Miss Welty: Well, I certainly do! The least you can do is to read something the second time!

Mr. Greenway: Well, I mean not to dismiss it, but if it doesn't say *anything* to you—the poet is supposed to communicate, at least. He put down something that communicates to him; if it doesn't communicate to the reader, do you think the reader should try and force it?

Miss Welty: Well, I think it's your privilege to not read it, but I don't think it's your privilege to say there's nothing in this. Of course, I think Shapiro—

Mr. Greenway: If it says nothing to him emotionally, do you think that if he gained something by poring over it and trying to get something out of it—

Miss Welty: I think that if there's something intrinsically in a poem, something is in there to be got out; I think if you can't get it out by one way, you might by another, and it would be certainly wonderful if it were opened up to you. I mean, you've gained that poem, if you want to try.

At this time Miss Rogers, the Moderator, gave the members of the audience opportunity to ask Miss Welty questions.

Audience: Does most of the creation come before you actually put the words down on paper? Or do you write and look at it and write it over again?

Miss Welty: Yes, I do do that all the time. That's an interesting question about what comes first. Like sometimes I know there's a word that belongs in a story—some key thing. I don't know where it's going to be—I mean really. Just some word, say "oblivion"—I mean just some word. I put that down; then when I get to it, I know it belongs there, just like W. C. Fields's desk where he had all his things where he could reach in. . . . I do a lot of rewriting.

Audience: Miss Welty, as to your Ford Foundation Fellowship— How do you feel about changing from short story to drama? Wouldn't you like to write a drama?

Miss Welty: Well, of course—yeah, I do know, partly. The first thing I know is that you can't make one into the other. I mean I'm pretty sure of that because I learned a long time ago that much that is useful in fiction does not play. I had that driven into me by watching *things;* and the second thing is what this scholarship is for, to go to learn by first-hand watching, by just looking and listening. The whole thing to me is to be an education. I don't believe anything I know will do me any good except, of course, a sense of character and theme— my subject.

Miss Rogers: Perhaps this question is not appropriate, but I'd like to ask it. There are so many different media of expression and you have written mainly in the short story. Do you think there are any advantageous ways of expression more so through the short story than through drama, or do you think that modes of expression vary between the arts?

Miss Welty: Oh, sure.

Miss Rogers: Is one more powerful to you than the other?

Miss Welty: None more powerful, just entirely different, and I think you'd have to learn such different things. That's why I want to learn to write the drama. I would love to be able to turn everything into terms of action and dialogue. Whereas now, I don't do that in a short story. It's interior. You have to show things all brought forth— have every action completed and carried through. It'll be a wonderful way to learn to—maybe to say the same thing, but in such different terms. I think they will be completely different. I expect it to be. Of course, I don't know.

Audience: I'd like to ask Miss Welty if she ever feels that there is a subconsciousness that sort of takes over when she writes?

Miss Welty: I think I feel that the subconscious has its help, but I don't want it to take over. I would put my hand down on it if it tried to *really* take over. I think you can trust things that you learned that way. I think some things you feel most sure of are way deep down. No, I want to be in charge of what I do.

Audience: I'd like to go back to the obscurity in art. I'd like to hear your opinion of what causes the obscurity and what you think about it.

Miss Welty: You mean in *art* art?

Audience: No, more specifically in written art.

Miss Welty: I don't know. I'm sure Dr. Boyd could answer that much better than I.

Dr. Boyd: She's not interested in how I feel about it.

Miss Welty: That's all I can say, what I feel about it. Of course we're living in a complex world, and all kinds of resources are available for us to draw words and terms and ways of thought—all kinds of science and psychiatry and one thing and another are all acting in us at all times, and I suppose there's a sense of complication and confusion that's in our minds because that's the way we live. Maybe some of that comes out through the various contortions that you go through in writing and produces something that's just a picture of what the mind is like. I don't know. That's very simple sounding. I still think that the history of all literature shows that the most profound thoughts can be expressed in the simplest ways, and we haven't really learned very much more. I mean we have other terms, but things have always been said in different ways always, and I guess there are millions more ways that we don't even know yet. They'll probably be the same things—don't you guess and—I don't know. That's not an answer to the question. I just feel that way.

Audience: Miss Welty, getting back to drama—I wonder, do you think (I know that of course that you're known as a short story writer going into this field of drama)—do you know of any dramatists that you would like to see go into your medium?

Miss Welty: Oh, that's an interesting question—yeah. Tennessee Williams has written some short stories, hasn't he—one novel, which I don't think shows up his—I think he's essentially a dramatist because on the written page his work seems terribly crude, I think. I mean what will "play," they always tell you, seems such a different thing from this calm page-to-eye business of reading. I can't imagine a dramatist even wanting to write a short story—isn't that funny. I think that they would be very bored with the idea of anything as calm a communication as that. I think there's a different talent entirely, and whereas we probably learn to write drama, I'll bet not a one of them could be bribed to write short stories. That'd just be an off-hand guess, but I don't know. Also they'd probably think there's no money—there isn't!

Audience: Miss Welty, I understand that you're working on the novels of Henry Green. Would you tell us why you consider him significant for consideration?

Miss Welty: I think that's *awful,* because I offered to read a paper on Henry Green and you said, "No thanks, no one would want to hear it. . . ." No, I didn't mean to tease you. If you really want to know, I've got a page of it right here. I just happened to have been reading his work all over again and I like him so much, and I just spontaneously began writing something about him. I think he's a writer of very tremendous imagination and is a unique writer, and I don't know—I just think he's such an extraordinary man writing, and he can also be very funny. You'll just have to read the piece—I can't even start on him. I'm in the middle of it. I wonder if many of you read him or like him?

Audience: Would you tell us something about him?

Miss Welty: It's too late. He's an English writer. I read his auto-biography called *Pack My Bag,* which he wrote during the war, thinking he would be killed any minute, and the first sentence is, "I was born in 1905, a mouthbreather, with a silver spoon in my mouth." Well, that places him.

Dr. Boyd: It seems to me I read *Loving* first and ended with *Nothing.* Is that possible?

Miss Welty: That possible? Yes.

Dr. Boyd: He has one-word titles.

Miss Welty: Most of them are some form of the verb. Everything about him is functional. He's stripped away everything. He doesn't use similes. He just finishes out images, just like this—Want me to read a page of Henry Green? Hot Dog! This is the way he writes— now listen. This is in the middle of the novel called *Concluding.* This is a sample of his writing.

[Here Miss Welty read from Green's *Concluding.* The Symposium ended when she finished her reading.]

An Interview with Eudora Welty
Comment Magazine / 16 October 1965

From *Comment: The University of Alabama Review,* 4 (Winter 1965), 11–16. © 1965 by Comment Magazine. Reprinted by permission.

Eudora Welty is recognized as one of the best short-story writers in English, not only in this country but also in Europe. She needs no introduction; however, in order that this interview may be read in the right perspective, some comments are called for.

Some readers perhaps will be disappointed with Miss Welty's unwillingness to talk dogmatically about her work and her tacit refusal to discuss her private life. Perhaps they have read too many interviews with other writers who not only "explain" their work in great detail, but also go into their private lives, sometimes with rather embarrassing results. (And this type of thing has become so dominant in the United States that many people read novels and poems and short stories not for their intrinsic artistic merit, but because they are interesting commentaries on their authors' private lives.)

Miss Welty does not do this. And we think the chief value of this interview is that in it she very gently forces us to question this confusion of "public" art with "private" life, and to make us distrust those writers who all too readily "explain" their work. After all, if a writer has to explain a work of art in terms of his private life, then something is wrong or missing in the work itself. For a writer to do such explaining is an admission of failure.

Also to be noted is her humility. How many times in this interview does she say, "I don't know," or, "I tried to do this or that"! One is reminded of that sentence in Henry James's short-story "The Middle Years": "We work in the dark—we do what we can—we give what we have. Our doubt is our passion and our passion is our task. . . . The rest is the madness of art." "The madness of art" is something about which one cannot talk in neat, sure terms. There is a certain element of mystery in it which will always defy complete explication, and Miss

Welty remains humble in the presence of it. She never
violates this fundamental mystery.

The interview took place at Miss Welty's home in Jackson, Mississippi, on October 16, 1965. Nearly all of the
stories discussed in it are found in the Modern Library
edition of her short stories.

THE EDITORS

Interviewer: First of all, may we ask you what are you working
on now and when is it likely to be finished?

Miss Welty: That is probably the last thing I could answer! I am
working on several things: an essay on Katherine Anne Porter for the
Yale Review, a short story and a novel. But the novel I have had
going for some time. I have done all the work on it; in fact, I probably
have done too much work on it. I hope to get it in final shape this
year.

Interviewer: What writers did you find helpful when you first
started writing short stories?

Miss Welty: Nobody really helps you when you work, as you
know. There are a lot of people that I admire and always will. But I
think any influence would have to be indirect. I should say this would
be true of most writers. While I'm really in the process of working, I
am not thinking about how anyone else does it or even how I ought
to do it. I'm thinking about the story itself in its own terms. But, of
course, there are many writers who have influenced my feeling about
the short story; Chekhov, William Faulkner, for instance. But I have
to answer vaguely about influences. It would be a good thing if you
could just go and influence yourself by the right person each time
you found something wrong. But that's not the way it's done!

Interviewer: Do you agree with Katherine Anne Porter's interpretation of "Why I Live at the P.O."? I think she says Sister is suffering
from dementia praecox.

Miss Welty: It never occurred to me while I was writing the story
(and it still doesn't) that I was writing about someone in serious mental trouble. I was trying to write about the way people who live away
off from nowhere have to amuse themselves by dramatizing every
situation that comes along by exaggerating it—"telling it." I used the
exaggerations and ways of talking I have heard all my life. It's just the

way they keep life interesting—they make an experience out of the ordinary. I wasn't trying to do anything but show that. I thought it was cheerful, on the whole.

Interviewer: Was your short story "A Still Moment" based on an historical incident?

Miss Welty: What I was really trying to write about was not anything that could have actually happened but about three attitudes of looking at life. I made the meeting up. Whether it happened or not doesn't matter. But all those actual people *were* wandering around down there on the Natchez Trace at the same time.

Interviewer: There is a sentence in "A Still Moment" which has always puzzled me. I wonder if you would say something about it. It is: "He could understand God's giving Separateness first and then giving Love to follow and heal in its wonder; but God had reversed this, and given Love first and then Separateness, as though it did not matter to Him which came first."

Miss Welty: Dow is speaking, isn't he?

Interviewer: Yes.

Miss Welty: I probably got that from reading some of his sermons. I think I was sort of quoting along from him and using his wild words to apply to the story. They were not my own words but the way he sermonized. Everything that I put in capital letters were the things Dow put in capital letters.

Interviewer: Do you have anything you would like to say about Flannery O'Connor?

Miss Welty: Of course I think she is just tremendous. I think she was a fantastically gifted writer. I have enjoyed everything she has done. I love it.

There are a lot of things I realize are a closed book to me in her work because of the Roman Catholic Church of which I'm ignorant. Certain things that I accept as symbols of the imagination are also symbols of her church, and would mean so much more to her than an ordinary reader would know about. Once I heard her speak and explain some of these things. That opened a great many doors to me and I read her work with renewed understanding. What I liked about her was her vitality, her great toughness, which was a spiritual toughness: I mean tough in the good sense of the word. Nothing could break it. It was the fiber you see in everything she wrote.

Interviewer: Those letters of Flannery O'Connor to Robert Fitz-gerald which appeared in the Winter 1965 issue of *Shenandoah* re-veal how brave she was in her last days.

Miss Welty: Oh, she was incredibly brave! She must have known she was going to die for as long as she was ill, which was a very long time.

Interviewer: I have always noticed in her work a certain conflict between the symbols of her church which she used in her work, and her characters who would reject such symbolism.

Miss Welty: Exactly. She has spoken about that. Of course, I think she did it as an artist. Maybe it's trespassing to say that, but it seems the way an artist like herself would work—simplifying for the sake of drama, reducing things to their essentials.

Interviewer: Do you think Southern writers have any peculiar ad-vantages over writers from other parts of the country?

Miss Welty: I don't think so, not any longer anyway. I think at one time you could find a reason (if you were looking for one) in the fact that people were more isolated then and amused themselves by family stories and things like that. But I do think we have retained, in our natural way of looking at things, the sense of the continuity of life, and the sense of the family. Southerners tend to live in one place, where they can see whole lives unfold around them. It gives them a natural sense of the narrative, of the dramatic content of life, a form for the story comes readily to hand. This is so generalizing. I don't think, just given that disposition, it would explain why they write. It might equally explain why they went crazy or anything else!

Interviewer: Do you think it is disappearing in the South today?

Miss Welty: Our life here is a great deal like life all the way up the Central Illinois line to Chicago, as far as I can tell. What is really the difference between Jackson, Mississippi, and Springfield, Illinois? Maybe Tuscaloosa is different but it looked a great deal like Jackson to me. I don't have any wish for a return of the old days. I think you have to be alive to what is happening today.

All the same, I think there still is in the South a great respect for, even reverence for, this life of the family, and the sense of history. I treasure that. I think we should treasure that, and keep it in our work.

Interviewer: You remember there is a white heron at the end of "A Still Moment." Dow looks at it for a long time; then he breaks away from it and calls it a tempter. By that, may we say that Dow considers the beauty of the natural world as something opposed to God?

Miss Welty: I'm not up on him any longer. And I can't jump in and tell you exactly what he meant because I didn't make him up. He was just a wild and strange and really half-mad preacher whom I used to put in juxtaposition with Audubon and the robber Murrell. Isn't there a reference to a white horse in the story?

Interviewer: Yes.

Miss Welty: Well, that's Murrell's own vision. Murrell thought he saw Jesus Christ standing across his path after he had committed a murder. He would write in his diary that he had seen the vision. So I used that vision, like Dow's sermon. Of course, "A Still Moment" is a symbolic story. I took the symbols all these people had used in their own work and put them together in my story. But I don't usually write about real people, so I can't talk about their minds so readily.

Interviewer: You have such a vivid sense of being in a particular place.

Miss Welty: I have a visual mind. That's the way I see things, so that's the way I write. I try to concentrate what I say in stories into visual images—landscapes, portraits, seasons, all the aspects plain to the eye. I work hard on these things.

Interviewer: But you don't treat these details naturalistically, that is, in the manner of strict realism.

Miss Welty: But I'm a great one for using what is natural and letting it function in the way it wants to.

Interviewer: To change the subject, may I ask you a question about publishing letters and private journals of writers? You know so much has been written about the demand of the American people for not only a writer's work but for his private life as well. Hemingway, of course, comes to mind.

Miss Welty: I don't think it's confined to America. I was thinking of Katherine Mansfield, all of whose letters and journals were the most agonizing, privately written things. They were published little by little so as to make book after book. They are fascinating to read, yet I don't know. There is something about reading something that the writer never meant others to read which is very disturbing. On the other hand, when Virginia Woolf's diaries were published and so much had to be removed because people were still alive, I was gnashing my teeth because of what I was missing! It both lures me and disturbs me.

Interviewer: Which of your stories do you consider your most successful?

Miss Welty: I'm afraid I don't think about them in those terms. I'm not even interested in them after I have finished them. I am interested in new things. I don't mean that I don't respect them as pieces of work, but that they were the best I could do and are gone.

I have naturally an affection for some stories that I don't have for others. And probably the ones I like best are the ones that you would not call successful.

Interviewer: As Faulkner said about *The Sound and the Fury.*

Miss Welty: Anyone feels that way. Something that really mattered more than the rest to you in your work may be the very thing you couldn't bring off.

I think I like the stories in *The Golden Apples* better than most of those I have written, though I still feel an affection for those in *A Curtain of Green* because they were the beginning. And I wrote them with a great deal of ease and should have gone back and worked on them. But I didn't know enough then. And now that I do know more, I have a kind of guilty feeling about some of them. I should not have let some of them be published.

Interviewer: *Death of A Traveling Salesman* was your first story to be published, wasn't it?

Miss Welty: Yes. In a magazine called *Manuscript,* published in Akron, Ohio. It was the first story I wrote. Naturally I was amazed.

Interviewer: You were also published in the *Southern Review* quite a bit, were you not?

Miss Welty: Yes, frequently. Everybody has been good to me in my whole life. They published things when I began to send them, and Robert Penn Warren and Cleanth Brooks helped me a whole lot. Katherine Anne Porter wrote me very kind and encouraging letters too. She was living in Baton Rouge.

Interviewer: You dedicated *The Robber Bridegroom* to her, didn't you?

Miss Welty: Yes.

Interviewer: What is your attitude towards that work?

Miss Welty: I had such a good time writing it! I had been working for the WPA or for the Mississippi Advertising Commission. In the course of my work I had to do a lot of reading on the Natchez Trace. I'm not a writer who writes fiction by research, but reading these primary sources, such as Dow's sermons, Murrell's diary and letters of the time, fired my imagination. I thought how much like fairy tales all of those things were. And so I just sat down and wrote *The Robber Bridegroom* in a great spurt of pleasure. You know something like that either stands or falls; you can't rework it.

Interviewer: There seems to be such a difference between the stories in *A Curtain of Green* and those in *The Wide Net.* In the first collection, you feel that you are in the objective world of ordinary human experience, but in all of the stories in *The Wide Net,* there is a dream-like quality. Facts and reveries seem to blend into each other.

Miss Welty: I don't know what would explain that except that the stories of *A Curtain of Green* were written over a period of six years and the stories in *The Wide Net* were all written in one year. It had taken me all that time to get anyone to publish my stories, and so I had accumulated a lot of work for *The Curtain of Green.* When you collect one book after six years and the next book after one year, there's bound to be a difference in at least their variety.

Interviewer: What actually happened in "The Wide Net"? Did he think that his wife was really at the bottom of the river?

Miss Welty: I didn't go into him, did I? That was on purpose. I was trying to write about it from the outside as well as I could because I wanted it to be a comic episode. The point I really wanted to make was that the whole thing was an adventure; they enjoyed dragging the river. I don't think he thought she was down there. But she could have been.

Interviewer: You remember he dived to the bottom and thought something which could lead the reader to believe that he knew all along that she was not there, that she had not committed suicide.

Miss Welty: I tried to suggest by that as much as I could, just to shade the story and make it not a heartless one. But at the same time, it was a story of a search and I tried to make it a joyous one.

Interviewer: You get such a sense of vitality in it. That river is such a powerful force in the story.

Miss Welty: Vitality is what I did hope to express. That hope is the kind of thing you remember about a story, even though you wrote it a long time ago. You may not remember how you worked it out but you remember what you tried for.

Interviewer: What is the King of the Snakes, which is mentioned in that story?

Miss Welty: Oh, it's just a great big snake. I wanted him to seem sort of extra powerful, a little more than life. I didn't want the story held bound to the exact. I tried to make it expansive by putting in different things from time to time. The reason I used the King of the Snakes was that I had heard the expression all my life and I was glad to be able to put him in.

Interviewer: What poets do you particularly admire?

Miss Welty: I like Yeats best, I think.

Interviewer: Early Yeats . . . ?

Miss Welty: I used to like the early poems when I was young. But now I love all the poems. I can see what he did continually with his gift. He made of himself a second poet out of the first.

Interviewer: What do you think the situation of the short story today is?

Miss Welty: I think it is getting along all right, don't you? I don't have any real opinion about trends or what is "happening" to stories today. And I don't always read what comes out new, not that I am against it. I'm always going back and re-reading what I like. But I don't see that the short story is anything to worry about.

Interviewer: It seems to me that you, Flannery O'Connor and Muriel Spark have in common the same sort of humor.

Miss Welty: Thank you for the company you put me in.

Interviewer: I mean a humor completely objective which sees the evils and shortcomings of man so clearly and yet does not scorn him. It is caustic and so human at the same time.

Miss Welty: I think objective is about the only way to be. As a writer, I try to see a person both as what he is and as what he thinks he is.

Interviewer: Sister is a beautiful example of this. At times you want to slap her, and at other times you sympathize with her. She had a lot to bear.

Miss Welty: She certainly did! I say that loyally!

Eudora Welty Talks About Her New Book, *Losing Battles*

Frank Hains / April 1970

From *The Clarion-Ledger Jackson Daily News* [Jackson, MS], 5 April 1970, sec. F, 6. © 1970 by The Clarion-Ledger Jackson Daily News. Reprinted by permission.

Publishers always speak of new books by established writers as "long-awaited events." But, on April 13, comes one that indeed is.

It's the first book—save her children's story, "The Shoebird"—in fifteen years by one of America's most important literary figures, Eudora Welty.

It's called *Losing Battles,* it's the first long novel in a body of work which has been most distinguished by some of the best short stories ever written in America, and it's already on sale in Jackson in advance of its official publication.

The book will be reviewed here next Sunday by Louis Dollarhide so it is not my purpose to anticipate that today.

But, in the meantime, I went this week to visit Miss Welty at her Jackson home and to talk about her feelings on the eve, as it were, of the book's publication.

It is almost 15 years to the day since my first meeting with Miss Welty and, this time as then, she was waiting on the stoop of her comfortable old English-flavored house on Pinehurst.

That time—at the publication of *The Bride of the Innisfallen*—I was very much in awe of one of America's greatest writers. The intervening years have served, if anything, to deepen the awe—not only of the writer but of the great and kind and warm and witty and thoughtful lady she is.

She is, she said, a bit apprehensive that some of the reviewers may criticize *Losing Battles* because of her apparent lack of concern for the preoccupations of today; where, she fancies them saying, is her awareness of black versus white, the degeneration of the family, all the "relevant" problems?

"I'm aware of what so many reviewers seem to be looking for,"

26

Miss Welty said, "but I'm content with the way I wrote it—it's the only way I can and it seems to me just as legitimate to write of people in a family group as in any more 'relevant' grouping.

"Human relationships are the same no matter what the context. It never occurred to me not to write it as I did, but now that it's about to come out"—she stopped and laughed wryly. "Well, you DO get jumped on."

Does the serious writer have any obligation to his society?

"To have deep feelings about it—to try to understand it—to be able to reflect on things—to know what's happening and to care.

"But, in a work of fiction, that can only come through in the mind and heart behind the work. One wants it to show through understanding of characters.

"A book should only reflect and present—not lecture people. I haven't got the presumption to feel you should lecture."

Losing Battles takes place in and around and through the recollections of those at a rural Mississippi family reunion. A large clan has gathered on Granny's 90th birthday and the major events surround the return from Parchman of the youth who is the apple of the family eye.

"I didn't know the title until the book was finished," Miss Welty says. "I never do. It's about all the battles which we always seem to be losing—battles against everything: poverty, disgrace, misunderstanding, and also funny battles I hope; trying to make a go of it, trying to survive. And old age. And the teacher's battle against ignorance.

"Oh, when you say all that it sounds like some kind of social science idea; like I was trying to give a lesson. I certainly wasn't. It's like all of our daily battles—when in an everyday way you feel like you might not make it.

"I hope that it's a comedy of one kind or another—not laughing at people," she hastens to interject. "But I think they're able to laugh."

The title might seem pessimistic?

"I didn't mean it to be. I think life is pretty darn hard and serious but—well, I think somewhere in there they said"—and she picks up the book and leafs through it—"Jack said, after he really loses everything:

" 'They can't take away what no human can take away. My family, my wife and girl baby and all of 'em at home. And I've got my strength. I may not have all the time I used to have—but I can provide. Don't you ever fear.'

"Oh, it's so darn hard to talk about. I can't express anything about my writing. I never have put it to myself what I was doing while doing it. When you get through, you can say SOMETHING but it really doesn't express it—to me."

And that seemed to me to express quite well the artist's inevitable and eternal dilemma when asked to talk about his own work—which has always seemed to me an unfair thing to ask anyway. It is not the author's obligation to talk about his work.

Of the questions she's continually being asked, the one that Miss Welty says she "really hates" is "did you mean that to be symbolic?"

"When symbols occur naturally within the content of a story, that's when the author recognizes them; after they spring up. I consider them legitimate because they function in the story. The other kind is pretentious and just in the way."

Her family in *Losing Battles* is not one she's ever known, but "I have travelled all over the state and I have seen places like this. I went to the "W" [Mississippi State College for Women] and worked for the WPA; I've known many families—families as families. I have known what poor families live like.

"The real reason that I used this family setting, and felt that the family should be poor, is that I wanted to reduce my narrative to the simplest denominators. The battles being lost seem so much more important when there is so little left to lose.

"And, I wanted to show everything outwardly if I could; rather than writing about what people were thinking, I wanted to show it in word and action.

"It seemed to me that comedy was best, and it seemed to call for a rural scene, a family scene, and a big day."

The book grew to be much longer than Miss Welty had originally intended. "As it grew, the parts grew," which called for constant rewriting and expanding of scenes; "I work in scenes." Usually Miss Welty says she "tears up as I go," but this time, "I kept thinking 'it really can't be this long: I'll probably go back and use the old one.' So when I finally finished I had a suitcase full of earlier drafts." Some have been given to the state archives, which has all of Miss Welty's manuscripts; some will not be: "I don't want people looking at my mistakes."

There are three other Welty books in the offing now: perhaps four, depending on whether one long story (which appeared in an entire issue of *The New Yorker* last spring as "The Optimist's Daughter") is brought out by itself or as the lead story in a collection.

The other two are a book of essays and a book of her photographs, for which she is writing brief captions.

While she's naturally interested in what the reception of *Losing Battles* will be, she herself is satisfied with it.

"And some of the people I like have liked it, and that's what matters most."

Meeting Miss Welty

Walter Clemons / 1970

From *The New York Times Book Review,* 12 April 1970, 2, 46.
© 1970 by The New York Times Company. Reprinted by permission.

By the information counter in the Jackson, Miss. airport waits a tall, plain, gray-haired lady with bright blue eyes and a droll, shy smile for an arriving visitor she's never seen before. When told earlier that he would land at noon and get a taxi to her house, she had refused to hear of it: "It's just a few minutes away, it's the easiest thing in the world to meet you." Now, no airport is just a few minutes away, but the first thing you learn about Eudora Welty is that one of the most admired of living writers hasn't learned to be a *grande dame.*

After a drive of greater distance, just as suspected, than she'd made it sound over the phone, she turns her blue Ford into a driveway on Pinehurst Street, across from the white buildings of Belhaven College. She lives, alone now, in her family's house, 1920's Tudor, of dark red brick, with camellias blooming around the cement front porch. No sooner inside the door than she's concerned that her guest must be faint with hunger, after the one hour time change from New York. "I've got ham and snap beans and grits and salad out in the kitchen, will that be all right?" She serves a drink, then lunch in the breakfast room, before settling down in the living room to talk about her first book in 15 years.

She says that *Losing Battles* took her six or eight years, though an old friend believes he heard her talk about it much longer ago than that, maybe 10 or 15 years ago. Both may be right. Speaking of *The Robber Bridegroom* to an interviewer back in 1942, she said, "I sort of hang stories in my mind for a long time. . . . Everything in it is something I've liked as long as I can remember and just now put down."

"I didn't write it in a normal way," she says of her new novel, "because I had private things at home." Her mother died four years ago after a long illness, and she has lost her two brothers, younger than herself, to whose memory *Losing Battles* is dedicated. "I originally saw it as a long story, the family telling a newcomer, while they waited for his homecoming, the tale of how Jack Renfro got sent to prison, and I saw it ending when he turns up on the front porch. I might not have had the courage to start if I'd known what I was getting into. It started out to be short and farcical, but as the people became dearer to me—it changed. When I got Jack home to the reunion, I realized I'd just begun."

The part of Mississippi in which the novel is set is one she's never written about before. When asked about the germ of the story, she talks of it only in terms of a technical choice: "I needed that region, that kind of country family, because I wanted that chorus of voices, everybody talking and carrying on at once. I wanted to try something completely vocal and dramatized. Those people are natural talkers and storytellers, in a remote place where there was time for that. I put in things I remember hearing about—like the dewberry picking. The hard thing, working on the book now and then over a long period, was to know what to discard. I deposited things I liked, and then last year I went through the manuscript from beginning to end and threw a lot away."

She is matter of fact about her art, like one of those good Southern cooks who have no written-down recipes. She dismisses the notion that her writing has made her a celebrity or a curiosity among her neighbors: "Oh, no, it's just what I do. I have almost the same friends I ever had." She mentions, with some asperity, a phone call from New York when "Where Is The Voice Coming From?" appeared in *The New Yorker* in 1963. The story was suggested by the murder of Medgar Evers, and a newspaper reporter wanted to know if Miss Welty had suffered any repercussions: "Had anybody burned a cross on my lawn, he wanted to know. I told him, No, of course not, and he wanted to know if he could call back in a few days, 'in case anything develops.' I told him I couldn't see any sense in his running up his phone bill. The people who burn crosses on lawns don't read me in *The New Yorker*. Really, don't people know the first thing about the South?"

She is anything but a recluse, as becomes apparent when, asked about her writing habits, she says she can write anytime, anywhere, even on the front seat of her car, "except at night." What's wrong with writing at night? "Oh," as if this were obvious, "I like to see my friends then."

Her phone rings in the front hall. "Curses," she says, but her voice brightens when she answers it. Two friends in Santa Fe are calling to thank her for a copy of *Losing Battles* she's sent them. "Why don't you come visit me?" she asks. "I was getting ready to write you." They are leaving for Europe, but it's settled that they'll try to come through Jackson on their way back. She entertains guests happily and often: Elizabeth Bowen was down at Christmas time, and Reynolds Price had recently spent a few days with her.

Her enthusiasms are varied. Besides the books neatly arranged by author (Faulkner, Elizabeth Bowen, Virginia Woolf) in the living-room shelves, there are others in stacks of twos and threes on tables and on an upright piano in the corner: C. M. Bowra's *Memories, 1898–1939, The Collected Stories of Peter Taylor,* Dwight Macdonald's *Parodies* anthology. And mysteries, which she reads late at night. She likes Dick Francis and Andrew Garve. Ross Macdonald? "Oh, yes! I've read all his books, I think. I once wrote Ross Macdonald a fan letter, but I never mailed it. I was afraid he'd think it—icky."

The theater is another love. "When I first went to New York, my father took me to the Palace, and I was a goner. I saw all the great acts, and I went to the closing bill." She mentions, among others, Fred and Adele Astaire, Nazimova ("You've probably never even heard of her? Oh, good!"), Beatrice Lillie singing "Snoops the Lawyer." Her own experience in the theater, when *The Ponder Heart* was adapted for Broadway by Joseph Fields and Jerome Chodorov in 1956, was a happy one. "They wanted to come down here, and I said I'd show them around. I was out when they arrived, they took a look around town, and when I got back to the house, here was a big bunch of roses, with a note from them: 'Welcome to Jackson. You'll like it here.' We had such a good time. Their first script was just awful, I didn't know anything to do but tell them the truth. I don't think I was much help, but we talked it over and they did it all again. I didn't interfere with the rehearsals or anything, I saw it for the first time on opening night, and I thought it was just fine."

Though she is thought of as a deeply Southern writer, Miss Welty points out that her mother was Virginian but her father was a North-erner, of German-Swiss ancestry. ("A Republican," she adds, in a mock hushed tone.) "It was a good family to grow up in. I learned there wasn't just one side that was right."

She was graduated from college before she was 20 (Mississippi State College for Women, University of Wisconsin) and went on to New York to the Columbia School of Business to study advertising.

Back in Mississippi during the early Depression years she worked for newspapers and radio stations and then as a publicity director, "on the road for the WPA," as she puts it.

Five years after her first story was published, her first collection, *A Curtain of Green*, came out in 1941, with an introduction by Katherine Anne Porter. "The strangest thing about my first stories getting published is that I never stopped to think how lucky I was. I just took it as a matter of course, sent them off, without any modesty or worry at all. It's only now, when I look back on it, that I'm simply amazed. Because I *was* very, very lucky. I didn't know enough to be scared."

A lesser-known episode of her career is her stint as a staff member of the *Times Book Review,* which she joined at the invitation of the editor, Robert Van Gelder, who had admired her first book and inter-viewed her in 1942. She was good at her job, according to a col-league of those wartime days: "Although the only battlefields Eudora had probably ever seen," he wrote recently, "were at Vicksburg and Shiloh, she turned out splendid reviews of World War II battlefield reports from North Africa, Europe and the South Pacific. When a churlish *Times* Sunday editor suggested that a lady reviewer from the Deep South might not be the most authoritative critic for the ac-counts of World War II's far-flung campaigns, she switched to a pseudonym, Michael Ravenna." Michael Ravenna's sage judgments came to be quoted prominently in publishers' ads and invitations from radio networks for Mr. Ravenna to appear on their programs had to be politely declined on grounds that he had been called away to the battlefronts.

Before the war's end, she decided to go back home to write fiction, and she has lived in Jackson since, though in the 1950's she made her first of several trips to Europe: "I was invited to lecture at Cam-bridge, and of course was scared to death. But if you're invited for six weeks, with a year to prepare, I just thought you're a perfect fool if you don't accept." One of her happiest meetings was with E. M. Forster, who invited her to lunch. "And the luckiest thing happened: our waiter was drunk, he came lurching on like a Shakespearian clown, and that put us both at ease and made our meeting so easy."

But then, how could a meeting with Eudora Welty be difficult?

Eudora Welty

Barbaralee Diamonstein / Fall 1970

A selection from *Open Secrets: Ninety-four Women in Touch with Our Times* by Barbaralee Diamonstein (New York: Viking, 1972), 442–45. © 1970, 1972 by Barbaralee Diamonstein. Reprinted by permission of Viking Penguin Inc.

This interview is Welty's response to a questionnaire originally sent by Diamonstein in fall 1970.

Eudora Welty has honored humility and heroism in plain people and recorded her view of the unchanging character of the South. With sensitivity and a sure comic sense, she has created two novels, two novellas, and four books of stories. She was awarded the MacDowell Medal, an honor from working artists to working artists, in recognition of her outstanding contribution to the arts.

Address: Jackson, Mississippi.

Job description: Writer.

Marital status: Single.

Age:

Educational background: Local grade and high schools; Mississippi State College for Women; University of Wisconsin (B.A.); Columbia University School of Business.

Previous experience: Self-taught writer.

I. **Women you respect most?** Georgia O'Keeffe, Martha Graham. For reasons plain to all—among them, common to both, an inviolate independence of spirit in pursuing their arts, the wholeness of their gifts of the imagination.

2. **Men you respect most?** Sir Kenneth Clark, for his vast knowledge and his generosity of mind and heart in communicating it to an audience of millions, who will now become a little more able to accept art and give it a place of meaning in their lives.

3. **Most gratifying aspects of work?** My work comes from the imagination. It gives me independence of range and habit and my choice of time and place in which to work.

4. **Least gratifying aspects of work?** Income is variable and

uncertain. One is asked to do too many outside things—a compli-
ment, but to respond politely even to decline takes time and energy
needed for sustained work.

   5. Satisfied with career? I would not be happy doing anything
else, never grow tired of it, never cease to learn from doing it.

   6. Person who has most influenced you? They can only be
multitudinous—the writers whose books from childhood on have
given me pleasure. As a great company they made me wish to do the
same.

   7. Men a help or hindrance? Writing is a profession outside
sex.

   8. Most important aspect of education? Reading.

   9. Most influential factors in choice of career? Loving to
read made me wish to write. Then I had a tolerant family—in particular a sympathetic, book-loving mother—and a quiet, congenial home
life which allowed me to try it.

   **10. For solving problems: (a) Psychotherapy. (b) Drugs.
(c) Group encounter. (d) Astrology.**
   With no familiarity with any of them, I still think very little of them,
and for myself should prefer to rely on self-examination and common
sense as resolute as possible.

   11. Most significant choice? I chose to live at home to do my
writing in a familiar world and have never regretted it.

   12. "Women's Liberation"? Noisiness.

   13. Unmarried women "bachelor girls" or "old maids"?
Just as women.

   14. Living in a man's world? Probably, in a good many respects.

   **15. Compared to men, women are more/less/about as
emotional, etc.?** As emotional; more competitive; less passive, ra-
tional, sincere; as strong, violent.

   16. Militant Women's Lib demonstrations? I'm not anxious
to have them as my representatives. I feel that their current acts,
usually rude, sometimes infantile, occasionally brutal, don't constitute
very valid reasons for giving women added respect. I would hate to
be respected, myself, for my power to embarrass.

   17. Men treat you as equal? As far as I know.

   18. Salary, compared to a man's, about equal?

19. Must a woman sacrifice femininity in career? No.

20. Meaning of "male chauvinism"? No idea.

21. Mother oppressed? Not at all.

22. Did she have a job? She was a full-time schoolteacher before her marriage.

23. Brought up to believe woman's place was in home? I don't think I was ever told where it was.

24. House-cleaning, cooking, laundry, etc.? I don't resent it. Accomplishment you can do fast and see finished gives me pleasure.

25. Men and women share burden of housework and child-raising? Share.

26. Ideal social unit in society? Family.

27. Marriage institution? Yes. For sake of emotional and social stability, for sake of the children.

28. Communal living? All right for those who want it. It has its element of fantasy and a pretty long history of not working.

29. Moral to bring children into our world? It's neither moral nor immoral to bring them into the world, but immoral not to accept the responsibility.

30. Have your job because you are a woman? Not in the case of any job I ever had.

31. Prefer company of men or women? In general I like them best together. In particular, according to the occasion, of course.

32. Speak freely when you disagree with a man? Probably more so.

33. Pretend to be dumber in presence of a man? No, but I might sometimes pretend to be smarter than I am. Because it would be desirable if I were.

34. How do you feel about living longer than most men? No better.

35. If equality achieved, would you be more or less successful than now? Compete better with men or women? Writing isn't competitive. Its success is probably a different personal matter with every writer; these are not matters to be compared.

36. If women had more political power? How to know?

37. Consider yourself successful? Yes, in that I can do the work I like and give all the time to it I want to.

38. Meaning of success? The above. The unattainable success would be satisfaction with any single piece of work, which can't happen; but I've found my ways to try.

39. Money important? Pays the way. For a writer it buys privacy and time.

40. Present job using full skills and educational background? It requires them—I try to apply them as I learn them.

41. Most worthwhile accomplishments?

42. Tempted to retire? No, I like doing my work.

43. Experiences compared with expectations? Always more interesting, whether to my sorrow or my joy.

45. Kind of community? City of 250,000 in the South.

46. Community problems? Education.

47. Most significant changes in society? Things opposing each other: destructiveness as a weapon and the genuine desire to make life better.

48. Changes please or upset you? Questioning our old acceptances pleases me—that's healthy and promising. Destruction of things for the sake of destruction upsets me, for the waste and stupidity of it.

49. "Law and order"? Lawlessness and disorder. The hysterical use and misuse of the words by political manipulators of all persuasions.

50. Strict enforcement of all laws? The basis should be that of reason, always in respect to humanity, and to mercy. If existing laws cost us humanity and mercy, they need to be changed, and changed along the lines of reason to better laws.

51. "All power to the people"? What any battle cry means. In this one all the words except "to" and "the" are suspect.

52. If child clashed with law over: (a) Civil disobedience. (b) Marijuana. (c) Hard drugs. (d) Traffic accident. (e) Draft resistance.
The danger of making a generalized answer to particular and individual questions lies exactly in the generalization—or so it seems to me. It's a popular habit in which loose thought, vanity of opinion, and dangerous judgment-passing all thrive. Human beings aren't in packages to be tossed into this pile or that.

53. Causes you would support? Peace, education, conservation, quiet.

54. Hopeless causes? The cause of yelling for what you want.
55. If you had real power? I cannot imagine.
56. The best years of your life?

"The Interior World":
An Interview with Eudora Welty
Charles T. Bunting / 24 January 1972

From *The Southern Review,* 8 (October 1972), 711–35. Reprinted by permission of Charles T. Bunting.

Eudora Welty has long been recognized as one of America's most distinguished women of letters. The recipient of numerous academic and literary awards, Miss Welty makes her home in Jackson, Mississippi, where this interview took place on January 24, 1972. The preceding day Miss Welty reviewed most of the questions which were to be asked. The interviewer wishes to express his appreciation for the graciousness afforded him by Miss Welty both during the interview and in the prompt return and careful editing of the transcript of our conversation. No alterations have been made to that returned manuscript.

Eudora Welty's contributions to the *Southern Review* (first series) include "A Memory" and "A Piece of News," which later appeared in her first collection of short stories, *A Curtain of Green.* The hard-cover edition of her latest novel, *The Optimist's Daughter,* was published last spring.

C.T.B.: What is the story regarding Ford Madox Ford's efforts to find a publisher for your short stories?

Miss Welty: Well, when I first began publishing in the *Southern Review* and other little magazines, I was still unable to get my work accepted in magazines of national circulation, like the *Atlantic* or *Harper's,* and, of course, no publisher wanted to take a book of short stories by such an unknown writer. I'm sure it was Katherine Anne Porter who called my stories to his attention. As you may know, Ford spent vast energies all his life helping young people. I was one of them, probably the last of a long list. It was just a great, generous spirit he had. He wrote to me out of a blue sky and asked if he could help in any way in interesting a publisher. Would I send him some of my work, which I did. And I suppose he wrote me altogether about six letters. He tried the stories on most of the publishers in England,

and they would send them back. He was in the process of sending my stories out at the time of his death. I never met him or anything. I wish I had. I owe him a great debt. Most of all, he gave me faith that people did care about beginning work, you know. A great person like him.

C.T.B.: Robert Penn Warren helped you, didn't he, especially by the publication of "A Piece of News" in *Understanding Fiction?*

Miss Welty: Oh, before that. He helped me from the time he accepted my stories for the *Southern Review*. He and Cleanth Brooks and Albert Erskine all were down at the *Southern Review,* which was published by LSU, and it was to them I sent my earliest stories. And they *accepted* them! *Helped* me? Why, it just gave me, you know, my life to get my stories into print at that time, and they printed a number of them. They were marvelous to me.

C.T.B.: Have you helped any aspiring writers along yourself, say, in the past few years?

Miss Welty: Not anything like that. I would like to do what I can. Now and then, when I was lecturing, I would run across, in reading manuscripts of students, things which were unmistakably good, and I would try to steer them to an editor or agent, something like that, but that was what anybody would have done. Mostly I think teachers are in a position to help young writers more than just another writer. They can say: *Read.*

C.T.B.: Where does a teacher steer these students? Don't you need an agent these days to get anything published?

Miss Welty: Well, you're talking now about selling. I was talking about writing, about getting good work done.

C.T.B.: And published?

Miss Welty: And in time published. In my case I got an agent after I'd been trying for about six years to place my stories in a national magazine. Diarmuid Russell wrote to me, again out of a clear blue sky, and asked if I needed an agent. He's the son of A. E., do you remember the poet, Yeats's friend? I'd never heard of an agent, didn't know what one was. But he had been given my name by an editor who came through Jackson on a scouting trip once: John Woodburn. And John Woodburn, who passed through here and spent the night in my house, took a whole bundle of my stories back to New York. He worked for Doubleday, who weren't particularly interested in the new, young short story writer. John, though, was a wonderful editor, the same kind as Max Perkins; he cared about work for its own sake. And he struggled very hard to sell the stories, but failed. Well, then he put me on to Diarmuid Russell, who succeeded finally in placing my stories in the *Atlantic* and *Harper's Bazaar* and *Harper's*. After which the publishers, the book publishers, were interested. So in the end he sold my book of stories to John Woodburn at Doubleday, so it was a perfect connected little story. And that's how it happened. But this isn't to forget that from the first I'd had instant acceptance from people like the *Southern Review* and the "little" magazines. I had encouragement important to me. That's what mattered, more than good fortune. Of course, as far as making a living out of writing goes, you can't. You always have to do something else, have a job or do assignments or teach or lecture or something. As far as making a living goes, writing stories is very precarious.

C.T.B.: While reading the article by Diarmuid Russell which you gave me [cf. *Shenandoah,* Winter 1969], it surprised me to learn that the first publication of *A Curtain of Green* sold less than three thousand copies. It was later sold to Harcourt, Brace, wasn't it?

Miss Welty: Yes, I moved to them when John Woodburn moved. I stayed with him because it was to him I owed my gratitude, before the publisher. I've forgotten what sort of sales happened after it moved to Harcourt; I mean to *A Curtain of Green. Low* would be the usual thing.

C.T.B.: I believe it sold a little less than seven thousand copies, according to the article.

Miss Welty: That book, of course, is included intact in this thing called *Selected Stories* [a reference to the Modern Library edition], which isn't really selected; it's just my first two books. I wish it could be selected. But they just buy plates of the books, and it has to be as is. And I suppose that's the one that stays in print. Well, I guess the Harcourt one is supposed to be in print.

C.T.B.: I think when *Delta Wedding* was published, then some of the other books were republished, weren't they? I believe they were out of print for awhile.

Miss Welty: No, I don't think they've ever been out of print. But now, the one I'm sorry about is *The Golden Apples,* which in a way is closest to my heart of all my books. Harcourt only issues it now as a paperback, but I am sorry about that because I like the book. And it was a beautiful hard-cover edition, just a lovely book; I mean, the job of bookmaking. It had a beautiful jacket. Everything about it I liked.

C.T.B.: You're fond of the work itself?

Miss Welty: Yes, I am. I was very happy working with that.

C.T.B.: Because of your use of folklore and myth?

Miss Welty: Well, in a peripheral way, it was that. That was one of the elements that went into it, but I mostly loved working on the connected stories, finding the way things emerged in my mind and the way one thing led to another; the interconnections of the book fascinated me.

C.T.B.: How long did it take you to write that work?

Miss Welty: Well, I don't know. Because I didn't begin it as a book of connected stories. I only realized the stories were connected after I was about halfway through the book. Some of the people I invented turned out to be not new characters but the same ones come upon at other times in their lives. Quite suddenly I realized I was writing about the same people. All their interconnections came to light. That's what I mean by the fascinations of fiction: things that go on in the back of your mind, that gradually emerge. And you say, "Well, of course; that's what it was all the time." It's not simple at all, of course, the working out of fiction in the mind. It's terribly complicated and not too well understood, I suppose.

C.T.B.: You mentioned yesterday that even your novels began as short stories, and that was true of *The Golden Apples* too, I guess.

Miss Welty: In *The Golden Apples* they exist on their own as short stories; they have independent lives. They don't have to be connected, but I think by being connected there's something additional coming from them as a group with a meaning of its own. I've had students write to me and say, "I'm writing a thesis to prove that *The Golden Apples* is a novel. Please send me. . . ." They want me to support them. So I write back and say that it isn't a novel, I'm sorry. They go right ahead, of course. It doesn't matter with a thesis, I guess.

C.T.B.: Do they get angry with you?

Miss Welty: I don't know what they get. (Laughing) And I'm sure they don't care what I get.

C.T.B.: When a school asks you to teach, do they assume that you will teach creative writing?

Miss Welty: *I* asked *them* for my only teaching job, at Millsaps. And they were marvelous about it. They found me the class; they gave me the time; I had a handpicked group of about seventeen very exciting young people, talented and good. We met once a week, sometimes twice a week, and I gave public readings and lectures on the side. I told them at the beginning I didn't believe in teaching writing. I don't think you can. It's something you have to learn for yourself. But I do think that it's helpful, perhaps—I was never in a writing class—that it may be helpful to write stories and read them aloud in class and then talk about them. And then have on hand certain stories written by real artists that we could read and talk about. So that's what we did. It was really a work class. Some people wrote three or four stories a year, and some wrote a dozen, just whatever they felt able to do. People have different capacities and different paces. I don't know what you think of that as a class, but . . .

C.T.B.: I think that having students actually write is the best way to teach such a course. Do you think that would-be writers should have a course in literary analysis? Does that help, or is that working in the opposite way?

Miss Welty: I wouldn't know because that isn't the way my mind works at all. Because writing is an internal process. You can't be helped from outside. It's interesting to see what people have done with analysis, but I don't think it helps you any while you're working because the craft of writing, which is constructive, moves in the opposite direction from the analysis of it. You don't start by saying, "These ingredients are to go in my novel: A, B, C, 1, 2, 3," and so on. It has to start from an internal feeling of your own and an experience of your own, and I think each reality like that has to find and build its own form. Another person's form doesn't really help. It shows what they've found, but that doesn't, may not, even apply. I know it doesn't help in the act of writing because you're not thinking of anything then but your story. You're not thinking, "How did Joyce do this?" That's fatal. It's all-absorbing, as it is, to bring about your own; your work needs all the sense you can master, and all the feeling, everything of yourself you can put into it. I don't mean self-conscious self. You don't think about your self either; you think about the work. To think "I, so-and-so, am writing this story" would just be fatal, more fatal than anything.

C.T.B.: Your fiction has frequently been praised for its lyrical quality. Did you aspire to be a poet when you first began to write? There were some poems of yours published in *Southern Humanities Review.*

Miss Welty: No, I can't write poetry at all. Of course, as a child of ten or twelve, like anyone, I would write jingles and stuff. *Southern Humanities Review* should have left them buried in the children's pages of *St. Nicholas Magazine.* But I know I have no connection with poetry. Of course, I'm pleased if a lyrical quality is felt in my stories because it does lie in my nature to praise and to celebrate things, but I try not to be "poetic." I think I'm trying to just write good prose, you know, explicit prose.

C.T.B.: What essential differences of technique and difficulty do you experience between writing short stories and a novel?

Miss Welty: Well, a short story to me, and I think to most writers, is a different kind of entity from a novel. Each form has its own organization. But a short story is more a single thing, more one sustained effort, which has a beginning, a rise, and a fall. And, of course, a novel has so much wider scope, greater looseness of texture, and so much more room to expand. Many rises and falls are possible, and even necessary. A novel's different from the very first sentence. It's as if you were going to run a race. If you just had to go two hundred yards, you would rely on a different takeoff and drive and intention, a different wind, than if you were going to run three miles. (This is someone who never does run, so I don't know why I choose that.) But it is a sort of a different girding up that you have to do. It's a different pace, a different timing. In the case of the short story, you can't ever let the tautness of line relax. It has to be all strung very tight upon its single thread usually, and everything is subordinated to the theme of the story: characters and mood and place and time; and none of those things are as important as the development itself. Whereas in a novel you have time to shade a character, allow him his growth, in a short story a character hardly changes from beginning to end. He's in there for the purpose of that story only, and any other modification is ruled out. In a novel you have time for subordinate characters, gradations of mood, subsidiary plots, other things that complement the story or oppose it. The difference is much more than a matter of length—it's a matter of organization and intention and in final effect.

C.T.B.: In your latest novel, *Losing Battles,* at what stage in the writing of this book did it become a novel? When did it depart from being a short story?

Miss Welty: I first thought of it as a story of the return of a boy from the pen, and I was going to end it when he got home. My idea was to show the difference between how people thought of him and what he was. It was to be just a pure talk story. Well, the moment he arrived, it became a novel. Because he was somebody. And the story was his. I realized the scope of the thing was a good deal larger than I had counted on. But I was still interested in trying to work something out in the technique I started with, altogether by talk and action, trying to *show* everything and not as an author enter the character's mind and say, "He was thinking so-and-so." I wanted it all to be shown forth, brought forth, the way things are in a play, have it become a novel in the mind of the reader, I mean, understood in the mind of the reader. The thought, the feeling that is *internal* is *shown* as external. I wanted the whole thing externalized. That was why it was a comedy. Because anything that's done in action and talk is a comedy. I wanted to see if I could bring it off. And it was a great job for me to do and very hard for me to do.

C.T.B.: Was it intentional to achieve such a unity of time?

Miss Welty: Yes, essential. Any novel that you write, of course, carries its timing with it. Its whole meaning and pace and setting and timing and all lie ingrained in the original idea. Any story or novel. I had originally planned *Losing Battles* to happen in one day, but you see it goes over the night into the next morning. That is probably a flaw, but I couldn't resolve it, mainly because the day was a Sunday. I had to have Monday morning. I realized it while I was working bcause I kept making notes, putting them in another folder saying, "Next A.M.," and then I realized that that was a whole section. I realized that I could not incorporate everything into the one day, so I had to have Monday. But everything does have to be compressed, of course, in any work of fiction. It has to have bounds. You can't begin without staking something off in time and place.

C.T.B.: Because of the longer time span in *Delta Wedding,* did you purposefully try to shorten the time in *Losing Battles,* or did that have anything to do with it?

Miss Welty: I'm sorry; I can't even remember planning *Delta Wedding.* But one piece of work doesn't affect another, at any rate. *Delta Wedding* did begin as a short story. It was Diarmuid Russell who told me it was a novel. I sent in something called "The Delta Cousins," and he read it and sent it back and said, "This is Chapter Two of a novel," which it is. It was about the little night light. When I say I don't remember planning *Delta Wedding,* what I mean is I don't remember any of the problems and the solving of them. What I remember about anything that's finished with or anything that I am not working on at present is its feeling and what I *tried* to do. But to answer your question, anything having to do with a wedding in the Delta couldn't be compressed into one day. (Laughing) I'm sure it's a much more loosely organized work than *Losing Battles.*

C.T.B.: Do you recall when you first began to write *Losing Battles?* Do you remember the genesis of the novel?

Miss Welty: I don't know how you would describe a genesis of anything. As I was just telling you, what I thought it was going to be was a short story. I think normally I would have just written it and finished it, the way I do everything else. But owing to personal responsibilities, I couldn't work at it with any sustainment or any regularity, so that what I did was mostly make notes and write scenes and tuck them in a box, with no opportunity to go back and revise, but writing a scene anew instead of revising it, so that the work prolonged itself. I don't mind any of this, because I was teaching myself all this time. And the fact that it stayed alive in my head over a period of years cheered me up because I thought that it must have some spark of vitality or it would have just faded away. But it kept staying with me; I only kept thinking of more and more scenes. So then when I did have time to work on it, I just had boxes full of scenes. Oh, I have a lot more than is in *Losing Battles,* which, Lord knows, is enough. There were extra incidents, which told the same thing in different terms, different scenes, different characters. And so, it took me a period of years, instead of, maybe a year. And all the time I was doing other things. I was writing lectures and giving lectures. I wrote a children's book. I did many book reviews, occasional assignments, and I was teaching. So it's hard to speak of a genesis or follow the growth of *Losing Battles,* and I don't really know what course it would have taken in an ordinary way.

C.T.B.: Would you comment upon the rather conspicuous absence of Negroes in *Losing Battles?*

Miss Welty: I didn't know an absence was conspicuous because I thought I had everything in there that mattered. It wouldn't have made any difference at all in *Losing Battles* because the same kind of battles were being fought by the white people as would have been fought by the black. So I don't think that there's anything missing, or anything avoided, there at all. But northeast Mississippi is not a part of the state where there ever were any black people because it's too poor. There weren't plantations where you had sharecroppers and a society like that. There are small, independent, poverty-stricken, white, red clay hill farmers up there, and Negroes never went there. There is, all the same, a very telling and essential incident in *Losing Battles* which is told about, that involves a Negro as such. Perhaps you remember.

C.T.B.: Miss Julia Mortimer has, of course, lost her battle to educate the Renfroes, but really it's a losing battle for everybody in the novel, isn't it?

Miss Welty: Well, you can look at "losing" in two ways: the verb or the participle. Even though you are losing the battle, it doesn't mean that you aren't eternally fighting them and brave in yourself. And I wanted to show indomitability there. I don't feel it's a novel of despair at all. I feel it's more a novel of admiration for the human being who can cope with any condition, even ignorance, and keep a courage, a joy of life, even, that's unquenchable. But I see human beings as *valuable.* Each life is very valuable in itself, regardless, and in spite of everything.

C.T.B.: E. E. Cummings wrote that "To be nobody but myself means to fight the hardest battle which any human being can fight." Is it this battle for self-identity, self-preservation, that you had in mind in *Losing Battles?*

Miss Welty: That could describe one aspect of it, I guess. Certainly, one battle was Gloria's for her own existence in that family of people she'd married into. But the feeling of the solidity of the family, which is the strongest thing in the book, is certainly not a battle of identity. The battle for identity is not even necessary. It's a sticking together. It involves both a submerging and a triumph of the individual, because you can't really conceive of the whole unless you *are* an identity. Unless you are very real in yourself, you don't know what it means to support others or to join with them or to help them. So it's a much more complicated business than identity-seeking, I think. To suggest to any of the characters in *Losing Battles* that they had to *seek* their identities would be a pretty good way to insult them.

C.T.B.: The Renfroes have such faith that with Jack's return things will be better; however, you get the feeling that they will not.

Miss Welty: That's part of the comedy. Their whole faith and trust in that, which they find necessary, is comic. And *his* faith, Jack's faith, which is where it all comes from: from his point of view, everything is going to be all right now. I think that's very comical and also very. . . . Well, far be it from me to put tags on my work.

C.T.B.: Don't you think that it's despairing for Gloria? You can't help but feel for her, particularly in that watermelon scene. I felt squeamish reading that.

Miss Welty: Yes, well, that's the way people are, though. No, I don't think she's going to win; but, still, she and Jack do love each other. She's the most naïve soul there; she's not Miss Julia Mortimer at all, by any means. And she totally lacks imagination. How could she have married Jack and thought she was going to change him? That's the comic side of her.

C.T.B.: And, of course, she tries to be aloof from the rest.

Miss Welty: Yes, but I also think their love was quite true, and there's a great deal of strength there, even though they haven't the faintest idea of the fallibility of the whole thing.

C.T.B.: Did you select the 1920s for *Delta Wedding* and the 1930s for *Losing Battles* to achieve a kind of aesthetic distance?

Miss Welty: Oh, no. I chose those for very particular reasons. In the case of *Delta Wedding* I chose the twenties—when I was more the age of my little girl, which was why I thought best to have a child in it. But in writing about the Delta, I had to pick a year—and this was quite hard to do—in which all the men could be home and uninvolved. It couldn't be a war year. It couldn't be a year when there was a flood in the Delta because those were the times before the flood control. It had to be a year that would leave my characters all free to have a family story. It meant looking in the almanac—in fact, I did—to find a year that was uneventful and that would allow me to concentrate on the people without any undue outside influences; I wanted to write a story that showed the solidity of this family and the life that went on on a small scale in a world of its own. So the date was chosen by necessity. In the case of *Losing Battles* I wanted to get a year in which I could show people at the rock bottom of their whole lives, which meant the Depression. I wanted the poorest part of the state, which meant the northeast corner, where people had the least, the least of all. I wanted a clear stage to bring on this family, to show them when they had really no props to their lives, had only themselves, plus an indomitable will to live even with losing battles, you know, the losing battles of poverty, of any other kind of troubles, family troubles and disasters. I wanted to take away everything and show them naked as human beings. So that fixed the time and place.

C.T.B.: In a criticism of *Delta Wedding* Louis D. Rubin, Jr., remarked: "The closed little world of Shellmound is doomed. The wide world will come in; there will be disorder, change." Is that a fair assessment? Is Shellmound with its way of life and its values doomed?

Miss Welty: Oh, yes. I think that was implicit in the novel: that this was all such a fragile, temporary thing. At least I hope it was. That's why I searched so hard to find the year in which that could be most evident. Well, you're living in a very precarious world without knowing it, always.

C.T.B.: Did you have Troy Flavin in mind as the outsider?

Miss Welty: Yes, in the Delta he was a hill person. He would be more like somebody out of the neighborhood of *Losing Battles,* although I don't mean as a character in *Losing Battles.* But his origins. You see, right outside the Delta there are the hills, and there are not very many miles difference there, but there's a world away in the kinds of people and their backgrounds. He was very different from anybody in the Delta.

C.T.B.: He has a strong attachment for his mother, who gives Troy and Dabney a quilt for a wedding gift. The quilt pattern, "Delectable Mountains," is the same pattern used for Granny Vaughn's quilt in *Losing Battles.*

Miss Welty: (Surprised) Oh, my Lord! Did I use the same pattern? I never realized that. I'm glad you told me. That's fascinating. I almost called the one in *Losing Battles*—for a time I did—"Dove in the Window." Once it was "The Rocky Road to Dublin." But I guess in both novels what appealed to me was the Pilgrim's Progress background of the Delectable Mountains name. And also the idea of the mountains, which would appeal to both those families. I'm sure I went through the same process without realizing I hit on the same quilt name. that's very funny. I know at least thirty other quilt names.

C.T.B.: You mentioned *Pilgrim's Progress*. In your first published short story, "Death of a Traveling Salesman," R. J. Bowman is journeying to Beulah. Of course, he never makes it. In *The Ponder Heart* there's the Hotel Beulah. And, then, of course, there's Beulah Renfro in *Losing Battles.*

Miss Welty: It's just a common name, but it also has in each case the right connotations, different every time, for where it's used. Beulah, as you probably know, is a name in use all over Mississippi. In a certain kind of Mississippi town, the leading hotel is always named after a lady. So I just named mine Beulah. There was a different reason for calling the town Beulah, in "Death of a Traveling Salesman"; in this case it stood for Beulah Land, in the old hymn. But I wouldn't ever use a name that was right in feeling if it weren't also typical of the kind of people. I'm careful as I can be about names, and I work hard at them. And I don't use anything that couldn't happen, that wouldn't be right for that part of the country or that kind of family, that time in history. I really do have those things as near right as I can get them because that matters to me. That's why it bothers me to get letters from people saying, "Did you call Phoenix Jackson 'Phoenix' in 'A Worn Path' as a symbol that she would make the trip over and over and over again the way the phoenix lives over and over and over again?" Very well, but I could not have called her that in the first place if the name "Phoenix" were not well known as a name for people she would have sprung from. She says in there, "I was too old at the Surrender," which put her back in slavery times. I wouldn't have called her that if nobody of her kind had ever been called Phoenix. So it's boring to think that things would be offered for symbolic reasons only, and it would be ridiculous too.

C.T.B.: Then there's Narciss in *The Ponder Heart.*

Miss Welty: Which is *not* symbolic. There are plenty of reasons for using names.

C.T.B.: When you are writing, are you conscious of your use of symbols?

Miss Welty: They occur naturally; they are organic. If they're a part of the story, they come readily to hand when you want them, and as often as you want them, and you use them with a proper sense of proportion, and with as light a touch as possible. There's a story that goes around—I'm sure it's true—about some students saying, "I've finished my story. All I have to do now is go back and put the symbols in." That isn't knowing what a symbol is. A book, a novel itself is a big symbol, and a word is a symbol. Color is a symbol. Anything can be a symbol if the way it's used refers us to the imagination. It's a vocabulary, and it's part of your equipment. But it does not exist for its own sake, something dragged in with a big, red "S" on it. That way, of course, it would have no effect.

C.T.B: Do you feel distressed when you see an article like "The Symbols in Eudora Welty's Works"?

Miss Welty: Rather helpless. Especially when they make them symbols of something that could not possibly be true. You know, as if I were really trying to write *Paradise Lost* in some little story about rural Mississippi. That's not a joke. I've seen people do things like that. It's a good reason not to read things.

C.T.B.: Do you plan to write anything else with a more contemporary setting, such as "The Demonstrators"?

Miss Welty: I've just written a novel, which is coming out in the spring, which takes place as of a couple of years ago. It too is a family story, but it's told from within. People who have read it and whose opinion I respect say it's different from anything else I've ever done. It's much more concentrated and headlong, and it's shorter; it's a very short novel. At all times, I'm interested in individuals, as you may have gathered, and in personal relationships, which to me are the things that matter; personal relationships matter more than any kind of generalizations about the world at large. So the date doesn't terribly matter. You can set stories at any time and place you wish. But since it is all an ordered world, any work of fiction, everything, including time and place, has to be directly applicable to the needs of the story. I couldn't have set *Losing Battles* in the Delta, for instance, where people are comparatively rich, much more sophisticated, where they come and go a lot, have everything to do with the outside world—at least they do now. *Losing Battles* had to be confined by its own world of poverty and isolation. The "contemporary" question doesn't matter in itself. The basic problem is *always* contemporary.

C.T.B.: What will the new work be called?

Miss Welty: *The Optimist's Daughter.* It was published in *The New Yorker* a year or two ago, but I've changed it some.

C.T.B.: What other plans do you have for your writing?

Miss Welty: Well, I'm supposed also to be getting my non-fiction together. I have accumulated a whole lot of things over the years—essays, lectures, various things—but I'm taking my time doing that. The thing I'd like to do now is write some more short stories. I have some of those still to be collected in a book, and I'd like to add three or four.

C.T.B.: Tennessee Williams once made the following remark concerning his writing: "I am not a direct writer; I am always an oblique writer, if I can be; I want to be allusive." Do you feel this same tendency to be "allusive"?

Miss Welty: Well, it's not a tendency; it's a technique. All fiction writers work by indirection; to show, not to tell; not to make statements about a character, but to demonstrate it in his actions or his conversations or by suggesting his thoughts, so that the reader understands for himself. Because fiction accomplishes its ends by using the oblique. Anything lighted up from the side, you know, shows things in a relief that you can't get with a direct beam of the sun. And the imagination works all around the subject to light it up and reveal it in all of its complications.

C.T.B.: Has your interest in painting and photography in any way paralleled your writing techniques?

Miss Welty: Well, I suppose they're all aspects of the visual mind. I see things in pictures. I'm not anything at all of a painter. I love painting. I have no talent for it. The only talent I have—for writing, I was blessed with it—is quite visual. And anything I imagine in what I read or write, I see it. I understand that's the commonest form of the imagination.

C.T.B.: Do you feel that your writing reflects a particularly feminine point of view?

Miss Welty: I am a woman. In writing fiction, I think imagination comes ahead of sex. A writer's got to be able to live inside all characters: male, female, old, young. To live inside *any* other person is the jump. Whether the other persons are male or female is subordinate.

C.T.B.: Why have there been so few really great women writers?

Miss Welty: Well, I think there have been not a few great women writers, of course. Jane Austen. I don't see how anyone could have a greater scope in knowledge of human nature and reveal more of human nature than Jane Austen. Consider Virginia Woolf. The Brontës. Well, you know as many as I do: great women writers. I'm not interested in any kind of a feminine repartee. I don't *care* what sex people are when they write. I just want the result to be a good book. All that talk of women's lib doesn't apply *at all* to women writers. We've always been able to do what we've wished. I couldn't feel less deprived as a woman to be writing, and I certainly enjoy all the feelings of any other human being. The full complement is available. I have the point of view of a woman, but if I'm not able to imagine myself into what another human being who is a man might feel, which I have to do all the time when I write, well, it's just from poverty of imagination. It's a matter of imagination, not sex.

C.T.B.: Commenting upon her art, Flannery O'Connor once said, "Mine is a comic art, but that does not detract from its seriousness." A critic for the *New York Times Book Review* wrote that "Eudora Welty possesses the surest comic sense of any American writer alive." Does such a statement make you wonder sometimes if the seriousness of your work may be overlooked?

Miss Welty: Of course not. No, I think Flannery O'Connor was absolutely and literally right in what she says: that the fact that something is comic does not detract from its seriousness, because the comic and the serious are not opposites. You might as well say satire is not serious, and it's probably the most deadly serious of any form of writing, even though it makes you laugh. No, I think comedy is able to tackle the most serious matters that there are. I'm delighted that the critic thinks that I have a good comic spirit. And I think that's taking me seriously.

C.T.B.: Do you discover something about yourself in creating your characters?

Miss Welty: Well, it isn't your object, of course. No, I don't think you're thinking about yourself at all when you're creating characters. What you do learn is something about the subject on which you're writing, through creating your characters; you learn more and more about human relationships through what you're doing. What you're trying to do is make a story, a work, a piece of art, if possible, in which lies all that you yourself have learned or experienced.

C.T.B.: William Faulkner remarked that Dilsey was one of his favorite characters. Have you created any characters whom you particularly admire?

Miss Welty: Well, I don't think of any characters as existing outside the book in which they happen, outside the story. I think you get very fond of the people in your work, but it has nothing to do with their artistic achievement. It's purely a personal thing, just as you like certain people in life; your love may not be a certification of their worth. But in the case of Dilsey, of course she was a magnificent and beautiful creation, a marvelous creation.

C.T.B.: Phoenix Jackson is too, I feel.

Miss Welty: Well, thank you. I love her.

C.T.B.: In your essay, "Place in Fiction," you state that "Making reality real is art's responsibility." Would you agree, then, with William Faulkner's contention that "The writer's only responsibility is to his art"?

Miss Welty: Well, I don't think those two statements are using the word "responsibility"—I don't think those are within the same category. The way I used the word in "Place in Fiction" was in a particular and specific connection: using place to make character believable and action believable and so on. I wasn't talking about art's responsibility. . . . I've forgotten exactly what his words were.

C.T.B.: "The writer's only responsibility is to his art."

Miss Welty: That's a very different kind of statement. The responsibility is a big general one. It's his *personal* responsibility, which is a very great one.

C.T.B.: Do you think there has been a decline in regional identification?

Miss Welty: Yes, because regions are no longer very definite, places are not as different from one another as they used to be. In the South or in New England or the Southwest, small towns still have a living identity, but I think you're certainly aware of the life of the country as a whole flowing through everywhere. You don't feel that you're cut off anymore, I'm sure.

C.T.B.: Were you pleased with the dramatization of *The Ponder Heart?*

Miss Welty: Well, I could answer that on several levels. I had nothing to do with the dramatization. It was done by two adapters, and it was completely changed from my book, of course, because the book existed as a monologue by one of the characters, Edna Earle Ponder. We see everything through her; what we are interested in is how she looks at things. Well, naturally, on the stage she was made a character at whom we are looking from the outside, and made subordinate to Uncle Daniel, the one who is the subject of her story. So that to an author is rather wrenching. And then by necessity the story itself was changed, and some of the characterizations. And they even took some lines from characters in my other short stories and put them into the mouths of people in *The Ponder Heart,* which was very strange. However, once I got used to all that, I rather enjoyed the play because of the performers, who were all very warm and understanding. They had read my novel, too, and were trying to use that to guide them in their characterizations, they told me. They were all terribly nice people, and they gave a gentle and warm performance, and I liked it for its own sake.

C.T.B.: Have you had any other offers to dramatize or film any of your work?

Miss Welty: Well, these arise every now and again, but nothing comes of it. That seems to be usual. So I've learned to not get excited when someone wires, "Do nothing until you hear from me." You don't ever hear anything.

There have been some interesting things done locally with my stories by New Stage Theater and by Educational Television. The groups really are quite imaginative and expert, and I'm awfully pleased to have been in such good hands. They did an evening called "A Season of Dreams," made of excerpts and scenes from my stories. This was done both at New Stage and on ETV. It's enjoyable to watch them work. It teaches me a lot to see things put together and watch something being made to work dramatically.

C.T.B.: In a recently published essay called "The Short Story," Joyce Carol Oates remarked that the short story is a "dream verbalized" and that "the most interesting thing about it is its mystery." Would you agree that these remarks coincide with your own feelings about the genre?

Miss Welty: Well, I don't know the context out of which those words came. "A dream verbalized" doesn't mean much to me. What's the other thing?

C.T.B.: "The most interesting thing about it is its mystery."

Miss Welty: I agree with that. Well, I don't know how Miss Oates meant this; I don't know if I'm agreeing with her opinion or not. I'm agreeing with the fact. The sense of mystery in life we do well to be aware of. And, of course, I think we do try to suggest that mystery in writing a story, not through any direct or cheap way but by simply presenting the way things happen. Mystery is a real and valid element, both in life and in fiction. I agree with that.

C.T.B.: Would you assess the importance that dreams seem to have for the characters in your fiction?

Miss Welty: I think dreams have an importance, but no greater an importance than many other things: ideas, meetings, letters, conversations. They're all component parts of the interior world, and if I've ever overemphasized dreams, I wasn't aware of it, although I've often written about people that might be over-given to dreaming, you know, young girls or old people. I've used dreams, of course, when I need to express something that's outside the range of what I can show otherwise.

C.T.B.: And dreams would be necessary for you because of your concern for the interior life.

Miss Welty: Right. They are. In the case of daydreams often. That's part of living. But I didn't mean to give an over important place to dreams.

C.T.B.: There is, then, no particular psychologist or philosopher whose ideas of dreams, such as Freud, has any especial influence on you?

Miss Welty: No. I don't think any ideas come to you from other people's minds, when you're writing, as directives. You can't take hints and suggestions from this person and that to know where you're going. It's just outside the whole process of writing a story. That all has to come from within. It doesn't mean that you haven't read things and understood things through reading and come to think things through reading that don't filter down and apply. What I mean is you're not using a snippet of Freud and a little piece of Jung or anything like that. Any more than a composer would take a piece of—Well, of course, they *do,* in popular music. (Laughing) That's not a good analogy. But you wouldn't take a scrap of someone else's painting and put it in your painting. You might both be treating of the same landscape, but you would put on paint as a matter of vision in both cases; your painting is your vision, not somebody's else's vision.

C.T.B.: Your influences, then, would be more cultural and imaginative than literary?

Miss Welty: When you're writing, your influences are by way of the imagination only. That doesn't mean that there couldn't be many unconscious forces at play. Of course that's true. But I think of my source as real life itself—nothing to do with reference books.

C.T.B.: What stories do you reread?

Miss Welty: I don't reread my stories. Giving readings on the lecture platform made me go back and reread stories to select from— the early ones were the only ones short enough. My reaction was how I could have made them better. I could see many faults that a little transposing and cutting would help. But I'm not interested in anything but the new, really. The only thing that absorbs me is what I'm working on, work ahead. I don't mean that I don't have affection and respect for the work I've done, and a wish that it had been better. But it's not an immediate concern to me.

C.T.B.: What other authors do you enjoy rereading?

Miss Welty: Oh, I love to reread so many authors. I'm just getting ready to read Jane Austen again. E. M. Forster. Henry Green. Virginia Woolf. Oh, there are so many people I love to read and reread.

C.T.B.: How do you feel generally about literary criticism?

Miss Welty: When can it be helpful to me as a writer? That I don't know. I do like to read the general literary criticism of good critics such as Edmund Wilson, just as I like to read good biographies or good anything else. I like the exercise of the mind and the fascination of learning, perhaps understanding new territories in other minds and hearts. I've just finished reading Robert Penn Warren on Theodore Dreiser, that long essay that was in the *Southern Review*, which was absolutely fascinating. It certainly showed me I had to reproach myself, since I'd never paid Theodore Dreiser any homage at all. It's brilliant and marvelous, profoundly instructive—a critic and poet offering his insight into another creative mind. Yes, I was thrilled by it, but not helped. What a waste of time and feeling to read for self-help! Maybe such a study will help me, by the exercise of my mind and the moving of my heart, but any "help" for my own work coming to me has to be by remote control and received by me all unknowing.

C.T.B.: In accepting the National Medal of Literature recently, E. B. White made this comment. "Today, with so much of earth damaged and endangered, with so much of life dispiriting or joyless, a writer's courage can easily fail him. I feel this daily. In the face of so much bad news, how does one sustain one's belief?" How would you answer his question?

Miss Welty: Well, I don't think it has any answer because it's certainly a fact of life; but just the fact that Mr. White said that is in a way its own answer. The facing of it and the grasping of it and the statement of it is in a way dealing with it, and a wonderful spirit like Mr. White's would always be capable of doing that very thing. All of our history must have been thought of, as we lived through it, as being the absolute worst or the lowest or the most threatening or the most something, and the human spirit seems to have survived many dark ages. And I think it's through the *individual* spirit, which is what Mr. White is, and what most fiction writers are, most artists. I believe the human spirit will survive, and that's not to minimize in the least, any more than he does, the existence and threat of all these horrors in the world.

C.T.B.: He concludes that the author must not despair.

Miss Welty: No, in fact I don't think you are despairing as long as you're working. Your work is an answer. I don't mean that working keeps you from thinking about it. I mean that working is the answer, in itself. By putting something on paper, and doing it well, making a meaning and an order out of some of the world in fiction. It's the human spirit answering in its own terms. I don't know if that's clearly enough put.

C.T.B.: Do you think that some fiction writers today have a tendency to emphasize philosophy too much in their works?

Miss Welty: Well, you can skip that. . . . I didn't mean to be flippant, but to me fiction isn't the place for philosophy. Philosophy has its own very great place, and we should consult it and learn from it as much as we can. But in fiction I think it's irrelevant and intrusive, when put in *as* philosophy.

C.T.B.: What have been some of your more distressing moments as a writer?

Miss Welty: I can't think of any, really. I love to write. I'm never happier than when I'm working. It doesn't matter how hard it is; in fact, I love hard things to write. I try harder and harder. I want to do harder and harder things because that's the fascination. I'm utterly happy when I'm revising. Throwing away gives me a great elation sometimes. So I haven't had any distressing moments, and I've had good luck in my writing life with good friends as editors and agents, and I've had a very happy time as a writer. I'm not bothered now and I was not deeply bothered then by the long periods of not being able to sell stories when I began; the fact that I never made much money doesn't have anything to do with it because the writing itself is the deepest pleasure to me. I love to read, and I love to write, and for the same reason, I think.

I get letters sometimes from students saying, "Can I come down and talk to you about this gut-tearing, soul-destroying practice of our craft, our art?" I don't want *them* to come. I have a good time writing.

C.T.B.: Do you feel that you have a built-in audience?

Miss Welty: I'm grateful for any audience I may have, but at the same time my real working life isn't affected by the thought of readers. I don't think about readers while I'm writing, but only of the story. Of course, I couldn't hope more strongly for the pleasure of good friends on whose judgment I rely, but that comes afterwards, when I've done all I can and stuck the story in the mail. I know I have good friends who understand my work, and I hope will tell me if they think I've made a disastrous mistake somewhere along the line. This is deeply important to me. I really don't know what you mean by a built-in audience.

C.T.B.: An audience who is eagerly awaiting the next Eudora Welty work.

Miss Welty: I'm grateful to think there could be such a thing. That's very comforting!

C.T.B.: We waited a long time.

Miss Welty: Well, thank them for waiting. I do thank them.

C.T.B.: What is your reaction to reading analyses of your work?

Miss Welty: It neither helps nor hurts. Because by the time something is in print, you've usually written it a while ago, and you're now working on something else. It's too late to—not that you would change anything—but it's too late even to have your mistakes pointed out and to have your virtues pointed out, which is usually just as mistaken as the mistakes. It doesn't help any. And it makes me very nervous to read. . . , especially some things that are so terribly farfetched. I get sent things, from time to time, and I will see how they start out, and then I feel that I would just rather not read on. I don't mean that to sound disdainful. It's just that I don't see the connection.

C.T.B.: It's difficult as a teacher, however, not to use analysis. Unfortunately, students seem to want some snappy epigram that will sum up the work for them.

Miss Welty: Well, what they ought to be given is some more stories by the same person. They should be advised to keep reading, is the way I feel about it. The horrifying thing is that they grew up in homes where people didn't read. They don't know what the imagination can tell you. They reach out for a snappy . . . whatever you called it.

C.T.B.: Epigram.

Miss Welty: At some future point, the students are going to descend on the writer with a tape recorder and tell him to justify that epigram. But the worst is that these students will later become teachers themselves, and pass on the stuff that's being fed to them now. I suppose you've thought about the consequences. What they need to do is learn to use their imaginations, to recognize imagination. They need to know the medium in which stories are written, which is again the imagination. I really don't know anything about teaching, but my firm inclination is to tell them to read more. But it really is too bad when you think of all they're going to miss the rest of their lives if they've never learned anything except a couple of snappy epigrams, which they think is an equivalent of the story. And, of course, it isn't. Nothing is, except possibly another story by the same person.

C.T.B.: Unhappily, students often come with the preconceived notion that if the story does not meet their demands then the story is no good.

Miss Welty: Well, it's just their loss, and that's all there is to it. They'll never learn by being collaborated with. And it seems to me a shame to risk a betrayal of art, to ruin art in order that a student will think he's getting something. In fact, I don't even think it's honest. To make a work of imagination out to be something in another category, that can be learned in capsule terms, as an algebraic, or mathematical formula, is not honest. But it's so sad; it makes you wonder what they will ever have in their lives to make up for that loss. But there will always be *some,* though. There will always be some. After all, we came along, we can read, although I think we came along in more congenial times, me much more so than you. But there will always be some.

C.T.B.: But don't you feel that there is a kind of prevailing anti-intellectual climate?

Miss Welty: Oh, yes, but there have been other anti-intellectual climates, and I don't think that that necessarily stops us. You could have an anti-intellectual climate and still have a climate that would accept works of the imagination. They don't necessarily cancel out.

C.T.B.: In a recent interview R. Buckminster Fuller remarked that "Science begins with the awareness of the absolute mystery of universe." Might the word "literature" be substituted for "science"?

Miss Welty: Well, I certainly think that poets knew it all along, the absolute mystery of the universe. That's what Shakespeare says in every word. I don't know the context of Fuller's remark, or exactly what he means by "science" here—whether he means knowledge, the knowledge of science, or the terrible power of science, which is what people think of these days, the frightening things. I think if he used it in the sense of knowledge, that is what literature is written in the sense of, an awareness. The power of science is a brutal concept. I don't want brutality dealing with mysteries.

C.T.B.: A difficulty arises when one tries to unravel the mystery in your story "The Purple Hat." It's a short story that many critics seem to puzzle over.

Miss Welty: That's a small mystery! (Laughing) I wish I hadn't written that story. I saw it dramatized last year, an off-Broadway thing, which only brought home to me its failings. It was just an odd story I wrote in an odd moment, about something I don't know much about: gambling. But I really meant it to be no more than a kind of playful ghost story.

C.T.B.: Some have read allegory into it.

Miss Welty: Well, I can't be responsible. I meant it to be a ghost story, a playful ghost story. I wasn't trying to be allegorical or anything else.

C.T.B.: What, perhaps, is the most outlandish interpretation of your work that you recall?

Miss Welty: Oh, let's not go into the outlandish. I don't mean to be disparaging about any criticism because I think it, some of it, can be valuable, extremely valuable. I only repeat that as far as helping the author goes, nothing helps in heaven or earth when you're writing. It's just you out there by yourself. That's the way you want it.

Eudora Welty: Rose-Garden Realist, Storyteller of the South

Henry Mitchell / 1972

JACKSON, Miss.—Some say Eudora Welty writes best of all, in all Hinds County, but she has never taken to prideful airs. Others say she's the best in all central Mississippi or all America.

"Shoot!" she says, or "Foot!" when the paid or as you might say store-bought critics start up their steady songs of praise.

"Now Eudora," a friend once said to her, "how come you read those reviews. Lots of writers don't read reviews at all."

"I know a lot of writers that don't," she said, "but I do. I've got too much curiosity not to."

Which is, as the Lord knows, true. Miss Welty has more curiosity than a tiger cat. Besides, though she won't exactly say so, it's fairly nice to pick up a paper or magazine and see them having consistent and urgent fits about both your last two books. She writes them for hours off and on in her bedroom right here in Jackson and they are, as some would say, a wonder to behold.

One fellow at the *Washington Post* (writer Reynolds Price) just flung up his arms in print and said there's no point comparing *Losing Battles* (1970) to other American novels. He suggested, for starters, you might compare it with *The Tempest* by the late W. Shakespeare, and then just took it on from there.

"Yes, I know he did," said Miss Welty when I had the pleasure of her company and her cooking for two days recently, "and I am really going to speak to him about it. Shakespeare is a bit much."

He was the worst, the *Post* reviewer, for making a decent person blush. The paper down in Houston just said the book was a "gigantic achievement" and at the *New York Times* they only spoke of their "general rejoicing" though they did add Miss Welty has the surest comic sense of any American writer alive. In Philadelphia where the cautious restraining Quaker influence is still felt they modestly called it a masterpiece and let it go at that.

"I do like to read blurbs," said Miss Welty. "And when I go through a book I look unconsciously for good ones."

"Ain't she kind of a recluse?" asked the cab driver that eventually showed up to carry me to the Weltys' house in the first place. He pronounced it "reckless." The idea of a reckless Eudora Welty is something to make a dog laugh. Reckless she is not. But then recluse she is not, either. It would irk the fire out of her if she knew that cab driver thought she was that.

It's a rare day she doesn't meet a friend (and when you're born and live 60 years in Mississippi and went to school and are still in the same not-very-big town, you have enough friends to get by on) for a small toddy or lunch or supper. Usually it's at home—theirs or hers—because Southern people are not much for wandering about in strange restaurants except in New Orleans where their origins are different.

Miss Welty's family had no Deep South background though she is famous for her Southern characters. Her father came to Jackson from Ohio and her mother from West Virginia. But Miss Welty has lived all her life in Jackson; she won a holiday from school once for learning to spell all 82 counties of Mississippi along with the county seats, and some of them are tricky—Oktibbeha, for instance. It is also known with certainty she used to purchase penny Tootsie Rolls and with equal certainty that even then she had a care with her writing and delighted classmates.

She still lives in the new Welty brick house (built scarcely 50 years ago), with spacious 1920-generous halls. Some of the walls have cracked—Miss Welty says Jackson is built on marl over shifting sands. It is somewhat like a time-lapse earthquake. You resign yourself to repairing cracked walls.

Miss Welty was pitched right out of a Jackson restaurant recently, though, which shows among other things she is no recluse. It was all because she was hostess to two young men with Jesus haircuts, and long hair is something the restaurant owner has a real thing about.

"But maybe you were mistaken—maybe you misunderstood the waitress," somebody asked Miss Welty since, after all, a restaurant is

no more likely to throw Miss Welty out in Jackson than Alice
Roosevelt at the Rive Gauche, it being an honor in both cases.

"I did not misunderstand the waitress," said Eudora, with just a
slight rise of tone, as if to say she did not go around misunderstanding anything humans are likely to do. "She said very plainly, 'you all
will have to go.' " But she did say not to feel bad about it—they
pitched customers out all the time for having long hair and the wonder of it is they have any customers left, barber styles being what
they are.

The humor was not lost, even at the time, on Miss Welty, but there
are times to express anger so she fired off a letter to the *Clarion-
Ledger* about it. The young guests weren't drunk or disorderly or
doing anything but sitting there like unshorn lambs hoping for a
shrimp cocktail. Eudora won't go back.

She stated her position right there in the letter. She acted and now
need not dwell on it further. She has no grudges. Or if she has, it's
not about restaurant owners but grand and immortal enemies like
death, yellow leaves or nematodes.

"You wouldn't know it," she said, "but this garden was once beautiful. My mother really kept after it." Both mother and daughter were
fine gardeners—the ones that really know, as distinct from the ones
that just have masses of color. They used to read V. Sackville-West in
the *Observer* and Elizabeth Lawrence and so on. And from those
excellent rungs they went right on up, to a garden that really meant
something.

The year the nematodes came things mainly died. Mrs. Welty was
ill—she died in recent years—and Miss Welty was writing *Losing Battles* at home with her and two nurses and laughing a great deal (the
book is beyond grief and funny as owls in heaven) and the nurses
did not approve of anything.

And right in the middle of it the nematodes did in the roses, which
had been packed in that garden tight as a trunk, but nothing that
could be tried availed at all. Miss Welty planted a crabapple at the
beginning rosebed to keep her mother from being too much aware of
disasters in the main planting.

Ordinarily an attack on her roses would have brought Mrs. Welty
right out of the kitchen, as they say, but she was past those battles
then. Many treasures went. The old "Gloire de Dijon" and "For-

tune's Yellow Climbers" succumbed, and so did even the great "Mermaid." But "Safrano," the old tea rose, is blooming yet, and "Silver Moon" pulled through and so did "Lady Banks."

Her characters in her stories are like the roses—some make it, some don't. Her first story, "Death of a Traveling Salesman" (1936, when Miss Welty was 24), is about a man whose vehicle doesn't work, who sees nothing the way it really is and who dies without having made much sense of himself or anything else in the world.

Her last novel *The Optimist's Daughter,* is also about people who are trying to figure out who they are (and who are commonly confused and mistaken) and one point of the story is that there is little difference among classes once the accents, the intonations and the other superficial marks of caste are allowed for.

That is why, probably, the story of Phoenix Jackson (in *A Curtain of Green* decades ago) is still admired, though few of its readers have any direct experience with the heroine, a very old black woman walking to and from the doctor's to get medicine for her grandson who swallowed lye.

Some of her readers think *Losing Battles* is her most typical and best book; though critics seem to keep hinting it's a tour-de-force.

It is the story of a white farming family in that part of Mississippi near the Tennessee-Alabama-Mississippi border. The time is the 1930s, the characters are of the poorest sort, but proud and self-reliant and highly conscious of the claims and bonds of family.

The author thinks nobody would believe it, if the setting were the present, and that is why it is set 40 years ago. "I wanted the characters to be down to bedrock—no money, no education, no nothing, except themselves—the rest being all cleared away to begin with."

Even so, the characters are complicated, and most of them misunderstand their roles. *Losing Battles* is partly about the battles they lose, and the title is partly ironic, about the battles they win, sometimes without knowing it.

The hero is named Jack, scion of the family, who has been sent to Parchman Prison for no good reason and who returns in time for the annual family reunion.

If a comparison to Shakespeare seems extravagant, and it does, one man who objected to that extravagance found himself comparing it to *The Iliad* and *Don Quixote.*

"It reminds me of *The Iliad,*" he said.

"*Everything* reminds *me* of *The Iliad,*" Miss Welty replied.

The speech of the narrative, the plainness and elegance of the language, the stripped quality of the action, the intense quality of the personal relationships and the occasional heightening of the dialogue for emotional effect—even to the extent of introducing an archaic note—all reflect the general method of Homer more than Shakespeare.

The comic element of this and many other stories is more like Damon Runyan or Cervantes than Mark Twain.

But just as one critic risked seeming like a fool by comparing it to Shakespeare's *Tempest,* many readers seem a trifle foolish recalling (as they read it) Cervantes and Homer. Just as the reviewers seemed generally to think in large terms and high precedents, so readers often seem to react as if Miss Welty were an oracle or a priestess rather than a good storyteller.

"I got a letter last week from a man in Taiwan," she said, "who for reasons best known to himself wanted me to be 'the grandmother' for his children. It's a warm nice letter, but how do you answer anything like that? I don't want to be anybody's damn grandmother.

"And here's a letter from a nun—I think nuns write letters a good bit—complaining some story I wrote is unfair to Campfire Girls or Girl Scouts. I don't know how to answer that. Here's another one, from a nun in India who has fallen in love with a priest and wants my advice. How would I know? I do so wish these people well, but I have no idea how to write them or even how to begin."

Another letter recently came from a nice person who wanted to know why her stories had not dealt with the Jews in the Mississippi ghettos.

"We have Jews in Mississippi as you know, but they don't live in ghettos. They are more likely to be mayor of the town. When I get letters that bewilder me—well, I'm thinking of getting some letter paper that says 'You Just Can't get There From Here.' "

But what many of the letters have in common is an unspoken assumption that Miss Welty understands all there is to understand about virtually any human relationship.

Her last two novels, like all her work, began as short stories. *Losing*

Battles was meant to end when Jack returned from prison to join the family reunion, but Miss Welty had fallen hopelessly in love with him by the time he made his first appearance on page 71, too many characters had already built him up as a hero.

So she allowed herself a few more pages to deal with Jack—436 pages, to be exact—and the result is her novel that she still thinks of in terms of a story rather than a grand panorama of the world.

Her last novel, issued this spring, *The Optimist's Daughter,* also began as a short story that wouldn't stop.

"It's the first thing I've ever done that has direct autobiographical information in it. I'm not sure that was right—the mother is based on my mother. The boys are her brothers—I think I may have added an extra one—and the West Virginia part is set in her own country."

The most notable thing in the book is a prolonged and lyrical coda (". . . His white shirt would shine for a long time almost without moving in her sight, like Venus in the sky of Mount Salus, while grandmother, mother and little girl sat outlasting the light, waiting for him to climb home . . .")

Few things are riskier than "fine writing," but Miss Welty has never been afraid to risk it. She spoke once in conversation of plant explorers who go to Nepal and Sikkim, risking their lives to introduce alpine flowers to gardens.

"Now that's something—discovering new primroses—that's worth taking trouble with, worth risking something for," she said.

She seemed to set the plant explorers bringing garden treasures from the Himalayas over against the ordinary world we all live in everyday:

"Words almost don't mean anything anymore. The meanings, anything can be a lie now. It doesn't make any difference whether something is fair or makes sense."

The decline of personal courtesy, the increasing power of pressure and loudness, the reliance on shadowy image rather than substantial reality, all disturb her.

But nothing, apparently, disturbs her comic sense, even when she alludes to politics, and she goes no farther than an allusion.

"All these people, come to think of it, so many politicians, people like Napoleon, are not much taller than short."

It was pointed out you couldn't say Lyndon Johnson was short.

"No," she said, "I guess you'd have to say he was not much taller than tall."

As a now-celebrated writer, Miss Welty tries to give herself time to think and feel—she has cut out lecturing since she no longer has to do it to earn money, and she does not usually see reporters, not out of snobbery, but because she is never sure what to say to them and because there is only so much time in life.

But if a reporter does get a chance to see her, she will talk for 12 hours and cook supper as well. She is fairly sure in the back of her mind that a visitor would rather eat a hamburger in the local Horror Room than dine at ease at home with Eudora Welty, but once she is persuaded that her visitor will make do with Eudora Welty's food as readily as the local hash house, she spreads a feast of cold consomme with avocado puree and cream in it and roast beef and other sliced meats and fine cheeses and a salad and tomatoes dead ripe and red as an Indian Cling (the peach of Southern childhood memories) and strong fresh coffee.

It tasted great—no danger of confusing it with something out of a vending machine.

Not only does she like to cook, and to cook without any interference or "help," she also likes to talk and refuses to let anybody help her with the dishes.

In her own reading, apart from garden books, cookbooks and virtually any other kind of book, she has a special enthusiasm for mystery novels or whodunits and for dictionaries. She has the great *Oxford English Dictionary* and wastes many delectable hours with it just for fun.

She likes poetry, especially Yeats, Donne and Marvell, but says, "I'm really afraid I'm not on the right wavelength for modern poetry. I'm a thoroughly visual person. I have to have a sensuous—is that right, sensuous?—yes, I always have to think—a sensuous image."

The fondness for visual images is constant throughout her stories. She compares such visual, if unlikely, things as fading red roses to the color of a bird dog's tongue and the locust's evening song to the sound of seed being poured into a tin bucket.

But always her taste for comedy breaks through. Apropos of nothing (except the American belief in signs) she mentioned her favorite sign, once seen in a train station: "No laughing or loud talking while train is in station."

And in spite of the intense admiration of many readers—the ones that ask her advice about falling in love with a priest, for instance—she sees no sign of becoming a "cult" writer with her own set of worshippers.

"I'd hate to be a sort of cult figure, and I've never seen any signs of it. It would be dreadful. First, you'd begin to believe it, then you'd get absurd and stupid. I've never been a big seller, not really a popu-lar writer, and most people never heard of me."

It's true that only in the last two years has she been able to support herself—in her 60s—by writing.

Her famous short stories at first were turned down endlessly and then published cheap. Her collection *A Curtain of Green,* with such famous stories as "A Worn Path," "Why I Live at the P.O." and "Petrified Man," has been in print since the early '40s but has sold only 6,700 copies in its first three decades and first two editions.

As Miss Welty's agent, Diarmuid Russell of New York, observed in *Shenandoah,* the literary quarterly, that is "not riches for author or publisher," or, for that matter, agent.

"I couldn't live without Diarmuid," said Miss Welty. (The name is pronounced Dermott.) He became her agent in 1940 and she's never had another. Russell is son of the writer A. E., and incidentally, is an authority on American wildflowers.

"When he offered to be my agent, I didn't even know there *were* agents. I just sent my stories off to magazines and when they came back, I sent them off somewhere else. It's still the best way. It's how everybody gets started. But now with legal things—permission to re-print and overseas rights—I could never keep up with all that.

"Until my last two books I never could live on just my writing. I was very lucky, I was able to lecture, and schools were good at get-ting me to come, sometimes for a one-shot lecture, sometimes longer. So I was always able to manage, but I never made any money. There was *The New Yorker,* though. They have the idea it's the writers who should make some money from the magazine. They pay well; yes, even when they know they could get a story for less. But of course the trouble was, you never know if you can write a story . . .

"You can't time that kind of work to fit in with when you need the money."

From one *New Yorker* story Miss Welty bought two Fords, one for a niece and one for herself.

Somebody once suggested that if she drove about in an amazing automobile and issued epigrams on television once a month she'd soon be thought an oracle.

"Oh, no, I've already tested that in a way. I had a 16-year-old Ford. It ran fine, I still don't know why I turned it in. But anyway, even when I had it, nobody thought I was an oracle."

When she sees her books newly issued she feels uneasy—"I'm never prepared for the reviews. I'm never prepared for anything, I mean I have no idea what people will think of the book.

"When I see my book for sale, I realize here's something I've been doing privately in Jackson, and now suddenly people anywhere can see it, what only I've seen. I feel very vulnerable."

Her own favorite author is Jane Austen, a writer she returns to again and again.

Unlike many Southern writers she has no special taste for Milton; she took a course in Milton years ago and has barely read him since.

"Are you trying to say you're not a Puritan?" she was asked.

"No, I'm a Puritan, all right. But I am saying if you substitute Jane Austen instead of Milton, you'll come closer. Sorry."

No sketch of a Southern writer in the past century has ever been written, so far as I know, without the writer adoring Milton. It was suggested that maybe Milton's influence is so pervasive that she has absorbed it by osmosis.

"Sorry. Jane Austen."

But then writers often are not aware of major influences, as we all know.

"And I've never read one word of James Fennimore Cooper. Yes, he's having a revival. I think that's sad. As if he had to be revived.

"I know a literary reputation is a fragile thing.

"Somebody told me once, watch out when a woman writer passes 50, they all turn on you. Sometimes I think they decide, 'Oh, we're so damned tired of saying she writes well.' "

She grinned and rose from her chair to fetch a private literary treasure somebody sent her—a student's essay question on Shakes-

peare. The allusion to critics made her think of Shakespeare and her
somewhat saucy humor made her think not of some great scene in a
play but of a Georgia boy's essay. It was clear the youth did not
know Shakespeare from a sack of vanilla beans but he did understand he was supposed to say something grand, so he wound up:

"Some say William was a moment without a tomb, star of the
poet, swan of the lake."

Miss Welty, reading it, laughed almost to limpness.

"Moment without a tomb—now there's a title for you," she said
between gasps. (Henry Miller once said he loved her stories but not
her titles). She is a connoisseur of titles and names. Naming her
characters is very difficult for her.

"There are some marvelous names right here in Mississippi. I used
to take a lot of the state newspapers and in the old days I loved to
read the Oxford *Eagle*. There was one woman whose name kept
turning up there, but I always felt any name around Oxford was
automatically the property of Mr. Faulkner. He had such perfect
names. I don't know if this is true, but somebody once told me they
mentioned a name to Mr. Faulkner and he said, 'Yes, I know the
name well. Can hardly wait for her to die' so he could use it."

Miss Welty now is thinking of publishing a book of lectures, but is
not sure—would there really be anything fresh and fine, would there
really be any point to it?

"Well, with two sensationally received novels in a row in two years,
had you ever thought of writing a flop just for a change of pace?"
somebody asked her.

"What would really bother me was if I wrote a flop and it was
praised—just out of habit. And I think things like that can happen."

Milton, of course, would have thought so, too.

The Art of Fiction XLVII: Eudora Welty

Linda Kuehl / 1972

From *Paris Review*, 55 (Fall 1972), 72–97. Interview with Eudora Welty reprinted in *Writers at Work: The Paris Review Interviews, Fourth Series*, ed. George Plimpton. © 1974, 1975 by The Paris Review, Inc. Reprinted by permission of Viking Penguin Inc.

Eudora Welty was born in 1909 in Jackson, Mississippi, where she has lived ever since, departing only for a rare visit to Europe, an annual trip to New York, an occasional reading at a college. During her brief stay in New York, we met in her room at the Algonquin Hotel, an hour or so after her train had arrived in Penn Station. She had given me the wrong room number, so I first saw her peering out of her door as the elevator opened. A tall, large-boned, grey-haired woman greeted me apologetically. She was admittedly nervous about being interviewed, particularly on a tape recorder. After describing her train ride—she won't fly—she braced herself and asked if I wouldn't please begin the questioning.

Once the interview got underway, she grew more at ease. As she herself might say, she was not *unforthcoming*. She speaks with a Deep Southern drawl, deliberately, measuring her words, listening, so it seems, to her own voice. She is extremely private, and won't answer anything personal about herself or about friends.

Interviewer: You wrote somewhere that we should still tolerate Jane Austen's kind of family novel. Is Austen a kindred spirit?

Welty: *Tolerate?* I should just think so! I love and admire all she does, and profoundly, but I don't read her or anyone else for "kindredness." The piece you're referring to was written on assignment for *Brief Lives,* an anthology Louis Kronenberger was editing. He did offer me either Jane Austen or Chekhov, and Chekhov I do dare to think is more "kindred." I feel closer to him in spirit, but I couldn't read Russian, which I felt whoever wrote about him should be able to do. Chekhov is one of us—so close to today's world, to my mind, and very close to the South—which Stark Young pointed out, a long time ago.

Interviewer: Why is Chekhov close to today's South?

Welty: He loved the singularity in people, the individuality. He took for granted the sense of family. He had the sense of fate overtaking a way of life, and his Russian humor seems to me kin to the humor of a Southerner. It's the kind that lies mostly in character. You know, in *Uncle Vanya* and *The Cherry Orchard,* how people are always gathered together and talking and talking, no one's really listening. Yet there's a great love and understanding that prevails through it, and a knowledge and acceptance of each other's idiosyncrasies, a tolerance of them, and also an acute enjoyment of the dramatic. Like in *The Three Sisters,* when the fire is going on, how they talk right on through their exhaustion, and Vershinin says "I feel a strange excitement in the air," and laughs and sings and talks about the future. That kind of responsiveness to the world, to whatever happens, out of their own deeps of character seems very Southern to me. Anyway, I took a temperamental delight in Chekhov, and gradually the connection was borne in upon me.

Interviewer: Do you ever return to Virginia Woolf?

Welty: Yes. She was the one who opened the door. When I read *To the Lighthouse,* I felt, Heavens, *what is this?* I was so excited by the experience I couldn't sleep or eat. I've read it many times since, though more often these days I go back to her diary. Any day you open it to will be tragic, and yet all the marvelous things she says about her work, about working, leave you filled with joy that's stronger than your misery for her. Remember—"I'm not very far along, but I think I have my statues against the sky"? Isn't that beautiful?

Interviewer: About your own work, are you surprised that *Losing Battles* was on the bestseller list—a first for you, I believe?

Welty: It occurred to me right at first it must be a fluke—that whoever had that place on the bestseller list had just got up and given me his seat—let the lady sit down, she's tottering. Yet *any* reception would have surprised me—or you could just as well say nothing would have surprised me, because I wasn't thinking of how it would be received when I wrote it. I thought about the opinion of a handful of friends I would love to have love that book, but not about the public.

Interviewer: Do you write for your friends?

Welty: At the time of writing, I don't write for my friends or myself either; I write for *it,* for the pleasure of *it.* I believe if I stopped to wonder what so-and-so would think, or what I'd feel like if this were read by a stranger, I would be paralyzed. I care what my friends think, very deeply—and it's only after they've read the finished thing that I really can rest, deep down. But in the writing, I have to just keep going straight through with only the *thing* in mind and what it dictates.

It's so much an inward thing that reading the proofs later can be a real shock. When I received them for my first book—no, I guess it was for *Delta Wedding*—I thought, *I* didn't write this. It was a page of dialogue—I might as well have never seen it before. I wrote to my editor, John Woodburn, and told him something had happened to that page in the typesetting. He was kind, not even surprised—maybe this happens to all writers. He called me up and read me from the manuscript—word for word what the proofs said. Proofs don't shock me any longer, yet there's still a strange moment with every book when I move from the position of writer to the position of reader, and I suddenly see my words with the eyes of the cold public. It gives me a terrible sense of exposure, as if I'd gotten sunburned.

Interviewer: Do you make changes in galleys?

Welty: I correct or change words, but I can't rewrite a scene or make a major change, because there's a sense then of someone looking over my shoulder. It's necessary, anyway, to trust that moment when you were sure at last you had done all you could, done your best for that time. When it's finally in print, you're delivered—you don't ever have to look at it again. It's too late to worry about its failings. I'll have to apply any lessons this book has taught me toward writing the next one.

Interviewer: Is *Losing Battles* a departure from your previous fiction?

Welty: I wanted to see if I could do something that was new for me: translating every thought and feeling into action and speech, speech being another form of action—to bring the whole life of it off through the completed gesture, so to speak. I felt that I'd been writing too much by way of description, of introspection on the part of my characters. I tried to see if I could make everything shown, brought forth, without benefit of the author's telling any more about what was going on inside the characters' minds and hearts. For me, this makes almost certainly for comedy—which I love to write best of all. Now I see it might be a transition toward writing a play.

Interviewer: Did you know what you were going to write before you put it on paper?

Welty: Yes, it was there in my head, but events proliferated as I went along. For instance, I thought all the action in the novel would be contained in one day and night, but a folder started to fill up with things marked "Next A.M." I didn't foresee the stories that grew out of the stories—that was one of the joys of working the novel out. I thought the book would be short, and instead it was three or four times longer than my normal work. There's no way of estimating its original length, because I had great chunks of things in paper clips which weren't numbered until they went to the printer. And I must have thrown away at least as much as I kept in the book.

Interviewer: Did you learn anything new about writing dialogue?

Welty: I believe so. In its beginning, dialogue's the easiest thing in the world to write when you have a good ear, which I think I have. But as it goes on, it's the most difficult, because it has so many ways to function. Sometimes I needed to make a speech do three or four or five things at once—reveal what the character said but also what he thought he said, what he hid, what others were going to think he meant, and what they misunderstood, and so forth—all in his single speech. And the speech would have to keep the essence of this one character, his whole particular outlook in concentrated form. This isn't to say I succeeded. But I guess it explains why dialogue gives me my greatest pleasure in writing. I used to laugh out loud sometimes when I wrote it—the way P. G. Wodehouse is said to do. I'd think of some things my characters would say and even if I couldn't use it, I would write the scene out just to let them loose on something—my private show.

Interviewer: Where does the dialogue come from?

Welty: Familiarity. Memory of the way things get said. Once you have heard certain expressions, sentences, you almost never forget them. It's like sending a bucket down the well and it always comes up full. You don't know you've remembered, but you have. And you listen for the right word, in the present, and you hear it. Once you're into a story everything seems to apply—what you overhear on a city bus is exactly what your character would say on the page you're writing. Wherever you go, you meet part of your story. I guess you're tuned in for it, and the right things are sort of magnetized—if you can think of your ears as magnets. I could hear someone saying—and I had to cut this out—"What, you never ate goat?" And someone answering; "Goat! Please don't say you serve *goat* at this reunion. I wasn't told it was *goat* I was served. I thought—" and so on, and then the recipe, and then it ended up with—I can't remember exactly now—it ended with, "You can do a whole lot of things with vinegar." Well, all these things I would just laugh about and think about for so long and put them in. And then I'd think, that's just plain indulgence. Take it out! And I'd take it out.

Interviewer: Are you an eavesdropper?

Welty: I'm not as much as I used to be, or would like to be, because I don't hear as well as I used to, or there's too much other noise everywhere. But I've heard some wonderful remarks. Well, in the South, everybody stays busy talking all the time—they're not sorry for you to overhear their tales. I don't feel in helping myself I ever did anything underhanded. I was *helping out.*

Interviewer: Do you think this oral tradition, so to speak, accounts for your vigorous use of dialogue?

Welty: I think it accounts for the pleasure people take in a story told. It's a treasure I helped myself to. I took it for my ways and means, and that's proper and justified: our people talk that way. They learn and teach and think and enjoy that way. Southerners do have, they've inherited, a narrative sense of human destiny. This may or may not come out in *Losing Battles*. A reunion is everybody remembering together—remembering and relating when their people were born and what happened in their lives, what that made happen to their children, and how it was that they died. There's someone to remember a man's whole life, every bit of the way along. I think that's a marvelous thing, and I'm glad I got to know something of it. In New York you may have the greatest and most congenial friends, but it's extraordinary if you ever know anything about them except that little wedge of their life that you meet with the little wedge of your life. You don't get the sense of a continuous narrative line. You never see the full circle. But in the South, where people don't move about as much, even now, and where they once hardly ever moved away at all, the pattern of life was always right there.

Interviewer: Would you say that Southerners—Deep Southerners—are more open than Northerners?

Welty: I think we have a sort of language we all understand and speak—a shorthand of some kind, based on familiarity—but I'm not sure we're more open. We may not tell as much as we think we do, and we may not hide as much as we think we do. We're just more used to talking—as you can see—and the subject doesn't especially cut us down.

Interviewer: And that profoundly affects your fiction?

Welty: I think that's what gives a pattern to it, and a sense of its shape to me. I do want to say that I'm only speaking for myself when I speak of Southern qualities, because I don't know how other people work. It may be entirely different, especially with a genius like William Faulkner, who had such a comprehensive sense of the whole deep, deep past, and more far-reaching, bred-in country knowledge than I have, which is so valuable, besides all the rest of his equipment that I don't need to tell you about.

Interviewer: Did you know Faulkner?

Welty: Slightly and over a long period of time, but not well. I liked him ever so much. We met at a dinner party in Oxford, just old friends of his and old friends of mine, which was the right way for it to happen, and it was just grand. We sang hymns, and we sang some old ballads—and the next day he invited me to go sailing. If we ever met in New York, we just talked about being in Oxford. *He* didn't bring up writing, and if he didn't, you know *I* wasn't going to bring it up! But when he was working in Hollywood, he once wrote me a two-line letter—this was long before we met—and told me he liked a little book of mine called *The Robber Bridegroom,* and said would I let him know if he could ever do anything for me. It was on a little piece of notebook paper, written in that fine, neat, sort of unreadable hand, in pencil—and I've lost it.

Interviewer: Did you feel at all influenced by his presence?

Welty: I don't honestly think so. It is hard to be sure about such things. I was naturally in the deepest awe and reverence of him. But that's no help in your own writing. Nobody can help you but yourself. So often I'm asked how I could have written a word with William Faulkner living in Mississippi, and this question amazes me. It was like living near a big mountain, something majestic—it made me happy to know it was there, all that work of his life. But it wasn't a helping or hindering presence. Its magnitude, all by itself, made it something remote in my own working life. When I thought of Faulkner it was when I *read*.

On the other hand, he didn't seem remote to everybody in being our great writer. I know a story about him, though he never knew anybody knew of it, I'd bet. Mississippi is full of writers, and I heard this from the person it was told to. A lady had decided she'd write a novel and got along fine till she came to the love scene. "So," she told my friend, "I thought there's William Faulkner, sitting right up there in Oxford. Why not send it to William Faulkner and ask him?" So she sent it to him and time went by and she didn't ever hear from him, and so she called him up. Because there he was. She said, "Mr. Faulkner, did you ever get that love scene I sent you?" He said yes, he had got it. And she said, "Well, what did you think of it?" And he said, "Well, honey, it's not the way I'd do it—but you go *right ahead*." Now, wasn't that gentle of him?

Interviewer: Do people give you unpublished manuscripts to read? I mean, women especially tend to write voluminous historical novels, and I wonder if any of them are in Jackson.

Welty: I wouldn't be surprised. I don't think there's any neck of the woods they're not in. Yes, I get sent manuscripts, but those historical and Gothic novels are really a subject on which I know nothing, and I say so. There is, in point of fact, a good deal of writing talent in general around our state now—a lot of good young ones, serious ones.

Interviewer: Did you ever feel part of a literary community, along with people like Flannery O'Connor, Carson McCullers, Katherine Anne Porter or Caroline Gordon?

Welty: I'm not sure there's any dotted line connecting us up, though all of us knew about each other and all of us, I think, respected and read each other's work and understood it. And some of us are friends of long standing. I don't think there was any passing about of influences, but there's a lot of pleasure in thinking in whose lifetimes your own lifetime has happened to come along. Of course, Katherine Anne Porter was wonderfully generous to me from the beginning. At the time I began sending my first stories to the *Southern Review,* she read them and wrote to me from Baton Rouge inviting me to come down to see her. It took me, I suppose, six months or a year to fully get up my nerve. Twice I got as far as Natchez and turned around and came back. But I finally did get there, and Katherine Anne couldn't have been more welcoming. Later on, she wrote the introduction to my first book of stories, and I owe her very much for that. We've been friends all these years.

Interviewer: How would you feel about a biography about yourself?

Welty: Shy, and discouraged at the very thought, because to me a writer's work should be everything. A writer's whole feeling, the force of his whole life, can go into a story—but what he's worked for is to get an objective piece down on paper. That should be read instead of some account of his life, with that understanding—here is something which now exists and was made by the hands of this person. Read it for what it is. It doesn't even matter too much whose hands they were. Well, of course, it does—I was just exaggerating to prove my point. But your private life should be kept private. My own I don't think would particularly interest anybody, for that matter. But I'd guard it; I feel strongly about that. They'd have a hard time trying to find something about me. I think I'd better burn everything up. It's best to burn letters, but at least I've never kept diaries or journals. All my manuscripts I've given to the Department of Archives and History in Jackson as they came out because that's my hometown and the director is a lifelong friend. But I don't give them everything. I must have a trunk full of stuff that I didn't give because I didn't think it was anybody else's concern, or that anybody would even care to see my mistakes and false turns. Like about eating goat and all the million things that I left out.

Interviewer: Why do *Losing Battles* and *Delta Wedding* take place back in the 1920s and 1930s?

Welty: It was a matter of setting the stage and confining the story. These are both family stories, and I didn't want them inhibited by outward events I couldn't control. In the case of *Delta Wedding,* I remember I made a careful investigation to find the year in which nothing very terrible had happened in the Delta by way of floods or fires or wars which would have taken the men away. I settled it by the almanac. It was a little inconvenient for me, because I myself was only a little girl during the era I was writing about—that's why I let a little girl be the observer of part of it. In the case of *Losing Battles,* I wanted to write about a family who had *nothing.* A bare stage. I chose the time that was the very hardest, when people had the least and the stage could be the barest—and that was the Depression, of course.

Interviewer: Do you prefer working with a bare stage?

Welty: In this case, it was in order to overcrowd it with people. I start with ideas about character and situation, and the technique grows out of these as I grow into the work. It's different, of course, for every story. In *Losing Battles* I wanted to write about people who had nothing at all and yet had all the resources of their own character and situation to do what they could about their lives.

Interviewer: Were you familiar with plantation life when you wrote *Delta Wedding?*

Welty: No, but I had some friends who came from there and I used to hear their stories, and I'd be taken on picnics and visits there. Family visits. The Delta is very rich and visually striking, but completely flat. I would find it maddening after days with nothing but the horizon. Just before you reach it there are high bluffs, and to get in you plunge down a deep hill and from then on there's nothing but flatness. Some of the things I saw and heard began to stick. Some family tales and sayings are right in the book, though by now I can't remember which are true and which are made up.

Interviewer: John Crowe Ransom wrote in a review that *Delta Wedding* might well be "one of the last novels in the tradition of the Old South."

Welty: I revere Mr. Ransom, but his meaning here is not quite clear to me. I wasn't trying to write a novel of the Old South. I don't think of myself as writing out of any special tradition, and I'd hesitate to accept that sanction for *Delta Wedding.* I'd hesitate still more today, because the term itself, "Old South," has a connotation of something unreal and not quite straightforward.

Interviewer: Your parents weren't from the Deep South originally. Do you think that contributed to your ironic perspective?

Welty: It may have given me balance. But other factors mattered more. My father's father owned a farm in Southern Ohio, and my mother's father was a country lawyer and farmer in West Virginia, and both my mother's parents came from Virginia families made up mostly of teachers and preachers. Some of these wrote for news-papers or kept journals, though none wrote fiction. But the family influence I felt came from the important fact that they all loved to read and that I was brought up with books. Yet my parents would have been the people they were, people of character, no matter where they were from, and I would have been their child wherever I was born. I'm a native Southerner, but as a writer I think background matters most in how well it teaches you to look around and see clearly what's there, and in how deeply it nourishes your imagination.

Interviewer: "Where is the Voice Coming From?" is about the Medgar Evers assassination and must be your only topical story.

Welty: I'm certain it is. It pushed up through something else I was working on. I had been having a feeling of uneasiness over the things being written about the South at that time, because most of them were done in other parts of the country and I thought most were synthetic. They were perfectly well-intentioned stories but generalities written from a distance to illustrate generalities. When that murder was committed, it suddenly crossed my consciousness that I knew what was in that man's mind because I'd lived all my life where it happened. It was the strangest feeling of horror and compulsion all in one. I tried to write from the interior of my own South and that's why I dared to put it in the first person. The title isn't very good, I'd like to get a better one. At the time I wrote it—it was overnight—no one knew who the murderer was, and I just meant by the title that who-ever was speaking, I—the writer—knew, was in a position to know, what the murderer must be saying and why.

Interviewer: Do real events hinder you in writing?

Welty: Well, if you write about an actual event, you can't shape it the way you can an imaginary one. In "The Voice" I was writing about the real thing, and at the point of its happening. I was like a real-life detective trying to discover who did it. I don't mean the name of the murderer, but his *nature*. That's not really a short-story writer's prerogative, or is it? Anyway, as events went to prove, I think I came close to pinpointing the mind, but I went a bit wide of the mark in placing the social background of the person arrested for it. As a friend of mine said, "You thought it was a Snopes and it was a Compson." However, in some ways, that isn't a very lasting distinction any more.

Interviewer: Do you see a difference between your early stories in *A Curtain of Green* and *The Wide Net* where you deal more with the grotesque and grim than you do in *The Bride of the Innisfallen?*

Welty: It's a difference not really in subject matter so much as in the ways I approached it. In those early stories I'm sure I needed the device of what you call the "grotesque." That is, I hoped to differentiate characters by their physical qualities as a way of showing what they were like inside—it seemed to me then the most direct way to do it. This is an afterthought, though. I don't suppose I did it as consciously as all that, and I didn't know it was the easiest way. But it is easier to show somebody as lonely if you make him deaf and dumb than if you go feeling your way into his mind. And there was another reason for making the boy in "First Love" a deaf character: one of the other characters—Aaron Burr—was a real person. I couldn't invent conversation for him as I could for an imaginary character, so I had him speak in front of a deaf boy who could report and interpret him in his own way—that is, to suit the story. It's instinctive for a writer to show acute feeling or intense states of emotion by translating it into something visible—red hair, if nothing else. But it's not necessary. I believe I'm writing about the same inward things now without resorting to such obvious devices. But all devices—and the use of symbols is another—must come about organically, out of the story. I feel emphatic about that.

Interviewer: Are you also talking here about other early stories like "Lily Daw and the Three Ladies" and "Petrified Man"?

Welty: Well, when I wrote my first stories, I wrote much faster and it failed to occur to me that I could write them any other way, and perhaps better the second time. They show all the weaknesses of the headlong. I never rewrote, I just wrote. The plots in these stories are weak because I didn't know enough to worry about plots. In the dialogue stories, they came into being exactly as the dialogue led them along. I didn't realize their real weakness until I began reading stories in public—and my ear told me. They could have been made

stronger so easily. Sometimes I fixed them up a little for my readings—cut, transposed—small things, just to see the difference.

Interviewer: What inspired "Powerhouse"?

Welty: I wrote it in one night after I'd been to a concert and dance
in Jackson where Fats Waller played. I tried to write my idea of the
life of the traveling artist and performer—not Fats Waller himself, but
any artist—in the alien world, and tried to put it in the words and plot
suggested by the music I'd been listening to. It was a daring attempt
for a writer like me—as daring as it was to write about the murderer
of Medgar Evers on *that* night—and I'm not qualified to write about
music or performers. But trying it pleased me then and it still does
please me.

Interviewer: Are there problems with ending a story?

Welty: Not so far, but I could have made mistakes without knowing it yet. It's really part of plotting to know the exact moment you're
through. I go by my ear, and this may trick me. When I read, I hear
what's on the page. I don't know whose voice it is, but some voice is
reading to me, and when I write my own stories I hear it too. I have a
visual mind, and I *see* everything I write, but I have to hear the words
when they're put down. Oh, that sounds absurd. This is not the same
as working with dialogue, which of course is another, specialized,
kind of hearing.

Interviewer: Your first stories were about Paris.

Welty: It's not worth remembering. That was when I was a college
freshman, sixteen years old. Oh, you know, I was writing about the
great world, of which I only knew Jackson, Mississippi. But part of it
stemmed from my sense of mystery in people and places, and that's
legitimate and lifelong. As for Paris, I remember a sentence I opened
one story with, to show you how bad I was: "Monsieur Boule in-
serted a delicate dagger in Mademoiselle's left side and departed with
a poised immediacy." I like to think I didn't take myself seriously
then, but I did.

Interviewer: When you sent out "Death of a Traveling Salesman," how did you know you had ended your apprenticeship?

Welty: I was just beginning it! I was thrilled to find that out. I
hadn't conceived of a story's actually being taken. A boy up the
street, an old friend, Hubert Creekmore, who's dead now, knew all

about sending stories out. He was a writer who started before I did and published many good novels and poems. I wouldn't let him read anything I wrote but just asked him, "Hubert, do you know where I can send this?"—and he said to John Rood of *Manuscript*. So I sent it off and John Rood took it, and of course I was flabbergasted. So was Hubert! I believe I've always been lucky—my work has always landed safely and among friends.

Interviewer: You were lucky to escape the novel-first requirement that publishers seem to impose upon young writers. They're wary of short story collections.

Welty: I owe that to John Woodburn, my first editor, who was then at Doubleday, and to Diarmuid Russell, my agent and friend of many years now. I owe it to my nature, too, because I never wrote anything that didn't spring naturally to mind and engage my imagination.

Interviewer: Compared to your stories, I see your novels as looser, freer, happier works which enjoy reconciliations and a final sense of communion.

Welty: My natural temperament is one of positive feelings, and I really do work for resolution in a story. I don't think we often see life resolving itself, not in any sort of perfect way, but I like the fiction writer's feeling of being able to confront an experience and resolve it as art, however imperfectly and briefly—to give it a form and try to embody it—to hold it and express it in a story's terms. You have more chance to try it in a novel. A short story is confined to one mood, to which everthing in the story pertains. Characters, setting, time, events, are all subject to the mood. And you can try more ephemeral, more fleeting things in a story—you can work more by suggestion—than in a novel. Less is resolved, more is suggested, perhaps.

Interviewer: You reserve the short story for the ephemeral and the novel for the resolution?

Welty: I can only say such things after the fact. If I'd known I was going to finish *Losing Battles* as a long novel, I don't know that I'd have begun it. I'm a short-story writer who writes novels the hard way, and by accident. You see, all my work grows out of the work itself. It seems to set its form from the idea which is complete from the start, and a sense of the form is like a vase into which you pour something and fill it up. I have that completely in mind from the beginning and I don't realize how far I can wander and yet come back. The flexibility and freedom are exciting to me, not being used to them, and they are hard to come by. But no one could have enjoyed more learning those lessons than I did. There's no end to what can be tried, is there? So better luck next time.

Interviewer: Do you think critics have made too much of you as a regional writer, taking off from your own essays on the subject?

Welty: I don't mind being called a regional writer. It's the critic's job to place and judge. But the critic can't really have a say in what a writer chooses to write about—that's the writer's lone responsibility. I just think of myself as writing about human beings and I happen to live in a region, as do we all, so I write about what I know—it's the same case for any writer living anywhere. I also happen to love my particular region. If this shows, I don't mind.

Interviewer: Is place your source of inspiration?

Welty: Not only that, it's my source of knowledge. It tells me the important things. It steers me and keeps me going straight, because place is a definer and a confiner of what I'm doing. It helps me to identify, to recognize and explain. It does so much for you of itself. It saves me. Why, you couldn't write a story that happened nowhere. *I* couldn't, anyway. I couldn't write anything that abstract. I wouldn't be interested in anything that abstract.

Interviewer: How about the function of place in "No Place for You, My Love"?

Welty: That story is the one that place did the most for. It really wrote the story. I saw that setting only one time—the Delta of the Mississippi River itself, down below New Orleans where it winds toward the Gulf—one time only. Which smote me. It started the story and made it for me—and *was* the story, really. At its very least, place is essential, though. Time and place make the framework that any story's built on. To my mind, a fiction writer's honesty begins right there, in being true to those two facts of time and place. From there, imagination can take him anywhere at all.

You can equally well be true, I feel, to an *impression* of place. A new place seen in a flash may have an impact almost as strong as the place you've grown up in, one you're familiar with down to the bone, and know what it's like without having to think. I've written about place from either one extreme or the other, but not from partial familiarity or guessing—there's no solidity there.

Interviewer: "Music from Spain" takes place in San Francisco.

Welty: That's using impression of place. I was in San Francisco for only three or four months—that's seeing it in a flash. That story was all a response to a place, an act of love at first sight. It's written from the point of view of the stranger, of course—the only way to write about a strange place. On the other hand, I couldn't write a story laid in New York, where I've come so many times—because it's both familiar and unfamiliar, a no man's land.

Interviewer: Where is Morgana, in *The Golden Apples?*

Welty: It's a made-up Delta town. I was drawn to the name because I always loved the conception of *Fata Morgana*—the illusory shape, the mirage that comes over the sea. All Delta places have names after people, so its was suitable to call it Morgana after some Morgans. My population might not have known there was such a thing as *Fata Morgana,* but illusions weren't unknown to them, all the same—coming in over the cottonfields.

Interviewer: Do you see a similarity between Miss Eckhart in *The Golden Apples* and Julia Mortimer in *Losing Battles,* both being schoolteachers who were civilizing agents and therefore outsiders?

Welty: It doesn't have to be "therefore"—though mine were indeed outsiders. I suppose they are kin, but teachers like those are all over the South and maybe everywhere else too—dedicated, and losing their battles, but not losing them every time. I went all through grammar school in Jackson under a principal all of us who went there still remember and talk about—Miss Lorena Duling. This isn't to say I based my character on her, but she gave me insight into what it meant to be a great teacher. And so was my mother one. All her teaching was done by the time I came along, but she told me stories about it. She taught in the little mountain schools in West Virginia, riding to her school on horseback and crossing the river in a boat, teaching children older than she was—she started at fifteen. I think it was my mother who made seventeen silver dollars the first month she taught, and after that they never could quite come up to that high a standard—which also happened to Miss Julia Mortimer. The shaping influence of teachers like that stays real for a lifetime.

Interviewer: I see another group of characters forming a pattern in your work. Virgie Rainey, in *The Golden Apples,* is an individualist and outsider and similar in that respect to Robbie Reid of *Delta Wedding* and Gloria Short of *Losing Battles.*

Welty: In looking back I can see the pattern. It's funny—when I'm writing I never see a repeat I make in large or small degree. I learn about it later. In Jackson they were recently doing a play of *The Ponder Heart* when I had just finished writing *Losing Battles.* The new novel was so fresh in my mind, whereas I hadn't thought of *The Ponder Heart* for years. But when I sat in at rehearsals, I kept seeing bits and pieces come up that I thought I had invented for *Losing Battles,* and there they were in another version in *Ponder Heart.* So I thought, it's sort of dismaying, but there it is. Your mind works that way. Yet they occur to me as new every time.

Interviewer: Do you write when you're away from home?

Welty: I've found it possible to write almost anywhere I've happened to try. I like it at home better because it's much more convenient for an early riser, which I am. And it's the only place where you can really promise yourself time and keep out interruptions. My ideal way to write a short story is to write the whole first draft through in one sitting, then work as long as it takes on revisions, and then write the final version all in one, so that in the end the whole thing amounts to one long sustained effort. That's not possible anywhere, but it comes nearest to being possible in your own home.

Interviewer: Do you typewrite?

Welty: Yes, and that's useful—it helps give me the feeling of making my work objective. I can correct better if I see it in typescript. After that, I revise with scissors and pins. Pasting is too slow and you can't undo it, but with pins you can move things from anywhere to anywhere, and that's what I really love doing—putting things in their best and proper place, revealing things at the time when they matter most. Often I shift things from the very beginning to the very end. Small things—one fact, one word—but things important to me. It's possible I have a reverse mind, and do things backwards, being a broken left-hander. Just so I've caught on to my weakness.

Interviewer: You rewrite considerably?

Welty: Yes, I do. Some things I let alone from first to last—the kernel of the story. You know enough not to touch something if it's right. The hardest thing for me is getting people in and out of rooms—the mechanics of a story. A simple act of putting on clothes is almost impossible for me to describe without many false starts. You have to be quick and specific in conveying that sort of action or fact, and also as neat and quiet about it as possible so that it doesn't obtrude. And I find that very challenging, especially to describe an action that I don't do very well myself, like sewing. I made Aunt Lexie in *Losing Battles* a poor sewer so that I wouldn't have to describe it too well. The easiest things to write about are emotions.

Interviewer: And yet, the most difficult thing would seem to be the hidden reaches of the human heart, the mystery, those impalpable emotions.

Welty: For a writer, those things are what you start with. You wouldn't have started a story without that awareness—that's what made you begin. That's what makes a character, projects the plot. Because you write from the inside. You can't start with how people look and speak and behave and come to know how they feel. You must know exactly what's in their hearts and minds before they ever set visible foot on the stage. You must know all, then not tell it all, or not tell too much at once: simply the right thing at the right moment. And the same character would be written about entirely differently in a novel as opposed to a short story. In a story you don't go into a character in order to develop him. He was born full grown and he's present there to perform his part in the story. He's subservient to his function, and he doesn't exist outside it. But in a novel, he may. So you may have to allow for his growth, and maybe hold him down and not tell everything you know or else let him have his full sway—make room for a hero, even, in more spacious premises.

Interviewer: Can you talk objectively about your language, perhaps about your use of metaphor?

Welty: I don't know how to because I think of the actual writing as having existence only in the story. When I think of something I put it into a narrative form, not in analytical form, and so anything I say would be artificial. Which reminds me of an Armenian friend of mine, an artist, who told me that his dreams all happened in the same place. When he went to bed he'd imagine himself on a sled going down a steep hill; at the foot of the hill was a little town and by the time he reached it he was asleep and his dreams happened right there. He didn't know why or how. And to go to the ridiculous and yet the sublime, there's W. C. Fields, who read an analysis of how he juggled. He couldn't juggle for six years afterwards. He'd never known that was how it was done. He'd just thrown up the balls and juggled.

"The Southern Imagination":
An Interview with Eudora Welty
and Walker Percy

William F. Buckley, Jr, / 1972
Panelists: Gordon Weaver, Jerry Ward, Dan Hise
12 December 1972

This is a transcript of the *Firing Line* program taped at WMAA in
Jackson, MS, 12 Dec. 1972, and originally telecast on PBS on
24 Dec. 1972. Reprinted in *Mississippi Quarterly,* 24 (Fall
1973), 493–516. *Firing Line* is a production of the Southern
Educational Communications Association, P.O. Box 5966, Columbia, SC 29250. All rights are reserved. Copies of this
transcript are available for $2 each. Reprinted by permission.

Mr. Buckley: The American South has always been a mysterious
generator of literary fire and beauty and pathos, for reasons that have
been endlessly explored, for reasons as simple as that men are endlessly curious about any cradle of genius. The new tranquility of the
South could conceivably put an end to it—one possibility. Another is
that it will bring on a spiritual peace that will permit a more un-
troubled pursuit of culture and art. But the question will be asked,
"What exactly is the Southern imagination? What does it come from
and why? Does it have anything distinctive to say? What are its particular attributes?"

There is no way that you can say about Eudora Welty or Walker
Percy that they are Southern writers in the sense that their work is
done for the benefit of a regional audience. Eudora Welty is as interesting to New Yorkers as Mary McCarthy is to Alabamians. Still, she
is a Southerner, born and educated here in Jackson, Mississippi, and
at the University of Wisconsin—a brief excursion out of state—then
back to begin writing those numinous short stories and novels that
have brought pleasure to a generation of readers and distinction to
her profession. Her current novel is called *The Optimist's Daughter.*
Other landmarks in her career include *Delta Wedding, The Ponder
Heart,* and *Losing Battles.*

Walker Percy went out of Mississippi to go to college, all the way up to what Senator Claghorn once insisted should be called "Upper South Carolina." After Chapel Hill, he went to Columbia and became a medical doctor. That was during the war, but before he had a chance to practice he contracted tuberculosis, which turned out to be a good excuse to do more reading. Years went by and suddenly there was a novel, *The Moviegoer.* It won the National Book Award in 1962; then *The Last Gentleman,* and a year ago the funniest, the shrewdest, the most poignant and jubilant novel of the decade, *Love in the Ruins.*

I should like to begin by asking Miss Welty: What is it you think you can see better for living in the South than you could living outside it?

Miss Welty: Well, as a writer, I think I see in the South what's the essential, because I take what I know for granted. So I see the new as the new and the old as the old and I feel I am a judge because my eye has been trained by experience so I know where I am. I have a base to see people moving in their true light.

Mr. Buckley: Is this an argument against novelists traveling?

Miss Welty: Not at all. No, I am all for that, too, because then you write from a different point of view—that of the outsider who sees things afresh. I mean *I* do. I am not speaking for anyone but myself.

Mr. Buckley: So, it isn't anything distinctive about the South that particularly endows your work; it is rather your familiarity with the region. It could as well be the Middle West.

Miss Welty: It endows me, and it enables me.

Mr. Buckley: Why?

Miss Welty: Because place does endow. I feel that I learn through my roots and understand better what I have lived with and come to know, and those are the tools you write with.

Mr. Buckley: I can understand that, but people, you know, don't much talk about the literary tradition of the Rockies—

Miss Welty: It may come yet.

Mr. Buckley: —or the Pacific Northwest and, quite apart from the fact that historically the South is an old part of this continent, what is it in the South that grabs people and causes them to want to write about it?

Miss Welty: Well, I don't know. I think this probably has been said a thousand times because all sorts of things have been said.

Mr. Buckley: Well, it could be true then, if it was said a thousand times.

Miss Welty: Yes. But I think the Southerner is a talker by nature, but not only a talker—we are used to an audience. We are used to a listener and that does something to our narrative style, I think. I think you could talk in the Rocky Mountains. You wouldn't get anything back but an echo.

(laughter)

Mr. Buckley: Well, does that mean that because you're talkers by nature you develop the art?

Miss Welty: Yes, we like to entertain and please, and we also rejoice in response, and I think that helps the narrative style.

Mr. Buckley: Whereas, say in New England people would be primarily taciturn?

Miss Welty: I don't know. That's what people *say* they are. I haven't noticed.

Mr. Buckley: I wish they were more taciturn in Massachusetts. Well, the art of communication, therefore, gets practiced in the South, does it, because people spend—

Miss Welty: From the cradle.

Mr. Buckley: Yes. Well, now, does television affect that, as far as you can see?

Miss Welty: I don't know. It probably does.

Mr. Buckley: Does that make people more passive in their social relations?

Miss Welty: Oh yes, I am sure that there are many other things to entertain us now, but in the early days of the South, people didn't have anything else to entertain themselves with except each other. That was in the days of the porch-sitting in the Faulkner stories. Don't you agree, Walker?

Mr. Percy: Yes. To me the advantages are what you say, coming from a region which has a tradition; but also from this tradition I think you have a perspective on the United States' culture which you would probably not have if you were born and raised in New York or Chicago. So I think one of the advantages of being a Southern writer is the advantage of a perspective so that you are in a subculture in one sense, and in another sense you are able to look at the main culture from outside. I mean it is possible to see the forest better from the outside than from the inside.

Mr. Buckley: Well, is the difficulty that we are trying to finger here, with some writers outside the South in particular, that of deracination? Is this what you mean by saying "talking from the inside"—the idea of roots struck, and productive?

Mr. Percy: Right. I don't think that you could recognize deracination unless you had some tradition or some fixed point from which to see it. Reminds me of a remark of Flannery O'Connor. When a New York critic asked her why she had so many freaks in her novels, she said, "Well, in the South we still recognize freaks, you see."

Mr. Buckley: As freaks.

Mr. Percy: As freaks.

Mr. Buckley: Yes. Because if the freaks are normal, then they cease to be freaks. Well, the fact that one develops roots in the South seems to me to escape answering the question of why doesn't one develop roots elsewhere that are as productive? Is there an obvious answer to that? Probably there isn't an obvious answer to it. Is there an unobvious answer to that?

Mr. Percy: Well, I think the obvious answer is the difference in the two cultures—Incidentally, the two cultures are merging now and there is less and less difference. I mean, Jackson is more and more like Cincinnati and more and more like Atlanta. But I think that perhaps it is still possible to characterize the South as having a tradition which is more oriented toward history, toward the family, as Eudora said, toward storytelling, and toward tragedy. I mean, we got beat and whereas the North—

Mr. Buckley: Was that a tragedy?

Mr. Percy: Well, that's a big question. We can take that up. But the North early on became a technological society, was less interested in roots and tradition. So I like to think of it as kind of a chemical reaction. What happened is you have these two cultures which were far apart in the beginning. They were too far apart, so far apart that there was not much interaction. So I think that for 100 years Southern literature, before and after the Civil War, was not particularly distinguished. It was ingrown; it was either romantic or it was defensive. It was trying to defend slavery as an institution and, later, trying to defend segregation. Then along about 1920, I think the cultures began to merge and you had a kind of spark jumping so that you had people like Faulkner coming on who began to write about their region but in such universal terms, neither romantically nor defensively, that it made itself understood to people from other parts of the country. And then, I think that this so-called Southern renascence probably lasted maybe 20 or 30 years. Now I think the two cultures have merged so that the South is more or less like the rest of the country. I don't really think there are probably any more Southern writers now than there are, say, in Chicago or—I mean young writers coming up.

Mr. Buckley: Well, I never meant the observation so much to be numerical as qualitative. Is it your guess that the quality of Southern literary art is going to cease to be distinctive?

Mr. Percy: I am not aware that the younger Southern writers are any better than younger writers coming from anywhere else. I don't know whether Eudora would agree with that or not.

Mr. Buckley: Would you, Miss Welty?

Miss Welty: I'm not sure I have seen enough, but I would agree so far as I know because I think their eyes are no longer self-conscious. I mean the art of writing as a Southerner would now be a self-conscious thing to do, don't you think? It never used to be. When we were coming along we just wrote because this is where we lived and what we knew. But to write strictly a Southern book now— I think you are quite conscious that you are seeing a segment and that people are going to look at it—

Mr. Buckley: If there is any Spanish moss there at all.

Miss Welty: I don't know.

Mr. Buckley: When you talk about the response of the South, how do you handle the generality? Or is there a generality—maybe it will become one now—that Southern writers are usually discovered by the North?

Miss Welty: Well, it's where the editors live. Is that what you mean?

Mr. Buckley: Well, also the book buyers.

Miss Welty: Yes. Well, to speak for myself, I—

Mr. Buckley: Do your books sell well in the South, compared to other parts of the country?

Miss Welty: Oh, they don't sell well anywhere (laughter). I mean I'm not much of a seller.

Mr. Buckley: That isn't what I heard.

Miss Welty: But actually though it was the Southerners who were first good to me and first published my work—*The Southern Review,* in Baton Rouge. It took me six years to sell a story to a magazine of national circulation, but from the start, *The Southern Review—*

Mr. Buckley: Was most hospitable?

Miss Welty: So I feel that I was discovered in the South. I *was.*

Mr. Buckley: In terms of this response, I understand what you mean by saying that the social contact between people in the South is more vivid than in the North, but I have not, in my own experience, seen that this transfers automatically on through the disembodied intermediary of a book.

Miss Welty: Well, I can tell you something that I think would apply; that is, if you grew up in the South when things were relatively stable, when there was a lot of talk and so on, you got a great sense of a person's whole life. This is because you know all of the families. You know several generations because they all live together. You know what happened to So-and-so clear through his life. You get a narrative sense of your next door neighbor instead of someone you just meet in the supermarket, which you do today, or you just see people in flashes. You had a sense of what happened to them and probably why, because look what happened to her grandmother—

Mr. Buckley: I see.

Miss Welty: —and you watch life and it is happening. Well, that is a novel. I don't mean you would take somebody's life and make a novel, but your turn of mind would be a dramatic one.

Mr. Buckley: Well, the dramatic turn of mind, of course, makes for readable prose, but it does not necessarily, or does it, make for prose that gets read by a society that doesn't read?

Miss Welty: No, I was really talking about subject matter, I guess, instead of—

Mr. Buckley: Appealing subject matter.

Miss Welty: Yes. I don't know, that's so individual. I don't see how you could ever make a . . . I feel like Walker—it doesn't matter where you were born in that respect.

Mr. Buckley: Pressing the point just a little bit, it is, as you know, widely believed in the North that the South is a Philistia, with two or three, or four or five oases, of which a solid minority are sitting here with me right now, and that you sort of reel drunkenly from Greenville and have to go about 500 miles before you find somebody else who is literate. This is, of course, caricature, but they like to buttress it with figures—book sales, for instance. What's the truth there?

Mr. Percy: It may be partly economic. You know, Faulkner used to say that he could sell more—he sold more novels in Japan than he did in Mississippi.

Mr. Buckley: Well, Japan's a lot bigger.

Mr. Percy: That's true. But the point is that it is true, maybe fewer people buy books in the South than they do in New York, but at $8.95 a copy, you know, fewer people can afford it in the South than in New York.

Mr. Buckley: Well, you're talking pre-paperback.

Mr. Percy: Yes.

Mr. Buckley: I'm talking about post-paperback.

Mr. Percy: I'm talking about those hard covers, where you make your money. What happens at home—for instance, I'll see somebody on the street and they'll say, "Look, don't worry, I'm going to read your book. I've got my name on the library list, so it's coming up," you see.

Mr. Buckley: Are you suggesting, therefore, that the libraries circulate much more here than they do in the North, that most of the reading is done here through library copies?

Mr. Percy: It certainly is done considerably here. I don't know how much is done in the North. A public library in a small Southern town is heavily used, I'll tell you that.

Mr. Buckley: Is there a sort of validating correlation between the increase of wealth in the South and the increase in reading?

Mr. Percy: I think so. I think more books are bought, particularly in places like Atlanta or Jackson or New Orleans, where there is more industry, more income.

Miss Welty: More book stores.

Mr. Percy: More book stores.

Mr. Buckley: Okay, let me ask this. The sensibilities of the Southern writer—well, I guess the sensibilities of any writer—are always one of the things he has primarily to offer, and the sensibilities in the

South must have inevitably in the past couple of generations, two or three generations, been deeply affected by what was then a distinctive problem here, which was the race problem. What one wonders, and what a lot of people have asked themselves, is how in the atmosphere, let's say, of the First World War or of the twenties, could a sensitive Southern writer have lived here? In the same way people are saying, "Why don't people leave South Africa? How is it possible to live in South Africa?" You wrote a very angry article for *Harper's,* in 1965, which was unfriendly to the then state of Mississippi. And it was so unfriendly to the state of Mississippi that one wondered, you know, is there a law that requires Dr. Percy to stay here? I don't have a position on this, but I am anxious to hear you both on the subject.

Mr. Percy: Well, I think you can say two things. I think you can recognize the injustice of the situation which existed at that time and still, to a degree, exists, but from a novelist's point of view the situation is much more—From a moral point of view, it is very simple. It's either right or wrong, and there was a lot wrong. From a novelist's point of view, human relations are much more complex than saying that the white racist is wrong and the black protester is right. I mean, Faulkner was always dealing with the complexities of human relations between white people and black people and between black people and black people. So he could create a character like Dilsey, in my mind one of the great characters of American literature, in spite of the fact that there was a great deal of social injustice in Mississippi at the time. I don't really see how one affects the other, you know.

Mr. Buckley: In the sense of continuing a front, isn't it hard to— Let's take a reductio ad absurdum. Let me say it explicitly so I am not misunderstood. I am not comparing life in Mississippi to life, say, in Germany during the thirties, but a lot of people left Germany during the thirties not because they were themselves being persecuted, not because they were Jewish, say, but because they simply didn't want to live in a society in which they saw that kind of thing countenanced. The question is: Was there an equivalent response by especially sensitive white people during the black days of the Southern experience?

Mr. Percy: Oh, I am sure some Southern writers did leave. I know quite a few who left and moved to New England.

Mr. Buckley: For that reason?

Mr. Percy: Not just for that reason. Strangely enough, many of the so-called "agrarian writers," members of the agrarian movement, who were defending the values of the old South, seemed to have ended up in Northern universities.

Mr. Buckley: At Yale.

Mr. Percy: So they certainly were not leaving in protest, but I think maybe what one does—at least for myself, the best thing to do is to stay where you are.

Miss Welty: I do, too, because I was here all that time and I felt the unreality of late night telephone calls from strangers asking me, "How can you stay in that place? Why don't you use all of your novelistic powers and so on and write some things against this?" And really, I assumed that my whole life I had been writing about injustice, if I wanted to, and love and hate and so on. They are human characteristics which I had certainly been able to see long before it was pointed out to me by what happened in those years. I was always against it, but what I was writing about was human beings. I put it in the form of fiction; that is, in dramatic form. I was writing about it from the inside, not from the outside, and when it was stated from the outside it seemed to me so thin and artificial.

I once did a story—I was writing a novel at the time, and when Medgar Evers was assassinated here—that night, it just pushed up to what I was doing. I thought to myself, "I've lived here all my life. I know the kind of mind that did this"—this was before anyone was caught. So I wrote a story in the first person as the murderer, because I thought, "I am in a position where I know. I know what this man must feel like. I have lived with this kind of thing."

Mr. Buckley: Did you sound like Beckwith when you were through?

Miss Welty: I think so. It was published in the *New Yorker* almost overnight. In the meanwhile, Beckwith had been arrested, so we had to change everything in it that would in the least seem to incriminate his trial.

Mr. Buckley: Was there a lot to change—which would be high tribute to your—

Miss Welty: Nothing was changed that mattered. The things that were changed would be like the color of automobiles—

Mr. Buckley: My point was did you end up knowing his profile so clearly that in fact—

Miss Welty: I think I had it on the inside, but as somebody said to me, "No, you thought it was a Snopes and it was Compson." (laughter) But at that time there wasn't too much difference, you know.

Mr. Buckley: Artistic license, yes.

Miss Welty: No, but I did know the inside and I wrote from the interior, because I felt that I could. That's the only time that kind of thing ever happened to me.

Mr. Buckley: That would not have been possible, let's say, writing about, oh, Speck in Chicago—

Miss Welty: Oh, no.

Mr. Buckley: —or any of those people?

Miss Welty: No. What I was writing about really was that world of hate that I felt I had grown up with and I felt I could speak as someone who knew it, and I didn't think anything else written about things like that *were* anything else but, more or less, tracts.

Mr. Buckley: Hatred can be useful too, can't it?

Miss Welty: Well, really, I just wrote from deep feeling and horror. You know, it was a real story.

Mr. Buckley: There was a reference in one of your pieces to the final evolution in the attitude of William Faulkner. I didn't altogether understand it, but I think you were saying that he had been latitudinarian in his attitude on the race problem and was finally catapulted out of it by some episode. Is that correct?

Mr. Percy: I am not sure I remember, but I think what happened was that he published a notorious letter in—

Mr. Buckley: Yes, in the *Reporter.*

Mr. Percy: Was it the *Reporter* or *Commercial Appeal*—about the time of the troubles in the early sixties, in which he said he felt his Mississippi rancor coming up and he said, "There's going to be some shooting in the streets, and Mississippians are going to be doing the shooting." And he seemed to favor it. But I think it is fair to say that in the last few years of his life he certainly reversed his attitude on that and was certainly on the side of civil rights, judging from repeated statements he made at the University of Virginia and also at West Point.

Miss Welty: Yes.

Mr. Buckley: If someone undertook the challenge of tracing the evolution of his position on it in his novels, would they come up with something?

Mr. Percy: Well, that would be hard to do because I think, here again, his attention as a novelist was not devoted to the issue, he was devoted to people. Nothing is more difficult to write than a good protest novel. The angrier you are, the worse the novel you are liable to write.

Miss Welty: That is true.

Mr. Buckley: Yes, you made that point in an essay, I know.

Miss Welty: Did I? Well, I believe it.

Mr. Percy: It's true. And the people who manage to do it, do it in spite of the fact that they are starting out to write a propaganda novel. Now I am thinking of somebody like Dostoevsky, who would start out to write a tract. He'd read something in the paper that made him mad and he would write an anti-revolutionary novel, but somehow or other the genius in the novelist took over and it became a great novel in spite of his strong feelings against a certain political or social issue.

Mr. Buckley: Has there been a good protest novel written in the South?

Mr. Percy: Yes, I can only think of one. Richard Wright's novel—well two, Ralph Ellison's, which I think transcends reason. It's a great novel. It transcends the protest and the character becomes a universal figure of modern alienation—which was a remarkable feat he pulled off, I think.

Mr. Buckley: In what category would you put Styron's *Nat Turner?*

Mr. Percy: Well, actually I did not think of it as a novel. I thought of it as a historical study—

Mr. Buckley: Great heavens, was it accurate?

Mr. Percy: Truthfully, I like it a lot less than I did his first novel and I have ambivalent feelings about it. I'm not sure it truly represented what Nat Turner was really like.

Mr. Buckley: Was that his objective?

Mr. Percy: I don't know what it was. In spite of the good things in it and the fact that I enjoyed it, when I finished it I couldn't help but wonder what Nat Turner was really like. Was he like this? Maybe I doubted it.

Mr. Buckley: I never got the impression that he was supposed to be like that. However—Well, you talk now about the merging of the cultures and I guess it was inevitable. I guess also everybody seems to agree on what one stands to gain from it. What does one stand to lose?

Miss Welty: Some identity, probably, but a different reaching identity. I don't know. I see the novel or literature, whatever, just as if it were an ocean and all these various things like the novel of protest, the novel of this and that, are just like little chips floating on it. But I feel that the novel itself, which is a work of imagination, is so much more profound and so much more full of monsters and beautiful things and just a big world in itself. That is the part that matters; that will always be there. And all these other things just come and go and float around on it. They are important, but they are not everything.

Mr. Buckley: Well, you are talking now exclusively *as* a novelist and—

Miss Welty: Well, that's all I am.

Mr. Buckley: Right. No, well, you are more things than that. You are also a human being and an American and a Southerner. I can imagine Caruso talking about the biological evolution of the Italian race based on whether "X" number of bel cantos would come from it. Let's concede that there will always be something for a novelist to do. I think that that, in fact, has been established. What is it that, in terms of that which is socially desirable, threatens now to go or to atrophy with the—I got a stuffy letter from a doctor saying I should say atrophy. Is that right?

Mr. Percy: That was the last way I heard it.
(laughter)

Mr. Buckley: —that threatens to go as a result of the merging of these cultures?

Mr. Percy: Of course, what we stand to lose, not just from the point of view of the novel but from the point of view of the culture, is a result of a homogenization—one excerpt coming to look just like another one, so that an excerpt of Jackson looks like an excerpt from any other city in America. The task of a novelist is something else. I think the task of a novelist—and I would like to think and I would like to hope that maybe the Southerner, with his peculiar tradition, might contribute to this—is somehow to humanize the new American culture. Maybe somehow he can bring his talents to bear on the supermarket and the shopping center and the shopping mall and treat it in ways in which, say, a Connecticut or New York novelist is unable to.

Miss Welty: Well, you wrote *The Moviegoer.*

Mr. Percy: Yes, of course, I think that is the task of the novelist. What we are seeing the end of is the end of the traditional Southern novel where you are dealing with small towns, country people, and in a few years there won't be many left. So, for better or for worse, we are going to have to deal with it with the new scene. It's going to be quite a trick.

Mr. Buckley: Yes. You will obviously have to do that and you have anticipated it in your last novel where you deal, I hope, with a world that we'll never have to deal with as a practical matter. But, in a search for the sources of the Southern imagination, one thinks of certain Southern strengths. You've named a couple of them. You name now only the loss of identity as one of those that will be dissipated by this fusion of the two cultures. What, as a practical matter, will this mean? Will this mean that people in their attitude toward Mississippi will exhibit less of the sort of Confederate syndrome? Will they care less to preserve the home of Jefferson Davis, or will they feel less of a sense of at-homeness when they are here? Is that what you anticipate?

Miss Welty: I don't know. I was just thinking from the workmanship point of view of the novelist—I mean, I am not a bit interested in preserving the home of Jefferson Davis.

Mr. Buckley: Why not?

Miss Welty: Because I am interested in human beings who are alive. I mean, I respect history for what it is, but I am speaking as a worker, somebody who likes to write. I like living life. What I want to do is find out what people alive today—

Mr. Buckley: But you were talking about the importance of the grandmother just a few moments ago.

Miss Welty: I know, but that is all part of it; I mean that's a—

Mr. Buckley: But she's dead.

Miss Welty: A character is a taproot that goes clear down. It used to be that it didn't have very far to go to get maybe something that was easier to see, but now there are so many layers of life, so many blurrings, so many homogenous things together that you have to send a taproot down perhaps deeper. But you are always going to get the same thing, because what you want is an essence, a dramatic entity, the human being to be shown as unlike any other human being. That's what human beings are, and you've got to show them that way. That Jefferson Davis doesn't have much to do with it is what I am trying to say.

Mr. Percy: Of course, I think the bad thing that has happened with the South has been the loss of Southern tradition in these magical 20 or 30 years which I think are more or less gone. The *best* thing that's happened, and in the past 10 years I think—and I believe people don't really realize this—is for the first time in Southern history, for the first time in 150 years, the South is no longer defensive. I mean for the first time since the revolutionary days, around 1820 or '30, the South is not trying to defend this peculiar institution or what followed it. I don't think we realize how much Southern talent and Southern brains went to defending this. I remember growing up when the best brains in the Senate and the House from the South were devoted to defending against the anti-lynch bill, devising parliamentary maneuvers to defeat the anti-lynch bill. That to me is a poor way to spend your time and energy. So now I think the rest of the country is in so much trouble, and the South knows this and whatever the good and bad of this, at least the guilt of the South is sufficiently assuaged so that it's no longer defensive.

Miss Welty: I agree.

Mr. Percy: I think this is going to lead to a release of Southern energy, both in the political field and, I hope, literary fields.

Miss Welty: I agree, and when I said that about Jefferson Davis, what I meant was that we do not have to go back to that to tell us anything. When I said I wasn't interested in Jefferson Davis—I mean we have other things. That lack of defensiveness I guess is what I was really meaning. We don't have to say anything except—

Mr. Buckley: I didn't really mean that the whole of the South was expected to focus on 19th century icons. I was using him purely as a symbol. Everybody in the South knows who Jefferson Davis was and this is one thing that distinguishes the South from other parts of the country. Now one talks about the South as the last true American

community, and a community has its myths, its history, that it
nourishes and cherishes and that, I take it, is going to be one of the
casualties. Perhaps you may say, in balance, worth losing, but it is a
loss just the same, right? That's why I am wondering whether 20
years from now the South will be literally indistinguishable from the
North with the single exception that the weather will be hotter, or
maybe they will change that too.

Mr. Percy: I don't know. That is a good question. I hope not.

Miss Welty: I hope not, too.

Mr. Buckley: You say you're not. I'll bet you're working on a
novel that gives all the answers and you're husbanding the details.
(laughter) Let's hear from the panel. Mr. Dan Hise of the English
Department of Millsaps College.

Mr. Hise: First, I would like you to say a few more things about
how the Southern writer can contribute to the rest of the country and
help humanize our culture. You've all mentioned shopping centers.

Mr. Buckley: By the way, are you against shopping centers?

Mr. Percy: No, no indeed. I will have to back up on that. You see,
I come at literature from a different point of view from Eudora Welty.
We speak of Southern writers, and we have something in common
and we have a lot different. She's a woman of letters in the best
sense of the word. She practices the art of the novel and practices—
She is about the best we've got. I practice a lower, a more bastard
art, actually. I came at it from science. I was brought up with a
scientific education and I'm not particularly well-read. So what happened to me—I did some science, medical school, and got interested
in the scientific method and I made what to me was a great discovery. It was nothing new—it was discovered before that by Kier-
kegaard—namely, that science, the scientific method, cannot make a
single statement about the individual man insofar as he is an individual. It can only describe a man insofar as he resembles other people. So science can say nothing whatever about the individual man.
So it suddenly occurred to me, "How do you go about talking about
the individual man?" Finally I came to realize that a novel could be
approached as a very serious effort—an extension of science, if you
will—to explore the individual man, what I call the post-modern man,
his predicament, his perennial predicament, his particular historical
predicament and do it in a very serious way. So, to answer your

question, my novels attempt to be an exploration of what it is to be a man living in a particular time in a particular place. If you are talking about making him human, this is part of the exploration. I am trying to explore what it is to be human, what it is to live in a certain place at a certain time.

Mr. Buckley: Professor Jerry Ward of the English Department of Tougaloo College.

Mr. Ward: Yes, Mr. Buckley, perhaps this was an oversight in programming, but as we try to find what are the sources of the Southern imagination, it seems to me that we should have considered the black writers from the South.

Mr. Buckley: Well, two of them were mentioned.

Mr. Ward: Now, we did mention Ellison and we did mention Richard Wright. We said nothing about Margaret Walker Alexander, for example, or Ernest Gaines or Alice Walker, who is from Georgia. It seems that if we are looking for something in the South that is new, a group of writers who have not decided that the South is really dead and who are still trying to find something there to hang onto, something that they can develop in their writing, it would be coming from the younger black writers and some of the older ones. Now there is something that Miss Welty uses quite a bit in her work that a lot of the black writers have been using and are trying to develop in a new way, and that is folklore—a feeling for the people, a feeling for those things that have been closest to the hearts of the people although they might not have received any kind of academic recognition. I am just wondering—I would like to address this to Miss Welty. In your own writing, do you feel that this is perhaps the one thing that marks it as Southern—a very fine feeling for the human being in a way that Northern writers or Western writers might not be capable of handling?

Miss Welty: I don't understand the question. Do I feel that what?

Mr. Ward: I am trying to find out what is the source of power in your own writing. Would you say that it is folklore?

Miss Welty: Well, I am certainly aware of all the existing folklore that is here; I mean, I will use anything, you know, whatever is about that I think truly expresses what I see in life around me. I have used not only Mississippi folklore but Greek and Roman myths or anything else, Irish stories, anything else that happens to come in handy that I think is an expression of something that I see around me in life. I don't start out just to write something and use folklore. It's just there to be plucked.

Mr. Buckley: What about the larger question of Mr. Ward, namely that the black experience in the South ought itself to be the source of a tremendous amount of artistic interest?

Miss Welty: I agree. I have read a good many of our new young black writers and think highly both of their work and their capacities. I think that's certainly a resource that is going to be very powerful in the future.

Mr. Buckley: Dr. Gordon Weaver, the director of the Center for Writers at the University of Southern Mississippi.

Mr. Weaver: I would like to address this question to both Miss Welty and Dr. Percy in going back to something that Mr. Buckley said. I recognize it's a spurious kind of comparison between Nazi Germany and Mississippi, but proceeding on that kind of fallacious basis, among the people who left Germany and suffered the suppression, to some extent, were writers. I am just curious if you ever felt, either of you, during the time of the more dramatic troubles in Mississippi or in the South, any kind of insecurity as writers; that is to say, the South was proud of you as writers and often times would hold you up to the North, I assume, as symbols of their culture, but did you feel that you were safe only so long as you might have stayed away from anything that was politically touchy or something? I don't mean to suggest that you did, but did you ever feel that there was an atmosphere coming out of, perhaps, the political superstructure that one had best stay away from these things if one was going to stay in the South and be comfortable there? Did you ever feel the hand, then, of government, however far back in the shadows, as a writer?

Miss Welty: I didn't feel any avoidance in anything I was doing and I might get just as mad as I could be about things at home and then I would go up to New York and the things that people would say there made me madder and I would feel defensive because there was a great void of ignorance between the two parts of the country. I think a writer, all his life, is aware of all sorts of threatening and menacing things going on. This time was very open and dramatized and the whole world knew about it, but there are always the human threats of people, of injustice and all these other things that go on through your whole life, and you can't run away from that. That's the life of which you are writing and of which you are taking part. I can't see that you ever avoid anything. As long as you are writing an honest story about human beings, you're writing about the same thing. Maybe I talk too much.

Mr. Buckley: When you say that you cease to be defensive—actually it was Walker Percy who first made the point—do you go on feeling some bitterness over the hypocrisy of the North?

Miss Welty: Yes, I—

Mr. Buckley: During the period that has ushered in the so-called "Southern tranquility," it has ushered in a national recognition of entrenched bigotry in other parts of the country that made a living off of moralizing at the expense of the South. Now, is this bringing on a vindictive reaction on the part of Southern intellectuals or a generous reaction?

Mr. Percy: Well, I think the point is that the North is so preoccupied with its own difficulties that the Northern moralists are no longer concerned with the South. They are too busy. They are very busy worrying with their own problems. And the old Northern habit, particularly New England habit, of using the South as the American demon and scapegoat, is no longer true. I, for one, feel no bitterness nor desire to redress grievances. I think that's the good thing about it—both sections of the country feel much more American in the face of our common problems, now, rather than in the problems that divided us before.

Miss Welty: I think so, too. Actually, I think you felt that all the time among individuals—I mean your friends in the North with everything always open, the understanding was always there. It was the casual person at the dinner party who never met you before who would say something that would really make your hair stand on end. I don't feel anything about that now either.

Mr. Percy: Strangely enough, even at the worst times, there was never a time when I felt that I, in spite of my opinions, should leave Mississippi or Louisiana. This may be hard to understand, but even at the worst times—I think paradoxically the South is known for its violence, a good bit of violence, but at the same time there is a certain tolerance and civility toward people and their opinions. Maybe it's because Southerners look on writers as harmless and eccentric and you're expected to say strange things—

Mr. Buckley: And do.

Mr. Percy: And do.

(laughter)

Mr. Buckley: Mr. Hise.

Mr. Hise: I was wondering, Dr. Percy, when you named your central character in *Love in the Ruins* Thomas More, whether you weren't intending to present a redefinition of America, since the original Thomas More, in a sense, defined America in the first place—Utopian myth, the new Eden.

Mr. Percy: No, that wasn't the reason. Unlike the first two novels, I wanted to establish a Catholic point of view and to identify the main character as a Catholic of a certain sort—not Irish, but English, which is a strange category in itself. It's a small minority. Here again, it's a question of perspective. I figured that the descendant of an English Catholic would be in a particularly advantageous position to see all around him, to see his fellow Catholics, his fellow Protestants, and other people. I wanted to establish a Catholic from a certain Catholic point of view from the beginning.

Mr. Buckley: Mr. Ward.

Mr. Ward: Yes. Mr. Percy, in an interview once you said some things about the loss of God. You didn't call it the death of God; you called it the loss of God, or the loss of man's power to believe in God. Do you see that this has been a kind of result in the South of some of the problems that we've had? Do you see that the young Southern writer, perhaps, is going to turn to other things, other than institutionalized religion or the old traditions, as a source of sustenance?

Mr. Percy: Yes, I think you're right. He certainly is. But if I recall the article correctly, I was defining religion in a very broad sense of saying that a writer is often addressing himself to ultimate concerns and he is a religious writer whether he is dealing with God or the loss of God. In either case it is a religious quest and, as Ptolemy once said, all issues are ultimately religious. So, whether the writer is dealing with God or the loss of it, to me it falls in the same category.

Mr. Buckley: Mr. Weaver.

Mr. Weaver: I'm wondering, given the tradition of fine Southern writers, is it possible that a number of writers who happened to be from the South and wrote about Southern subjects, stories located in the South, may have been overrated by the rest of the country because there were so many good ones? Have bad or mediocre writers crept into national literary reputation on the shirttails of writers like yourself or Faulkner?

Miss Welty: Are you asking me?

Mr. Weaver: Yes, either or both of you. Miss Welty.

Miss Welty: Who are we to say? I mean, I would hate to think that anybody was trying to—

Mr. Weaver: I don't mean a self-conscious plan, but just that the non-South may overvalue any writer from the South.

Miss Welty: No, I don't know of a single case myself, but I don't think so. I don't see how that could well be.

Mr. Weaver: Well, there have been, for instance, writers from the South who have very explicitly exploited, for instance, the troubles of the sixties and that kind of thing. I don't want to name names, but there are some who have written novels about—

Mr. Buckley: Go ahead, you may if you like.

Mr. Weaver: I would rather not. But you said before—

Mr. Buckley: Is that Southern civility?

Mr. Weaver: —that these concerns with social protest struck you as being somewhat outside what you thought were really the profound and valuable things in literature, and I just wondered if you would agree that the Northern critics, and so on, may look at all Southern writers in a lump and it may have the effect of giving cachet of a kind to some mediocre Southern writers?

Miss Welty: I am not familiar with whoever it is you are talking about, I guess, but I think—

Mr. Buckley: That's because you are too choosy.

Miss Welty: No, but I think the thing is general, anyway. The whole country is full of people who are jumping on bandwagons every time they go past the corner in every concern. But I don't think you can blame any section of the country—I mean, put the cause of it on any section of the country. Those things are either good or bad according to their own merits. I don't feel—

Mr. Percy: I think it would be a question in terms of people who

were influenced by Faulkner, Southern writers who were influenced
by Faulkner. Incidentally, I think this is the reason Faulkner has been
both a blessing and a curse to the South—a blessing because he is
probably the greatest American novelist of this century and a curse
because he was so powerful and influential that many Southern
writers, younger writers who came after him, were influenced even to
imitate his idiosyncrasies and his styles and his sentences. I can think
of a few writers, whose names I will not mention, who have published as imitation Faulkners.

Miss Welty: But that is a different kind of influence.

Mr. Percy: Yes.

Miss Welty: That's an honest kind and a benign one, even if it
does not work out very well.

Mr. Percy: But I think that it is important to get out from under
the big name.

Miss Welty: I do, too. I mean one is a fashion and the other is a
serious attempt.

Mr. Buckley: Mr. Hise.

Mr. Hise: You never did, Dr. Percy, get to the question of the
Civil War as a tragedy. Shouldn't it be thought of more as a sort of
fortunate fall in C. Vann Woodward's sense that the South could no
longer participate in the American myths and it has taken the rest of
America 100 years to find out what the South found out at the time
of the Civil War?

Mr. Percy: Well, in the last novel I wrote, the novel ended on the
hope that the South could do for the country what the North did 100
years ago. The North saved the Union, which is probably a good
thing and I was hoping—in the novel, the country falls apart again
here. In this case, it is the great Northern cities which break away
from the rest of the country. It was hoped in the novel that the reconciliation would take place in the South and extend to the black-white
reconciliation, liberal-conservative. This was a hope and it would certainly be poetic justice if this *would* happen.

Mr. Buckley: Does that answer your question or does that evade
it?

Mr. Hise: So it's not really a tragedy? Hopefully.

Mr. Buckley: When you say that much of what happened to the

South is the result of its having got beat, do you mean chastened?

Mr. Percy: No, I was thinking of the novelist's equipment and maybe a tragic sense of life being an indispensable part of this equipment. And the North, never having lost a war, didn't have it and so, if this is the case, then the South certainly had a tragic sense of life for a long time after the Civil War.

Mr. Buckley: And why did that not, during the 19th century, result in interesting novels? You said because it was over-defensive?

Mr. Percy: I think it was defensive. It was either romantic or defensive and there was too much hurt and too much anger. I think it took a while to be digested and I think it happened along about 1920 or '30.

Mr. Buckley: Would you say that Japan and Germany will need themselves also to pass a couple of generations before their writers can write interestingly?

Mr. Percy: Well, they got help from the United States in their reconstruction.

(laughter)

Miss Welty: Yes.

Mr. Buckley: And your point was that that sapped the bitterness? Well, what about the defensiveness?

Mr. Percy: You mean in Germany and Japan?

Mr. Buckley: Yes. In the American South, there was a lot of antebellum enthusiasm, but there isn't in Germany very much enthusiasm for their experience.

Mr. Percy: Right. History seems to be accelerating. Things happen so much faster than they used to. World War II seems to have been forgotten by the Japanese and the Germans. Of course, they don't like to think about it—and as I say, the material effects—

Mr. Buckley: But the old order was all that the South had left, wasn't it?

Mr. Percy: For a long time.

Mr. Buckley: And, under the circumstances, mooched on it in every sense of the word.

Mr. Percy: Yes.

Mr. Buckley: In sum, commendable?

Mr. Percy: I would like to think that the Southern literature in the

19th century was good, was first class, but I don't think it was. I can only think of one or two writers who compared with the New England writers.

Mr. Buckley: Thank you, Dr. Percy. Thank you, Miss Welty, and gentlemen of the panel, ladies and gentlemen.

An Interview with Eudora Welty

Charlotte Capers / 8 May 1973

From the Mississippi Department of Archives and History, Oral History Program (OHP 046), Jackson, MS. Transcribed by Mary H. Mingee from a taped recording (TR 149). Published by permission.

Capers: This is Charlotte Capers, at my home, 4020 Berkley Drive, Jackson, on May 8, 1973, and I am about to interview Miss Eudora Welty, who yesterday, May 7, 1973, received the news that she had won the Pulitzer Prize for Fiction. Miss Welty has previously won many honors, and only last week was honored by the State of Mississippi, when Governor William L. Waller declared Wednesday, May 2, 1973, as Eudora Welty Day in Mississippi.

I'd like for Eudora to tell us something about the book for which she was awarded the prize, and her reactions on being informed that she had won.

Welty: Well, the book is a short novel, really a novella, I should say, which is not much different from a long story. I wrote it in 1969 and it was published in the *New Yorker* magazine. It was changed a little bit when I wrote it over for a book, but I suppose I changed every sentence with one word or two that no one would notice but the author. It was published in 1972. The title was *The Optimist's Daughter,* a title which I kept thinking I would change but never did. It's really an interior story of what went on in a young widow's mind in response to grief and loss and her adjustment to facing up to it, and acceptance of the meaning of the love in her life and affection. All this is shown in a family tangle of relationships.

Is this going into too much detail?

Capers: No.

Welty: It's all done by a series of confrontations, of only four or five people, plus a chorus of small townspeople who come to a funeral and come from here, there, and everywhere to speak as a chorus about love and death and so on.

Capers: I have heard it said and I have read it—that of all of your books, this was perhaps the most autobiographical. Is this correct?

Welty: Well, all my books are autobiographical in that I never have made up the feelings in them. I think that you have to experience emotion before you write about it, but usually I have the emotions acted out by a cast of characters and through situations that are better dramatic vehicles than my life happens to be, which is rather calm, but in the case of *The Optimist's Daughter,* I did draw on some of the childhood and early married experiences of my own mother. That's the only thing that is "factual"; and the character of Becky, the mother, is not the character of my mother, but it draws upon it. At any rate, there were letters and events and traumatic things in the life of my character, Becky, which came from my knowledge of my mother. This made it both meaningful and instructive—and hard for me to write.

Capers: I was going to say, I think it would be extremely hard . . . . so close to you that it was painful.

Welty: I don't know. It was very painful; but also, it helped me to understand and so I don't know whether you'd call that autobiographical or not. The situation is made up, characters are made up.

Capers: Did it not help you to work through your own emotions after the death of your mother?

Welty: I think it did; although, I did not undertake it for any therapeutic reasons, because I don't believe in that kind of thing. I believe in really trying to comprehend something. Comprehension is more important to me than healing; but, I suppose the by-product of that was being able to understand something better—my own feelings about it. It was helpful to me. But that's not important, really, because the important thing is if the novel itself was able to show these feelings I'm talking about, and what happens to people in such circumstances, and how they react on one another. It was just a story of relationships.

Capers: Well, it was, of course, beautifully done, and I think that the recognition it has been accorded proves that; but the thing that really rings so true to an old home-town girl is the chorus. I feel that I know a good many people in the chorus, but I think that these are almost typical people that do come to funerals, and that do stand by you and support you, and drive you mad and love you and worry you. The chorus you could pretty much spot, couldn't you, if you tried?

Welty: You mean, actually? No; you can spot that kind of person who goes on forever and ever.

Capers: Yes.

Welty: But the important thing again, to me, is that they are there, that they exist, and that they do come forward . . . I mean, the important thing to the story. It was an inevitable part of the story. Of course, it was the easiest to do.

Capers: Because there they are.

Welty: There they are, and you don't get on the inside of these people, they're self explanatory; so you're only on the inside of the figures through whom you're writing and you see these people through their eyes.

Capers: Well, do you feel that in *The Optimist's Daughter,* the place—the sense of place, which you have written a lot about and which I know you feel very strongly—is this very evident? Could these people have just as well been anywhere, or do you think these people, the principals and the chorus, are peculiarly Southern or peculiarly Mississippian?

Welty: I don't think, perhaps, they're peculiarly Mississippian. Well they may be, but I use place in this as I do in everything, but in a more complicated way; because the characters in it were not all of the location where the story happened. The character of Becky, the mother, has her deepest roots in another place, and that's the thing that most changed her life—a feeling of being out of place, in a place to which she has never really resigned herself; and the girl through whom the story is told, Laurel, has come from Chicago where she has attempted to change her life back into the past. She's coming from the opposite direction and must make her decisions in respect to the future, here, whereas the people who live in the little town have never changed. There's also the doctor who has left there and become another kind of being in a city. So I was using place in many ways—to define people, to explain them, and to be their lures and their despairs, etcetera, a little more complicated than having a story set in a place which never moves or changes.

Capers: Eudora, thank you very much for these very revealing remarks about your book. I would like to ask you now, since this is the book that has been recognized by the awarding of the Pulitzer Prize, if you know how the Pulitzer Prize is awarded, and by whom?

Welty: I got a telegram, which is all I know, saying that the Trustees of Columbia University had awarded it, and it was signed by the president of Columbia. Those are the only facts about it that I know.

Capers: Would they have a committee?

Welty: I don't know. I asked some friend yesterday, and he said, "We've always understood that it's been very secret." Oh, this was someone I asked over the telephone. I believe it was Albert Erskine, somebody in New York.

Capers: Albert Erskine, who is your editor?

Welty: My editor at Random House. He telephoned me to tell me that he had heard the news, and I said, "I think it's wonderful," and he said, "Well, it won't do any harm."

Capers: (Laughter) Well, it won't!

Welty: So I asked him how it happened, and he said that it's all very secretive.

Capers: Does a cash award go with this?

Welty: That's what the paper said. I just read the paper and it said a thousand dollars went with each award.

Capers: Oh. Well, this is a marvelous thing for Mississippi, and as we have said previously, Mississippi has produced a few Pulitzer Prize winners before, but I don't think ever one for fiction. But you think William Faulkner, for fiction?

Welty: Well, it just seems natural that it would have been William Faulkner. I would love to get hold of some information about the whole thing. (Laughter).

Capers: (Laughter) I bet you would. Well, what do you do? Do you go somewhere to receive an accolade, or something?

Welty: I have no idea.

Capers: You don't know about ceremonies or—

Welty: The only thing said in the telegram was just what I told you. They didn't even say "letter follows," so I don't know if they'll ever tell me! (Both laugh).

Capers: Can you quote the telegram?

Welty: Yes, I think it said, "The Trustees of Columbia University have today awarded you the Pulitzer Prize for Fiction. Congratulations." Signed, the President, Mr. McGill, I think.

Capers: Dear old Mr. McGill!

Welty: That's all it was. It took ages to get here. By that time, I'd known it for about half an hour—or had been told it for about half an hour.

Capers: And you had been on television, and you had been interviewed.

Welty: And everything; and this was just people appearing at the door to tell me, and Frank Hains over the telephone.

Capers: And Frank Hains over the telephone was your first word?

Welty: He was my first word, so of course I was thrilled, but I was confused . . .

Capers: I'm sure.

Welty: And Winifred [Cheney] was visiting me at the time.

Capers: How happy that must have made her! Your winning the Pulitzer Prize has made Mississippians—your friends, and so many people in Mississippi—so happy. We have just had an occasion I'd like to talk to you about, which I think is unique, and that is the recognition of *you* by your fellow citizens of the State of Mississippi, and the great events associated with that recognition only last week. At that time, Governor William L. Waller, Governor of the State of Mississippi, proclaimed Wednesday, May 2nd, as Eudora Welty Day in Mississippi; and I do not know of another literary personality or another artist who has been so honored by any state; and this has made us all very happy. And I think the occasion itself was felicitous in the extreme. It was also historical, and if you don't mind, I'd like for you to tell me about your friends from Jackson and from out of the state who came to honor you. I believe the people started coming in on Sunday before Eudora Welty Day on Wednesday. Is that correct? Would you tell me about some of the people?

Welty: Yes, this was the most marvelous part of all, because it was really a gathering of my closest and oldest friends, throughout my whole life, both in Jackson and from away. I'd been hesitant to send them invitations. It seemed like such a long way to come for something; and then I thought, no, I'll just make my ideal list of who I'd most like to have, and ask them. I couldn't have lost by that, and it was marvelous how many people came. The ones that did come on Sunday were Diarmuid Russell, from New York, who is my agent, and has been since 1940, and his wife, Rosie. They stayed all week with me in Jackson. The first time they'd ever been to Mississippi. That was just wonderful!

Capers: I think they were delighted with Mississippi, and to be here. I'm interrupting you to say that for the benefit of the tape and transcription, this was all part of the Mississippi Arts Festival, Inc., for 1973. The Mississippi Arts Festival, Inc., sponsors a magnificent week of cultural events each spring, and the idea of Eudora Welty Day, I believe, was initiated by the Executive Committee of the Mississippi Arts Festival, Inc. Is that correct? This was part of the Arts Festival, and I wanted to make that reference for historical purposes, that the great feature of the Arts Festival, which each year brings celebrated people in all of the arts to Mississippi . . . that the special honoree this year was Miss Eudora Welty.

Welty: Yes, and really what made it so wonderful besides the fact of all the people gathering for me, was the really beautiful way it had been planned and carried out by these girls. I've never seen anything so lovingly planned, so thoughtful—just perfection was all you could call it. This was felt by all the guests.

Capers: Would you explain, amplify, about having friends meet friends at the airport?

Welty: Yes. Well part of their arrangements, which were complete, if there were ever complete arrangements, every guest was met at the airport; they were taken to their rooms in motels which had been set aside for them, and in the rooms were little bouquets of garden flowers, which I later heard many of them took back with them when they left. The little roses would have opened, but they said that they were going to carry them back. They were taken to functions and taken home again. They were taken riding in cars and shown everything, taken to lunch in someone's home in little groups of six or eight. There was no end to the courtesy and to the pleasure that was given to them.

Capers: Well, it was a great pleasure for the people here who did it.

Welty: They showed that; and I think they all liked each other— that was the best thing. All my friends liked each other. That's something that happens in Paradise!

Capers: It really is.

Welty: For the time it lasted, it was just beautiful.

Capers: Well, I interrupted you when you were telling about Rosie and Diarmuid coming first. Rosie and Diarmuid Russell came and they stayed in your home, and they were the only out of town guests in your home. Then, other early arrivals were . . .

Welty: John and Catherine Prince, from Washington, who are young-old friends. I mean—they're old friends who are young. They live in Georgetown, and I've been to see them lots of times. I don't know what to tell you about them.

Capers: Well, that's enough—old friends.

Welty: Anyway, yes, old friends. Then, Reynolds Price, a young writer from Durham, North Carolina, who's been here many times, came, and, gee, I can't go down this whole list.

Capers: Well, you can if you want to. Where's your list? Let's see. . . . What about . . . did Mr. Downs come?

Welty: Mr. Downs came.

Capers: I never met Mr. Downs.

Welty: Well, no wonder you never met him, because he never got my letter. Mr. Downs is from Denison University, and I've worked for him three or four times . . .

Capers: What is his job at Denison?

Welty: He's in the English Department there; and he said he thought the way to come would be by bus because that's the way I went to Columbus, Ohio, although I came to Columbus, Ohio, from Kentucky, which is a little easier. So he arrived by bus, and my letter didn't reach him so he didn't know he was invited to a party at my house for the out of town guests. All I knew was that he didn't come. He said he walked up and down in front of my house looking in and thought that must be my house.

Capers: He never got to your house?

Welty: He never got to my house . . . never got to my party! I saw him the next morning. That was the one sad story.

Capers: And his name is Mr. Linfield Downs?

Welty: Linfield Downs.

Capers: Lin Downs. Well, I'm sorry about Mr. Downs. Well, now, Mr. and Mrs. Lambert Davis got here.

Welty: They got here. He used to be my editor at Harcourt, Brace.

Capers: Say his name. I'm not sure I heard.

Welty: Lambert Davis. He retired from New York and publishing up there at an early age, because he couldn't stand New York any more; went down to Chapel Hill and became editor of the University of North Carolina Press, where he's lived happily ever after.

Capers: They're very nice.

Welty: They're so nice.

Capers: Now, the . . . Mr. and Mrs. William Meacham

Welty: They didn't get here . . . that's my relations. . . .

Capers: They were afraid of the flood.

Welty: They were afraid of the flood, and called up and said, "But it's flooded down there." I said, "No, it isn't." They said, "Well, you must not have been listening to the national news."

Capers: I heard that their travel agent warned them it was dangerous.

Welty: I don't know. She wrote to me after talking to me and said that they got phone calls and everything from people saying, "You don't dare go."

Capers: So they didn't come?

Welty: So they didn't come.

Capers: Well, that's real sad. Nona Balakian is an old friend?

Welty: She's an old friend on the *New York Times Book Review*.

Capers: Did you work with her?

Welty: I worked with her.

Capers: On the staff?

Welty: Yes, the time I worked there—one summer. And we're old friends. She had a lovely time, I think because she knew so many people.

Capers: She was real thrilled, though. She kept wanting to tell Nash Burger everything!

Welty: I know.

Capers: Michael Newton.

Welty: Michael Newton.

Capers: What is his official capacity? In the Arts?

Welty: Well, at present, I think he's vice president of the Associated Councils on the Arts. But I invited him here because he's an old friend from England whom I knew.

Capers: Oh! He's an Englishman?

Welty: Yes. I knew him when I was at Cambridge.

Capers: I didn't get to talk to him. I really didn't know much about him.

Welty: He's visited me in Jackson two or three times—so it has really nothing to do with the Associated Councils on the Arts. But that's what he is, at present.

Capers: How about Joan and Olivia Kahn?

Welty: They're old friends of mine, and they're sisters, in New York. Joan is the mystery editor of Harper's Publishing House, and Olivia is a reader for several publishing houses and a fine painter.

Capers: Is E. J. Kahn their brother?

Welty: Their brother, yes.

Capers: Who writes short stories for *The New Yorker.*

Welty: Yes, and reports, too.

Capers: Well, of course, Mary Lou Aswell is one of your dearest friends.

Welty: One of my dearest friends, and, I guess, one of my oldest . . . since 1940. She was fiction editor of *Harper's Bazaar* when I first met her. She published my early stories.

Capers: Do you know the first story she published?

Welty: Oh, I can't think what it would be. I have such a poor chronological sense.

Capers: I knew she had published some of your earlier stories.

Welty: She published some of the stories in *The Golden Apples*— about three of them, I think—long stories which she had to get down on her knees to Mr. Hearst to save her space for.

Capers: Isn't that . . .

Welty: Wonderful!

Capers: Wonderful! doesn't she feel good today!

Welty: Oh! Yes! And so do I! (laughter)

Capers: Yes. Agnes Sims is a friend of Mary Lou Aswell's, and a friend of yours, of long standing. And a friend of mine, also.

Welty: And a friend of yours . . . and a painter.

Capers: Who lives in Santa Fe.

Welty: Yes, both she and Mary Lou come originally from Philadelphia.

Capers: Did they know each other in Philadelphia?

Welty: Yes, they knew each other long ago.

Capers: Well, now, we have known William Jay Smith in Jackson, Mississippi, before, but he appeared with Mrs. William Jay Smith this time.

Welty: Right.

Capers: And he is an old and close friend of yours.

Welty: That he is.

Capers: When did you first know Bill Smith?

Welty: I met him in Florence—Italy, not Mississippi. He had just gone over after being a Rhodes Scholar, and had been two years in England, then had moved on over to Italy. We've known each other in many parts of the world since, and he's now poetry consultant for the Library of Congress, and teaches at Hollins half the year, this summer at Columbia. We're old friends and he's a very fine poet.

Capers: Yes. I saw his thing on Venice in the *New York Times*.

Welty: Yes, beautiful!

Capers: Beautiful, very beautiful! Mr. and Mrs. Gwin F. Kōlb, and I said, "No, that is not your name, it's not Kōlb, it's Kŏlb." He's an old Jacksonian. Was he a friend of yours in Jackson?

Welty: No. I never did know him in Jackson. But he is at the University of Chicago, and when I went there to lecture, of course, he became my shepherd. We've been friends a long time. His wife, Ruth, is from here, too. Her name was Ruth Godbold, I think. They went to Millsaps, and met each other there.

Capers: I see. Mr. William McCollum—do I know him?

Welty: He came. He and Mr. Napier Wilt are both friends of the Kolbs.

Capers: I don't believe I met them.

Welty: Napier Wilt has retired now, but he was also on the English faculty at the University of Chicago.

Capers: I would like to ask you about Kenneth Millar, whose pseudonym is Ross Macdonald. He is a celebrated detective story writer, or writer, and is a friend of yours, and I'm interested in how you two met.

Welty: We met because he wrote me a letter after I had said, in an interview published in the *New York Times* with Walter Clemons, that I admired his work and had written him a fan letter, but had not risked sending it to him. So he wrote me a fan letter, which I answered, and we began to write letters over, oh, quite a while. Then I reviewed a book of his, *The Underground Man,* and we got to be friends again.

Capers: That was on the first page of the *New York Times Book Review.*

Welty: The *New York Times,* yes. I think so much of his work, and he's such a nice man. Then, in a typical Ross Macdonald fashion, we, unknown to each other, turned up at the same time in the same hotel in adjoining rooms in New York.

Capers: At the Algonquin?

Welty: At the Algonquin—and met then, and had some good conversations, and walked, and talked, and so on, and got to be good friends. So, I felt that he was almost like an old friend, especially after he dedicated his new book to me; so I invited him to come to this wonderful occasion for me, and he came, which I think was just wonderful—from Santa Barbara. I was sorry his wife couldn't come. She had planned to.

Capers: What's the title of his new book?

Welty: *Sleeping Beauty.*

Capers: I'm his fan, too. I can't wait to read it.

Welty: Oh! I know it! I'm going out today to try to buy some copies. Rosie wanted to take my inscribed copy home on the plane, but I wouldn't let her.

Capers: I don't blame you. Well, I thought he was a most attractive man, and I'm delighted that he came. Mr. and Mrs. Richard Ader were very nice people. They're from New York City, and I believe he's your lawyer. He's our lawyer.

Welty: He is. He is of the firm of Greenbaum, Wolfe and Ernst, and has been helping Charlotte and me over our literary matters. He had a wonderful time. He loved Mississippi—drove to Jackson by way of Columbus in a car, and then went on to Natchez. He telephoned me after they got back to New York that they had had such a wonderful time they only made the plane by seconds, and wanted to come back. I can't tell you how everybody was so sweet to them.

Capers: Who are the Brainard Cheneys? And the Lewis Simpsons? I didn't meet them.

Welty: Well, the Cheneys—I've known them a long time, too. They are from Smyrna, Tennessee, and their association is with the old Agrarian group. They're old friends of the . . .

Capers: The Vanderbilt people.

Welty: Yes. And I think she is the librarian at Vanderbilt, or was at one time, and writes book reviews. He's in politics somehow, in Tennessee, but he's also a novelist. They're old friends of Caroline Gordon's, and Robert Penn Warren's, Cleanth Brooks's and Allen Tate. At the time I made my list, they were all hoping to come, so I invited the Cheneys because I thought it would be good for them to see all of their old friends again.

Capers: I wanted to ask you about Robert Penn Warren.

Welty: Robert Penn Warren would have come, but he had a lecture date as close as Alabama on the night of this, and so, of course, he couldn't come.

Capers: And Allen Tate didn't get here.

Welty: Allen Tate had meant to come, but his health is frail, and he had spring flu just before. He had accepted . . . Caroline Gordon had accepted.

Capers: Yes. Where are they now? Caroline Gordon is in the East.

Welty: She's in Princeton. They're no longer married to each other.

Capers: No, I know. But is she writer-in-residence, or lecturer, at Princeton?

Welty: No. She's been writing up there, but she's just beginning a new sort of life out in Dallas, Texas, at the University of Dallas, where she's going to teach a course in Creative Grammar, which I think sounds wonderful.

Capers: Well, lots of grammar is very creative.

Welty: Yes, and there mostly isn't any grammar.

Capers: I know. Well, isn't she rather—isn't she of advanced years?

Welty: I think she's the oldest of that group, although I'm not quite certain how old she is. But she's of great vitality and vivacity.

Capers: Now, who is Mr. Shattuck?

Welty: Charles Shattuck is from the University of Illinois at Urbana, and my connection with him is that years ago, he and Kerker Quinn edited a well-known little magazine called *Accent*.

Capers: How do you spell "Kerker"?

Welty: K-e-r-k-e-r Q-u-i-n-n. He died, but Charles is still at the

University of Illinois. But *Accent* had a long and honorable life, and they published a piece I wrote. Charlotte, you may know, on Ida M'Toy.

Capers: Oh, yes.

Welty: And we all got to be such friends over that. Then they invited me to come and lecture, and we've kept an acquaintance and friendship up, you know, over all these twenty-five years or so, and I was delighted he came; even though the Ozark Airline struck at the last minute, and he had to go to Chicago and down. He's a delightful person, and he had a wonderful time.

Capers: Now, we did miss Mary Mehan.

Welty: Mary Mehan is an old friend also, in Santa Fe, who was struck down with a virus before she and her husband, Aristide—they would have loved to have come.

Capers: Well, it was a marvelous occasion. It was wonderful for us to be honored by the presence of these distinguished people. Most of all we enjoyed their demonstrated affection for you.

The day itself, I think, deserves some comment—Eudora Welty Day. And the reading in the House of Representatives of Mississippi's Historic Old Capitol, I don't think there's ever been such a crowd in the Old Capitol. It was a real tribute to you. I thought that it should also be noted that Governor Waller awarded you a "Distinguished Mississippian" plaque, which is well-deserved. Would you care to comment on the confusions of the day?

Welty: Well, the whole thing was so overwhelming to me. It also was beautifully run. I was the only one that didn't know quite what to do, and Charlotte is the one who should comment on this, but any-way . . . there in one room, semi-circular . . .

Capers: I'd like to know how you felt about it, because I will comment that I thought the arrangements were not good, there was a great deal of unnecessary confusion with the press and the televi-sion people. There should have been better planning, but as all these things did not work out—the main thing is how did you feel about it? It was your day!

Welty: I felt wonderful about it, and I was surprised by the lights and the TV and so on, but it just seemed like a dream in a way, in which various unexpected things turn up and it doesn't seem to bother you—you just go on. What really was present with me at every moment was the fact that in that one room were my oldest and best friends in Jackson and from around this country, all in one place for probably the only time in anyone's lives. How could they ever be in any one place again? Everything had converged that meant happiness and pleasure and joy for me, along with my family, and a beautiful day. And . . .well, I just thought it was beautiful.

Capers: Everyone thought you were beautiful, and your graciousness, under what must have been terribly straining circumstances, was remarkable. I felt that the arrangements for the press—well, apparently they hadn't been made at all, and it was bad to have all that interruption and confusion . . . but it did show one thing, and that is that you're the biggest "draw" we've ever had in Dixie! (Laughter). The night the lights went on in Mississippi! The day the lights went on in the Old Capitol! But, anyway, following the reading from *Losing Battles,* Eudora went to the Archives and History Building and received her fans, and was most gracious, and signed autographs for little children who'd come great distances to see her; and was joined, somewhat unexpectedly, by Mrs. Waller, who was very gracious and nice and is the wife of the governor, and who received with her. After this occasion, which was given by the Mississippi Arts Festival, Inc. (I think we should try to make this clear all along—the way that these things were planned by the Mississippi Arts Festival through its committees, some of which functioned a great deal better than others), then we moved on to the night, which was the climax of Eudora Welty Day. This was a big party, a lovely party given by the Mississippi Arts Festival, in the home of Mr. and Mrs. Arnold Turner, Jr., on Crane Boulevard, in Jackson, following a performance of *The Ponder Heart,* which was really a gift of love from New Stage Theatre to Eudora, because they gave her one whole night to ask her friends to be with her there. I enjoyed it more than the Old Capitol because I wasn't so tense about it. Would you like to say anything about the people that came to *The Ponder Heart?*

Welty: Well, it was all the same wonderful crowd that had been together all day. The Festival girls provided a bus. That was the only time we had any rain and it fell just as we were going to the theatre. They took everybody there dryly and securely in a chartered bus. The performance was wonderful, and I think everybody loved it . . . I'm sure they did.

Capers: And the whole house was yours for the night?

Welty: Well, except for the people that had their regular seats that night.

Capers: Did you have some regular ticket holders there?

Welty: Yes, no one was put out, but those who did not have season tickets for that night. Room was made for everybody, and it was just a beautiful performance.

Capers: And you had your old friends from high school and . . .

Welty: I had my old friends from high school—from Sunday School, Davis School, high school, everything. And they all came, and when someone who was an old friend couldn't come, then their family came in their place—like Lehman Engel. I asked his three girl cousins. I would have asked them anyway, but I mean, they all came because he couldn't, and they wanted to see me too, I know it. But it was all in the same spirit . . . I mean it was like some kind of reunion. I think we left out, Charlotte, back at the Old Capitol, about the exhibition . . . or do you want to go into that?

Capers: Yes, everything that you'd like to comment on.

Welty: Well, I thought that was beautiful!

Capers: I did too. I'm real delighted with it.

Welty: The Archives—as you know, having done this—has manuscripts and a lot of letters pertaining to things that happened in the course of my writing life, and these were all beautifully arranged by Patti Black, and they were heartwarming to me. When I saw those letters from John Woodburn . . . and also from a number of the people who were present—it was wonderful for them, they just kept going back and looking at it because it was strange—it was like looking into a prism or something. It gave you so many faces of things that everybody had had a part in . . . so really all of it belonged to everybody. It was really unique.

Capers: Well, the people at the Old Capitol really did work hard on that exhibition.

Welty: I know they did. It was obvious.

Capers: It was fine, I thought.

Welty: It was fine. They also had samples of the photographs they have, which was one more aspect of things. I don't see how anyone could have a more moving and meaningful tribute paid to them than my friends and fellow Mississippians did in this. I just can't conceive—I can't imagine people going into the detail and into the care and the study that brought all this about. It was really overwhelming.

Capers: It was really heartfelt, and I do not know of as many people anywhere who really wanted everything to be just right for you because they love you, and because they're proud of you. And so far as our collection goes, I think it's the greatest thing we have in the Department of Archives and History; and I'm really indebted—the State of Mississippi is really indebted to you, which I might as well say here, for the collection. I think you're about out of time, and I think we've hit the high spots of the day.

Welty: We'll have to . . .

Capers: We haven't gotten to the party but the party was great. I'd like to say that myself. It was a beautiful—what would you call it—it was an after-theatre black-tie supper.

Welty: It was an after-the-theatre, after-the-rain, after-everything, end-of-the-whole-beautiful-day party.

Capers: We had such a good time that we stayed till about two-thirty.

Welty: We stayed until about two-thirty. Every room in the house was filled with . . .

Capers: "The odor of roses and sweet girl graduates?"

Welty: Yes, and Becky Turner played the piano. It was in Jean and Arnold Turner's house, and given by her and Arnold, and Tay and Guy Gillespie (for the Arts Festival). They were the co-hosts and hostesses. It was a perfectly beautiful and perfect party. It was lovely. What else can you say about a party? It was also lively and animated. It was fun, it was beautiful!

Capers: Eudora, I thank you so much. I know you're in a great rush because you're just between all the excitement of receiving yet another distinguished award, and getting ready to go to New York Friday to attend—well, tell me where you're going.

Welty: I'm going to the annual ceremony of the National Institute of Arts and Letters in the Academy, and to a party being given for Diarmuid Russell in New York.

Capers: We'll take this up when you get back. Thank you ever so much for your time, and for being what you are.

Eudora Welty: An Interview

Alice Walker / Summer 1973

From *The Harvard Advocate,* 106 (Winter 1973), 68–72. ©
1973 by the Editors and Trustees of The Harvard Advocate.
Reprinted by permission.

*Eudora Welty was born in Jackson, Mississippi, and pres-
ently lives there. She studied at the Mississippi State Col-
lege for Women and graduated from the University of
Wisconsin in 1929. She has been a professor at Smith
and Bryn Mawr and a lecturer at Cambridge University.
Her novel,* The Ponder Heart, *was awarded the Howells
Medal for Fiction by the American Academy of Arts and
Letters. She has also been the recipient of the Hollins
Medal, the Brandeis Medal of Achievement and a Guggenheim Fellowship.
Alice Walker was born in Georgia in 1944 and has lived
and worked in Mississippi for several years. She is the
author of* Once, *a book of poems and the novel,* The
Third Life of Grange Copeland. *Her new works,* Revolutionary Petunias *(verse) and* In Love & Trouble: Stories
of Black Women, *will be released next year. She is currently a fellow at the Radcliffe Institute and a lecturer at
Wellesley and the University of Massachusetts on Writing
and Black Woman Writers. She is also completing a biography of Langston Hughes.*

It is a hot summer day in Jackson—97 degrees. In Eudora Welty's front yard the tallest oak tree I have ever
seen in a yard covers the whole house with shade. It was
planted by her father when she was a child. Inside, in the
room she has chosen for this interview, a coolness comes
from an air conditioner in the window, but also from the
cool neutral colors of the room: white, eggshell, beige—
dark brown floors and picture frames. There is solid quiet
here, and space and light.

When we face each other, talking at first in starts, I
think how odd it is that I feel entirely relaxed, entirely
comfortable. Considering how different we are—in age,
color, in the directions we have had to take in this life, I
wonder if my relaxation means something terrible. For
this *is* Mississippi, U.S.A., and black, white, old, young,

Southern black and Southern white—all these labels
have meaning for a very good reason: they have effec-
tively kept us apart, sometimes brutally. So that, although
we live in the same town, we inhabit different worlds.
This interview itself is an accidental meeting. Though we
are both writers, writing in some cases from similar experiences, and certainly from the same territory, we are
more strangers, because the past will always separate us;
and because she is white and not young, and I am black
and not old. Still, I am undaunted, unafraid of discovering whatever I can.

She is modest, shy, quiet, and strong as the oak tree
out in the yard. Life has made a face for her that concen-
trates a beauty in her eyes. They light with directness, and
will not be moved downward or to the side. She speaks
softly and says she is hard of hearing. When the tape
recorder collects nothing after spinning pleasantly for half
an hour, she is sympathetic. Her understanding helps me
recover from embarrassment. We go over, as best we
can, the parts the tape recorder missed.

AW: How many books have you written?

EW: Well, I believe I've written eleven, counting the collections of
short stories.

AW: Do you write mostly short stories? Novels? Which do you like
to write best?

EW: I think I'm more of a natural short story writer. I've written
many more short stories. In fact, the novels I've written usually began
as short stories. And I then realized they were developing beyond the
bounds of a story . . .

AW: Do you feel that all short stories are potential novels?

EW: No, they are two different things. I think that one of my faults
as a novelist is that I don't think as a novelist does. I think the short
story is a sustained thing, all in one piece, and compact. You don't
have any of the expansion and scope that the novel can have. So
any time I've made the mistake of writing a short story that became a
novel I've had to go back and start at the beginning again. It's like
starting for the long jump or the short hop. You don't have the same
impulse.

AW: Do you ever write poems?

EW: No.

AW: Never? Not any? Not even one or two?

EW: Oh, maybe one. I don't think I count as a poet. I think poetry takes a very special gift. I do think the lyric impulse, which is in poetry, is also in the short story. I mean I can see the affinity, but I've never been led to try the other form.

AW: Do you like any poets?

EW: Oh yes, I do. I'm not too up on the new ones, although I've read a good many of the new ones. But I mostly turn to poets I've liked all my life, such as Yeats, John Donne . . . I tend to go back to them, no matter what else I read.

AW: How long did you live in New York City, and when was that?

EW: Well, I went to school there for a year, at Columbia, which was the longest I've ever been there. And I have gone up and stayed many times for several weeks. Then one summer I worked on the *New York Times Book Review* for about three months; that was the longest time I've been there since I began working for my living.

AW: You know Langston Hughes spent a year at Columbia too, in the twenties; one year. He hated it. He said the teachers were dull and the buildings looked like factories. Did you like it?

EW: Oh, I enjoyed it. What I really went for was to learn my way around New York. I was taking a business course which took up almost no time and so I could go to the theatre every night!

AW: A business course! I don't understand. Why did you take a business course?

EW: Well, I'm glad I did. My father, when he learned I wanted to be a writer, very wisely said that I could never hope to earn a living at it, which turned out to be absolutely true. He said I should learn a business or profession that would keep me going. When I came home during the Depression I got a job at the radio broadcasting station and I also worked for the WPA.

AW: And you took the pictures you collected in *One Time, One Place* while working for the WPA?

EW: Yes. My father died that same year. I was thankful to get a job. Of course I was writing, at the same time. But although my stories from the first were given an encouraging welcome in college quarterlies and the so-called "little" magazines, they took six years of trying to find a place in magazines of national circulation. It wasn't until the *Atlantic* took two and published them that the charm was broken. After that, some of the same stories that had been rejected by magazines before were accepted by those same magazines. Over all, I've always been lucky in publishing—in the people I've worked with, I mean, especially.

AW: What did your parents think about you going to New York?

EW: They knew it was what I wanted to do. They'd always believed in the value of gaining new experience. They were extraordinarily sympathetic parents, both of them.

AW: Did you think there was anything *wrong* with Mississippi [in terms of race] in those days, when you were young? Did you see a way in which things might change?

EW: Well, I could tell when things were wrong with *people,* and when things happened to individual people, people that we knew or knew of, they were very real to me. It was the same with my parents. I felt their sympathy, I guess it guided mine, when they responded to these things in the same way. And I think this is the way real sympathy *has* to start—from direct feeling for something present and known. People are first and last individuals, and I don't think of them in the mass when I feel for them most.

AW: How does living in Jackson affect your writing?

EW: It's where I live and look around me—it's my piece of the world—it teaches me. Also as a domestic scene it's completely familiar and self-explanatory. It's not everything, though—it's just a piece of everything, that happens to be my sample. It lets me alone to work as I like. It's full of old friends with whom I'm happy to be. And I'm not stuck, either, not compelled to stay here—I'm free to leave when I feel like it, which makes me love it more, I suppose.

AW: What do your friends think of your writing? Do they read it? Do any of them ever creep into your fiction?

EW: Oh yes. They do read it. But they don't creep in. I never write about people that I know. I don't want to, and couldn't if I did want to. I work entirely in terms of the imagination—using, of course, bits and pieces of the real world along with the rest.

AW: Do you write every day?

EW: No, I don't write every day—I write only when I'm in actual work on a particular story. I'm not a notebook keeper. Sustained

time is what I fight for, would probably sell my soul for—it's so hard
to manage that. I'd like to write a story from beginning to end right
through without having to stop. Where I write is upstairs in my bedroom.

AW: In bed?

EW: Oh no, I write at a desk. I have a long room with six big
windows in it, and a desk and typewriter at one end.

AW: What does it overlook? A garden? Trees?

EW: It overlooks the street. I like to be aware of the world going
on while I'm working. I think I'd get claustrophobic sitting in front of
a blank wall with life cut off from view.

AW: Do you have a "Philosophy of Life"? Some pithy saying that
you quote to yourself when you seem inundated with troubles?

EW: No. I have work in place of it, I suppose. My "philosophy" is
like the rest of my thinking—it comes out best in the translation of
fiction. I put what I think about people and their acts in my stories. Of
course back of it all there would have to be honesty.

AW: Many modern writers don't seem overly concerned with it.

EW: It's noticeable. Truth doesn't seem to be the thing they're
getting at, a good deal of the time.

AW: In fact, much popular poetry, some of it black, engages in
clever half-truths, designed to shock only. Or to entertain.

EW: Some of the black poets I've read I have not been able to
understand. It hasn't so far as I know anything to do with race. I
don't quite understand the virtue of the idiom they strain so over, the
language—I don't see the good of it. I feel *tactics* are being used on
me, the reader—not the easiest way to persuade *this* reader. It's hard
to see the passion behind it.

AW: Oh. I understand the idiom and the language; I can see the
passion behind it and admire the rage. My question is whether witty
half-truths are good for us in the long run, after we've stopped laughing. And whether poetry shouldn't stick to more difficult if less funny
ground, the truth.

EW: That's its real business. I don't believe any writing that has
falsity in it can endure for very long. It's end will take care of itself.

AW: Let's hope. What are your thoughts on the Women's Movement?

EW: Well, equal pay for equal work, and so on, fine. But some of the other stuff is hilarious.

AW: Hilarious? Oh, you mean "the lunatic fringe," the flamboyant stances used to attract attention.

EW: Some of the effervescences. Of course, I haven't any bones to pick, myself. A writer never has the problem to face. Being a woman has never kept me from writing or from finding publication for my work.

AW: That's interesting. In the course I teach on black women writers I find that in critical studies black women writers are always given scant attention and sometimes none. They may have published with ease, as Zora Hurston did, but later they were forgotten. Until quite recently, of course. Of course, to many women your life would seem ideal. You have your work, which is substantial, both in what it gives you and what it gives others. You have a house of your own— a lovely one—and all the freedom you want. You are rare, a success- ful writer who is a woman!

EW: Well, I do have freedom. The successful part is not so much to the point. I think that any artist has it over other people.

AW: Well, some women artists feel that when they marry they must share too much of their time with their husbands and children. They feel they lose single-mindedness, energy they need to put into their own work.

EW: That of course I couldn't say—about husbands and children, I mean. But my tendency is to believe that all experience is an en- richment instead of an impoverishment. My own relationships with people are the things that mean the most to me. I couldn't say what marriage and childbearing would do, of course.

AW: But have you regretted not having been married and not having children?

EW: Oh, I would have been glad if it had come along. Yes I would have. Of course. It wasn't a matter of choosing one thing in place of the other. I think the more things the better.

AW: Over the years have you known any black women? Really known them.

EW: I think I have. Better in Jackson than anywhere, though only, as you'd expect, within the framework of the home. That's the only way I'd have had a chance, in the Jackson up until now. Which doesn't take away from the reality of the knowledge, or its depth of affection—on the contrary. A schoolteacher who helped me on weekends to nurse my mother through a long illness—she was beyond a nurse, she was a friend and still is, we keep in regular touch. A very bright young woman, who's now in a very different field of work, began in her teens as a maid in our house. She was with us for ten years or more. Then she went on to better things—her story is a very fine one. She's a friend, and we are in regular touch too. Of course I've met black people professionally, in my experience along the fringes of teaching. Lecturing introduced us. The first college anywhere, by the way, that ever invited me to speak was Jackson State—years ago. I read them a story in chapel, as I remember. Now I don't count meeting people at cocktail parties in New York—black or any other kind—to answer the rest of your question. But I do know at least a few black people that mean a good deal to me, and I think they like me too.

AW: Have any of them ever crept into your fiction?

EW: No. As I said before, I never write about real people. You know, human beings are incapable of being made into characters, as is. They are so much more fluid, and so opaque in places where they need to be transparent and so transparent in places where they need to be opaque. But I think that what I put into a short story in the form of characters might be called certain *qualities* of people in certain situations—no, pin it down more—some quality that makes them unique. I try to dramatize something like this in a way that can show it better than life shows it. Better picked out.

AW: Has it ever been assumed that because you were born and raised in Mississippi your black characters would necessarily suffer from a racist perspective?

EW: I hardly see how anyone could claim that. Indeed to my knowledge no one ever has. I see all my characters as individuals, not as colors, but as people, alive—unique.

AW: Have you ever been called a Gothic Writer?

EW: They better not call me that!

AW: No?

EW: Yes, I have been, though. Inevitably, because I'm a Southerner. I've never had anybody call me that to my face. I've read that I'm Gothic, or I get asked by students to explain why I am.

AW: Why do they try to put all Southern writers in that mold?

EW: I don't know. It's just easy.

AW: I was never even sure of what it meant, exactly.

EW: I'm not sure either. When I hear the word I see in my mind a Gustave Dore illustration for "The Fall of the House of Usher." Anyway it sounds as if it has nothing to do with real life, and I feel that my work has something to do with real life. At least I hope it has.

AW: Do you do much publicity for your books?

EW: No, I don't do any. Never have done. I've had sympathetic editors who wouldn't try to get me to "appear."

AW: Did you ever meet Langston Hughes?

EW: No. I guess he would have been before my day, really.

AW: But he just died in 1967. He was sixty-five, but he never grew old.

EW: I wish I had. He was the first, one of the first, poets, I ever read, down here at the library, and I loved his work.

AW: What are you working on now?

EW: Well, I'm not doing anything except thinking. I haven't got anything on paper yet. I've got many things that I want to write, and expect to write.

AW: How long does it take you to write a novel like *Losing Battles?*

EW: Different things take different lengths of time. It took me a long time to write *Losing Battles . . .*

AW: It's a long book.

EW: . . . and I was doing a lot of other things too. I do rewrite a good deal and I write carefully and I'm not satisfied with things for a long time. Maybe I keep things too long. You have to know when to quit, you know. That's one of the things I'm least sure about in my work, one of the most important things.

AW: Are you leaving your books and papers and manuscripts to a school?

EW: Well, the Department of Archives and History here in Jackson has everything. I started giving them my papers a long time ago. That bunch of stuff over there on the table is on its way to them. I like having my things in Mississippi. Of course many universities do try to collect a writer's papers and books, and that's a good thing. I think the important thing is to try to have everything in one place.

Think about Mr. Faulkner, whose work is spread from one end of the country to the other.

AW: Yes. Or of Richard Wright, whose work is spread all over this country and France too, from what I hear.

EW: Or many others.

AW: Was *The Optimist's Daughter,* the whole thing, in the *New Yorker* before it became a book?

EW: It was the finished story, but I later worked on it some more. I mean I didn't take out any of the book to publish it in the *New Yorker.* I wrote it first just as it came out in the magazine. But I still had that feeling that I didn't want to let it go. I added a little to it, eventually expanded it—in the interests of precision, really. It's the same story, just more so. And I suppose too there are millions, well, hundreds, of small changes that nobody would know but me. Maybe just a modification of a word, the transposition of a sentence—important to the author, though.

AW: Have you gotten many awards and grants?

EW: Yes. I've been lucky that way, which is a fine thing. Now, I think, authors get paid tremendous sums—I don't mean writers like us (laughter) . . . but you know it was a great help back in the forties, fifties and sixties too, to have a grant. What it meant was that that year you wouldn't have to teach a class or give lectures or something. It buys you time. And anything that buys you time is God-given, God-sent.

AW: Are you able to support yourself entirely by your writing?

EW: At the present I am. Because this last book *(The Optimist's Daughter),* and the one before that *(Losing Battles)* did very well— I'm still speaking in terms of the kind of writer I am, not as a "seller." I just mean that I can get along all right this year. I think. Touch wood. But I hope to keep on, selling stories . . . writing.

I think it's possible to support yourself by writing, but it is the most precarious livelihood in the world. Of course, my father couldn't have been more right. For example, I said that my novel, *Losing Battles,* did very well, but I suppose it represents eight or ten years of work. During which time you don't get anything. You get a lump sum of money for a novel but that could be five years of work during which you have to support yourself, so it really isn't a way to earn a living.

AW: Did you teach at a local college at one time?

EW: At Millsaps. I asked them for a job, because it was when my mother was ill and I couldn't leave home to do lectures. I needed a job of that same sort that I could do and still live at home. So it was *just* wonderful.

AW: They must have been delighted to get you.

EW: Well, *I* was delighted. I had a grand class. Just grand. I had about sixteen students. And I still see lots of them, too. They look me up when they come through town. One of them brings me a big watermelon from Smith County every summer. That makes a writer feel good!

Eudora Welty: "I Worry Over My Stories"

Don Lee Keith / 1973

From *The Times-Picayune* [New Orleans, LA], 16 September 1973, sec. 3, 8. Reprinted by permission.

The voice, even filtered through telephone wires, is gentle. Its inflections are casual, comfortable, not bothering with widened vowels or distinct consonants. Words tumble out easily; they flow unstumblingly over each other, yet are sharply defined. And she is direct, especially with directions.

"Well, let's see, if you're on North Street, just keep on it and when you get to Pinehurst, go right. You'll know it. There's a church on one side and a graveyard on the other. After that, it's four blocks, on the right. Mine's the only two-story house on the block. The first floor's brick; the top's speckled. You can't really see the number, though. It got broken off. No listen. What I'll do is go outside in a few minutes and wait for you. If you see somebody in a checked dress waving from the doorstep, that's me."

And sure enough, there she is, Eudora Welty, framed somewhat lopsidedly in the doorway's brick arch. She smiles a pleasant smile. One hand is on a hip, the other digs deeply into an apron pocket, fingering a crumpled Kleenex. The handshake is firm, a statement. Her gestures are explicit and gracious, a class trait of that last American generation to be steeped in the true tradition of hospitality.

The motion is toward the open door, and inside, housed so securely by the walls that have been her ramparts of stability for several decades, Miss Welty is at ease. Even before she has offered the comforts of the living room sofa, she has suggested, perhaps, a biscuit with butter and some fresh preserves? And a cup of coffee? Or would you rather have iced tea? Just made it. Coffee? Fine. Come on back to the kitchen and you put in the sugar and cream. I always get too much or not enough, one way or the other . . .

And so she stands in front of the white stove, her angular frame tall and proud, her head tilted down at the warming coffee pot, her steady fingers reaching out twice, a third time, tapping the lid, just to

make sure it's on tight. Now, trying as politely as possible to divide
her interest between the coffee and the chance of showers for the
roses outside the window, and in the meantime, keep up a decent
conversation, she becomes a favorite aunt, an aunt given to special
favors. Her offhandedness detours you around the expected eccen-
tricities of the literati, sidetracks you from remembering that she is,
after all, the first lady of American letters.

Despite the honors and awards and the multitude of devoted fans
who sang hosannas last spring when she finally won the Pulitzer
Prize, she knows no pretensions. Unlike some less respected authors,
she does not wear an ego on her lapel, nor is she one to mention,
much less discuss, her literary stature without being prodded. For
decades, newspaper reporters and other journalists have been dis-
concerted by her hesitancy to grant interviews. Some said she
shunned the press; others insisted she was a recluse. Neither was
right. The truth is that Eudora Welty, in the peace of her brick and
speckled home in Jackson, Mississippi, is an uncommonly modest
woman. And perhaps she has always suspected that all too many
interviewers, some doubtlessly spurred by curiosity, never quite
understood what she was trying to say, even after she had said it
again.

"Besides," she begins, seated at last on a Victorian sofa, her feet
placed firmly on the purplish oriental rug of long use. "I have no
patience with those people who talk about creativity being the result
of the need to communicate, the product of some freak psychology.
They're always saying this about Southern writers, saying that's why
there are so many of them. Don't they know that everybody's born
with the need to communicate? It's natural. To hide this need, to
refuse it as an outlet, that would be the freak thing.

"As it happens, we in the South have grown up being narrators.
We have lived in a place—that's the word, Place—where storytelling
is a way of life. When we were children we listened a lot. We heard
stories told by relatives and friends. A great many were family tales.
We naturally absorbed not only the fairy tales, but the sheer nature
of telling them.

"So, when Southerners write, they are doing what comes naturally. Their stories have been a part of their lives, and maybe they do

tell them more convincingly, more freely, as some say, but if that's so, it has happened because the writer has been a part of The Place.

"Of course, it is true that a lot of history has happened in many of our front yards, but also, the person was there to see it happen, watching and being part of it over long periods of time, passing it carefully to the next generation, telling the stories which always grew, never got smaller.

"We've known a community of life, as I say, through the years. If we weren't around when something happened, way back, at least we think we know what it was like, simply because we've heard it so long. We tend to understand what's tragic or comic, or both, because we know the whole story and have been a part of The Place. Our concept of Place isn't just history or philosophy; it's a sensory thing of sights and smells and seasons and earth and water and sky as well."

When she was born, in 1909, the Weltys lived in another house in another section of Jackson. Her parents weren't really Southerners, in the sense that term is most often applied. Her father had come to Mississippi from Ohio, her mother from West Virginia, and they stayed in Jackson the rest of their lives, rearing two sons and the daughter who is now the sole survivor of the three children.

Since the Pinehurst house was built, well before World War II, she has lived there, where the shades of the tall yard trees play their patterns on the sidewalk, regardless of the day time. The front of the house stretches suddenly skyward up to the green gabled roof of the second story. Further back, the house drops to a single story, making it seem smaller inside than out; in actual count there are only six rooms and a sleeping porch. Her upstairs bedroom is where she writes, mostly in the mornings. Across the street sprawls the campus of Belhaven College; strangers might easily mistake the Welty home as that of a ranking college official.

The first Welty house, however, was the scene of her childhood, a time she recalls with no obvious anxiety. "Growing up, I had an enormous appetite for reading, and although we had plenty of book-shelves, amply filled, before long I had been through them all. My main disappointment was always that a book had to end. And then what? But I don't think I was ever disappointed by the books. I must have been what any author would consider an ideal reader; I felt every pain and pleasure suffered or enjoyed by all the characters. Oh, but I identified! Or tried to. Right in the middle of *The Five Little Peppers*—you couldn't possibly remember them—I suddenly decided that we had to be poor, and I hoped and prayed we were, just so I could do like Polly Pepper and bake a cake in a stove that had a hole in it. I asked my mother, 'Rich or poor?' but she wouldn't answer. She was smart. I must have been nine or ten at this time; I'd already discovered the public library, and once I'd looked up at all those shelves, all of them filled, I was assured that I was no longer in danger of running out of reading material. That meant a lot to me. I was so relieved.

"I never hesitated, if I happened to finish a particularly wonderful book, to turn around and read it again, right there. I devoured them so quickly, one after another, I'm sure the librarian eyed me as quite peculiar. And you know, I think part of my love for books had to do with what they looked like. I simply adored the printed page, just loved it."

Reading remained a major interest, but before long, she had decided she wanted to become an artist. In her head, she says, it all looked very good, but when it came time to put it on canvas or paper, her powers of execution were found lacking. (Later, in college, she drew the cover for an abortive attempt at establishing a statewide literary magazine called *Hoi-Poi-Loi*.) After art, her attention switched to writing, and she wrote a nostalgic piece for the employee publication of her father's insurance company. Those were the Sundays when young Eudora and her brothers would ride along with their daddy to his office, where he opened his weekend business mail. The two sons would swing on the mahogany gate in front of the safe, but their sister headed straight for the typewriter. "Once that limp black cover was spirited away, and the roller could be persuaded to chew in a sheet of Lamar Life Insurance stationery, there were all those polished keys which, if only hit right or long enough, might write anything at all."

After two years at Mississippi State College for Women, she went north to get her diploma from the University of Wisconsin. "It must have been then, gosh, so long ago, I was right out of college, when my daddy asked me what I wanted to be, and I said, straight away, a writer. He said that was okay with him, but I'd better learn something

else, just so I could make a living. I went off to New York and Columbia Business School to study typing and other stuff. Thank
goodness I did, although I had an ulterior motive. I wasn't crazy for
the idea of a degree from Columbia; I just wanted to live in New
York for a year. Well, I had to pick a major subject and I picked
advertising, which wasn't awfully good because all at once, when the
Depression hit, nobody had any money to advertise with. For that
matter, nobody had any money to do anything with. Now that I think
back on those days, I know they must have been very bad times
indeed, but actually, I'm not sure we realized it, my friends and I. We
were all so naive, so inexperienced, right out of school. We sort of
found our own ways of having fun. We invented methods of entertainment, things that didn't cost anything. You could go on a picnic,
a dozen people, for practically nothing."

It was because of the Depression, however, that Miss Welty returned to Mississippi, and it was here that she was to stay, except for
occasional professional excursions. When *Book Week* polled the na-
tion's leading authors, critics and editors several years ago, seeking to
determine which 20 writers had written the most distinguished fiction
during the period 1945–1965, Eudora Welty was 14th on the list,
one of only three women. The concluding comment was: "As did her
fellow Mississippian, William Faulkner, Miss Welty chooses to live
close to her sources, which she mines and polishes scrupulously for
the novels and short stories that have gained her the reputation of
being our most distinguished woman writer."

At the time she went home to her native state, she recalls, radio
was the major competition of newspapers. "So, the papers didn't
publish the schedule of radio programs. It just happened that my
father, being rather progressive, had helped start the station in Jackson, and since they needed somebody to write and circulate those
radio programs, I got hired. Maybe you'd call it nepotism, but it
wasn't, not really. Besides it didn't last long, because I got other jobs,
in fact, a lot before I was finished."

Between those jobs, her spirit of adventure began to surface.
"Back in the '30s, you could go from Jackson to New York and stay
three weeks on a hundred dollars. The train (it later was called the
Pelican) would take you to Washington, where you could get that
special round trip fare to New York for three dollars and fifty cents.

When I got there, I'd stand in Penn Station and sell my ticket back to Washington. All you had to do was wave the ticket in the air and somebody would snatch it up. They were as poor as I was, and with my deal, they got a ticket cheap and I made a little profit.

"I stayed at this place called the Barbizon, a hotel for women. It was $9 a week. Very strict: no men allowed above the mezzanine. It was a grim place then. I'd hate to see it now.

"That was when I was trying to peddle a book of my short stories. I'd go in and leave the manuscript on some publisher's desk, and I'd fully expect him to have a yes or no by the next day. After all, the stories were short. But it never worked like that, and I'd have to stay on a few days longer so I could take my manuscript to another publisher.

"Since the hotel was cheap and they gave you breakfast, I think, you could really save some money. Why, the train fare was only $17.50, or thereabouts." (Officials of the Southern Railway System, researching records which indicate the company had lowered its rate to one cent a mile in 1933, report that because of special fares designed to encourage round trip travelers, Miss Welty's rate estimate is entirely within reason.)

"Back home, for a while," she says, "I had been working as a publicist for the WPA. I'd been taking pictures for them, going all over the state with a camera. They weren't special pictures, but pictures of life as it was. Nobody really knew anything about Mississippi back then. I was practically grown, myself, before I found out the Delta was north of us, not south. Anyway, I guess everybody thought I was crazy. If I saw something happening that I wanted to take a picture of, I'd just go up and tell the person to keep on doing what he was doing while I took a picture. And they always did! You couldn't do that today, you know.

"So, when I went to New York, I'd take with me my pictures. And I'd always leave them with the publisher, along with my stories. I don't know why I thought it would be a good idea to have the pictures illustrate my stories. Oh well, none of the publishers ever thought so either.

"But there was a little gallery, Lugene's, up on Madison, that liked my pictures. They showed things like that. And I had a show there."

In 1936, she sent a story, "Death of A Traveling Salesman" to a small magazine called *Manuscript*. The editors liked it and printed it. A few other such sales followed. "None of those publications paid, not really. Oh, I think maybe the *Southern Review* was giving $25 a story, but it took two years, almost, before an agent could place one of my stories in a national magazine. I think it was *Atlantic Monthly*. I was ecstatic. I didn't know what to do. And after that sale, things went just great. I never had any more trouble finding a publisher."

Her early stories were collected to form her first book, released in 1941. Since then, there have been 11 books, including novels, short story collections, a children's book and a book of her Depression photographs. Intermingled were various essays, articles, reviews and personal remembrances, scattered through numerous publications.

It is possible, even probable, that she was unaware of the growing cult of Welty lovers who, since the war years, had been waiting in the shadows silently, most of them, somewhat reservedly. They had been the unknowing founders of an unchartered fraternity, dedicated to the author, a diverse selection of strata-slicing readers, content and grateful for the occasional offerings she made, often hesitant to discuss their devotion to her, perhaps for fear that Eudora Welty was still a bit esoteric, not yet really fashionable, rather private. Eventually, the individual allegiance became a collective one. It began to spread, steadily, easily, undaunted. Like the slow but indelible movement of volcano lava, the effect of her work started to cut its swath of attention.

She was to rack up an impressive track record of recognition from foundations, writing under grants from the Rockefeller and Merrill Foundations and the National Institute of Arts and Letters. She received a Guggenheim Fellowship and held notable professorships at Smith and Bryn Mawr and served as writer-in-residence at Millsaps College. Too, there were honors and awards—four O. Henry first prizes for stories, the Brandeis Medal of Achievement, the Howells Medal for Fiction from the American Academy of Arts and Letters. Even honorary degrees from Smith, the University of Wisconsin, Western College for Women, Millsaps, Sewanee.

For an increasing number of college students, exposure to Welty was more widespread because anthologies in literature courses often included her stories. Academic coffee clatches were frequently sprinkled with Welty quotes, and The Serious Person—whoever that was—for years had known the strength of her efforts.

But the world, The World, didn't know, didn't even pretend to. It wallowed in the successfully saccharine sunshine beamed by such best-selling typists as Catherine Marshall and Frances Parkinson Keyes.

Miss Welty's first book, *A Curtain of Green* (containing some of her most beloved stories), was published in 1941. After 30 years and two editions, it had sold only 6,700 copies.

Even in her native state, everybody was proud of their first Miss America, Mary Ann Mobley. Elvis Presley they called their own. With some reluctance, they admitted to having heard of William Faulkner. But Eudora Welty? Well, I'm not really sure . . . Part of the transgression may be excusable. Until 1970, a whole generation in this country had passed puberty without a single novel having been forthcoming from the Welty pen. From 1955 until then, silence.

The publication of the 1970 novel, *Losing Battles,* forced open the eyes of an entire public, their lids having previously been sealed by literary apathy. Persons who'd never read a line of hers swore they'd known her for years. The critics, so anxious for the world to love her and settle the debt of past ineptitudes, uncrated their supply of superlatives. Hyperboles flowed with the fervor of tent meeting testimony.

Ever loyal, the swelling ranks of longtime Welty fans felt that at last, she would be exalted to the pedestal she deserved. But after the book came out, some of them confessed that they couldn't even finish it. Kinder ones, while feeling that praise of most critics had been excessive, said they found the new work pleasant. Others, more vehement, complained of the lack of judicious editing. The novel, a product of so many laborious years, had been expected to win either the Pulitzer Prize or the National Book Award, maybe both. It lost both. And now, clearing houses for publishing firms advertise the much-touted book for $1.99, soberingly below the original price asked by Random House, her new publisher.

A year later came the book of her photographs, *One Time, One Place,* and another year brought another novel, *The Optimist's Daughter.* It was the story of a clash between the daughter of a dead judge and his new, callous, self-centered wife. It was only 180 pages long; *Losing Battles* had been four times that. But *Optimist's Daughter* was tighter, clearer, a truer indication of the Welty force. It was awarded the Pulitzer last May.

In a typically gracious, soft-spoken reaction to the announcement, Miss Welty replied: "I'm just overwhelmed, dumbfounded and delighted. It is just like a dream. That sounds trite, but that's what it is. It just makes me want to work harder and faster."

There is already an expanse of evidence to prove she has always, right from the first, worked hard, if not necessarily fast. "I worry over my stories," she says, getting up from the sofa, her lengthy frame unfolding like parts of a string-pulled marionette. She goes over to straighten wayward volumes on the bookshelves. Row after row are the works of favorite writers such as Katherine Mansfield, Jane Austen, Katherine Ann Porter (who wrote the introduction to the first Welty collection), Virginia Woolfe, Reynolds Price, Peter Taylor, Faulkner, Elizabeth Bowen (who was a treasured friend of Miss Welty's).

"Sometimes I go around for a long time with a theme or point in my mind. And then, suddenly, I hear something or see something, and I know in an instant that I have a bottle for the theme I've been thinking about."

"But what I'd really like to write is a movie. From scratch. I don't think I could ever do an adaptation of my work for the screen; I'd be too involved. I'd like to try an original screenplay, because I feel there is such a close kinship between movies and short stories, rather than novels, because short stories, like movies, have only a set space or time in which to prove themselves.

"Neither could I have adapted anything of mine for the stage. They asked me to do that with *The Ponder Heart,* but I said no. I didn't know anything about stage techniques and directions and the like."

She goes into the bathroom, plucks a framed picture from the wall, and brings it out. It is signed by David Wayne and other members of the stage version of her novel, *The Ponder Heart,* which enjoyed a modest Broadway run in 1956.

"Just look at the expression on David's face. He was so good. Fortunately, I didn't see the play until opening night. Maybe I had been too accustomed to the idea of Edna Earle (the novel's narrator) being a big part. Maybe that's why I was taken aback when I first saw it on stage. Then, too, they had done all kinds of things, like pick out quotes from other stories and stick them in the play. Edna Earle was reduced to the background, sort of whimpering on the porch as Uncle Daniel goes through his antics. As I had written it, the whole story was seen through the eyes of Edna Earle. On stage, they had done something else. There were times I thought I was in the wrong theater, that perhaps my book was being done as a play in another theater down the street.

"But the actors and other folks were so warm, so kind. They had all bought copies of the book, just so they could get the feeling of the characters.

"I went back to see it three or four times. And after a while, I began to understand that they couldn't possibly have gotten the book into a play without changing it. The stage is a totally different concept. When you write, you can get the feeling you want by telling the reader things. On stage, it's dialogue and action, action and dialogue.

"With stories, I think of readers and how they interpret the words. Punctuation for me is very important, even more important than names. It accounts for the rhythm of a story. A comma left out can mean an entirely different feeling, and one put in can mean disaster, if it doesn't belong there.

"I don't think I've ever counted rewrites, but I do a great deal of polishing. After that, I polish some more, so that by the time I put them in the mail, I'm sure my stories are as good as I can make them.

"Years later, of course, I may or may not still like them. I still like particularly some of the stories from *The Golden Apples* (the collection published in 1949), I like 'Wedding Day' ["June Recital"], which was originally called 'Golden Apples.' And although it's not from that book, of course I like 'Why I Live at the P.O.' (perhaps her most famous story).

"Occasionally, when I read stories in front of an audience, like in a lecture, which I've practically discontinued, I may see changes I'd lke to make if I could do it over. 'Petrified Man' for instance. I think now I would cut it some, especially the part about the Siamese twins pickled in a jar. That goes on too long. That story is sort of vulgar, and I meant it to be. Certainly, it doesn't always lend itself to being read aloud. Particularly by me, in front of an audience."

As could be expected, most of Miss Welty's stories, many of them in first person, are told from the feminine viewpoint. But not all. "Right after Medgar Evers got shot, I had this idea about a story told from the viewpoint of the murderer. Of course, it was a man, and I really cannot envision my telling something from the male viewpoint. But somehow, this was more than a man; he was a murderer. Now, does that make me more of a murderer than a man?" She chuckles at her own mocking logic. "So, I wrote the story. And then they caught the man who did it. *The New Yorker* called and we spent hours on the telephone, changing places and times and makes of cars and all sorts of details, just to avoid a possible libel suit. I was wrong, it turned out, about the psychology of the person who did it. But the principle was correct."

Even that story, with its intense theme, could not be construed as a "message" story or one with underlying chants for a cause. The author has always been adamant in ejecting the role of crusader, despite the commercial success of other writers who capitalized on the game. First off, she thinks it important that people not confuse the purposes of a novelist with those of a crusader. "Fiction is one thing; journalism's another. The distinguishing factor is that in the novel, there is the possibility that both writer and reader may share an act of imagination.

"But just because an author chooses not to crusade doesn't mean he has no conscience, not by any means. All my life I've been opposed to such things as racism and injustice and cruelty. Back when the civil rights movement was heating up, I used to get midnight phone calls from strangers, demanding to know why I was sitting down here, allowing such awful things to go on and why I didn't make amends for my shortcomings by writing something that would teach those devils a lesson.

"It bothered me, sure. But that's not the kind of writer I am. Whatever wrongs there are, I want my stories to show them as they are, to let them speak for themselves. I don't want to preach, I'll leave that to the editorial writers and essayists. In my wildest dreams I could never come up with something that would do what those telephone callers wanted. And even if I could, if I tried to write it, it would be contrived. Not only that, it would be artificial. And what's more, and I guess this is more important, it would be dishonest."

The angry calls have stopped, her telephone number has become unlisted, but the postman seldom fails to deliver a batch of mail that gets to be somewhat unnerving, often from readers who want her answers of wisdom to their questions of stupidity.

"My God, I don't know what they're trying to say, very often, or what they're trying to say I said. Some time ago, I got a long letter from some graduate student who had 'perceived' this parallel between my work and, of all things, Dante's *Inferno.* Or was it Milton's *Paradise Lost?* Oh, something. I never answered the letter. No need to. Whatever would I say?

"And soon afterwards, there was a letter from somebody else who was certain there was a connection between Beatrix Potter's Peter Rabbit and something of mine. I loved it, I thought that quite wonderful, to be put in that class. But it was hardly valid. I wish I could have been clever enough to come up with something like Peter Rabbit, but I had to disappoint the girl who wrote; I had to beg out.

"All this symbolism they find! All the things they say you're really saying! They get so clinical about it. Others, I couldn't know, but for me, writing doesn't work like that, not at all. You don't just read some definition of anger or love or hate, and say, 'Here, I'm going to write about this character who symbolized a particular emotion, or who personifies something else.' You can't make up how people feel! If you don't know what it feels like, you can't really describe it."

And for sure, there's always somebody who writes to comment, or is seeking a comment, on the death of the novel. "If it's not the novel, it's the short story. And I wonder if it's all that bad. Oh, it's not a secret that young, unestablished writers certainly have practically no market for their stories anymore. And it's sad. Back in the '20s and '30s, there was an abundance of small magazines for that. Like I said, they didn't pay anything, but it was publication. Now it's to the point where even the big magazines run so little fiction. I guess television has had something to do with it, people not reading as much, I mean. But somehow, I just can't believe that the novel or the short story will die, or has died, as some say. People will always read. Am I naive to think that way?"

Hopefully not, Miss Welty.

Not as long, Miss Welty, as there's still left a writer whose sentences reflect the compassion our emotions need to know exists in the privacy of silence, whose chosen themes are as timeless as agriculture and sin, whose dedication to the integrity of creativity must often seem lonely in an age when modes and matters are ruled by mediocrity.

Not as long, Miss Welty, as there's still left a writer who, at a summer day's twilight, can stand in her rose garden, holding a wilted blossom, and offer such a simple but profound insight as:

I shall always keep my belief that good literature is always about one subject—mankind. We in the South may portray the South, Northern writers may portray the North; indeed, Chinese writers may portray China. But if their works are good, they are really about mankind, everybody everywhere.

"Time will not diminish such works. Things like love and hate, justice and injustice, good and bad, truth and lies, they endure, they are still the same, no matter the skin they wear, no matter the year they were written about."

A Visit with Eudora Welty

Bill Ferris / Summer 1975 and 1976

From *Images of the South: Visits with Eudora Welty and Walker Evans,* Southern Folklore Reports, No. 1 (Memphis, TN: Center for Southern Folklore, 1977), 11–26. © 1977 by Center for Southern Folklore. Reprinted by permission.

In 1929, my grandparents moved to Jackson and bought a home on Laurel Street. Three blocks away, the Welty family lived with their children, Walter, Edward, and Eudora. My grandmother often spoke to me of the Weltys who were among her closest friends in Jackson.

After Grammie and Granddad moved to the farm where I grew up, Eudora and her friends sometimes visited our home to picnic and sketch the landscape. I remember them seated one spring day on a hillside below our home. I was twelve years old, and when they left, my mother told me one of the group was an important writer.

I first read Eudora's work in high school, and in my senior year at Davidson College in North Carolina, I invited her to be our Book-of-the-Year Speaker. She accepted and arrived by train late one night at the Charlotte depot. The next morning she read "A Worn Path" before the student assembly in her soft voice, and during the afternoon we walked around the campus where wisteria vines were in full bloom.

Four years later I was reading folklore materials at the Mississippi State Archives when Charlotte Capers, the director, showed me unpublished photographs which Eudora had taken for the Works Progress Administration. Her photographs explored the faces and landscape of Mississippi with an honesty which became a standard for my research as a folklorist.

During the summer of 1975 and again in 1976, I visited Eudora at her home on Pinehurst Street, and we spoke about those photographs and her writing.

BF: I want to start with your work in *One Time, One Place* and how you happened to travel around Mississippi and take those beautiful photographs.

EW: It was part of a job I had which was with the WPA—the Works Progress Administration. I was in the state office, called Junior Publicity Agent. And that meant I had to travel around the state looking at and talking to the people on the various projects. That was every sort of project—farm-to-market roads, juvenile court judges, air fields being made out of old pastures, library work and Braille—all sorts of things that were going on, even setting up booths at county fairs.

And so I would go on the bus to Meridian or Forest or somewhere like that. Then I also remember I went to Tupelo soon after the devastating tornado that was there, because I think the WPA was helping them furnish men to help build it back. And scrambling over the ruins up there.

So that took me to practically every county in Mississippi. And it was an eye-opener for me because I'd never been in those places before, and it just hit me with a great impact, to see everything firsthand like that.

BF: Was it a discovery?

EW: In my case it was. I was so ignorant to begin with about my native state. I was in my early twenties. I had gone to MSCW [Mississippi State College for Women] for two years, and that should have taught me, because I met girls from all over the state.

But I didn't really get an idea of the diversity and all the different regions of the state, or of the great poverty of the state, until I traveled and until I had talked to people. I don't mean schoolgirls like myself that were at college with me, but *people,* you know, in the street. And the great kindness of everybody. They were all so glad to see someone in those days, you know—somebody from away coming through. They were glad to see them; hospitality everywhere. Nobody was suspicious. And I would have been amazed if they had been because I wouldn't have expected it. It was just innocence on both sides. That was lucky.

And so I began taking the pictures, not in connection with my job, but for my own gratification on the side. Oh, some were used, but I was not the photographer of the WPA. I was a journalist, and I was doing a newspaper job, really—interviewing. So, everybody I had to see generally lived in the courthouse towns like Canton in Madison County, and Yazoo City—you know, county seats.

BF: What were the courthouse towns like?

EW: Usually, there is just one good-sized little town—there was then—in each county. That's where everything converged on Saturday. That's where the stores were, and the hub of life. If you went on Saturday, you saw everything going on.

We usually stayed in a hotel. I can remember the electric fan I would have to turn on me all night in some little hot town, the telephone out in the hall or down in the lobby, which didn't matter a bit.

You didn't have to plan ahead; that was one thing. You could just hit town and everything opened up for you. You could always get a room. That was before people stayed in tourist courts or motels, except for nefarious reasons. So, you'd stay in hotels.

I began with no end in view, I just took the pictures because I wanted to. Just impulse. I was not trained and had no good camera. But for that reason, I think, they may constitute a record. I think that's the only value they could have now. I had no position I was trying to justify, nothing I wanted to illustrate. They were pictures because I would see something I thought was self-explanatory of the life I saw.

BF: I wanted to ask, in those travels, did any of your fiction grow out of the people and places?

EW: Well, I think it's bound to have, indirectly. Never in my work have I used actual happenings transposed from real life into fiction, except perhaps once, because fiction amalgamates with all kinds of other things. When it comes out as fiction, it's been through a whole mill of interior life, you know. But I think that nothing could have been written in the way of a story without such a background, without the knowledge and the experience that I got from these things. Of course it did. It provided the raw material. And more than that, it suggested things in a valid way that could never have been made up without this reality. It was the reality that I used as a background and could draw on in various ways, even though indirectly.

BF: When you traveled and were doing your photographs around Mississippi, did your parents appreciate that? And did they share that interest?

EW: Well, my father had died by that time. But my mother was very interested. She wanted me to be a writer. I mean, she knew my wish to be one. But I had to have a job. This was the Depression. I was lucky to have a job. I could have done it better, probably, in better-off times—if, for instance, I could have had a car instead of having to go by bus or train and catching rides and so on. But I couldn't take the family car away for a week at a time. And a lot of the pictures that were taken when I was in my car were close to Jackson for that reason. I would just go out to Raymond or Utica or Port Gibson, or somewhere that I could drive to and come back in a day. And the farthest places I went to, I was not my own commander of where I went. You can't stop a Greyhound bus to take a picture. And so some of the things I could have done better. That doesn't matter.

My family always thought learning was a good thing. I was brought up in a good household, because we always had books, and we always believed in learning, and that nothing would be wasted that was spent finding out things and learning about them. That was a marvelous background. Both my parents had that feeling. And we were brought up with the encyclopedia in the dining room, you know, always jumping up from the table to settle an argument, you know, and look up things in the unabridged dictionary and haul out the atlas.

BF: Do you remember any of the experiences when you were traveling and taking photographs? Were there people that stood out? Or places?

EW: One thing I remember, because it did have an effect later in a story. One of the things was we had to put up booths at county fairs, as I was saying just a minute ago. I loved that because I've always loved fairs and being on the midway and hearing things. And I heard about an act that was almost like "Keela, the Outcast Indian Maiden." I didn't see such a thing, thank God. And that was not my story, although it was the background of the story. My story was the three different reactions of people that have come in contact with such a hideous human event. But I heard that, and sometime later on I made it into a story because it bothered me for so long—how people could put up with such a thing and how they would react to it. That's one thing I remember, because I did some work that came out of it.

But mostly I remember things visually. I remember how people looked, just people standing against the sky sometimes, at the end of a day's work. Something like that is indelible to me. But most of the conversation I had was, of course, in the way of business, like interviewing people and writing them up. They were telling me about the project but not about their lives, except indirectly.

BF: When did you first begin to write, Eudora?

EW: I did stories in school, but they weren't any good. There weren't any courses given in so-called creative writing when I was in college, which is probably just as well. I think you have to learn for yourself. Oh, you could be helped, certainly. I could have been spared a lot of mistakes, but I think you have to learn from your own mistakes too. I believe 1936 was when I sent my first story out, and it was published that year. And I was working on the WPA right up until it was disbanded. Our office was disbanded with the reelection of Roosevelt—our state publicity office. We were through on the day he won. We didn't know that was going to be the end, but it was. So I was working then, and the same year I had a story. I don't have a very good memory by years, but that coincided so I must have been working at the same time, at night—but secretly. I always had jobs and was doing journalism at this time. I was in print, but nothing to do with fiction.

BF: You once said you felt it was not a good thing to try to do both.

EW: Not for me. It may be for other people. I mean, everyone has to find out. I'd rather do something unconnected with words to earn my living—just because I like to keep my tool for one thing. But that doesn't mean it would trouble the next person, or the next. You just have to go by your own wishes.

BF: You've talked about a sense of place in fiction, and I wonder if you feel Mississippi is a special place?

EW: Oh, absolutely. Since it's the only one I really know, it's the whole foundation on which my fiction rests. It's a test. It's a way to test the validity of what you think and see, and it also sets a stage. It helps to identify characters . . . helps you to make up characters. Because your characters grow out of place, and that's the way you test them as to their validity and their propriety in your work. I haven't read the essay I wrote about place in fiction in an awful long time. I can say anything much better on paper than I can in conversation. But I thought over that quite a lot and tried to express my feelings about it . . . which I still believe.

BF: Do you think a place shapes the people in it—that geography and climate shape characters?

EW: I don't see how it can help it, do you? Something shapes people, and it's the world in which they act that makes their experiences—what they act for and react against. And, with its population, a place produces the whole world in which a person lives his life. It furnishes the economic background that he grows up in, and the folkways and the stories that come down to him in his family. It's the fountainhead of his knowledge and experience. I think, of course, we learn to grow further than that; but if we don't have that base I don't know what we can test further knowledge by. It teaches you to think, really.

BF: Getting back to Mississippi, in an interview on the local television here, you talked about the sense of continuity in a community where you know the grandparents and the parents and the children in a family. And you can understand the people better when you know them in the context of their families.

EW: Exactly. That's probably changed some now, as you know. We move around a lot more than we used to, and that continuity has been broken in lots of places. But I still think the sense of it remains in all of us. We know that there is such a thing, because we have family memories and family things even if we ourselves move around more. I do think that the sense of a person's full life and what happens to him in the course of it, and then how that influences his children's lives, and how that influences on and on and on . . . which is part of a place and part of time—the two things working together. And just the knowledge that another person has all this behind him which can help to explain him and give a background to his opinions and his feelings—it's such an easy way to understand, to begin to understand other people. You miss that in our urban life where you meet somebody cold, have no idea of his background. Everything has to start from scratch and for that reason can remain more superficial unless you really work at it. With your best friends you overcome everything, no matter where. But just the ordinary acquaintanceship of life is so much easier in a place with continuity. I think not only Southerners but New Englanders and many other people feel the same way.

BF: There seem to be so many writers who, like yourself, have grown out of Mississippi.

EW: I haven't any explanation of that. Of course, all Mississippi writers are asked this, and some people have come up with theories. But I don't know. I think one of the great mysteries of life is how, in some centuries, some section of the country will just produce every-thing—like New England at one time, the Middle West at one time, then the South. Who knows why these things happen? I don't know, but I'm glad they do.

BF: If you put your work together, Eudora, it's sort of a portrait of the state in a way—Natchez and the Delta and Jackson and small towns. Do you ever think of your work as sort of a map of Missis-sippi?

EW: I think of it more as an internal map. I mean it's a map of minds and imagination. Of course, it has to be laid somewhere. But what guides you is what is inside of the characters, to show what they're doing.

No, I know what you mean. I mean Faulkner's marvelous work, which really is just a triumph of the first order, and what he did in that respect. But I have no such abilities or ambition. I locate a story, but that's all.

BF: In much of your work I have a feeling that I really am hearing the voice of the people, hearing words as they are spoken. "Why I live at the P.O.," I guess, is the most famous. But you use the voice of the characters very often, and I wonder if you feel voice—the spoken word—is important for a writer?

EW: I think the ability to use dialogue, or the first person, or any-thing like that, is just as essential as the knowledge of place and other components of a story. But I think it has a special importance, be-cause you can use it in fiction to do very subtle things and very many things at once—like giving a notion of the speaker's background, furthering the plot, giving the sense of the give-and-take between characters. Dialogue gives a character's age, background, upbringing, everything, without the author's having to explain it on the side. He's doing it out of his own mouth. And also, other things—like a character may be telling a lie which he will show to the reader, but perhaps not to the person to whom he's talking, and perhaps not even realize himself. Sometimes he's deluded. All these things can come out in dialogue. And you get that, of course, by your ear, by listening to the rhythms and habits and so on of everyday speech everywhere.

I listen all the time. I love it. I don't do it because I have to, but because I like to.

I do not think you can transfer anything, as it's spoken, onto the page and have it come out at all convincingly. As you know from much of your work with the tape recorder, what comes out as a sound is not really at all what the speaker thinks he said, or really what he did say in context. It has to be absolutely rewritten on the page from the way it happens, but if you didn't know how it happened you couldn't start. It's a matter of condensation and getting the . . . oh, I don't want to say "universal" about the character, but getting his whole character into a speech about a little thing, perhaps. It's a shorthand. It's like action. It *is* a form of action in a story. And people don't talk that way. You've got to make it *seem* that they talk that way. I'm sure that you, of all people, will agree, because you've had so much experience with interviews.

BF: In a way, you're giving what seems to be reality, but it's really an artistic illusion.

EW: But you have to know that, just the way you have to know other things in a story to make them seem believable. And yet, they are not duplicates of life but a rendition of it—more an impression, I guess.

BF: Could you tell me the background of "Why I Live at the P.O.?"

EW: It doesn't have any, I guess, except I once did see a little post office with an ironing board in the back through the window. This was in some little town—less than a town—some little hamlet in Mississippi. And I suppose that's what made me think of it. Suppose somebody just decided to move down there.

But mainly, it was an exercise in using the spoken word to tell a story. And I more or less made it up as I went along. It was quite an early story. It would have been improved by more thought, better construction.

BF: For me as a folklorist what's interesting and especially important is that you, as an artist, often choose the spoken word as your primary literary vehicle rather than a more abstract literary frame.

EW: Well, it's interesting to me. I could go on to say that while you don't use exact things people say in a situation, you can often use an exact thing someone has said—adapt it to your situation where it's the perfect way to say it. And you do that by a fund in your head, having heard people talk and noted in your mind all your life the way people say things. And it will come back to you at the right time. Whereas you are using real life, it's not taking it out of one box and putting it in another, you know. It's a transformation, a magician act—if it's good, I'm talking about.

BF: One thing that strikes me about your work is how attention is drawn to the detail that seems insignificant, but is very important to the character and to the artist.

EW: Yes, I want everything to be right. It makes me feel better when I work to think these things are right, and then I know very well that so much of the belief of a reader depends on not having things wrong.

An editor a long time ago told me, "Don't ever have the moon in the wrong part of the sky." And that's important. And I notice when I read other people's works, often a man will have something blooming at the wrong time, because he never has been out in the garden. He doesn't think it matters; he just names some flowers.

Well, that destroys something for me when I read it, and I try not to make these mistakes. You can't always know that you've made a mistake. But I do believe in accent. And not only that, but I just am a natural observer, and to me the detail tells everything. One detail can tell more than any descriptive passage in general, you know. And that's the way my eye sees, and so I just use it.

It goes back to place again. You've got to have everything truthful. And by having the world truthful—the setting—that helps to make your story more easily believed.

BF: My grandmother, who is 90, reads every book that you write. She's a great garden person, and she loves to read your work because you describe flowers so carefully. She thinks you have almost every flower in Mississippi in each book.

EW: I hope it's correct, because that would be the kind of thing that would shame me if I made mistakes in that way. And she would know if I slipped on that. That really does please and honor me that she thinks that.

When I first began to write, I hadn't worked in the garden the way I came to do later, and I may have made plenty of mistakes in those first stories which I don't know. I once got a letter from a stranger after I published a story called "The Wide Net," I think. Anyway, it was in that first book, and he wrote and said, "Dear Madam, I enjoyed your stories, but bluejays do not sit on railroad tracks." And sure enough, they don't. But you know, I didn't think anything of it. I didn't know anything about birds. Probably bluejay was the only name I knew at the time. But that's the kind of thing that you don't want to get wrong. And that was somebody that that offended, and rightly.

BF: I'm working on this book on Ray Lum, a mule trader. He has an extraordinary eye for detail, in some ways similar to an artist's. In his stories he may describe a dog on the road. And he can tell if that dog's been a long way off and is headed home by the way it walks. That's the kind of detail I see coming through in the works of both folk and literary artists . . . both coming out of a sense of place.

EW: Absolutely. That's strange that you used that example, because one of the things that I've overheard and have used in stories is exactly that, that "he looked like he was going home." I think I used it in *Losing Battles*. You know: "Which way. . . ? Did he look like he was going home?" "Yeah." They really knew.

I've heard people say, "He looked like he was going down the road to turn around and come back." It was knowing this person and how they drove. These were people, not animals; but also it was animals, too. So if Mr. Lum really knows, it means that they really do know.

BF: Mr. Lum admires Indians who had what he calls "an instinct" about nature. He used the phrase, "When you've slept on the ground covered with stars, you know a lot more than most folks do about life."

EW: Oh, I don't know. Since I'm not an outdoor person except by love of it, mine has come the hard way, I guess, by just observation and wish to know, and so on. To have slept on the ground covered with stars the way Mr. Lum means—that's growing up in intimacy with the earth. I wish I had. Both my parents did, because they both

came from farms in a different part of the world—Ohio and West
Virginia. And they knew; they knew everything. A lot of what I know
probably comes from my father, who could predict the weather. He
had all these signs, you know. "It's all right to play golf, because if
the birds begin to sing it means the rain will be over in a certain
number of minutes." I just heard things like that all my life; and he
knew that from a boyhood on the farm.

It used to upset him, being from Ohio, to see how farmers in Mississippi never planted their corners. They'd let everything straggle
out. They didn't have everything neat and in rows. It was done so
slap-dash. He would say, "That's a sorry way to plant a field."

But my mother was like your grandmother—a great gardener, and
really a horticulturist by inclination and study. She taught herself.
And so, I grew up in a house that liked things growing.

BF: There was a story you told me of your mother, Eudora, planting the oak tree in the yard, and how it grew, and how she explained
to you that it was a small oak tree. . . .

EW: This big one—out here in the yard. Yes, she refused to cut it
down, although we had seven giant pines standing around it. Now
the pines are gone, and the oak tree is majestic. And she said,
"Never cut an oak tree." And that's the fact.

BF: In a place like Mississippi, people have such intimate knowledge about each other. In some ways it's shocking that they know so
much about their parents and grandparents and all the details. Like
the Irish, they say, we have a long memory, and that memory seems
to be reflected in a lot of your work.

EW: Well, we probably have some of the same background of
those Irish and the Scots and the other people that have long
memories in this part of the world. It has been said by people that
know more about it than me that one of the reasons Southerners
have this to talk about is that they don't have much else to talk
about. It's their source of entertainment besides their source of
knowledge. The family tales while away a long winter evening, and
that's what they have to draw on. I think you feel that in Faulkner a
lot, you know, especially in the little hamlets where people sit on the
store porch and talk in the evenings. All they have to talk about is
each other, and what they've seen during the day, and what hap-

pened to so and so. It also encourages our sense of exaggeration and the comic, I think, because tales get taller as they go along. But I think beneath all of that is a sense, really, of caring about one another. It is a pleasure and an entertainment, but it's also something of deep significance to people. Don't you agree? In a way, I think Southerners care about each other, about human beings, in a more accessible way than some other peoples. We can reach our feelings more easily.

BF: Do you find that Southerners are more talkers than others are—that they love storytelling especially?

EW: Well, I know they used to be. I don't know whether they are now, or not. I guess we're getting more and more like people any-where else. I don't mean we ourselves, but the people who have come along. I think we have a native love of the tale. I remember once Robert Penn Warren was at my house, and there were a lot of us sitting around talking. And he laughed so hard, and he stayed so late. And when he left he said, "I had a perfectly wonderful time— not a serious word was spoken all evening." *(Laughs)* I thought he had something there. Oh, we had told so many tales! He had Ken-tucky ones, and I had some from West Virginia and Mississippi. I think Charlotte [Charlotte Capers, former director of the Mississippi Department of Archives and History] was here, and she had some Tennessee ones.

BF: Let me ask you a more general question about the artist. Do you feel the artist has a political role to play in a society?

EW: I don't believe that a work of art in itself has any cause to be political unless it would have been otherwise. I think there are places for political outspokenness, but in my mind, it should be done edito-rially, and in essays and things that are exactly what they seem. But I think a work of art, a poem or a story, is properly something that reflects what life is exactly at that time. That is, to try to reveal it. Not to be a mirror image, but to be something that goes beneath the surface of the outside and tries to reveal the way it really is, good and bad. Which in itself is moral. I think a work of art must be moral. The artist must have a moral consciousness about his vision of life and what he tries to write. But to write propaganda I think is a weakening thing to art.

I remember I got lots of phone calls in the bad 60's when we were having all the troubles here. People saying—especially from Boston somehow, which is rather laughable at the moment—saying, "What do you mean sitting down there and not writing stories about your racial injustice?" Well, I think I've always written stories about that. Not as propaganda, but I've written stories about human injustice as much as I've ever written about anything. It was not anything new to me that people were being unjust to one another then, because I had written about that in all of my work, along with other things people have been. I was looking at it in the human, not the political, vision, and I was sticking to that. I didn't want to be swerved into preaching disguised as a work of fiction. I did not think that was required of me, or necessary. I was glad to say what I thought about anything straightforwardly, but not to write a story as an illustration of some-thing *per se*. And I still feel that way. All great, great works have been moral documents in their way, too. And it's nothing new. You know that's the part that seems so strange: that people would say, "Have you ever thought before about such things?" They didn't mean it that way, but that's the way it sounded, coming in the dead of night.

BF: Do you think there's a sense of community among the south-ern writers? You spoke of Robert Penn Warren and others?

EW: In my case, no. I'm very fond of the ones I knew, but I didn't meet them till much later on. I'd been writing for 23 years, I guess, before I met "Red" Warren who was one of my first publishers. He was editor of the *Southern Review,* and had written me letters and accepted my work and encouraged me. But it just hadn't worked out that I met him until he came to lecture across the street at Belhaven College, and I was delighted. Of course, I met Katherine Anne Porter earlier. She invited me down to Baton Rouge, but "Red" had been away. I met her and Cleanth Brooks at that time. But you know the South is a big place. As Reynolds Price points out, it's as big as France. *(Laughs)* And we don't just live in each other's parlors, you know. I'm fond of them, and eventually I got to meet a good many of them just as it turned out. But I came along a little late for the Allen Tate-Cleanth Brooks-Robert Penn Warren group, and the Fugi-tives. They had already formed and dispersed before I came along. They *were* a community, you know. I love to see writers when they coincide with my friends, but not just *as* writers. You work by yourself. And I'm grateful to a great number of them, and love many of them as friends now.

BF: What about the Southern black writers? Like Richard Wright and Margaret Walker and others?

EW: I know Margaret Walker and Alice Walker. There are two Walkers here, and Margaret is the only one I really know—the one out at Jackson State. I like her very much. They've nearly all been here in my house. I know Ralph Ellison. I've known him over the years, since the 40's in New York, and like him very much. He's a fine, delightful man and a good writer.

BF: There's a young, black writer, Ernest Gaines, who did *The Autobiography of Miss Jane Pittman,* and who came to Yale and spoke to my students. He told me that over his desk he has a portrait of Faulkner. And he's written a lot of short stories, and I asked him what he admired, and he mentioned your short story "A Worn Path."

EW: Is that so? Well, that really pleases me. I'm surprised, because I didn't know. Well, he's done very well and got much appreciation, hasn't he?

BF: It's interesting to me in his work *Miss Jane Pittman,* and in some of the other more or less folklore-type works of fiction that have been done recently, there is what I would call a dramatic monologue approach. It's fiction, but it reads as though it were being recorded and transcribed.

EW: And that's very hard to do, too. Because you're doing much more than that. It takes art to make something read as though it were spoken—of a very high kind, I think.

BF: Once when we were talking about "A Worn Path," you mentioned having seen a woman at a distance and, not knowing anything about her, the vision for that short story came.

EW: That was out on the Old Canton Road at the time the Old Canton Road was in the country. I was with a painter friend who was doing a landscape, and I just came along for company. I was reading under a tree, and just looking up saw this small, distant figure come out of the woods and move across the whole breadth of my vision and disappear into the woods on the other side. And it's just like your friend, Mr. Lum, said—I knew she was going somewhere. I knew that she was bent on an errand, even at that distance. It was not anything casual. It was a purposeful, measured journey that she was making. And what I felt was—of course, that was my imagination I suppose, since I never knew—was that you wouldn't go on an errand like that, so purposefully, unless it were for someone else, you know. Unless it were like an emergency. And so I made it into a story by making it the one you'd be most likely to go for—a child. And so I wrote that. But another time, on this same road and in similar circumstances, an old woman came down the road—I don't know whether she was the same one or not. But she stopped and talked to us, and she used the words to me, "I was too old at the Surrender." Which was about something else—maybe it was learning to read and write. I don't know. But that was indelible in my mind: ". . . too old at the Surrender." And so I put that into my story because it belonged in it. It was a case of joining two things that I had thought of, and making them into one. And that's a very simplified way to state it, but it's a good example because it's explicit.

BF: Your description of that lady crossing the field was presented as fiction. But that is the sort of validity you also captured in the photographs that you did, and hopefully it's captured in the films and in other work that folklorists are doing. To document something is not enough. It's not a living thing unless we can draw some sort of relationship beyond that, to the people, to make the document more of a work of art.

EW: Well, folklore and fiction are different branches of the same thing. And I think I agree with you that there are many connecting lines between them, which you have made a life of studying and finding out. But you know all those ends, and I just know my end.

BF: But to me it's important and really exciting that you as an artist worked in several forms of media . . . as a photographer and then as a writer, and more recently you've been working with films.

EW: Well, I haven't really worked in film. I've just been a subject. I haven't done anything on my own in film, although I would like it. I think film is a marvelous thing. I have been interested in it in the past, and once tried to write a scenario, but I didn't think it was worth even showing anybody. I didn't know enough. I see a relationship between film and short stories. I don't know if you do.

BF: What sort of relationship?

EW: In technique. I'm thinking about film, not in the documentary sense now, but in a film play with, for instance, the use of flashbacks and memory, of a dream sequence—things you couldn't show on a stage, that you can show in a fluid form of a film which can move back and forward, and back and forth in time, and can speed up life, can slow it down, just the way you do in a short story. It can elide, and it can compound, and it can exaggerate. It can do all the things you do as a short story writer to bring out what you are trying to do. And I think as a short story writer I feel that I must have absorbed things. I've been a constant moviegoer all my life. I must have absorbed some of the lessons which have come in handy. I don't mean anything I can put my finger on. I never think of it. But it's just like, in the way of folklore, these things come into your mind, and you learn from them without really knowing.

BF: What sort of films do you like?

EW: I haven't seen any recently, I may say, that make me want to be an avid moviegoer—except *The Return of the Pink Panther,* which I think is marvelous. Do you remember the French film *Breathless?* I think it's a beautiful film. I saw it two or three times. I felt very strongly when watching that, how those techniques are like a short story writer's—not novels, short story. And for that reason, I think most films that are made from fiction do better to work from the short story than to try to condense the great ramifications of a novel into a film. It's better to expand them from a short story.

BF: I've been amazed at how much my father remembers from the films, and how importhant they were when he was a young man.

EW: Absolutely. We never missed one. And part of my life in New York was spent running out to the Thalia and all those places, every little foreign film place in New York, seeing all those films. And of course Hitchcock. I mean, I like detective stories, and I don't think in general they make good films. They can't do it. But Hitchcock had something you could learn. He's a trickster and a magician, but so are writers, in technique. For instance, his transitions, which are old-hat now, but at the time he began them were something new: showing, for instance, a person screaming, and all of a sudden that scream turns into a train whistle which is the next scene of a train going along. A short story writer uses transitions like that in a less obvious

way, more in some symbol or some detail of observation which becomes a figure in the next section. You use something that will
transport you from one scene to another, even if you don't know it,
even if you don't realize it. That's like a film. Or else Hitchcock was
using short story techniques. I don't know who thought of it first. It's
been there forever.

I think the lyric film teaches you more than the adventure film or
anything like that. The mood films show you what is focused upon
and how atmosphere is used. The French always do it better than
anyone. They've got so many people who were trained in a world of
art—like Jean Renoir. How could he have escaped a great knowledge of the making of a film from the painter's household he grew up
in?

BF: How would you describe Jackson as a place, when you were
growing up? What sort of community was it?

EW: Oh, when I was growing up, it had much more of an identity
than now because it was smaller. And it was so small that one knew
everybody practically. Also, it was a very free and easy life. Children
could go out by themselves in the afternoon and play in the park, go
to the picture show, and move about the city on their bicycles and
everything, just as if it were their own front yard. There was no sense
of danger or things happening in town. No one had to really take
care, so we felt. That was a nice way to grow up.

The town was easier to know, easier to get a sense of place. All of
which is gone now, of course, because Jackson is a city.

BF: You grew up in an artistic community, as I recall. Weren't
there writers and artists that were friends in Jackson here?

EW: I knew lots of painters, but Hubert Creekmore, up the street,
was the only writer I knew. There weren't too many people writing
around here. But Hubert started before I did, and was a good friend
and a very talented and wonderful person, and that was a big help.

I knew a lot of people interested in writing, which was good. I
never did show anybody my early work. I was too shy to show it to a
human living being. When I asked Hubert to whom I could send
these he gave me some addresses, and that worked. Once they were
in print I wouldn't mind showing it to someone.

I feel I'm just about talked out.

BF: I appreciate your taking time to help me understand.

EW: I think I've been a lucky person all my life. I seem to have always had around me congenial, helpful, sensitive people. And I was lucky in my agent and my publishers. Everything worked out beautifully, and I'm grateful.

An Interview with Eudora Welty

Jean Todd Freeman / 29 July 1977

Eudora Welty was interviewed by Jean Todd Freeman on the morning of 29 July 1977 at the Welty family home, which parallels the Belhaven College campus in Jackson, Mississippi. Miss Welty had just returned home from several hectic months of traveling and said she was "burning" to get back to work on a piece of fiction. She sat on a small, pale yellow sofa next to a table on which several books rested, including the latest publications of Reynolds Price and Katherine Anne Porter.

Conversations: I read your collection of stories, *A Curtain of Green,* shortly after it came out; then I read *The Wide Net;* and, unfortunately, I missed *The Robber Bridegroom* somewhere along in there—

Welty: Everybody did; I swear everybody did.

Conversations: Although your latest two books have been novels rather than short story collections, I think of you primarily as a short story writer.

Welty: Thank you, so do I. I certainly do. My novels have happened by accident. Every single one.

Conversations: Katherine Anne Porter in her introduction to *A Curtain of Green* has suggested that you might get pressure from publishers to write novels.

Welty: Oh no, there never was that. That's because, I think, Diarmuid Russell stood between them and me.

Conversations: Diarmuid Russell was a wonderful agent, wasn't he?

Welty: He was wonderful and, of course, if it hadn't been for him, I wouldn't have ever been published anywhere. That's true.

Conversations: How did that come about?

Welty: Well, I was his first client, I think. I believe I was. He wrote me when he first opened the agency, just as he wrote to lots of young writers whose works he'd read that he liked and whom he thought might not have an agent. And I had had some stories in the little magazines and the quarterlies. He wrote and asked if I would like him to be my agent. I'd never heard of a literary agent, but I liked his letter so much that I wrote back by return mail and said, "Yes! be my agent." Well, his first letter showed me what he was like. And also his second because when I wrote and said, "Yes, be my agent," he wrote back and said, "Now don't be too quick. You don't know anything about me; I may be a crook for all you know." He spent about a full year or maybe two full years trying to get my stories in national circulation magazines and finally made it with the *Atlantic.*

Conversations: The *Atlantic,* then, was the first major magazine that published your stories?

Welty: Yes, through his work.

Conversations: Which story was that?

Welty: That was—they published two. One was "Why I live at the P.O."; and one was "A Worn Path." As soon as that happened why then the way was clear for other magazines to be interested. And that made the first book possible, which would otherwise never have happened, you know, never.

Conversations: You had been published before in literary magazines?

Welty: Yes, I'd been sending these stories around about six years. I'd had good luck being published in the *Southern Review* and little magazines—*Accent, Prairie Schooner.*

Conversations: I think your first story was published in a magazine called *Manuscript.*

Welty: Right. The man who did it, John Rood, has been dead for quite awhile now, and he left publishing anyway and became a sculptor. I owe *Manuscript* a great deal.

Conversations: I'd like to go back a little bit and talk about your childhood. This is a beautiful house we are sitting in. Is this the house you grew up in?

Welty: It's the second house my family built, but I was in school by then. This was sort of in the country when we built it in 1925, I guess. Before that I lived in the house in Jackson where I was born.

Conversations: You had two brothers, is that right?

Welty: Yes. They were younger.

Conversations: Do you consider that you had a normal kind of a childhood?

Welty: I had a happy childhood and I was very fortunate in my family. It was always a congenial house with plenty going on. But, also, we always had all the books we wanted. We always had books and my earliest presents were books, which I loved. And I remember we had an encyclopedia always, and it used to be in the dining room; if someone asked a question at the table, you could jump up and prove right away that you were right or find you were wrong. It's always been a family full of curiosity and interest in the world.

Conversations: Did your brothers read, too?

Welty: They didn't read as much as I did; they were more athletic. They liked reading, but one of my brothers became an architect and he was musical; they were other things.

Conversations: Was your mother interested in artistic pursuits?

Welty: She was a teacher when she was young but she was also a great reader all her life, and, even after her eyesight failed, loved books. And so did my father. So, what hopeful writer could be more lucky? From the first I was able to read.

Conversations: Who were your favorite authors back then?

Welty: Of course, I read lots of fairy tales and all the childhood books. And I also liked Mark Twain. We had a set of his work; it's still over there in the bookshelves. I read practically everything, the way I do now. You know, a ferocious, voracious reader.

Conversations: I notice there's a new book by Reynolds Price right here on this table. He's another Southern writer.

Welty: Absolutely, and a good friend.

Conversations: Did you have a large peripheral family of cousins and aunts and uncles or was it rather small?

Welty: No, not in Jackson because both of my parents came from away. My mother came from West Virginia—

Conversations: That's pretty obvious in *The Optimist's Daughter.*

Welty: Yes. That was literal memory, up on the mountain and the sounds and sights up there.

Conversations: I've always been curious as to how West Virginia got in that novel so strongly.

Welty: Well, we spent every summer visiting the families. My father was from Ohio and we went to his father's farm down in southern Ohio, and to the house on the mountaintop in West Virginia. That's where all of our kinfolks were, not here. Not any here, except the immediate family.

Conversations: So you never had the experience that many Southern children have of being "trapped" in a room where all the relatives are talking and telling family stories.

Welty: I've experienced that but only as a treat, you know, in the summer. I had to make all that up for *Delta Wedding*.

Conversations: How did you manage to cope with such a large cast of characters in *Delta Wedding?* Have you ever counted them?

Welty: I wonder, myself. I had to make family trees and chronologies, to be sure I had everything right. But you touched on a tender subject when you asked had I ever counted, because when Edward Weeks serialized *Delta Wedding* in the *Atlantic,* he found out, as my editor, that I had miscounted the children, and set me right. It was a stern lesson to me; I made my mind up never to let that happen again. I said, "Here I've had nine children" or whatever it was, and it was really ten. Of course I knew them all, but I hadn't really said one, two, three, four, five, six. . . .

Conversations: When did you actually start writing?

Welty: You know how we all write when we are little. I think always I loved writing because I loved reading. I don't mean I get my stories out of books—I don't. They spring from living. And not that I literally take things from real life, but it's living that makes me want to write, not reading—although it's reading that makes me love writing.

Conversations: You have never consciously emulated another writer?

Welty: No. It is a way to do, but I have never . . . I don't think consciously that I've ever used that method.

Conversations: Can you remember the first piece of writing—a story or something—that you did as a very young child?

Welty: You know how you made up little booklets to give your mother for a present. Mine were surely sappy. It seems to me I can remember my illustrations more than what I made up. I seem to remember an Easter rabbit on the telephone, that kind of thing.

Conversations: You were interested in both painting and drawing, weren't you?

Welty: I have a visual mind but I had no gift for painting.

Conversations: This may be why the imagery in your writing is so vivid.

Welty: It may be. I *am* interested in the visual world.

Conversations: Have you always been interested in people, in what makes them tick, and in what brings them together or drives them apart?

Welty: I think so. I was probably a troublesome child with my curiosity, because I asked a lot of questions and I loved to just sit in a room with grown people talking, anyone talking. My mother has told me how I would sit between two people, setting off for a ride in the car, as we used to do on Sunday, and say, "Now start talking!" My ears would just open like morning glories.

Conversations: You have an awfully good ear, too, for dialogue; you're universally praised—

Welty: I do work hard at that. Of course, a lot of conversation in the South, as you know, is of a narrative and dramatic structure and so when you listen to it, you're following a story. You're listening for how something is going to come out and that, also, I think, has something to do with the desire to write later. We would listen to talk forever. When you go up North, they don't want to hear it, you know. They don't want to hear in the starting-at-the-beginning-going-all-the-way-through style. They just want to hear the results.

Conversations: You went to public schools in Jackson and then to Mississippi State College for Women.

Welty: For two years, then I went to the University of Wisconsin.

Conversations: What steps took you there?

Welty: That was my father's preference. He was from the Middle West, and he had the idea that the big Middle Western universities were the most progressive. I think at that time he was probably right. I was considered too young to start off there. You know, in those days we went to college at sixteen, which I was, and I would have been too much of an infant to go to the University of Wisconsin. Well, I think I was too much of an infant to go to college.

Conversations: Did you like MSCW?

Welty: I liked it; I had a good time.

Conversations: After you went to the University of Wisconsin, you then went to Columbia and studied advertising?

Welty: That's right. Well, by that time, I knew I wanted to be a writer. Again, my father who always was pretty wise said, "You'll never make a living as a story writer"—prophetic words. "You'll need to be able to support yourself." I said, "I'm not going to be a teacher." So he said, "Well, then, it should be business." I had longed to go to New York for a year, so that was the answer: I went to Columbia School of Business and had a year in New York.

Conversations: Where did you live in New York?

Welty: I lived in Johnson Hall. All female graduate students under twenty-one had to live there.

Conversations: You didn't do the Greenwich Village scene?

Welty: We didn't live down there, but we went out nightly, you know, to something: the theatre, to dance up in Harlem, down to Greenwich Village. Well, it was the heyday—1931.

Conversations: Did you meet some of the literary people there at that time?

Welty: No, no. I didn't mean we knew anybody. We would just go down there, wandering around in Minetta Lane, to Romany Marie's, and places like that. In that year the theatres couldn't have been more wonderful.

Conversations: Is this when your interest in the theatre started?

Welty: I'd always been interested. On trips with my family, we'd go to the theatre wherever we were. And plays used to come here, you know. In the days of train travel and road companies, Jackson was the stopover between Memphis and New Orleans, so we got a lot of shows here, the so-called Broadway shows. Our parents always took the children; that was another good thing.

Conversations: There was really quite a lot of cultural life in Jackson, then?

Welty: Well, we thought there was. And I think that we really did have people come through here that were first-rate.

Conversations: After you left Columbia you came back to Jackson?

Welty: Yes, because the Depression happened. There was no more advertising being done; there were no jobs.

Conversations: Is this when you started working for the government with the WPA?

Welty: Pretty soon. That was also the year my father died—he was fifty-two. My mother was left with two sons in high school and college, so I came home and worked in Jackson at whatever I could do. You know, it was poor pickings in those days. But I, again, was lucky. I worked for the radio station here and did, oh, various meager work on newspapers—whatever I could get. Then when the WPA came along, I was offered a job as a publicity agent.

Conversations: What exactly did you do? I know that you took pictures.

Welty: I did reporting, interviewing. It took me all over Mississippi, which is the most important thing to me, because I'd never seen it—except Jackson and Columbus—never. And the coast, I guess, once or twice.

Conversations: Did the people that you met become "characters" in some of your early stories?

Welty: Not as themselves, and not directly. But some of the places are real—and the landscapes. And you're certainly right in that that experience, I think, was the real germ of my wanting to become a real writer, a true writer. It caused me to seriously attempt it. It made me see, for the first time, what life was really like in this state. It was a revelation.

Conversations: Did you really get to know people like the characters in your stories, like "Keela, the Outcast Indian Maiden" and "Petrified Man"?

Welty: Not the particular people, but I got an insight into human beings that I'd never had. I realized later what a protected life I'd led. You know, I thought I had been so sophisticated in New York, and didn't know a thing. I didn't know what people were really like until then.

"Keela," which you mentioned, came about in a special way. In my job I would go to different county fairs and put up booths for the

WPA. Once some of the people on the midway—I used to go out and drink coffee with them and so on—they were talking about the sideshow act of something *like* Keela, the outcast Indian maiden. I don't remember now, but it involved a little black person that had been carried off. Well, of course, my story is not about that; it's about the moral response to it made by three different people. It troubled me so and I tried to write my story in response to that situation. In a way that's a very simple example of the way I always begin in making a story.

Conversations: You don't try, then, to take a person you have met and put that person, exactly as he is, on the printed page?

Welty: It would be impossible. You never know enough for that, to begin with. But also, you have to invent the character to suit the purpose of the story that you are trying to tell. That is his circumference and his point and his reason for being. I mean the character of a short story, not a novel.

Conversations: In your introduction to *One Time, One Place* you say: "I learned quickly enough when to click the shutter, but what I was becoming aware of more slowly was a story-writer's truth: the thing to wait on, to reach there in time for, is the moment in which people reveal themselves." Would these people that you met open up to you and talk?

Welty: Maybe I considered that they had, because I began to understand a little. I hadn't thought of this until you asked me, but maybe I was speaking too subjectively in that remark. Of course, some people did open up; you got an idea of their lives anyway, by one way or the other, by something they'd said, something you saw, something that made you feel where your sympathies were going.

Conversations: I know you dislike the tag of "regional writer."

Welty: Oh, I don't mind.

Conversations: Most of your fiction is set in the South and your writing conveys a strong sense of place. Do you consider this an important element of your work?

Welty: It seems very important to me. I think Southerners have such an intimate sense of place. We grew up in the fact that we live here with people about whom we know almost everything that can be known as a citizen of the same neighborhood or town. We learn significant things that way: we know what the place has made of these people; what they've made of the place through generations. We have a sense of continuity and that, I think, comes from place. It helps to give the meaning—another meaning to a human life that such life has been there all the time and will go on. Now that people are on the move a lot more, some of that sense of continuity is gone, but I feel . . . I believe it will always be in our roots, as Southerners, don't you? A sense of the place. Even if you move around, you know where you have your base. And I just think it's terribly important.

Conversations: On the inside of *Delta Wedding* there's a map—

Welty: Well, that was just done as a decoration by Doubleday. But maps—they're of the essence. I drew my own map for *Losing Battles.* I had to; I used it when I was working. I had to be sure just for one thing that I had people turning left or right correctly, when they charged up and down. To be sure I got all those routes right. Oh, it was just a delight. I loved being able to do my map.

Conversations: Was *Delta Wedding,* your second novel, fairly easy to write, after having written mainly short stories?

Welty: Yes, well, again, that's something I owe to Diarmuid. I sent what I thought was a story in to Diarmuid called "The Delta Cousins," and he wrote back and said, "Eudora, this is chapter two of a novel. Go on with it." He recognized that it had a possible scope to it or something. It hadn't occurred to me; it might never have occurred to me. And it never occurred to me that I could write a novel, but he spotted it. His judgment was so acute and I trusted everything that he said, absolutely. You know, I would have given it a try after he'd said that, no matter what had happened. So I just went on from there, and "The Delta Cousins" became *Delta Wedding.*

Conversations: Many of your books center around an incident and involve a great many people, all commenting on that central incident almost like a Greek chorus.

Welty: I know. I seem to have these unconscious patterns. Does everyone? I didn't realize that myself for quite awhile. I suppose it's more or less an obvious kind of way to bring people together and have things emerge.

Conversations: It's like writing a play, especially in *Losing Battles* where you use so much dialogue and your point of view is objective.

Welty: I really do work at it, do a good deal of rewriting. I didn't do so much in *The Optimist's Daughter,* but it's never as hard for me to write something that's an interior story. Although it was a more complicated and deeper story, *The Optimist's Daughter,* and it meant more to me personally, it was easier to write. But I had set myself to do *Losing Battles* to see if I could, to try to see if I could do everything objectively. I wrote, oh, so many scenes over and over again to condense them, shape them to sharpen up what I was trying to do.

Conversations: Didn't it take you about fifteen years?

Welty: Well, I wrote it over a period of ten years, but then, of course, I was working on other things too. I couldn't work on it consecutively because of affairs here at home. I worked on short things and I was giving lectures. I also wrote *The Optimist's Daughter* before I finished *Losing Battles.* I really loved writing *Losing Battles* because of the problem it set: trying to do something strictly through dialogue and action. And another problem was to keep the spark, you know, that was what scared me when it took so long. I thought: the spark may have died; it may not still be alive, and there was no way to know until someone had read it.

Conversations: I felt that there was a shift in style in *Losing Battles.* The first part seems to be very poetic; and then it seems that your book becomes less poetic, less concentrated. The narrative moves faster forward. Were you aware of this? Was this something you had in mind?

Welty: I must—no, I think that's astute on your part. I can think of two reasons why that would be true. First, I thought it was going to be a short story—I do every time. I wrote the first part thinking that was to be the story: the family gathered and telling the story about Jack, what he had done; and then I was going to end it with Jack coming home and asking them what in the world is the matter with *them.* It ended with his appearance, that is. Well, goodness, by that time—

Conversations: You were hooked on him.

Welty: I was hooked. Also, I went back at the very end and rewrote that very beginning many, many times. It was the hardest thing in the world for me to lead into what had come out of it, and it may be too rewritten, you know. In the opening part that you're talking about, with all the similes and so on, I was trying to see if I could

condense all that was ahead into just such terms, in a very concentrated way to give a picture. I could have overwritten it and overdone
it; some people didn't like that beginning. Whether people liked it or
not was not the thing I was worrying about; that never enters your
mind.

Conversations: Have you ever written any poetry?

Welty: No, I can't write poetry at all.

Conversations: In reviewing *Delta Wedding, Time* took you to
task for writing about an aristocratic Southern family without criticizing the aristocratic Southern way of life. The reviewer closed with
something like, "Such writing is to be expected from one who is the
daughter of an insurance company executive and a member of the
Junior League." Does this sort of comment make you angry?

Welty: Sure. Sure it made me mad. I used to get mad at *Time* for
everything they said about the South in those days; it was a good
deal of a pattern. I never write stories or novels with the object of
criticizing the people. I want the reader to understand the people,
and people as individuals. I'm not condemning people at all and
never have. I think it's the business of a fiction writer to reveal life as
he sees it by letting the characters reveal themselves and letting the
reader draw his own conclusions. It doesn't matter whether I live and
write in the South or East India or the North Pole, I would still feel
that way.

Conversations: Yet in your earliest collection, *A Curtain of
Green,* there are stories which show people being exploited, people
suffering; these were hardly "Junior League" stories.

Welty: Yes. And when I was one of the writers who was receiving
middle-of-the-night, dead-of-night telephone calls about the troubles
in the sixties, when I was harangued by strangers saying, "Why are
you sitting down there writing your stories instead of out condemning
your society," I felt like saying I didn't need their pointers to know
that there was injustice among human beings or that there was
trouble. I had been writing about that steadily right along by letting
my characters show this. I don't believe in pointing my finger and
shaking a stick at people and saying,"Look here—" As a fiction writer
I never would do that.

Conversations: Didn't you write an article defending this position?

Welty: In 1965 I wrote a piece for the *Atlantic Monthly* called "Must the Novelist Crusade?" in which I tried to express this. Not only on my behalf, but on the behalf of all writers at all times. Some writers may see that as their business, which is their privilege, but I see as my privilege writing about human beings as human beings with all the things that make them up, including bigotry, misunderstanding, injustice, and also love and affection, and whatever else. Whatever makes them up interests me. I try to write as I see real life, which doesn't allow stock characters who get up and illustrate something in the abstract—that was going on a lot at that time.

Well, one thing that I did do which pertains to this, I guess, was in result of the one really bad thing—one of two really bad things—that happened in Jackson during the 1960s as far as race incidents went. It was the murder of Medgar Evers. I did write a story the night it happened. I was so upset about this and I thought: I live down here where this happened and I believe that I must know what a person like that felt like—this murderer. There had been so many stories about such a character in the stock manner, written by people who didn't know the South, so I wrote about the murderer intimately—in the first person, which was a very daring thing for me to do.

At that time, of course, he hadn't been caught; I mean, no one had been arrested, much less tried. In between my writing that story and its publication, which was done very quickly in *The New Yorker*— they set it up and printed it almost right away, just two pages long— there had been an arrest. William Maxwell, my editor, called me up and we made the changes over the telephone. The story had to be gone over with a fine-toothed comb by the magazine's lawyers in case I had inadvertently jeopardized somebody. And it was odd how many things I had guessed right, though I was wrong in the social level of the man accused—that's interesting, isn't it?—but, I think I still knew what the man thought. I had lived with that kind of thing.

Conversations: First person was a very daring approach.

Welty: Well, I felt that desperate about it.

Conversations: That story should have silenced some of your "social" critics!

Welty: Well, but that was using my skill as a writer and not lecturing. I was trying to let the story itself speak for its point, you know.

Conversations: I noticed that your number is no longer in the phone book, whereas it was for a long time.

Welty: Well, that was sort of as a result of those midnight calls. I'm sorry not to have it in there, although it helps me in a way, because I work at home and I like to work pretty concentratedly through the day. I try to give my number to everyone who could possibly want it, but sometimes I miss out on the visit of a friend who is unexpectedly passing through and I'm sorry.

Conversations: Various people have commented on how accessible you are as a writer—

Welty: Real accessible.

Conversations: You give interviews—maybe you don't like to, but you do; you give lectures—you have just come back from a lecture tour.

Welty: Well, it really wasn't a lecture tour. That is, I came back to home base in between everything. There was a time when I did a lot of this, and it pleased me to get invitations from some of the same places where I went before. It's mostly readings from my work and answers-to-questions periods. I like best the give-and-take with the students. I enjoy it but I don't try anymore to write and do that at the same time.

Conversations: You appear on educational TV; you appeared with Jim Hartz when NBC's *Today* show came down here to Mississippi—

Welty: I know, but I was so disappointed in their idea of coverage. It was just that they had such a chance to find out things for the rest of the country about Mississippi. I told Mr. Hartz and some of the others that in one or two sentences I, for instance, could give them a picture of the great amount of work in the arts that's been going on here—writing—painting—music—and they said, "Well, we don't have time to go into anything. We've got to get to Arkansas." I really was so cross, because everybody here was trying and ready to help them with things: show them the backgrounds and give information.

Conversations: How do you manage to keep out all the people who make you mad, or do you?

Welty: Oh, I really do what I like to do. For instance, I wanted to see you, but I don't have time or energy to give many interviews. And when I work, I do nothing else. For instance, after we finish our interview I'm going to dive right in. I've not been able to wait to get home from these lectures and so on, and get into some work which I interrupted to go off—some writing.

Conversations: Well, when you don't want to see people, what do you do? Do you take the phone off the hook?

Welty: Oh, no, I answer the telephone. I can't not do it. And, of course, I want to see people and my friends; I can do that in the evening. My friends are understanding: if they know I'm working on something, they usually don't call me in the morning—that's when I like to work. People have always been understanding of me here in Jackson. But it is necessary, as you know, to have consecutive time ahead. You can't take an hour this morning, an hour this afternoon, thirty minutes after supper.

Conversations: How do you work? Do you have any peculiarities?

Welty: Oh, no, I don't think so.

Conversations: You do work on the typewriter?

Welty: I work either way, but I have to type it early in the process. I guess my journalistic training taught me to want to see something on the page, objective, in type.

Conversations: Do you do any revision as you're working or do you tend to go clear through a long chunk of writing, and then go back and rewrite?

Welty: I guess a combination of both. Or either, depending on how I worked at it. I revise a lot, at one time or another.

Conversations: Did Diarmuid Russell ever, ever, ever send you anything back and say, "Brood over this for a while"?

Welty: That's his favorite word, isn't it? I don't believe he ever sent a story back; I don't believe he ever did. But, you know, his terms were not uncertain; you knew how well he liked something or how well he didn't. I just can't tell you what it meant to me to have him there. His integrity, his understanding, his instincts—everything was something I trusted.

Conversations: You never had the feeling that he would sell a shoddy piece of work just to make money.

Welty: No, nobody's. And neither would he send a publisher a shoddy piece of work. They knew he was going to send good things; the writers knew he would send it to the right place. Editors and publishers have remarked to me that they opened his things first. It's so nice to know that two people who started off with those wonderful ideas succeeded. You know, Diarmuid and Henry Volkening started off on a shoestring and just the two of them—they always wanted to keep their own clients; they kept the firm small; the client list small; so they could always handle it personally. And can you imagine anything more lucky than just walking into their agency?

Conversations: Was there anyone else—what about publishers—who helped you?

Welty: Are you old enough to have known John Woodburn? Well, he was marvelous. He was with Doubleday to begin with. He gave my name to Diarmuid Russell when he was starting an agency. Diarmuid finally sold my first book of stories to John Woodburn. And, you know, for Doubleday to publish a book of short stories by an unknown writer was really extraordinary in those days. Or, maybe, at anytime for anyone to. So when John moved to Harcourt, Brace I moved with him, because it was to him that I had the allegiance.

Conversations: And you stayed with Harcourt, Brace until—

Welty: Until *Losing Battles.* That came after such a long interval and everyone I knew at Harcourt had left. And I didn't feel close to them anymore, whereas at Random House there's Albert Erskine, who was on the *Southern Review* when they published my beginning stories. So when I came to Random House it was another full circle. I really have been a lucky writer as far as my professional associates have been concerned, all the way through.

Conversations: You never have had any bad experiences with publishers and certainly not with Diarmuid Russell.

Welty: No. And then, Mary Louise Aswell, who was on *Harper's Bazaar* and still a close friend of mine, published some of the early stories. She was so good; she would keep the powers from cutting her fiction to make room for an ad, you know, that kind of thing. She fought for her writers. William Maxwell is close to me as my editor and my friend of many years.

Conversations: Well, you've had a lot of friends but I don't know that you really needed much help—

Welty: Oh, boy, who doesn't! Who doesn't.

Conversations: *The Ponder Heart* was produced in 1956, wasn't it?

Welty: I believe it was. I didn't write the play, as you know.

Conversations: Have you ever written a play or tried to write a play?

Welty: Not to show other eyes. I've worked on it, but torn up everything. I discovered exactly what my trouble is: the difference between dramatic dialogue and dialogue on the page. You know, it's completely different in function and everything else.

Conversations: And yet, I would think that anything from *Losing Battles* could be read straight out and would sound like stage dialogue.

Welty: I don't know—but think how short a play is and how every single line of dialogue has to advance the plot. You can't have any digressions and—

Conversations: You're very good at digressions!

Welty: Well, my great weakness! And also, it was a liberty I could take in *Losing Battles;* in a play you could take no liberties. I would love the discipline of writing a play; I still would like to do it.

Conversations: There were two versions of *The Ponder Heart* produced, were there not? Wasn't one done by Frank Hains here in Jackson?

Welty: Oh, yes, absolutely. At New Stage.

Conversations: Which one of the versions did you think was truer to your novel?

Welty: Oh, Frank's. Of course, we gave it paying our royalties to Chodorov and Fields and so on, because it wouldn't be allowable to write or publish another version. I loved the one they did here; I wish you could have seen it. They've done it about three different times. Frank wrote it; directed it; made the sets; wrote the music for it—did everything. He said he knew that he broke every rule of dramatic construction, but it seemed to work.

Edna Earle, who is the chief character in my story, was still the chief character and what happened was all presented from her point of view. The Broadway play made Uncle Daniel the main character and Edna Earle receded to the background. It was perfectly legitimate for the play to do that, but it was not my story.

Conversations: No, well, the whole strength of *The Ponder Heart* is the central intelligence which is Edna Earle telling the story—

Welty: The way she saw it. It was done as really a labor of love by

New Stage here; Frank and the whole crew, and the beautiful performances—especially by Jane Petty and Tom Spengler who acted
the leads. That story was very blessed.

Conversations: Have you had any other theatrical productions?

Welty: Well, *The Robber Bridegroom.* I, of course, didn't write
that either. That was this past fall; I gather it's about to go on tour.

Conversations: Wasn't there a ballet based on your juvenile
book, *The Shoe Bird?*

Welty: Oh, yes, there was, by the Jackson Ballet Guild.

Conversations: I think that was charming, too.

Welty: It really was. Rex Cooper and Albia Kavan did the choreo-
graphy, and Lehman Engel wrote the music for it. The costumes
were charming. I was very proud that they did it—and pleased.

Conversations: In earlier interviews you have warned readers
about the dangers of overanalyzing stories. Yet a lot of critics have
talked about the mythological content in your stories, such as the
name "Phoenix" in "A Worn Path," and in "Death of a Traveling
Salesman" the idea of Sonny as Prometheus, the bearer of light, and
his wife as the great Earth Mother. Are you consciously using this
material symbolically?

Welty: Yes, I know. I think that sounds like a literal way to take it.
In the case of "Death of a Traveling Salesman," I had no idea of any
of that which you were just saying.

Conversations: When the mule's face looks in the window
there's been. . . . Somebody wrote a scholarly article about just what
this mule's face meant.

Welty: It meant a mule was looking in the window. Well, the thing
I feel about all symbolism, in general, I can easily say very simply and
that is: if a symbol occurs to you organically in writing the story, you
can use it. For instance, I wouldn't have used the word "phoenix" in
"A Worn Path" if it hadn't first come to me as an appropriate Mississippi name. I'd heard of old people named Phoenix; there's a
Phoenix town. I thought it was legitimate as a symbol, because it is
also true. I couldn't have called her "Andromeda" or something like
that, you know, in order to make her a symbol. It would take away
her life. If it comes in naturally, then it can call up some overtones
and I don't mean to do any more than that.

Conversations: Would that also apply to "Beulah" as the name of the town that Bowman is heading for in "Death of a Traveling Salesman"? "Beulah Land" has a biblical connotation, but there is a Beulah, Mississippi, isn't there?

Welty: Mississippi is full of Beulahs. I used it again in *The Ponder Heart* without remembering that I'd used it before—it doesn't matter. The Beulah Hotel—and someone wrote in to ask me if the whole thing was a Christian allegory. That kind of thing makes me uncomfortable. You try to suggest, to arouse people's imagination. But then, I don't like to be held responsible for making their ideas neatly work out. Some are far-flung! There's the sense of proportion to go by, too, in letting in symbols.

Conversations: I was going to ask if you had read a lot of mythology.

Welty: I certainly am interested in myths and I've always used them; I read and loved them as a child. In *The Golden Apples* I used mythology, but the stories weren't meant to illustrate a myth. I just used mythology, just as I used Mississippi locations and names. In *The Robber Bridegroom* I used fairy tales and real folklore and historical people and everything alike and simultaneously. I think it's there; I think it's right there—so why shouldn't I avail myself? But it is kind of frightening to think that people see ponderous allegorical meanings—

Conversations: And even would take to worrying about that old mule looking in the window.

Welty: I know; I don't think that's fair; I really don't. Not fair to that mule. This isn't to say I don't appreciate genuine criticism—

Conversations: You have been praised for your ability to reconcile the tragic and the comic and to balance them simultaneously. Do you see life basically as a comedy or a tragedy or, perhaps, as a tragicomedy?

Welty: Well, I guess it's like what I just said about the myths and the folklore and everything; it's there. It's in the fabric of life—and I try to show what I see or find there, sometimes comedy, sometimes tragedy, and sometimes both. I don't see what else you can do, except try to show in the most honest way you can what you see.

Conversations: You have also been accused of being obscure. Would you agree with this criticism?

Welty: Well, I think it would be the worst sin I could commit, if I were. I certainly don't do such a thing on purpose. If I'm obscure, it's where I've made a mistake somewhere in trying to be clear, because I abominate deliberate obscurity.

Conversations: When you're dealing with what Robert Penn Warren has called "love and separateness," you can't help being a little bit mysterious—

Welty: Well, mysterious is something else; I don't mind being mysterious. I think life is mysterious. But to be obscure would be a fault in the teller of the story; and that is something I would have avoided, or overcome, as far as I'm able.

Conversations: Would you agree with Robert Penn Warren's statement that your writing is often about love and separateness?

Welty: I guess it is. He's a most marvelous critic. I haven't read that piece in a long time because he wrote it a long time ago, but I'm grateful to him for whatever he would say. I would trust him to be right.

Conversations: It seems to me that "At the Landing"—

Welty: *That* has lots of faults to it; *that's* obscure. I was really trying to express something that I felt in that *place*. It used to be really lost down there. A ghost river-town. It was magical to me and I was trying to express some of that lostness and the feeling of enchantment. Maybe I got too carried away by my own words.

Conversations: Another thing that you seem to come back to besides love—the expression of or the failure to express—is family loyalty and unity. Would you say that this is one of your recurring themes?

Welty: Well, I think it goes with your sense of family, however that loyalty or unity works out. In *The Optimist's Daughter* there is Laurel's loyalty to her father and her mother, and Fay's family swarming in is another aspect of the same thing. They are together, for heaven's sake—a knot. Just as sure as Laurel's family is a knot. I do think the family unit can hold just about all the stories of man, don't you? It can embrace them.

Conversations: You've won a staggering number of awards and prizes, including the Pulitzer Prize in 1973. Would you go out on a limb and say which of these awards meant the most to you, personally?

Welty: I don't know; I don't know. Of course, I was so *astonished* at the Pulitzer. I had no—

Conversations: How did you find out about it?

Welty: Frank Hains down at *The Daily News* called up and said, "Well, how does it feel—" or something. I thought he was talking about something else and while I was talking to him I saw these two strangers with a camera coming up my walk. I said, "Frank, what's happened?" He told me it came over the AP wire. About two or three days afterwards, I think, I got a telegram. So that was my biggest shock, the Pulitzer Prize.

I was very proud of the Gold Medal for Fiction from the National Institute of Arts and Letters, because this is a body made up of artists who are my own contemporaries—people doing what I'm doing. And also because it was for a body of work instead of for something that—some one effort. It meant a great deal to me for those two personal reasons.

Conversations: When was this?

Welty: I think it was in 1972. I've had great descents of good fortune.

Conversations: Well, but you do work at it!

Welty: I do work hard; I do work hard, but it doesn't always follow, you know, that people even read your work, much less like it. The whole world could have been like *Time* magazine in 1943.

Conversations: Have you served on any boards that grant awards?

Welty: Well, I am a member of the Institute and the Academy and we all do a shift at some committee like that, and I have been a judge on their awards, and a number of others.

Conversations: Does this mean you're reading a great number of books?

Welty: Yes, constantly, constantly reading.

Conversations: Could you give a rough estimate of how much?

Welty: I don't know. If I'm serving as a reader for such a thing, it seems to me that wherever I go, like to get my hair done, wait in the dentist's office or anywhere, I try to get a part of a novel read. I don't know how people who review regularly in a weekly do it. It's different from constantly reading on your own.

Conversations: You do a lot of reviewing, too. Do you work exclusively for *The New York Times?*

Welty: I do do a good bit of reviewing. No, they're the ones that seem to ask me the most. I've just finished reviewing Katherine Anne Porter's book which she wrote on Sacco and Vanzetti. Did you see— it came out in the *Atlantic.* I didn't know that she was one of those writers who went up to Boston and demonstrated with Edna St. Vincent Millay and John Dos Passos and all of them. She took notes at the time, but had not found herself able to really make a book, a complete thing of it until now, this last year.

She's eighty-seven years old and this is an extraordinary book: it's sixty-three pages long—utterly concentrated and pure and honest and straightforward reporting, in the light of her subjective feelings which she has tried to clarify through the years. It was a privilege to review it. I just mailed it yesterday.

Conversations: Have you and Katherine Anne Porter been friends? I know that there's a disparity in your ages, but I also know she was one of the earlier writers to recognize your talent.

Welty: She was one of the first people. She was living in Baton Rouge at the time that I was sending my first stories in to *Southern Review.* She wrote me a letter out of the clear blue sky and said that she liked my work, and invited me to come down to see her, and offered anything she could do. Isn't that amazing? It was just wonderful. It was also her way. So, of course, we've been friends ever since. I owe her a great deal and admire her whole life's work a great deal and, of course, love her.

Conversations: Which of your stories is your own personal favorite and which of your novels?

Welty: Whatever I'm working on at the time seems to matter the most with me, and all the others are forgotten. But I think really that book of stories called *The Golden Apples* is, on the whole, my favorite. Somehow that's very close to my heart. It has some of the stories I most of all loved writing. And then it excited me, because I discovered only part way through that the stories were connected. All this time in the back of my head these connections had worked themselves out. I had just to get the clue like a belated detective: this story's people were that story's people at a different period in their lives.

Conversations: That's fascinating.

Welty: It was to me. And also, Diarmuid liked that; he even telephoned me, which is very unusual for him, you know. After he finished reading it he said, "I think this is a very, very good book." That meant a lot to me—the reader, you know, speaking from the other end. It stayed with me as something that really made me happy.

Conversations: So things do happen in your writing that you are not expecting to happen, such as these connections.

Welty: Yes and I trust them.

Conversations: So you don't go through and plan, plot out everything exactly as you expect it to go. Then how do you know if a story is going well?

Welty: You do get a story to a point where it, on its own momentum, can sort of work for you. That's a mark that you are doing it right. I do think that if the story is any good, it has a life of its own, don't you? And a momentum. And it helps you and you help it sort of at the same time. I find in every story that I write it's teaching me how to work it out as I go, which is why I love to write. I really love the work involved and what happens.

Conversations: A lot of writers claim to write with pain and agony—

Welty: It's hard, but I like it to be hard. In fact, that's another mark that it's any good, but I love it. Really, it just delights me to write. Sometimes I think about P. G. Wodehouse, who was said to laugh as he wrote. Well, sometimes I do too.

Conversations: What do you think about the current literary scene? Are there any writers whom you are particularly interested in right now?

Welty: That's a hard thing to answer off the top of your head. I think it's very important to us what is going on today, and I am interested in finding out about young writers coming along. As well as the new work of us older ones.

Conversations: What do you think about Walker Percy?

Welty: He's very interesting to me. I don't always understand his work right off and have to go back and read again. Or that's the way I read *Lancelot.* I still prefer *The Moviegoer* to all of them. When I was reading *Lancelot* it interested me and compelled my admiration, and still I kept thinking, "But I like *The Moviegoer.*"

Conversations: I think Walker Percy has a philosophical idea that he's trying to express through fiction. Do you have that feeling?

Welty: I do too, and I'm sure that whatever it is it's full of interest and complications. I'm just not certain I can follow. I thought he did something of the same thing, but more by suggestion, in *The Moviegoer.* In *Lancelot* it's sort of wide open: actual symbolic playing with things, and the movie mechanism of pictures within pictures within pictures, and media being the meaning and so on. I admired how he was able to do this. I'll be interested to see what he will do next.

Conversations: And Reynolds Price?

Welty: I am deeply interested in him. He's just rewritten or reconceived his first book as a play. I read an earlier version of it, but not this finished one that just came out, *Early Dark.* Yes, I think he's full of books to come. With all his fine accomplishments, his absolutely first-rate work so far, you feel there is so much more there. He teaches at Duke University and he's a person of great vitality and independence of mind, who knows exactly what he wants to do. I feel the same way about Elizabeth Spencer, you know: she's just a born writer with all sorts of resources already shown and to come. Abundance!

Conversations: What about Ellen Douglas, who you think is a fine writer.

Welty: Yes, I've read all of her work. She has so much power, hasn't she? Tremendous strength. She writes with a lot of passion, too, which is the essence. A passion of knowing and understanding, able to give a true reflection of life in a particular part of the world. Peter Taylor has it too, another writer I like enormously—he finds his essence in the life he knew in Tennessee.

Conversations: I kept trying to make Peter Taylor a Mississippi writer, but he's over the border.

Welty: Oh, he's over the border, very much so. If you'd say Mississippi to him, he would say, "Are you crazy? It's Tennessee!"

Conversations: Of course, there are other writers besides Southern writers—

Welty: There are indeed.

Conversations: I was thinking of Saul Bellow, for instance, who is another Russell and Volkening client, is he not?

Welty: Yes, he is. I think he was Henry's. And, of course, he is a very knowledgeable and skillful writer. He has won all the honors in the world.

Conversations: What do you read for pleasure?

Welty: I've just finished reading a whole year of Chekhov which was pure bliss. The one lecture I gave this year was on Chekhov, so that gave me a wonderful reason to—as if you needed one—to re-read everything and track down everything that I had not read. Reading Chekhov was just like the angels singing to me. Often, if you're asked to do a piece on somebody, I think the reason you accept is that you know it's your chance at something that you've always wanted to do: that is, read one person through and no one else and everything they've written. I did the same thing with Willa Cather, to my great delight.

Conversations: I have never done that with Cather.

Welty: Neither had I before. You know, I hadn't even read all of her books. I thought I had, but had not. So that was a wonderful new experience.

Conversations: I did that with Jane Austen once. I understand that she is one of your favorite authors.

Welty: She is. And I did the same thing. More than once, because she only has a short row of books and you can't stop when you start her anywhere. If you ever start her, you read them all.

Conversations: It is astonishing to me in this day and age of explicit sex, violence, and so forth, how Austen can keep you hanging, waiting for the hero to call the heroine by her first name.

Welty: Absolutely. Exactly. Well, it's symbols either way—the whole thing means coming intimacy or intimacy arrived. Today's explicit sex and Jane Austen's calling by the first name speak of human beings reaching the same thing, within the dramatic possibilities of the day. So there you are.

Conversations: Who are some of your other favorite writers—not necessarily contemporary?

Welty: Henry Green! I'm crazy about him. I just got hold of his first novel—the one he wrote while he was still at Eton—called *Blind-*

ness. I knew he had written it, but, to me, it was a mythological book that had never reached this country. I knew it had been out of print in England for ages. While I was in Santa Barbara a friend who has a bookstore told me that he had come by this book, and so I bought it from him. I don't usually buy rare books, per se, but I just had to have this, and now I've read it.

It really is extraordinary. Only a seventeen-year-old boy would have the daring to start off like that: his hero, a young boy, is blinded when struck by a child throwing a stone through the glass of a moving train. And the boy's ordeal . . . his going on home and trying to adjust to his life. This is the novel. Isn't that amazing? I've heard it said that afterwards Henry Green disowned it; I don't know on what basis. Anyway, I've read everything that he's ever written, closely and with love.

I love E. M. Forster and Elizabeth Bowen very much. I revere Virginia Woolf but I don't want her preeminence now—everyone reading her and writing about her—accidentally to put Elizabeth Bowen in any kind of shadow because I think she was fully as good. And, in a rewarding way, more robust, human, and rounded. I'm not dreaming of trying to see them as competitors, which they *never* were. You can't look at writing like that. But Elizabeth died recently, and I don't want her books suddenly for that reason to drop behind, even briefly.

Conversations: Well, it's a little unfortunate that we get these cult figures—

Welty: It's not fair to either one.

Conversations: No, not fair to the person who inspires the cult, either. I am thinking of Sylvia Plath and, of course, Truman Capote for a long time. And I've wondered if Harper Lee was stopped from writing more by having so much attention, so early on with *To Kill a Mockingbird.*

Welty: I know nothing at all about her case, but I do know that this happens because I've seen it. It could be the most unfortunate thing in the world, I guess, to have something happen to you too soon. It's a matter of timing in your life. It's really not fair, either, that somebody's first book, written at a very tender age, gets the acclaim it deserves but yet at the wrong time for that person; so that whatever happens after that, people will always say, "Yes, but it's not what we expected when we read so-and-so." Why should it be?

Conversations: I suppose nothing could be more maddening for a writer than to have his or her very first work praised over anything he writes during the next fifty years.

Welty: It's happened to us all, including me. Somebody told me— Reynolds Price told me this past spring that he thought "Death of a Traveling Salesman" was the best story that I had ever written, the first one that I ever wrote. Anyway, it's nice to know that people still like your old work. I guess you don't think of it in chronological terms much. That is, I don't consider that I am progressing or regressing from story to story; I've just reached something different.

Conversations: You've done a great deal of experimenting with point of view.

Welty: Well, I feel that each story has its own demands and that's why I say: it may not be better or may not be worse; it's just something new. I mean new to the writer, not necessarily to the reader. That's the fascination of working with the short story.

Conversations: You did recently write an essay for a book about short story theory edited by Charles LeMay. In it you said that the short story was vital and was going to last partly because of the short story's infinite variety which offers so much scope for experimentation.

Welty: I do feel that very strongly.

Conversations: Well, there are a considerable number of people who feel that a short story is somehow inferior to a novel, simply because it's shorter.

Welty: Isn't that a bore? "Well, I couldn't find *anything* at the library; I just had to bring home some short stories." I love the short story!

Conversations: Then you plan to continue to write short stories?

Welty: Yes! As I told you, I've never started a novel knowingly. What I thought *Losing Battles* and *The Optimist's Daughter* both were going to be is really my favorite form which you can call the "long short story." I guess *The Ponder Heart* is really that and *The Robber Bridegroom* as well—they aren't novels. Ninety pages or 100 pages, that is my favorite length. But I write them as I do a short story, in a sustained, one-piece manner.

Conversations: Whereas with something like *Losing Battles,* obviously, you could not do that way. *The Optimist's Daughter* is a very, very strong novel.

Welty: Thank you. It came to be a kind of essence of what I've been trying. . . . I was glad that I wrote it. Oh, you know, I can see things that I wish I had been able to do better in it. But I felt that I . . . I guess through discipline or experience or something, I had learned a little bit about how to give the story the shape I wanted. I felt that it was cohesive.

Conversations: I assume that you will go back to working on a short story, and not a novel.

Welty: I hope so. It's begun and it's in lots of pages and notes. What I want to do with it is to look at it fresh and to start from the beginning, and get it all in one. I have just finished making a collection of my nonfiction, which I had to get off first. Pieces that I wrote all through the years starting back in 1944, reviews and lectures and what they call "occasional pieces."

Conversations: That's quite a job to get all of the material together, isn't it?

Welty: I had to hunt everything up and make Xeroxes.

Conversations: Will this be a Random House book?

Welty: Yes. They've got it up there now. I have a couple of stories that are still uncollected that have been in *The New Yorker,* but never have been in a book; so I have a start on a book of stories. Now to write my new story.

Conversations: You have taught writing classes; you've been the writer-in-residence—

Welty: Something like that.

Conversations: Do you really think that writing can be taught?

Welty: No, I don't and I always say that at the beginning. I don't think you can tell anyone how to do it, but I do think that with specific works it may do something for a writer to have his work put out on the table, out before him in the open. Once he's finished it. I think that the writer helps himself; I've seen this work and I'm sure you have too.

I had a little class like that at Millsaps for a year and a half. A nice group of about sixteen people, talented, bright. They would bring their stories in, and I was trying to learn as well as they were how to proceed in class. They would read them out loud and the rest would respond. That was it. As the writer reads his own work out loud, he hears it objectively for the first time. And you begin that way to teach yourself. I found that out, too, when I began reading my stories out loud, on my college visits. I could see all these weaknesses that had been in there all these years and I didn't know it. You know, sentences that should have been cut; paragraphs, bits of narrative that should have been transposed—mistakes that were just as clear as day. Finally!

Conversations: You feel that not only poetry, but short stories, too, should be read aloud?

Welty: Well, I find that for me that's a way to learn. No. I think their place is really on the page. That's their destination. But before that's reached, learning by reading aloud seemed to work all right in our class. Since the class was an excellent one, there was a good playback, you know, a good sounding board.

Conversations: Then do you feel that a writing class has its value, has its place?

Welty: Well, they seemed to think that it went off all right.

Conversations: Did you ever take a course in writing?

Welty: No. I didn't write any stories while I was in college—well, I don't think so.

Conversations: You were preparing to be a businesswoman.

Welty: No, I mean, I was thinking about my major. I was majoring in English literature, and I'm terribly glad I had the sense to.

Conversations: But there was no class in "creative writing"?

Welty: No. I was from the start on my own. And that's the way it needs to be. I think it's so much a personal matter. As you know, writing's an interior business, and you have to tell yourself, in the long run, only you can help.

The Town and the Writer:
An Interview with Eudora Welty

Jane Reid Petty / Summer 1977

From *Jackson Magazine* [Jackson, MS], 1 (Sept. 1977), 29–35.
© 1977 by Jackson Magazine, Inc. Reprinted by permission of
Jane Reid Petty.

"It's so hot, the typewriter keys burned my fingers!"

Eudora Welty stood in the high doorway of her house
on Pinehurst, welcoming. Above her the windows were
raised to the room where she writes, the white curtains
still as the summer air.

"Come on in, I've moved downstairs to work. This
heat wave."

Her temporary work place in the library was a card
table set in the middle. Bright books lined every wall. Her
own were leather-bound, a gift from her publisher. A
porcelain Shakespeare reigned on the mantelpiece where
she had placed the day's mail.

"I must show you this photograph that came today,
from the university . . . so funny. I seem to have a little
nanny goat goatee the way the tassel falls from the mortar
board. They sent it to me framed and everything."

Her laughter was refreshing as the cool breeze she'd
waited for. The Washington and Lee University degree is
one in a long list of honoraries awarded the Pulitzer Prize
winner. She had received it with a grace that allowed
room for high spirits, too.

"I appreciate it, but the picture *is* funny."

She sat in the corner of the Queen Anne loveseat,
pretty pillows all around. Across the room stood a piano
reminiscent of Miss Eckhart's stern lessons in the Welty
masterpiece, *The Golden Apples*. A series of framed
etchings and woodcuts hung above the bookcases, with
family treasures on the top shelves and everywhere
books, from writers wanting a reading, editors an opinion, friends begging their books to be hers.

JRP: Is it true that during the thirties this house was something of
a literary salon?

200

EW: A literary salon? We'd never heard the word. Somebody was being ironic.

JRP: Nash Burger, a Jacksonian who later went to the *New York Times,* said that.

EW: Oh Nash *was* being ironic. He says outrageous things to get a rise out of me so I'll scream "What!" He's always done that, you know. We grew up together in the same neighborhood and went to Davis School and Central High.

JRP: He said writers flocked here then as now, and would-be writers, journalists, friends.

EW: Yes, oh yes, the whole town was filled with imaginative activity in those days even, with everybody excited about things like we were. There were all kinds of people who passed through here, even in the thirties.

Just this summer I saw a man who remembered those days. He teaches at Kent State now, but he's from Natchez country. He said "Do you remember George Marion O'Donnell?" and of course I did. He was one of the legends in this part of the country. He died young. He was from Blue Ruin Plantation up in the Delta and knew everyone. He would come through here on the train and come out to this house and regale us with anecdotes—about all the great Southern writers. He knew them all, we didn't know any. We'd feel we'd been in the company of the great. We'd all drink whiskey and then go and help him onto the pullman as best we could, and he'd go on his way. Robert Penn Warren and others said he wrote the very first discerning critical piece on William Faulkner.

JRP: Did Henry Miller come to Jackson about the same time?

EW: Henry Miller! I don't think he knew *where* he was since he didn't know we took him to the Rotisserie for supper three nights in a row. He said "Imagine a town like this having three good restaurants." He never took his hat off for three days, even on picnics. He had written he was coming in a glass automobile, the better to see; he said he'd be coming to Jackson in a glass automobile and wanted to see me. My mother said "Not in this house."

She didn't give a hoot what he'd written in his books, it was what he had written to me. He had offered, some time earlier, to put me in touch with an unfailing pornographic market that I could write for if I needed the money. It could have been a stranger's idea of a charitable suggestion to the author of a first book of short stories (which I was) but neither my mother nor I saw the suggestion in that light. When he got here he didn't have any car at all and had to depend on our family Chevrolet. I took him to Windsor and around. Nash and Hubert Creekmore went everywhere with me. I didn't want to be alone with him in the misguided belief he'd be something like *The Tropic of Capricorn*. Of course he wasn't. He was the most boring businessman you can imagine. He didn't say a word about Jackson in his book, and he was supposed to be writing up his trip.

Now I'll fix us a drink, but the ice may melt in this heat.

(Down the hall to the big kitchen that overlooks the Welty garden, lushly green even in the summer drought, with a little formal bench beneath the oak tree. Laurel Hand might have knelt there beside the walk, dividing the iris bulbs in the Welty novel, *The Optimist's Daughter*.)

Nash could tell Henry Miller everything. He might have worked at the Archives, he knew so much about Mississippi.

JRP: Did you always plan to be a writer?

EW: I worked at other jobs.

JRP: What sort of jobs?

EW: The WPA, the *New York Times Book Review* one summer. And the radio station—Jackson's first—in the Lamar Life Building downtown.

JRP: The one your father built?

EW: Jackson's first skyscraper, thirteen stories high! My father wanted to build something on that land that didn't conflict too much with St. Andrew's Church, which he thought was a beautiful structure. He talked to Dr. Capers about it. He had a sense of building it on that good block, across from the mansion and next to what was then the First National Bank building, a pretty little classical structure. He had it designed in the gothic mode and was very proud of it.

The architect did the gargoyles in the shape of Mississippi alligators. I thought it was clever to make it Mississippi gothic. I'm sorry they blasted the gargoyles off when they remodeled.

JRP: Your father also founded the radio station?

EW: Yes. He was all for the new media, communications. Back in 1925 that was quite forward-looking.

JRP: What was your job?

EW: I wrote the schedule for the radio programs.

JRP: A paying position?

EW: Yes, I think it was sixty-five dollars a month, though that may be what I got from the WPA We had to print our own schedule because the *Jackson Daily News* wouldn't carry it. Fred Sullens fought us from the start, called us traitors, said we were trying to take away their advertising and their news. So I wrote the schedule to mail out to people with feature stories about the Leake County Revellers. . . .

JRP: Who?

EW: The talent we had to get on the radio station to fill in when we didn't have NBC. We had the Leake County Revellers (which is exactly what it sounds like) and the Venetian Trio, consisting of Mr. Coullet and Betty Sue Hutcherson and a third who played "elegant music" on the strings. Also Lois McCormick and her accordian. We had lots of local talent. Another part of my job was writing letters.

JRP: To listeners?

EW: To ourselves. "Dear WJDX, I *love* getting the opera on Saturday. Don't *ever* take it away!" We wrote all the letters and mailed them in. It was in a good cause.

We worked up there in the clock tower. It was our office and about as big as a chicken coop. There was just enough room for Mr. Wiley Harris, who ran the station, and one other person—that was me. Mr. Harris was the announcer and the manager and everything. He'd go in the clock tower and start cleaning out the canary bird's cage and somebody would yell: "Mr. Harris! Mr. Harris!"

(Down the hallway, the telephone rang. She returned quickly and gaily.)

I must finish about the canary bird's cage because Mr. Harris, bless his heart, was the most absentminded man. Across from our office they'd be making frantic signals to him that it was time to announce the station, and at first he wouldn't notice because he was cleaning out the bird cage. Finally they'd get his attention, and he'd go in there and say, "This is Station . . . uh, this is . . . This is Station . . ."

(Eudora Welty giggled.)

We'd finally write it on a piece of paper and hold it up to him—

WJDX—and then he'd say it. Oh, he was utterly polite and every-thing, but he just couldn't remember the name of our station. Everybody adored him.

JRP: What was his background?

EW: He had a great Mississippi background. The Harris ancestors were great statesmen in Mississippi history. And he was so genial, a friend of my father's, and he knew everybody. My father thought he would be absolutely first rate to run WJDX—and he *was*. It was just that he was absentminded.

When he would drive out to the transmitter station (I've been with him in the car) he'd forget to shift gears. And he used to ride these little airplanes, going on business trips to Atlanta and so on. You could stick your neck out of the plane . . . like this . . .

(She did a Mr. Harris imitation.)

. . . he'd forget to pull his head in. The pilot would yell from the cockpit, "Mr. Harris, Mr. Harris, there's a bad storm out there!" Then he'd notice and bring his head back. And he'd say "Yes, oh yes, I did see a good many leaves flying around."

They'd be flying low.

(Like all superb storytellers, Eudora Welty inhabits the character she describes. Genial and forgetful, Mr. Wiley Harris made his brief appearance in the Welty kitchen to remain, at the very least, a light-hearted and affectionate memory.)

JRP: You mentioned a job with the *New York Times Book Review*.

EW: Just for a summer. But speaking of the *Times,* once I think there were six or seven people from Jackson with reviews in the same issue . . . George Stephenson and William B. Hamilton, Hubert and Nash and me—oh, and Ralph Hilton. Ralph edited a newspaper in Jackson for a while, and we all worked on it. He got hold of some space up over a store—and under that flat hot tin roof it was like working inside a popcorn popper. But we survived briefly, even if we never put Fred Sullens and the *Daily News* out of business. Ralph went on to the Associated Press, the State Department, and upwards.

He's retired now and lives on Hilton Head Island (his Hiltons from early days) and edits a country newspaper.

These were all people in my class at Central High School or the one above me. All in the same issue of the *New York Times Book Review*. It was funny.

JRP: How do you account for the exceptional literary talents in your group. Was there a particular teacher who inspired all of you?

EW: We had hard teachers, and I'm very grateful for all that. I think it may have gone back to Miss Duling at Davis School where we really had the fundamentals drummed into us. And in high school we had good teachers.

Of course our set hadn't thought of dropping out. Davis School? You couldn't even have left the classroom without a written excuse from home, and then you'd still have to get past Miss Duling in the principal's office. You couldn't. Miss Lorena Duling could freeze you, maybe kill you, with the look of her eyes. She'd have stared down a drop-out the way Saint Peter would if he caught one trying to get out of the gates of Heaven!

Davis School was right across the street from our front yard, and after school we were within a child's walking distance of everything—the ice cream parlor, the grocery store, the two movie houses, Smith Park. In our Davis School days, Jackson didn't spread very far, and somehow that size gave us more scope.

On summer nights there were band concerts in Smith Park, and whole families—mine included—would stroll there after supper and listen, and let the children dream in the swings, run up the seesaws, climb the statues, and drink lemonade while the band played selections from *William Tell*.

Without the exact approval of home, we children made free of the nearby State Capitol too—riding our bicycles down the steep terraces or the long flights of steps, flying our kites or playing ball on the lawns. We'd skate *through* the Capitol, skimming over the marble floors (very desirable echoes in the rotunda) and rounding a circle in the Hall of Fame, in the center of which, for some unknown reason, was exhibited an Indian mummy in a glass case. It was about the only inaccessible thing I can think of in Jackson, and *it* was a fake.

In the summers we swam in the Pythian Castle swimming pool. It was downtown where Deposit Guaranty Bank is now. They had a public pool and I learned to swim there with water wings. And there was a summer camp for children, as written down by me in a story

called "Moon Lake," with the orphans one week and other people
. . . it happened exactly like my story.

In those days the honor roll of the public schools was considered
news and was carried in full by both daily newspapers. Maybe that
attitude gave us all a sense of the fitness of things.

(Again in the library, "where it's cooler and the ice won't melt,"
talk was of another Southerner, now president of the United States.)

I was trying to explain (as if it were necessary) Jimmy Carter to
some people at Harvard last month. "How do you account for
Jimmy Carter?" they asked. "Do you know people like him?"

I said well I don't know people like him exactly, but I certainly am
familiar with the kind of background he came from. I think that it
could be a lot like the people I knew. We could do things because we
didn't know we couldn't.

You know, when he went to school and he studied hard and he
went to Annapolis . . . he was determined to learn things and he was
bright and he learned them. And there wasn't anybody there saying
"you can't."

At Harvard, they said, "Extraordinary!"
(She laughed, affecting a perfect mimicry of Eastern speech.)

But I didn't think it was extraordinary, she added softly.

You know, he thanked one of his teachers in his inaugural address,
and that's the way we feel about Miss Pearl Spann and others. We've
always thanked our teachers . . . and my own mother was a wonderful teacher, and I lived with her!

JRP: You probably have some interest in saving Central High.

EW: Oh yes, can anything be done? The year we graduated, they
were remodeling. We studied our whole last year with crashing bricks
and timbers. They left all the thick walls, but it was the facade they
were interested in. I think I wrote an editorial for our school paper
about that . . . what will happen to the wisteria vines . . . very sentimental.

JRP: Did you keep a scrapbook as a teenager? Do pieces like your
editorials still exist?

EW: I hope not. They couldn't have been more sentimental and
sloppy.

(The telephone rang again in the hallway, and Eudora Welty went
to answer, closing the library door "to keep the cool air in for you."

Soon she was back.)

JRP: You've participated in the theatre world of New York as well as the literary, haven't you?

EW: I've always been stagestruck.

JRP: Your *Robber Bridegroom* was a hit Broadway musical last season, and *The Ponder Heart* had a successful Broadway run, but both were adapted by other writers for the stage. Is it the same as writing the play yourself?

EW: Not at all. I felt much closer to the New Stage production of *The Ponder Heart* here in Jackson. That seemed mine, and it was an entirely different feeling.

JRP: Have you written plays?

EW: I wrote a lot of musical sketches that were done at the Phoenix Theatre in New York, and then Hildegarde Dolson, a delicious writer, teamed with me to write a musical. We worked all one summer in New York but Lehman Engel, another Jacksonian, read it and said, "You'll never get anywhere because there's not a blackout in it." And you know, he was right. We never did get anywhere. But it was a wonderful excuse to see all the shows on Broadway that season.

JRP: Did you know Lehman Engel as a child?

EW: Oh yes I did, and I knew his three cousins, the Lehman girls.

JRP: There's another exceptional Jacksonian.

EW: Exactly! When I went to New York, he did for me what he always did for everybody from Mississippi who came there—invited them in, took them to lunch, introduced them around, gave them praise. Lovely.

She paused.

Lehman took music from Miss Evelyn Spickard.

JRP: Who was Miss Evelyn Spickard?

EW: A lady in Jackson who gave lessons.

JRP: Did you take piano lessons?

EW: I took from Miss Amanda Stewart Buck. Of course I didn't copy the tragic character of Miss Eckhart (in *The Golden Apples*) from her, but simply her recital and the way she taught. I don't know very many teachers who hit their pupils with a flyswatter like Miss Eckhart did in my stories.

JRP: How early did you want to be a writer?

EW: I don't know. I loved to write, but also I loved to do some other things. I don't think I could say I seriously wanted to be a writer when I got out of college. I was too young and dopey—and ignorant.

JRP: When you were traveling for the WPA writers' project and taking your photographs, had you started to write?

EW: I kept thinking in secret about doing some things. I wanted to write when I went to Columbia. I went there to graduate school with the idea of learning a job to support myself while I tried to be a writer. I studied advertising. My father was exactly right. He said you can never earn a living by writing stories.

Of course he wished I could write everything for the *Saturday Evening Post,* but he gave up on me for that. I was writing all this time but I never showed anything to anyone.

JRP: But it was very soon that your stories were accepted?

EW: I had wonderful luck. The first one I sent out, "The Death of a Travelling Salesman," was accepted. I sent it to *Manuscript* at the suggestion of Hubert Creekmore, my friend and neighbor up the street, and they took it! That was a great day in my life because for the first time something was being looked at critically.

This was from afar, an objective point of view, and they liked it and were going to print it. I didn't care a hoot that they couldn't, they didn't pay me anything. If they had paid me a million dollars it wouldn't have made any difference.

I wanted acceptance and publication. Then other magazines accepted my stories, *The Southern Review* and little magazines like *The Prairie Schooner* and *Accent* at the University of Illinois. I really was very lucky, so much luckier than young writers today who don't have near the kind of people waiting to help them. It's really very troubling.

JRP: Reynolds Price said you have the keenest eyesight in American letters. Do you think of yourself as a visual writer?

EW: I do have a visual mind. I see when I'm reading—pictures. The sounds come more slowly.

JRP: Yet your dialogue, the sounds and cadences, are very true.

EW: Faulkner taught me that, by reading him, that you can much better suggest the way we speak by cadences and punctuation than by any sort of spelling. Faulkner did it so perfectly.

JRP: "Powerhouse" was another early story, but it made the rounds before being accepted by a magazine. Was it at Bread Loaf you said everybody agreed no one would ever publish it?

EW: I'm not sure. It was a story about Fats Waller, you know. I heard him at a dance in Jackson. I remember it was *The Atlantic Monthly* that published it first. I remember because they censored it. They censored my selection of a song that ended the story. It was "Hold Tight, I Want Some Seafood, Mama," a wonderful record. They wrote me that *The Atlantic Monthly cannot* publish those lyrics. I never knew why. I had to substitute "Somebody Loves You, I Wonder Who" which is okay but "Hold Tight" was marvelous. You know the lyrics with Fats Waller singing "fooly racky sacky want some seafood, Mama!"

I read "Powerhouse" aloud to a group in Santa Barbara this summer because I was in a nest of jazz loving people who knew Fats Waller's records. The young ones didn't know them, but the older ones did. It was fun, because when you read it aloud you sort of get into the rhythm of the jazz. I guess it was in the story all the time and was driving me on when I wrote it.

JRP: Are you working on both fiction and non-fiction now?

EW: This is something you need for the interview?

JRP: If you don't mind.

EW: That's what I was doing yesterday, copying a piece on the machine at the public library to send up for the non-fiction book that's to be out soon. I'd come across a review I'd done of Faulkner's *Intruder in the Dust* back in the forties. I thought Albert Erskine (editor at Random House) might want to include it.

It will go over about thirty or more years of writing lectures, book reviews, occasional pieces like that. I keep taking things back and putting more things in. It will be my only book of non-fiction, but maybe I ought not inflict that on people.

JRP: It's eagerly awaited.

EW: I don't know how interested the public in general will be in reviews and lectures on the craft of writing.

JRP: Is your recent Chekhov lecture included?

EW: Yes that's in it, and there are pieces on Willa Cather and Jane Austen and a few others. Not many because I've only done pieces when asked or invited. I haven't a title! Can you think of a title?

(The telephone was ringing with final details about videotaped interviews with Welty and Shelby Foote, scheduled in Jackson.)

After the taping, they want to drive down to the coast for shrimp, she said. "I hope it cools off."

(The book will also include "A Sweet Devouring," an autobiographical piece about a child's reading experience, with the Jackson Public Library as a setting.)

I loved writing that—about Miss Annie Parker.

JRP: She would only let you take out two books at a time?

EW: Right. Until you were dead. You could be eighty-five years old and could still just take out two books. I always wanted more.

JRP: If you read them fast and brought them back, would she let you have another?

EW: She would not! She'd send me home again. "What do you *mean* coming back here on the same day?"

JRP: Is there fiction in progress, as well as non-fiction?

EW: The fiction book has been put off until I get the other done.

JRP: A novel?

EW: It's a long story. I want to have a book of stories. I've written some that have never been collected, and I want to write some more, some short stories. I don't know when I'll finish the fiction book, but I will.

JRP: That's exciting news.

EW: Oh, I look foward to it. One of the things I've been doing is buying the time for it . . . you know, by doing the lectures, which I won't have to do. No book reviews and stuff for a while.

I can just write fiction.

The gift of new Welty fiction was a joyful goodbye. Out on the dark green lawn and into the evening the air was cool. The heat wave had broken.

An Interview with Eudora Welty

Jan Nordby Gretlund / February and June 1978

This interview is the result of two conversations Miss Welty granted to Jan Nordby Gretlund, currently a professor at Odense University, Denmark, at her home in Jackson, Mississippi. Although Mr. Gretlund's questions range widely over Miss Welty's fiction and non-fiction, her personal experiences in Mississippi and New York City, her beliefs about social issues, sin, and Adlai Stevenson, Miss Welty returns again and again to a common theme, a topic that is obviously of pressing concern to her. This theme, briefly, is that the relationship between the author's "real life"—her family, her town, her beliefs—and her fiction is much more complex than most readers are willing to admit. Again and again, Miss Welty reminds us that fiction for her is not a recording of experience nor a statement about life, but that it is, rather, a craft. As Miss Welty tells it, her experiences furnish raw material for her imagination; the imagination then makes the artifact which is the short story or novel. To her, the power of the imagination and the power of language are central.

Other common themes which emerge in her answers are her sense of a rapidly changing South, her continuing curiosity about life, her excitement about the story, and her unbounded admiration for those writers of fiction who are true craftsmen, who know how to make us see and hear. Her own self-awareness, her wry self-irony, is most engaging. Hers is a distinctive and distinguished voice, and we take pleasure in presenting it.

THE EDITORS

Jan Nordby Gretlund: In an essay on Jane Austen, in 1969, you wrote that "the interesting situations of life can, and notably do, take

211

place at home." Was your childhood home full of "interesting situations"?

Eudora Welty: No, not especially. My family wasn't the usual kind in the South, because both my parents came from away. So there were no blood-kin—aunts, uncles, grandparents and so on. Different ones came from time to time, but in those days people couldn't lightly travel from Ohio and West Virginia to visit. So it was mostly our immediate family circle. Of course there were things going on. I had two younger brothers. But in the homes of my friends, who grew up with large families around them, that's where I got that insight—and when I went to my parents' homes, especially my mother's in West Virginia, where she had five brothers. But in the Jane Austen essay, I was writing a generalization of something I believe; I wasn't drawing it out of my own life in particular.

Gretlund: It's obvious from your fiction that you take great pleasure in oral narratives. Was there a tradition of story-telling in your family?

Welty: Yes, on my mother's side they were big story-tellers. When her brothers came here to visit, they would renew the stories of their youth, funny things that happened in West Virginia out in the country. They grew up on a farm. Every name they mentioned would bring out gales of laughter and reminiscences—and there would be songs: "Remember how we used to sing. . . ?" So they would all sing it.

Gretlund: In *Delta Wedding,* Laura says that Uncle George "evidently felt that old stories, family stories, Mississippi stories, were the same as very holy or very passionate, if stories could be those things." Can they?

Welty: To some people. Oh yes, sure—Laura is trying to comprehend that sort of thing. Family stories are where you get your first notions of profound feelings, mysterious feelings that you might not understand till you grow into them. But you know they exist and that they have power.

Gretlund: Some of Laurel McKelva's memories center on the library of her childhood home. Were the classics mentioned in *The Optimist's Daughter* (i.e., Tennyson, Dickens, and Gibbon) in your parents' library?

Welty: Yes, they were. Besides Mark Twain, Henry James, and

Ring Lardner—he's a classic to me. My parents always had books, for which I am deeply grateful. I grew up in a family of readers. No book was prohibited to me. As far as Dickens goes, he meant a great deal to my mother. She had been given a set of Dickens as a little girl, as a reward for having her hair cut. She had chosen that over a pair of golden earrings to pierce her ears, in those days much favored by little girls, especially in Virginia and West Virginia. Her father was very poor, a country lawyer with a large family, but he ordered the books from Baltimore, and they came up the river packed in a barrel. She adored those books, so that later when she was married she brought them to Jackson. When our house caught on fire, she went back into the burning house, although she was on crutches at the time, and began throwing that set of Dickens out the window to save it.

Gretlund: You have said recently that parts of *The Optimist's Daughter* are "literal memory." To what extent are the West Virginia scenes literal memory?

Welty: The physical memory of how it looked—the shoals, the mountains—and how it sounded; the memory of the entire setting.

Gretlund: You have mentioned that *The Optimist's Daughter* meant more to you personally than *Losing Battles.*

Welty: Yes, because of the strictly personal memories. The way my uncles looked coming home at night through the far-off fields, just white shirts showing down the mountain. And the sound of the horses. All the physical sensations were memories of about age three, when you really have very sharp sensory perceptions. I still recall this, and I just put it all in there.

Gretlund: You have often pointed out that you never write about people you know, about real people. And you take great pains to stress that Morgana and its inhabitants are fictitious. Miss Katherine Anne Porter (for one) has not accepted your disclaimer in *The Golden Apples.* Below it, in her copy of the book, Miss Porter has written: "All right honey, we shorely believes you!"

Welty: Well, this is the first time I heard about *that!* Of course, any character you write has bits and pieces of somebody; but they are really conceptions of the imagination, which are invented to carry out what I want to do in the story. Of course, I endow them with things I have observed, dreamed or understood, but no one represents a real person. I couldn't do it; it would defeat me in my fiction. I'm sure Katherine Anne was not being literal in the way you imagine. "Morgana" is a made-up name in the tradition of Delta names. I made it Morgana because of the Morgans that were there, although I made it Morgana first and *then* got the Morgans to name it from. I also like having the idea of *fata morgana,* to show that they were living absorbed in illusions. It all went of a piece like that.

Gretlund: If your fiction is not autobiographical, will you accept it if we call it very personal?

Welty: Oh yes, it is very personal; they aren't the same thing at all.

Gretlund: Do you feel that a critic has any right to be interested in your personal life?

Welty: It all depends on for what purpose. If it is about my work and if it bears on my work—but not just an idle question. It always reaches the point where people begin to ask you out of curiosity. That gets me edgy.

Gretlund: In 1951 you said that "in a story, character and place have almost equal, or even interchangeable, contributions to make." Do you still feel that this is true?

Welty: Now I wouldn't say "interchangeable"; but I think that place can be almost a character in a story. Place can have really important and even dramatic significance.

Gretlund: Obviously, Jackson, Mississippi, is a place that's meant a great deal to you. Is that what is implied by the famous statement, supposedly first made to Miss Porter and later quoted by Flannery O'Connor, that you are usually "locally underfoot" in Jackson?

Welty: That is just an expression—it means I am always moving around here. "Underfoot" just means "present." It is just a localism, and it carries some tinge of being in the way.

Gretlund: I admire your house here in Jackson and also the Southern houses in your fiction. Do buildings like the Shellmound Mansion, the MacLain House, the Renfro Farmhouse, and the McKelva House have a special meaning for you?

Welty: They have a value in the work of fiction because they convey, I hope, the kind of person, the kind of background, the kind of economic background, to which they belong. It is just as evocative to a knowing reader as saying "they never went to school," "they make so-and-so much a year," or "they are poor whites," or "they are ambitious people on the make." You can't make a mistake in something like that and write well. I think it is important, not strictly that you see the house in your mind's eye, but rather that you know these facts.

Gretlund: Mr. Walker Percy has written that "town and writer sustain each other in secret ways." Jackson, Mississippi, has obviously sustained you all your life; but is it necessarily "in secret ways"?

Welty: No. Unless he means that the ways are not very easy to communicate, and they probably have no bearing on what the writing is. The relationship exists, but it should be of no interest to the reader of a piece. I certainly agree that the ways are many and profound.

Gretlund: Do you feel that the essential part of what you say about your fellow Mississippians could have been said with equal validity about anybody else?

Welty: Think of it like this: What I was trying to say about Mississippi was like being drawn to a magnet of that one place—well, there's another magnet in the *next* place! I think the same kind of relationship exists, but the things related wouldn't be the same things. Mississippi and Alabama and maybe parts of Georgia would be sort of alike. Tennessee is very different. Louisiana is totally different. Virginia is different. They all have their own truths. I think the same relationship would exist, but not the same bindings would be there. Of course, this country, as you can see everywhere, is changing. Places are not as different as they were when I began writing.

Gretlund: Is it still possible here in Jackson to send your taproots down far enough to give you a sense of origin?

Welty: I don't know about the ones coming along now. But everybody I grew up with has that same feeling of roots. Children growing up now have lived in five or six houses by the time they are ten years old.

Gretlund: Does that make the children rootless and restless?

Welty: I suppose, and every place is getting to be somewhat alike. In the future, it's not going to be the same, but I think there will still be a deep sense of family to people who have grown up with that. I can't help but think that.

Gretlund: Judge McKelva is buried with a view to the new interstate highway under plastic poinsettias by Fay, his second wife. Is the portrait of Fay, "the little shallow vulgarian," a portrait of the future?

Welty: God, I hope not! But I did mean to suggest that she might have that element in her.

Gretlund: Fay does not seem to have a past.

Welty: And she doesn't miss it! She doesn't know what it is. I don't know if you happened to see the French reviews of *The Optimist's Daughter* when it came out in France? I am not a very good reader in French, but I did get the point—which was that the only sympathetic character in the book was Fay!

Gretlund: Are you fascinated by the Stovalls, Peacocks, Chisoms, Sistrunks, Reids, etc.?

Welty: Oh yes, I love them all!

Gretlund: Are you a little bit horrified also? It has been suggested that you're "looking down your nose" at these people.

Welty: Suggested by whom? That's absurd! I understand them very well indeed. I love them. I know just what's going on in their minds. I don't look down my nose at anyone among my characters. I wouldn't invent somebody in order to look down my nose at them. No, I see the absurd qualities in everybody, and it doesn't matter who they are. I saw the absurd qualities in Judge McKelva, who was of a different order. And in Edna Earle, who is sympathetically telling the story about all the people she herself looks down on.

Gretlund: Is Judge McKelva a "Compson"?

Welty: Oh yes.

Gretlund: Are the Stovalls "Snopeses" who are taking over the South?

Welty: Let's not be literal about things. People won't stand for being divided up like that. In the red clay hills, which is farther to the north and east of Yoknapatawpha, there is quite a different social structure. There is nobody else except what you'd call poor whites. Yoknapatawpha has an entire gamut running from Compson down to Snopes, with many in between. So there is the friction of Snopeses trying to take other people's places. Nothing like that goes on in the red clay hills because nobody has anything. The only reason that Stovalls are different from the others is that they are just *meaner*. None of them has a dime.

Gretlund: You have said that in the early 60s there wasn't much difference between Compsons and Snopeses.

Welty: It was not I, but a friend who made the remark. That was when I was talking about my character in "Where Is the Voice Coming From?"—when someone told me that I had made my murderer a Snopes and he was a Compson. The remark meant that some of the people who are born so to speak in the Compson neighborhood or family had just as rotten ideas about race at that time as the Snopeses. People who could be racist could be in any part of society. It was meant only in that respect and only at that time, I think.

Gretlund: In her story "An Exile in the East," Flannery O'Connor called New York "no kind of place." You have called it a "no man's land," and you have said you can't write stories which take place in New York. Would it ruin your sense of place if you were to use a Northern setting?

Welty: All I meant was that you could not confine anything that you said if you wrote about New York. I love New York; that's why I wouldn't call it "a no man's land" except in the depiction of a character in a story. It was not out of my lack of affection. But as far as using it as material, I find even a town like Jackson too big for me to manage. I have to have a small enough stage, a small enough arena, to confine it and to be able to manipulate what I am doing.

Gretlund: You were in New York at the beginning of the 30s. It seems to have been a good time to be there.

Welty: It was indeed. It was a good time for me. It was my chance, the first I had ever had, to go to the theater, to the museums, to concerts, and I made use of every moment, let me tell you. I was taking a business course, which meant I didn't have to study at all, so I went to the theater. In those days there were many theaters running, the way there are in London now. And you could go on the night you decided to go. Furthermore, you could get a ticket for $1.10 for the cheapest seat, at the cut-rate drugstore in Times Square. You could buy tickets for a show and rush straight over and see it. Also I didn't mind standing up for anything.

Everybody that was wonderful was then at their peak. People like Noel Coward, all the wonderful music hall stars—Beatrice Lillie, Bert Lahr, Fred Allen, both the Astaires, Jack Benny, Joe Cook, and Ed

Wynn. Wonderful dramatic stars, even Nazimova! Katherine Cornell, the Lunts—if I sat down to it, I could make a list of everybody on God's earth that was playing. Martha Graham was dancing solo in a little cubby-hole somewhere. I would go and watch her dance. And Shan-Kar! Everybody was there. For somebody who had never, in a sustained manner, been to the theater or to the Metropolitan Museum, where I went every Sunday, it was just a cornucopia. We had a good group of people from Jackson there at Columbia to start with, so we had company for everything we wanted to do. We could set forth anywhere. We could go dancing in Harlem to Cab Callo-way. We went a lot to Small's Paradise, a night-club in Harlem where all the great bands were playing then; whites were welcome as any-body else.

I was there at the opening of Mercury Theater, during the WPA days. I remember seeing the opening of the black *Macbeth,* which was put on in Harlem, directed by Orson Welles. The play's location was changed from Scotland to Jamaica. The witches were voodoo priestesses. The Queen wore crinolines, the banquet was outdoors under swinging paper lanterns, and the witches were playing the voodoo drums. Hecate was played by a black man dancing on a drum without any clothes on. After the opening night I believe he was made to wear something.

Gretlund: In a *Paris Review* interview (1972), you said that you do not think of yourself as writing out of any special tradition. Do you acknowledge a kinship with other Southern writers?

Welty: Oh yes, I feel that we are all like bathers in the same sea. We all understand and know what we are partaking of. But I think we're each going about it in our own way. So far as I know we haven't had any definite effect on each other's work. There could be many unconscious effects; I read all the time, I love to read, and I live in books a lot. But as far as the act of writing goes, I have never felt the touch of any other imagination on mine as I write. I think that must be true of all of us. I can't imagine, for instance, three more different writers than Katherine Anne Porter, Flannery O'Connor and myself.

Gretlund: Do you still keep up with Miss Porter?

Welty: Yes. She is a dear friend. She is a great lady, whose work I admire from the bottom of my heart. She came here to make a lec-

ture at a college in March 1952. I drove her down to the Gulf Coast.
We looked up Elizabeth Spencer—she lived down there— and we all
had a good time together. We drove round the Coast, then pretty
unspoiled; it bears no resemblance to what is there today after hur-
ricane Camille. Katherine Anne loves that part of the world, we were
getting near—you know she is from Texas near Louisiana—so driving into Southwest Mississippi and Louisiana, we were nearing her
baliwick and I think she felt that. And she lived in Baton Rouge a
long time, where I first met her. All of that country meant something
to her, which Jackson didn't.

I saw her a couple of years ago in Maryland after she had been ill.
She had moved to the apartment out near Silver Spring where she
lives now. She had had cataract operations and a broken hip, but
had most courageously and indomitably recovered from these. She
couldn't see very well yet, but she was getting used to her cataract
glasses. She had a secretary to help with her work, she was keeping
up with everything. I was in New York and asked if I could stop by
and see her. "Darling do you like catfish?" she said. At that time I
had never eaten a catfish in my life. I don't know why, I lived in
catfish country where you could get all you could eat for a dollar
eighty. But she said she was going to cook some. She is a wonderful
cook. So when I came down from New York, Katherine Anne had
been cooking all morning. She had cooked these dainty little catfish
fingerlings, I guess you call them, little tiny things which you dip in
something. She had fresh asparagus, it was early spring and we had
champagne and strawberries. We celebrated. We sat and talked, ate
and drank champagne all afternoon. It was an affecting, really an
indelible visit, and we laughed so much all the way through. It was a
wonderful reunion. I haven't seen her since she had her strokes. But
I have talked to her on the telephone. Yes, I keep up with her.

Gretlund: From an unpublished Flannery O'Connor letter, it ap-
pears that you were on a program with her in November 1962.

Welty: That's right. That was in South Carolina. That's how I met
her. I admired her work a lot. She "hated me" she told me, because I
was supposed to have gone to University of Chicago once and had
illness at home and couldn't leave at the last minute. Flannery went
in my place, and she said, "It was the most awful blizzard I landed in
and I got pneumonia." She had an awful time, and she said, "I ought

to hate you, really." But we turned out to like each other. We got to talk, but *never* did I get to talk to her just by herself, it was always in a crowd or a group. We wrote now and then. I always had it in my mind that we were going to get to talk again. I felt I knew her well and loved her work. I always regret that I didn't have that next meeting.

Gretlund: During a press conference at Oxford, Mississippi, in 1977, you were asked if you had been influenced by William Faulkner. You answered briefly, "Not any!" Is it as simple as that?

Welty: Of course not!

Gretlund: Are you simply fed up with the question?

Welty: I was sort of fed up with the question, and at a press conference how could I go into that? I think the answer is *no*. The answer is no, because I think what was meant by the question was whether or not he had helped me in specific and personal ways. It was a sort of arithmetical question. Just his existence and his works mean a great deal to me. Certainly they influenced me; they meant so much to me. He also in very specific ways taught me so much; how he had done things just dawned on me. I was telling you a while ago about houses. He showed me above all in his work how in Yoknapatawpha *every* single segment of society is represented by place and house and so on. He knew so *much* about all that. He wrote about a much vaster world than anything I ever contemplated for my own work, and he made all of that so visible and so exactly right. Every speech that comes out of a character's mouth *would* be made by a person in that situation, in that kind of family, at that time. He can't go wrong. He showed me the marvelous usage of dialogue and, well, of everything.

Gretlund: Have you consciously tried to avoid rewriting Faulkner?

Welty: No, I think that was what I was answering, too, when I said, "Not any!" It is not so self-conscious a process as that when you write. I think in the act of writing, "how I am going to handle something," and *not* "how would so-and-so have done it," or "I mustn't fall into this pitfall here." It is just trial and error on my own.

Gretlund: Two of your stories particularly remind readers of William Faulkner's work.

Welty: What are they?

Gretlund: "The Burning" and "Clytie."

Welty: As for "The Burning," I think that is a bad story. I don't know why I tried to write anything historical. It is almost the only time I ever tried to write something which is not in our time and place. But I certainly never consciously thought—Heavens! I would hate to be assigned: "try to write something influenced by Faulkner." My pen would drop from my hand.

Gretlund: In retrospect, can you see why some critics would be tempted to see the Faulkner influence in those stories?

Welty: I think that my faults in "The Burning" were the kind of things they blamed Faulkner with. I think the story is too involved and curlicued around with things. I haven't gone back to read that story, but recently Shelby Foote, who is getting together an anthology of Civil War stories, wrote and said he wants to use "The Burning." I wrote back, "I hate for you to use it; I think it is the worst story I ever wrote." He said, "I think it is a good story, and I'm a Civil War expert; you're not." I still didn't go back and read it, but I thanked him and told him to go ahead.

As far as "Clytie" goes, I am sure the answer is that there is "not any" Faulkner influence. I have seen here and there a family going to seed right in the public eye. These things exist in life; of course, Faulkner saw the same kind of thing in Oxford.

Gretlund: It has been taken as proof of the value you place on the concept of the family bond that Robbie Fairchild returns to the family in *Delta Wedding*. Is this justified?

Welty: Is proof needed? Without realizing it, I seem to have repeated a pattern like that in many stories. It is partly because for my point of view in that novel, I have to have an observer come in. In *Delta Wedding* it was the child; Robbie was another outsider. I think the Fairchilds would have accepted her as much as they could accept anyone. The same way that Gloria in *Losing Battles* and Fay in *The Optimist's Daughter* are different types of interlopers with different results.

Gretlund: Is it the purpose of the watermelon fight in *Losing Battles* to point out the negative side of a close family life?

Welty: I wanted to show that the relationships run the whole gamut of love and oppression. Just like any human relationship has the possibilities of so many gradations of affection, feeling, passion, resistance, and hatred. But "negative" is not the word I would use.

Gretlund: The families of *Delta Wedding* and *Losing Battles* are united. But in middle class Morgana this is not so.

Welty: *Delta Wedding* was very middle class, it was just a different kind of family from those in *The Golden Apples.* All those in Morgana seem to have been smaller families, and they weren't isolated on a plantation, they were living in a town. The Fairchilds had a sort of family kingdom in the Delta. And the people in *Losing Battles* had a sort of kingdom in the poor red clay hills, but they were isolated from community life. The family is what they had nothing else but. But Morgana was a whole town and everybody was sort of like a family itself.

Gretlund: Is it fair to say that it is the community that makes Virgie "a little tart" and drives Miss Eckhart to madness?

Welty: I suppose in a superficial way it is. A community that tightly knit can be very exacting of penalties and especially for someone who doesn't belong. And both Virgie and Miss Eckhart qualify. They had more power of feeling than the other people did, and they were pecked down.

Gretlund: You once said about a plot: "There has to be a story, to bear it." Did you worry about the plot when you wrote *Losing Battles?*

Welty: Yes, I did, because, owing to circumstances, I wrote it over an extra long period of time. So things had time to worry me at the intervals when I was not working. I had so much more than I needed, I could have said things in a hundred different ways. So the plot worried me in that respect, how best to show it.

Gretlund: I know you cut *Losing Battles* substantially. Did you cut it enough?

Welty: I think so. But I haven't read it again; I don't like to read my work over. I think there were complaints that it was too long. I am sure that disturbed some people. To me everything in there had its place, or I would have cut it. I can be very ruthless in cutting. I don't put in things because my loving hand wrote it. I felt they were there for a reason.

Gretlund: You have said that you feel more comfortable with the long short story. And you indicated that this is because you feel that less is resolved, more suggested, in a short story.

Welty: That's true, and yet in the short story you don't have the demands of a novel, where everything has to be accounted for. The short story can be suggestive for its own sake. You don't have to develop what you don't need. Whereas in the novel you have to carry everything through. Short-story writing is a freer, more imaginative way to work. Yet it is even tighter knit than a novel because it has to keep its sustained quality. You can't let it down in the middle. It has to be just right.

Gretlund: One of the differences between a short story and a novel is supposed to be that the characters in a short story are born "fully grown." Yet the characters in *Losing Battles* seem "fully grown" from the very beginning.

Welty: Some are and some aren't. You know, the E. M. Forster classification, some are round and some are flat. The flat ones never change, and there are plenty of flat ones that don't ever change in *Losing Battles*. But all the main characters have many possibilities. There is a character like Aunt Beck, who is always gentle yet puts her foot in her mouth when she says things. The very time she wants to be the most tender, she says something that can really hurt, without knowing that she does it. There is Miss Lexie, who started out as a flat character. But all kinds of complications come in when we know about her life in nursing Miss Julia. All the torments she went through—I considered that *that* happens to her. I think Miss Julia is the factor that shows the depth of the others—the ones that were touched by her. And Judge Moody, who might have started as a flat character, is far from it. Everything is aroused in him by what happens. And Jack, who is not by any means just a straight hero-type, has deep feelings. He is deeper than Gloria, who claims to be the sensitive one. He feels where she can't. If she hadn't had that shallow streak, she would have done better by Miss Julia.

Yes, I feel that *Losing Battles* did give me room to develop the characters.

Gretlund: Do you still feel that "character is a more awe-inspiring fish" than situation in a short story?

Welty: A novel can do so many more things and develop so many more things than a short story. Its situation and scope, all of that is a different kind of thing, so that you might have more important things you can develop in a novel than you could in a short story. But character is a more profound subject than situation in either short story or novel.

Gretlund: You once said that "in a story character and place have almost equal, or even interchangeable, contributions to make."

Welty: Now I wouldn't say "interchangeable." But I think that place can be almost a character in a story. Place can have really important and even dramatic significance.

Gretlund: To what extent do you make conscious use of Greek and Roman mythology in your writing?

Welty: It is conscious, clearly. I've lived with mythology all my life. It is just as close to me as the landscape. It *naturally* occurs to me when I am writing fiction. It is not a far-out, reached-for something. I feel no sense of strain when I use mythology. Maybe I use too much of it; I don't know. I have grown up with legends and fairy tales and I've always loved them. I still like to read folk tales from all kinds of other lands.

Gretlund: Critics have been quick to refer to Frazer's *Golden Bough* and Bulfinch's *Age of Fable* for many aspects of your fiction. Are the critics overdoing it?

Welty: I have read the one-volume edition of *The Golden Bough,* but I didn't read that till I was out of college. But myths themselves I've read all my life. Many of my childhood books were of Greek and Roman myths, also Norse and Irish. The whole Andrew Lang series of fairy tales and fables, and *Aesop's Fables* were in my house.

Gretlund: Did you read Bulfinch's *Age of Fable?*

Welty: Never have read that one. I am interested in fables as *told.* I truly haven't read enough of the critics to make a sweeping statement. But I think that anyone who attributes my stories to myths very specifically and thoroughly is overshooting it. I would rather suggest things.

Gretlund: The ending of *The Golden Apples* is a case in point. When Virgie is sitting alone on the Court House steps, she is joined by a black woman. One critic has seen the black woman as Minerva, the stealing servant, *and* Minerva, the goddess of wisdom.

Welty: Oh, that really drives me crazy. It makes me sort of frantic. The end of my book was the most natural thing in the world. It was just a drawing together of two people without a roof. The old black woman, who has nothing, and Virgie, who is bereft at that moment. Yet they both have something; one of them's got a chicken, and the other has got all these things in her mind. No! When I hear something like that, it drives me to the other extreme of saying something literal, like I have just said.

Gretlund: In an introduction to an interview with you, Ms. Alice Walker has maintained that "the past will always separate" the races. Do you believe this to be true?

Welty: I don't think so. I have black friends who agree with me that it isn't so. Recently I was at Yale with some humanities scholars, answering questions. The woman sitting next to me was black, and they were all talking about the problems of the 60s. Several of the scholars were from foreign countries, asking questions about the situation here, how strained it was. And the black woman said to me, "You know, during it all, when it was just at its worst back in the 60s, and I was a school teacher, my mother said to me, 'Why aren't you all upset about this?' and I was laughing. I said, 'I guess it is because I am a Southerner.' " Which I really loved. I, too, always knew we would understand each other; we always have in the past.

Gretlund: Your 1942 essay, "Ida M'Toy," is one of your great portraits of black women, but where is genuine black and white friendship in your fiction?

Welty: I see it in a good many places. I meant to convey that Missouri, in *The Optimist's Daughter,* is a true friend of Laurel's. Missouri is her maid in the household, but they were also big friends and both of them knew it.

Gretlund: Does Missouri help Laurel much?

Welty: I think she does. When Judge McKelva's body is being carried out, it is Missouri that stands with Laurel and helps her. She helps her with the bird too, doesn't she? I mean, in these really wrenching experiences that Laurel is going through by herself, Missouri's instincts are perfect. She is always sensitive to what is going on. In *The Ponder Heart,* too, Narciss is the mainstay of the family.

Gretlund: In one of your manuscripts for *The Ponder Heart,* you wrote: "I think they only asked [Miss Teacake] because she was somebody white, the rest of their testimony was black as midnight." Was this deleted for artistic or for political reasons?

Welty: It isn't good writing. Nothing political had anything to do with the case. I am sure the reason I took that out was that it was out of character for Edna Earle to say that.

Gretlund: In the early 50s you showed great political interest in the career of Adlai Stevenson. Has there been anything in politics to be enthusiastic about since then?

Welty: Neither before nor since. He just really touched my mind and heart. I was so enchanted, to have a person like that wanting to be in public life. I happened to be in New York at the time he was running so that I got to hear him in person. I think a lot of people in this country felt the same way I did, wanting so much to help Stevenson be elected. When he didn't win, I lost interest again.

Gretlund: It has been claimed that you are indifferent to the larger social and political problems of your region. Is it true that you overlook the regional problems?

Welty: Whoever has claimed this, it isn't accurate at all. What is true is that I don't think of myself as a writer of fiction who seeks to make it a platform for my opinions. I am a very interested citizen and try to keep informed on everything and to vote. But I don't think fiction is the place to air those principles, except for the moral principles of right and wrong—and these I try to let characters show for themselves. I tried to put all this in a piece I wrote for the *Atlantic* [Oct. 1965] called "Must the Novelist Crusade?"

Gretlund: It is clear that the object of your fiction can't be social criticism, but can the novelist *avoid* crusading?

Welty: You can't avoid dealing with moral matters, because that's what life is about. But I think it is wrong when somebody like Steinbeck crusades in his fiction. That's why Steinbeck bores me so. The real crusader doesn't need to crusade; he writes about human beings in the sense Chekhov did. He tries to see a human being whole with all his wrong-headedness and all his right-headedness. To blind yourself to one thing for the sake of your prejudice is limiting. I think it is a mistake. There's so much room in the world for crusading, but it is for the editorial writer, the speech-maker, the politician, and the man in public life to do, not for the writer of fiction.

Q: How can you say that fiction is "stone deaf to argument" and then go on to write "The Demonstrators"?

Welty: I think that was right and true, because I was letting all that speak for itself. "The Demonstrators" is written right out of that kind of situation, in the thick of it.

Q: And the issues are implicit?

Welty: Yes, and the fact of the great complexity of it, how inexpressible some things are. And how so many of the people who would feel the most are powerless, and so many of the wrong-headed people have all the power. To me it was consistent to write "The Demonstrators" and say what I did.

Gretlund: Yet readers of your well-known fiction find many topical elements. In *Losing Battles,* for instance, you deal with electioneering, depletion of woods, bad teachers' training, and a poverty-stricken orphanage, just to mention some of the potentially political issues.

Welty: These things are there. And there are people there who are living with all these handicaps and things that should be righted. *Losing Battles* was written about the 30s, when nobody had anything with which to do it. Injustice was staring everybody in the face—and they were living in spite of it and through it and with it. I am not saying that is a good way to be; I am saying it is a terrible way to be.

Gretlund: You do not seem to be interested in the concept of "sin" or in the idea of "evil." This is so uncommon in an American writer that perhaps it deserves a comment.

Welty: I am, though. *Not* in "sin"—not from a Roman Catholic point of view like Flannery O'Connor, because I am ignorant of that religion. But I do believe that there is "evil." I believe in the existence of "evil," or else your reaching for "good" could not mean anything. I do feel there is "evil" in the world and in people, very really and truly. I recognize its power and value. I do! I thought there was "evil" in Fay in *The Optimist's Daughter.* And there is "evil" in a society that does wrong things.

Gretlund: It seems that you think very little of organized religion.

Welty: I don't know where you got this opinion. I am not a frequent churchgoer, but I am a reverent person.

Gretlund: In your fiction you have always treated the prejudice between denominations with scornful humor.

Welty: Or amusement, I'd say. Up in the East, when Carter was running for President, everybody said, "How could a Baptist ever be President!" In the South, that is the structure of the society of a small town. It is in a churchy society that most Southerners are brought up, and it is what they mention in every other word in their conversation. In a small town like Banner, if the Baptists couldn't be against the Methodists, they'd have nothing to talk about. My amusement has nothing to do with reverence or with God, it is *society,* and I am writing about it in that aspect.

Gretlund: It is obvious that you don't like it when critics use novels as "fishponds" for their criticism. Isn't it surprising then that you yourself have written so much criticism?

Welty: Not especially, because I do think I write out of a fellow feeling for fiction writers. I'm really trying to get at what I think they were trying to do. I am not trying to take something there and put it here; I am trying to understand what *they* did. I like it when someone writes that way about me, which many critics do. On the whole I feel that I really do approach other fiction writers with the feeling of a fiction writer, instead of the feeling of a critic. I like to write about the process of writing that I have discovered through my work, and what I think I have learned reading others.

Gretlund: In your new book of non-fiction, you chose not to include pieces like "The Abode of Summer" and your little essay on the nature of the fairy tale. Why did you leave them out?

Welty: Only because I thought they repeated material already in the collection. I took out the one on fairy tales because I had a piece called "Fairy Tale of the Natchez Trace." I cut a great number of things because I wanted to make a sort of balanced selection. I liked "The Abode of Summer," too, but I thought I had enough on Mississippi, such as "Notes on River Country," a more considered and longer piece. I chose among things of a kindred type and tried to take the one that I thought well-developed.

Gretlund: You have included most of your purely critical essays in the collection, such as "Place in Fiction," "Words into Fiction," and "The Short Story."

Welty: Yes, just about all of those, because they were considered essays on my part. I really worked on those; they were my long-time thoughts about fiction. Whereas a review is something done with a deadline. You do the best you can, but it is not something you've worked over for months.

Gretlund: There isn't anything by "Michael Ravenna," your World War II pseudonym, in your book of non-fiction.

Welty: No. I didn't save any of those reviews because they weren't worth saving. I don't even know what they were.

Gretlund: For how long did you write under a pseudonym?

Welty: This is to exaggerate my signing another name to an occasional book review. I didn't work at the *New York Times* very long, through a summer (1944). And I was writing reviews under my own name at the same time, holding down a full-time job. So I didn't have too much time to be "Michael Ravenna."

Gretlund: Has your book-reviewing stolen time from the fiction you wanted to write?

Welty: I like reviewing books. I take my pick. I couldn't write about a book I really don't like, you know. It is a source of pleasure to write about books I do like, and I do that and other things to earn a little money on the side. That includes going around lecturing. I have had a year of that, which is unusual. I like it, but it takes a great amount of time and still more energy.

Gretlund: Are you working on any fiction at present?

Welty: That's what I'm waiting to do. I have just now finished writing a piece for Mr. Bruccoli. This was an "Afterword" on a novel called *The Great Big Doorstep* by E. P. O'Donnell from 1941. This is in the Lost American Fiction Series. I was asked if I had a nomination for such a series, and I nominated this book. I was thrilled when I was asked to write the "Afterword."

That's all. That is the last assignment that I promised. I can get back to my fiction—after this interview!

Eudora Welty in Type and Person

Reynolds Price / 1978

From *The New York Times Book Review*, 7 May 1978, 7, 42–43. © 1978 by The New York Times Company. Reprinted by permission.

R.P. Are you aware, as you turn from writing fiction to prose essays, of different problems? Are they two entirely different processes for you?

E.W. I think of writing stories as going *south* and writing essays as going *north*.

R.P. Against the wind?

E.W. No, just two different directions—upstream and downstream. I can't work on them simultaneously. I like both. I think it's more natural to me to write stories, but I like writing essays. I think I'm not a born critic, but I may be a born appreciator. I like to write about things I like.

R.P. The liking is steadily reflected in this present selection from nearly 35 years of essays and reviews. With the single exception of your review of a biography of Ford Madox Ford (a writer you do admire), you haven't written about any writer or any thing that you haven't at least 90 percent liked. Has that been a conscious choice?

E.W. Yes, it has. I don't accept the review of a book that I know I'll dislike. I don't enjoy it. I really write for pleasure in reviewing as much as I write for pleasure in writing stories. I like the work of doing it, so I prefer to write about something that strikes my imagination or that I can admire. I felt at one time that I should have written a preface to this book to say that the essays and reviews weren't written with a whole in mind—since I'm not a professional critic, I don't write to compare one person with another person. I write each one only about that subject. I wasn't setting out to put Willa Cather and Jane Austen into their related levels of excellence.

R.P. Some hierarchy of genius.

E.W. That is not my way of reading or thinking or anything else. I like each thing for what it is. But I didn't think it was necessary to explain that; anyone would see it if they began to read. I only regret, even though I chose these out of a great number, that I'd never written some that I wish I had—on P. G. Wodehouse, V. S. Pritchett, Edward Lear, travel books about places that I love. I wish I could have written more; I still intend to just because I love them.

R.P. Have you ever wished you could make a statement against a book? Have you ever felt that a book was dangerous and should be combatted?

E.W. I don't feel like setting up as a moral judge of anything—no, I don't. I never felt that any book was dangerous, that I can think of right off the bat. (However, my mother thought that the Elsie Dinsmore Series books would be dangerous for me and forbade them to me as a child.) I don't feel that it's up to me to pronounce judgment on whether somebody should have *written* a book; *that* would be dangerous. It's O.K. with me for people to write anything; I don't have to read it or agree with a word.

R.P. Whenever I read a book by a good writer, I'm always fascinated when I think I begin to discover the one word that's recurring, almost unconsciously, as a kind of secret motto or emblem for the book. The word I noticed most frequently, even in this selection from years of work, is *radiance* in its various forms. It recurs a dozen or so times and clusters round the writers who seem closest to you, both as reader and writer—Jane Austen, Chekhov, Willa Cather, E. M. Forster, Katherine Anne Porter, Henry Green, Elizabeth Bowen. And it seems to me that the word contains and summarizes an important theme of all the essays—that the writer is a visionary, whose gift is a gift of actual and internal vision; that the writer is someone who both sees and radiates. Well, the point of the speech I seem to be making is this—have you found in your own writing of fiction that a story comes to you entire or do you find that you get a piece, a *glimpse,* and that the story radiates from there; that it manufactures itself around a fragment of vision?

E.W. I never had thought about it as seeing it from a piece, but of course that may precede the way I think of myself as seeing it. I do see a story, feel a story, as a whole before I ever begin the process of thinking how to work it out; and, as you know, I do a lot of revision, but it's always toward getting closer to the original—I hate to use the word *vision* in relation to my process of writing—the original perception of what it is I want to do. It *is* a whole, but also, if it has any vitality, it allows changing in working toward it. It has to be flexible. To be alive it has to remain always capable of moving and growing itself, in the work. I didn't know I used the word *radiance* all the time; but I can understand why I might have—having a visual mind (literally visual) and a pretty good observing eye, through having trained it over the years. But the way of perception, that a writer must learn, is also an act of vision; and it's the act you can recognize in the writer you're reading—it's like visions meeting (isn't it?), which is what you seek.

R.P. Yes, and more—as your uses of *radiance* began to mount, I came to feel that the essays combined to advance a concept of the great writer as a kind of nuclear power plant, a large center of energy, radiating for us; and that the nuclear fuel is love, a deep tender fascination with human life.

E.W. That *is* what it is. It goes to the center of my being, my feeling for what I've read. It's a *vital* force.

R.P. Well, you know I agree; but it's worth considering that there almost always have been sizable writers who could hardly be said to work out of love for the human species and that there are many such younger writers working today. Perhaps you and I and certain writers in older traditions had kinds of *luck* which made tenderness come more naturally to us than it does to young people today.

E.W. I think that's absolutely true. I don't think we ever questioned it. What young writers are doing today is questioning. They tend to doubt the truth of something that doesn't hurt pretty badly; there's a sort of distressing feeling that if you admire or like something, there's a *lie* in it somewhere—either in it or in yourself—which is such a frightening prospect when you think of all that can be missed out of life if you can't embrace a little more of it than comes in through such a narrow squint-hole, like the leper's squint in a church. Not like Swift! He hated but saw everything. I feel now sometimes that so much is being left out, and so many young writers feel that their proper place is one of isolation from what they're writing about that there's no sense of anything *joining*. I'm not saying this in a condemnatory way, but in a concerned way, though I do often get the terrible feeling "How facile!"

R.P. The chanting of *Woe!* as if woe were new or perpetually appropriate.

E.W. It's not that I don't feel sympathy and try to understand—I think I do to some extent—but I also get impatient because I think: "How long will this go on? You'd better hurry up, kids. There's a lot to be seen out there." When you're playing with stakes that are all dynamite, all cruelty, all hideous fate, what takes the trick is something even more violent, more hideous. You could need to get back with another set of ingredients to work with. You can say the same things with anything in the world. They're not saying anything new; they're just saying it more violently. There's plenty of violence in life, and I would be the last to deny it—none of my fiction does deny it—but it comes from within human beings. *That's* its source, and you can write about that source with any set of tools you wish. The novel has got to reflect life—life is violent and it has to show violence, but the novel doesn't have to show it in a self-defeating way.

R.P. You point out in one of the essays that the novel and life are in many ways opposites of one another, that form and order are not delivered to one on a seashell by the waves but are made out of life. However great its need to reflect, are there certain things you can't imagine the novel reflecting, doing? Are there subjects or themes which you've found the form itself to be resistant to?

E.W. I think the novel can do about anything it wishes to do, but I don't think it can stand still. I don't think it can be static, and I don't think that it can get along without finding a line of communication that is indelible, something that has always been there in human emotions. I don't think you can write about something that is not felt. If a novel does not *connect* with us, it's lost.

R.P. Maybe the one thing it can't do is *not* be about interesting people.

E.W. It can't be about un-people—abstracts.

R.P. The great writers you've written about and that we've discussed were certainly people; and if they were big repositories of energy, then it would seem to follow that everything about them might conceivably be of value to us. Yet I think I can detect in your reviews of the letters of Virginia Woolf and Faulkner, in your review of the posthumous stories of E. M. Forster, that you have a deeply

instinctive repugnance for examinations of the private lives of the
recently dead. Am I right?

E.W. You're certainly right—especially in a way that seems without relevance to their work. I think a writer's life does belong to the
writer, as any human being's life does; and, as I think you'll agree,
you spend your life transmuting all you've been able to understand
from the experience of living into your work. To me, *that* should
stand for what your life has meant to you; and the part that does not
appear to a reader, I think, should remain a part of the writer. I
agreed with W. H. Auden, who in his will directed that everyone
destroy his correspondence. I thought that was right, and I was mad
when people didn't do it and went on and printed things anyway—
that's accepted as the thing to do, with just a shrug. I don't think it's
morally right to do such a thing.

R.P. Have you ever thought of an *auto*biography?

E.W. Who, me? No. I've had a very quiet life, on the surface; and
I don't think anyone would be too fascinated by that *per se*. I cherish
many things in my life that I would like perhaps to write about sometime—I've done it.

R.P. What wasn't on the surface is in the work anyway, isn't it?

E.W. Yes.

R.P. You do have two essays in *The Eye of the Story* which ex-
amine stories of your own. In the one which looks at "No Place for
You, My Love," you say, "It seems likely that all of one writer's
stories do tend to spring from the same source within him. . . . All of
one writer's stories carry their signature because of the one impulse
most characteristic of his own gift—to praise, to love, to call up into
view." It's a hard question to ask, but do you have a sense of a single
source within yourself from which the stories come?

E.W. Well, I could answer generally. I think it probably is a lyrical
impulse, to—I don't know if the word *praise* is right or not.

R.P. It's the word I was thinking.

E.W. That's as near as I can get—I think it's probably that. I imagine again that must be the most common impulse that most of us do
share, and I think it's a good one to share.

R.P. What particular skills flow out of that single source in yourself?

E.W. I don't know. I think it presumes that you will be *attentive* to life, not closed to it but open to it—to genuinely try to see it for what it is *to you,* without gross distortion (there has to be the distortion of passing through any personality). So I also think attentiveness and *care* for the world, a feeling of concern and a wish to connect with it. I suppose all of this sounds very primary, but it is primary—it goes right down to the source. It's getting something right—not making mistakes about facts, about people, and the wish not to make mistakes extended as far as you care to go. I think really below everything—or above everything; which is more fundamental to say?—is the caring to be right and the caring for what is *there,* feeling that life is worth your giving everything you have to it. That all sounds so simple.

R.P. So do the Ten Commandments. You say in one essay: "Willa Cather used her own terms; and she left nothing out. What other honorable way is there for an artist to have her say?" You've certainly used your own terms, in a crowded field; and you've had quite a say—and are still having it. Are you conscious, after so many books, of having left out some important piece of knowledge—some important source that you'd like to get at?

E.W. I can well believe that there are many; there are plenty of things I don't know. We all work with what we have; and, even if you leave something out in a literal sense, you have probably put it in, in another sense to you—what stands for it, in other terms. You need to know what *is* there. It would be very different if you left something out because you never realized it was there in the world. That would be a very serious omission. Everyone has something to deal with. You can't live without having limitations that you're aware of, but I'm sure it's been often said that the limitations themselves are the, well, shall I say springboard?

A Conversation with Eudora Welty

Martha van Noppen / 9 August 1978

From *The Southern Quarterly*, 20 (Summer 1982), 7–23. Reprinted by permission.

The following interview is part of a taped conversation with Eudora Welty at her home in Jackson, Mississippi, on 9 August 1978. I arrived at Welty's Tudor-style home at 1:30 in the afternoon, after receiving perfect directions from her over the phone, and was warmly greeted and shown to a sofa in front of a large window. Miss Welty, sitting in a wing-back chair, immediately put me at ease with her lyrical, distinctly Southern voice. Beginning the interview with a reassuring "Don't worry," she generously discussed her work and beginnings as a writer. Excerpts from that discussion follow.

MvN: In *The Optimist's Daughter* you've used the limited omniscient narrator, through Laurel's point of view. Did that story give you any trouble, as far as viewpoint or narration is concerned?

Welty: No, because the whole story's conception was in the character of Laurel, so I didn't have to work to get it into her point of view. I thought of it and wrote it out of that point of view. It was my given—my set of circumstances out of which I wrote it, so it didn't cause me trouble. It was my real method of working it out. . . . It's told through her point of view and there's no other point of view.

MvN: Does that mean that Laurel's a totally reliable character?

Welty: What do you mean by "totally reliable?"

MvN: Can we believe her perceptions?

Welty: Well, I certainly intended for you to believe her. She may be mistaken in some things, but the whole story is a growth of her understanding, so she understands much more at the end than she did at the beginning. But there isn't any lying going on. She is writing, speaking in good faith all the way through. It all depends on what your intention is. I wasn't trying to play tricks. I've seen that used in the detective story; the narrator who may be a villain is consciously trying to trick the reader. Well, that has nothing to do with the kind of thing that I was doing in this novel. I was writing with a passionate conviction on the part of one who is telling it that she was trying to get at the truth, so it was the complete opposite of any chicanery.

MvN: I particularly like the way Laurel is revealed—slowly.

Welty: It is gradual. I think some people said that it was a surprise to find her emerging as she did, but naturally I wanted her quiet in the beginning before the situation was revealed. She was present and tense, and you knew that it all mattered to her. But she herself didn't move into a prominent position until the story progressed.

MvN: Would you call the scene with the breadboard the epiphany of that story?

Welty: Well, I don't use such terms to myself much. I mean, it's a Joycean term. It's much more dramatic in the sense Joyce uses it and has more reverberations. I suppose you could call it that, but I don't like pretentious words. I suppose it was more of a means of revealing what I was trying to do, and in a sense it was symbolic in the gesture, but also it was a very real material thing, and everything was sort of brought together, into focus, with that. In that sense, you could call it, I suppose, "epiphany." If you wanted to force a word on it, you could call it that. I didn't call it that to myself.

MvN: We, the reader, know from Laurel's memory in the course of the novel that she has lived through the deaths of her husband, mother, and now father, but we aren't actually present with her husband and mother, as we are with her father. I thought that the moment with the breadboard, when Laurel says to Fay, "I see the whole solid past," was the point of recognition or self-realization for Laurel, when everything comes together for her.

Welty: Yes. Exactly. That's what I was trying to do. That describes it much better than a word like "epiphany." Really, it was a focusing and bringing together and revelation—self-revelation—when everything cleared for her. She realizes a great many complicated things at once about herself and her parents, and about Fay—all together.

MvN: In "Place in Fiction" you say that place lies in the fact that it has a more lasting identity than we have and that we attach ourselves to it. I believe this, and also believe that's how we come to understand who we are in all our connections in the world. But doesn't there come a time in some people's lives when they no longer want to be attached to the very things that helped shape their identity, a time when they want to create new identities? I'm thinking now of Laurel, who at the beginning of *The Optimist's Daughter* has already been away from home for some time.

Welty: No, because what meant the most to her, I think, was her identity down there. That didn't mean that she couldn't fall in love and marry and live somewhere else, but that wasn't breaking with her family. I don't think that one means denying the other. I think there are people such as you describe, but it was not true of Laurel.

MvN: I meant to suggest that, rather than breaking with anything, Laurel might have needed to see herself identified with something else—particularly for the reasons that her own community in Mount Salus sees her differently. Mrs. Pease says, "If you come back you'll be a stranger."

Welty: People always say that. But she knew where she was—her identity was always clear. . . . If you go away, you know, people always think you must be somebody else if you come home again. At least they used to. You used to always need to explain why you'd been away. But I think that's a Southern small town characteristic. She herself was quite secure in her identity, and she did have a definite, strong sense of identity with family and place.

MvN: Laurel gave her mother so much credit—sometimes more than herself, it seems, for that kind of strength. Even though Becky's not present, except in Laurel's memory, I felt that Laurel has as much strength as her mother.

Welty: Well, I don't know. I think she was getting ready to have it, anyway. She was learning to have it because she'd had to be strong for her mother and for her father. In the end, she had to support them with her own character, although she was taking support from them too. In this three-way interchange of everybody giving everybody something—some taking something just when they all were by Becky's bed, all holding each other's hands—I tried to give that feeling of support and dependence that just ran in an endless line among the three of them.

MvN: Walter Sullivan, in *A Requiem for the Renascence,* says that when a writer's society becomes fragmented, an uncertain moral vision is reflected in the writer's work. Speaking about the South, he suggests that Laurel has an excess of virtue for this reason, and that she has nothing to sustain her. Did you mean to suggest that Laurel represents the decay of moral certainty for the South?

Welty: No, that never occurred to me. I wasn't using her as a figurehead. I wasn't writing anything about the South. She is a person, a human being.

MvN: I wonder if you would mind saying anything about the role or the function of "memory" in *The Optimist's Daughter?*

Welty: I've said all this the best I can, and I've already written it, you know, in the novel. I worked so hard on what I said about memory. . . . I can't put it into words in a spontaneous conversation in a way that says something I worked very hard to make clear and plain in my work. It's just not easy to do. I do think memory is of the essence—it's the organ that accounts for our continuity of feeling and understanding.

MvN: I brought up the subject of "memory" in *The Optimist's Daughter* because I think that some of the things you do with memory in that novel are similar to what Shakespeare does in *The Tempest.*

Welty: Oh, my.

MvN: I remember that somebody compared *Losing Battles* to *The Tempest.* For me, the comparison can be made for *The Optimist's Daughter.*

Welty: I don't know—that just leaves me floored. Thank you for your generosity. I appreciate that very much.

MvN: It's just such a magical kind of thing. Much of what Shakespeare uses Prospero for, with respect to "memory," is very much like what you do.

Welty: Following through on what you said—the end, with the bubble, is like a memory, which is like a bubble that holds all this. Well, it's a form of not only storing things, but of cherishing things. It's the organ for all of that, so it's connected with—

MvN: Preservation?

Welty: Yes, preservation, and with love. Also, with patience and endurance. With all those things.

MvN: I want to ask about Laurel's parents in *The Optimist's Daughter.* Both had eye problems, but Laurel suggests that there was a difference. She says to Miss Adele in the kitchen, after her father's funeral, "It wasn't like it was with Father," that is, her mother's death, I think you meant.

Welty: I think she was referring to her mother's mental wanderings and troubles, which were connected with her lack of vision, you know. She got confused and distressed. Her father didn't have that. . . . Where a quotation comes in a story means everything—it's all interlaced with the whole story. It has all these other meanings, too, that come through the context. . . . They were two different kinds of deaths, both with the eyes and so on, but her mother died in distress of thinking she'd been betrayed. Her father was just patiently enduring it, and dying, you know. There are a lot of differences.

MvN: Did he actually die from the retina problem?

Welty: Well, it was so complicated. You can't just say it was this, that, or the other, because the way Fay treated him also had something to do with it. She came in and tried to jerk him off the bed. And in those days, when you operated for cataracts, you couldn't move the head for a long time. You can now. I mean people get up and walk out, more or less. He also was old and he made a mistake, I think, in his marriage, and he wasn't too ready to go on with everything. I think it was a whole lot of things together.

MvN: Did his realization of what he had done in marrying Fay bring on his death?

Welty: I didn't want it to be just absolutely arithmetical, you know, like this plus this plus this equals that. I did want to suggest all kinds of complications. I don't want to say it's this either, or that, because I wanted to *suggest*.

MvN: Fay didn't intend to kill him in her selfishness. I didn't think the novel said *that*.

Welty: No. But her whole attitude—like "Get up"—was enough to shock and to hurt. No, she didn't physically attack him.

MvN: I loved the irony of Judge McKelva's remark when Dr. Courtland is showing Fay something on the wall chart about the eye. Judge McKelva looks at Laurel and says, "That eye wasn't fooling, was it?"

Welty: (Laughs.)

MvN: Did you mean to suggest something symbolic about the birds in this novel—the pigeons and the bird in the house during the storm?

Welty: Yes, I did mean to suggest. In the case of the pigeons, of course, this very young child was really horrified by all the acts that pigeons went through—regurgitating and reaching down each other's throats. You know how pigeons do.

MvN: No, I didn't. Is that how they eat?

Welty: Well, they feed each other, and especially when they're courting. Oh, their acts are really just revolting to the aesthetic sense. It would be very startling to a little girl.

MvN: Laurel drew a connection immediately from what the pigeons were doing to what people do.

Welty: Yes. Her mother, the grandmother, said, "They're just hungry like us." It's all nature and so on, and then in the end, when the bird does come in the house, it's just like a return of everything to her. It is terrifying to think of anything with wings that can't get out—the caging of anything, a spirit. I have a terrible panic in a crisis when a bird gets in this house. That was written out of real fear. And, it's also a superstition that a bird in the house means death. Did you ever hear that?

MvN: You said it was more than a superstition, but, yes, I have heard of that superstition.

Welty: Oh, it was. I mean, there are all kinds of things you could bring to bear on it. Again, I've tried not to be too specific, but just to suggest the menace of things, and the presence of something, and the difficulty of an imprisoned spirit. She herself was trying to get out.

MvN: At the end of the story, when Laurel releases the bird, sets it free, she sees, we are told, not the body or tail of the bird, but the shape of a crescent moon. I really like that.

Welty: I'm glad you liked it. You try to make anything you use suggest lots of things, you know, not just one thing, but a whole lot of things.

MvN: I felt that in this novel more was given to the memory of Laurel's mother than to her father—that I knew more about her mother, even though the part about her mother came from her memory, and her father was an actual character in the book.

Welty: Well, I think the mother was the one who influenced both

Laurel and her father. So they both referred back to her. We don't
know what Laurel and the father meant to her firsthand. We could
tell her effect on his life and her effect on Laurel's life. It was sort of
the focal point of the influence. So, it was more important to the
novel to have the strength of that understood. I hadn't thought of it
in that respect, but you're right. So much went back to Becky.

MvN: You wrote *The Optimist's Daughter* first as a short story?

Welty: *The Optimist's Daughter* was very close to me personally.
It meant a lot to me in a way that some of the others hadn't, and
when I sent it to the *New Yorker,* I stipulated from the beginning that
I didn't want it to come out in book form until some time had passed,
and I could revise it as I wished to. That's what I did. I just went
through on the typewriter, and I typed and changed as I went along.
I did change it and enlarge it a little bit. I guess there are many small
changes that probably no one but me would notice. But it was important to me to get another chance to shape it and sharpen it. In
fact, I think I deepened it in some ways. I tried to because things
happened to my thinking in the meanwhile and I could see it more
clearly.

MvN: You added something toward the end.

Welty: I added that part about the "confluence" of the waters. I
love that part.

MvN: When Laurel and her husband were crossing the bridge, on
the train?

Welty: Yes, crossing the bridge at Cairo, Illinois. I wanted to have
a meeting of everything.

MvN: That is a wonderful word—*confluence.* I love it.

Welty: I love it too. I'm crazy about that word.

MvN: When Laurel says that Becky "predicted" Fay, and that
what Becky had been afraid of might have existed in the house all
along, could you say what it was that Becky was afraid of, or was it
anything in particular?

Welty: She distrusted because her mind began to be suspicious
and distrustful. She had predicted nothing definite, like, "You'll fall
for somebody" or something like that, or "You're not true to me."
Nothing that literal. . . . The judge couldn't have been truer to her, at
the time. He was always true to her, but he was seeking solace. She
had predicted that he would. "You'll all go off, you'll all desert me."

That's all I meant. She didn't predict Fay herself.

MvN: That comment shouldn't be construed, then, as a social commentary, something about social change, since Fay did represent a displacement of the established order?

Welty: No, I don't think so. It's just her distrust of the whole world, that she couldn't count on anything anymore, that nobody was true to her.

MvN: It was attributable to her condition?

Welty: Yes, her distress. And, of course, it was completely unfounded at the time she said it.

MvN: When Judge McKelva was at a loss for any way to answer—

Welty: He would walk out. That was just to get his mind cool again, obviously, but he was not in any way unfaithful. I didn't mean to suggest that.

MvN: Laurel said he needed spiritual guidance.

Welty: Well, he was in distress, too, you know.

MvN: This story, in particular, sparked my interest in the writing process, I think because of the poetic reverberations. In one of your essays about writing, "Writing and Analyzing a Story," you refer to your own story, "No Place for You My Love," and discuss the creation of a "third character." You say that between the writer and the story he writes is the undying third character. You're not talking about the narrator here are you?

Welty: No, I was talking about the relationship between the characters in that story.

MvN: At one point you refer to your having to say "they" instead of "he" or "she."

Welty: Yes. Of course that was a story unto itself. I don't do that in all stories. I was using that in that story because I wanted to indicate that this relationship was a presence to these people who were strangers.

MvN: In the relationship of the reader to the work of fiction, I often find readers who don't trust themselves to have an understanding of the work, particularly what was intended by the author. Students often turn to interpretation and scholarly criticism. Perhaps that's part of the reason some of us are fortunate enough to have interviews with writers.

Welty: Well, every writer takes a chance with everything he writes that it will be understood. Also, a writer is learning all the time he's writing, and things are being suggested to him in the work. Everything I write teaches me how to do it as I go. All kinds of things open up. Something I write today, I didn't even know about yesterday. I don't meant a fact in the plot, but just an insight into something, and so it's a constant learning process with me when I write, I'm not surprised what any reader may go through, just as I feel when I read something.

MvN: You do bring things to the reader that you're probably not even aware of.

Welty: Yes, I'm sure that happens.

MvN: Would you say that most of your revisions are extensive?

Welty: I'm a heavy reviser. I guess I am. I don't know. I never have compared my revisions with other people's. I do revise a lot. I work out a lot as I go, and then I go back and type that up, and then I tear up as I go, too, so I won't have these things reproaching me lying around, and also so nobody else can read them.

MvN: And you use pins too?

Welty: I don't know. I write with anything.

MvN: I mean pins, instead of paste.

Welty: Oh, P-I-Ns. Well, that's an easy way. I never heard of cut-and-pin. I just made it up for myself, but I suppose a lot of other people must have thought of it too. Have you ever worked on a newspaper?

MvN: No.

Welty: When you throw something away, you just tear the strip off across the bar at the top and throw it away. I got in the habit of tearing off the strip, both what I wanted to save and what I wanted to throw away; so that I ended up with strips—paragraphs here, a section of dialogue, and so on. I pin them together and then when I want to cut something, I cut it with the scissors.

MvN: I really like that idea of pinning. That means you can move it around.

Welty: You can move it, you can transpose. It's wonderful. It gives you a feeling of great moveability.

MvN: How did you get the idea? Were you ever a seamstress?

Welty: Oh, I have cut out things with patterns. No, I'm not a seamstress, but I have made things, and that is the way you make things, of course. On a dining room table, too.

MvN: I thought you used to do that with your mother.

Welty: Yes. Both of us used to cut out, back in the Depression. When you grew up in the Depression, you learned all kinds of tricky sorts of things. I mean, I made my clothes. They must have looked like the end of the world, but that was a good way to do.

MvN: In your essay, "Writing and Analyzing a Story," you say that fiction writing and criticism travel in opposite directions and involve different choices. You chose "No Place for You My Love" to discuss in connection with analyzing a story, and you call what you did with that story "a piece of hindsight from a working point of view." Did you feel that you were in the position of the writer analyzing her own work?

Welty: What can I say to that? I wasn't really criticizing my story, which I wouldn't attempt to do. It's like people telling you to review your own book, which I'm often asked to do—of course I've never done it—like estimate your own character. I was trying to analyze it, and the only reason I chose one of my own was that it was the only one I felt that I really knew the answers to. I could really give a first-hand account of it because I didn't believe that we could tell very much about another writer's work through analysis. Therefore, I used my own. It wasn't because I thought my story was a glorious example. It's just because I had firsthand information about it.

MvN: What do you think the critic's role should be, and how is it an art?

Welty: I do think criticism is an art. I don't claim to have it. I like to read good criticism, you know, by marvelous critics. I think criticism is very valuable and that it is an art, and what makes it valuable to me when I read criticism is simply the enlightenment that it gives and its quality of suggestion. It opens your imagination; it gives you a new insight into what someone has interpreted from a person's work. You may or may not agree, but it adds another peephole into a writer's work, which is always interesting. And some of it is inspired. Some of it is a brilliant work of art in itself. I do not mean book reviewing and so on, such as what I did, which is just to take something and write about it as well as you can—a specific work—but, I mean real criticism, and I think it is very valuable. I don't think it is like writing fiction. It doesn't attempt to be, and it's wrong for people to confuse them. You know, a lot of people nowadays who don't really understand much fiction because they haven't read very much can't even tell the difference between fiction and fact. They often believe that a story that's written is something true and condemn a character because he has ideas that are not in accordance with what they think, when the whole reason for having put a character like that in was to show that point of view. I think it's extremely hard for non-readers, which a lot of students are—non-readers of fiction—to comprehend what fiction is.

MvN: I think that's especially true when they're just learning to read it themselves, with a critical eye—something beyond reading for pleasure, or even reading for pleasure. If they miss things that might have to be looked for, it might be because they're not getting a lot of guidance in the schools.

Welty: Well, I expect not. I think really the best guidance you get is the way I did and probably you did—just by reading, growing up reading.

MvN: Do you think critics can influence a writer's success, harm her reputation?

Welty: Do you mean by something unfavorable?

MvN: Yes.

Welty: I hardly see how it can be harmful unless it would serve to destroy someone's reputation for good, which I don't think could be very frequent. A critic can hurt your feelings, but I don't know that anything else can be done. It usually is not the only voice speaking of you, you know. I suppose what could really hurt a writer worse than unfavorable criticism—I'm talking now about book reviewing—that would be the only cases I think in which this would apply—would be the ignoring of a book, saying nothing. If there's no notice taken, it's as if a book sinks without a ripple. That's often happened. A book may come out in the year that war was declared, when no one is thinking about new fiction. If it had come out the year before, everybody would have been in an uproar of excitement about it. There are some books that have come out during the newspaper strikes. They never get reviewed. And those things can really hurt later. Much worse than an unfavorable review.

MvN: I've been told that there are critics who don't look favorably on Southern writing in general. Do you believe this, and what do you think about such critics?

Welty: I suppose so. They expect a certain thing. I remember that review of Reynolds Price's *The Surface of the Earth* in the *New York Times Book Review,* which angered me so that I wrote a letter to the paper. The reviewer didn't actually review the book. He reviewed the fact that a family novel had been written in the South, and he said that was antideluvian, that no one could possibly be interested in the family anymore, and that this kind of writing just ought to be buried and forgotten. That's a case of what you mean, I think, a perfect example of it. I think they're fairly rare. Those things are a matter of fashion. When I was growing up, it was the same way with Southerners' being popular as Southerners in the North. When I first went to New York to school, Southerners were just thought to be the most attractive, cutest things in the world. You know—"Oh, she's a Southerner, ask her." Great heyday. Then afterwards, it got to be, "Oh, watch out, you know they're from the South." Well, all those things are frivolous and passing. Neither one means anything.

MvN: I think there are places where Southerners, particularly women, Southern women, would not be expected to do anything with any validity.

Welty: That's too bad. I don't think serious people, no matter where they live, hold it against any other person for where they come from.

MvN: But I have been shocked at the number of educated people—

Welty: Yes, exactly. I've been asked the most astounding questions from very educated, worldly people. Astounding.

MvN: Do you generally read the critical articles on particular works of yours?

Welty: There are a lot of critical articles that are written about my work, and I have read some that are very valuable to me. There are a lot I have not seen, and some that I've been sent that I keep that I haven't yet read. I appreciate the critical attention. A lot of it is very helpful to me. Yes, I do read them. I don't read some of the very technical, analytical things that seem to me far afield. At least I read part of them—enough to see that I don't really understand them. But it's all right with me if that's what they want to do.

MvN: Do you ever feel compelled to answer a critic?

Welty: I never have done it. I would like to write an appreciation to some people who have said some good things. That's what I ought to do. But, I would never argue with their judgment on something. They're perfectly welcome to their judgment, and it's their valid judgment, and what good does it do to object to a review? I can't see the point in that.

MvN: Do you think that luck or good fortune, or a "break" played any part in your getting started with your writing career, or anywhere along the way?

Welty: Oh, sure it did, because I had good luck getting things published from the start, not in selling things which took quite a while, but in getting accepted by small magazines which did not pay, but which published. That was very lucky. Then to run into *Southern Review* down in Baton Rouge with Robert Penn Warren and Cleanth Brooks and Albert Erskine, who took my work almost from the start and published it. That was wonderful luck. What could be better? I also was lucky in my agent, who sold my work to begin with to the *Atlantic Monthly*, the first paying magazine with national circulation. *Southern Review* paid, you know, a lump sum—twenty-five dollars, or something—but it was not a national magazine. It was a university quarterly. I had a lucky editor for my first book, John Woodburn, who persuaded Doubleday to publish a book of short stories by an unknown writer, a first book, which was almost unheard of. What could be more lucky?

MvN: So you feel fortunate?

Welty: I certainly do. I know to what I owe a lot. All those people were of the greatest help, not only for publication but by their encouragement, you know—liking my work and thinking well of it. Making me feel that I was professional.

MvN: In the beginning of your career, did you seek out any of these people, or did they seek you out?

Welty: Well, that kind of thing wasn't done in my day. Now everybody looks up people and wants to see them and all that. I was very close, from here to Baton Rouge, but it wouldn't have occurred to me to go down there. Later, I was invited to come and see Katherine Anne Porter, which I did, and I met them, but it wouldn't have occurred to me to write. Nothing was wrong with that, but it just wasn't the way it happened with me. It wasn't the way I did, and I don't think it was the way they did.

MvN: Do you think a lot of gifted people fall by the wayside because they don't have lucky breaks?

Welty: I happen to believe that most people that really have what it takes to be a professional writer are going to do it. If you're easily discouraged, it's not a very strong gift, I feel. When I wrote six years before I was published in a national magazine, I wasn't discouraged. Of course, I had things to encourage me. But I loved to write, and I was determined to do it. So, I wasn't to be discouraged by being constantly turned down by the national magazines all those years.

MvN: When Tillie Olsen came to the State University College at Brockport, N.Y., to do a reading, she talked about the real hardships in people's lives, in women's lives particularly, that prevent them from writing. Did your own environment make it easier for you to be able to write?

Welty: I've heard her speak on that—at a writer's conference. I was on the panel with her at the University of North Dakota. She's so absolutely in earnest, and she has suffered so much. She's very touching, but she will brook no disagreement. Well, she has got a point, she certainly has. I have her new book, *Silences.* I know it's part of her passionate advocacy.

MvN: She makes the plight of women, particularly, who would be—or would have been—writers seem very real to me. The kinds of responsibilities and commitments women have believed themselves to have—

Welty: Well, I've had plenty of responsibilities—always have had. And I've had, mostly, a job to support myself. And although I didn't marry, I had a family that I was working with and helping to take care of, and people who were ill, and different things, and it didn't occur to me to mind this, you know.

MvN: Or that it took anything away?

Welty: No. My own feeling is that human responsibilities come first. That would be blaming another person if you didn't get your writing done. I'm speaking absolutely personally. My life was easier than hers [Tillie Olsen's], I'm sure, but I grew up in the Depression, which wasn't too easy, and my father died the year I got out of college, which wasn't too easy, but that was just all in the way life was, you know. I think you can write no matter what goes.

MvN: A lot of people would agree with you, but, whereas I don't think everybody in the world is gifted or is an artist, I do believe, as Tillie Olsen does, that women have always been at a disadvantage.

Welty: I do too. I certainly do, but what I mean is, it needn't paralyze you.

MvN: I believe it can, that it's a very real thing. It must just depend on the circumstances.

Welty: It depends on the circumstances, on the person, on the degree of talent. I mean by degree, on the *vitality* of the talent.

MvN: I think it took Tillie Olsen a period of twenty years, writing on little scraps of paper which became her first and only novel.

Welty: Well, *Losing Battles,* which I wrote among difficulties, took about ten years, and it was written—

MvN: On scraps of paper?

Welty: On a combination of scraps of paper, and on different things. You can write in any way. At the same time, I was doing lecturing to earn money. I just take for granted you have to manage, you have to learn some way.

MvN: I think of Laurel McKelva in *The Optimist's Daughter* as a "liberated" person, woman. Do you? And what sympathy do you have for the Women's Movement?

Welty: Oh, well, I didn't mean Laurel to sound—I know you didn't mean that, but I have been asked that, believe it or not. I get asked that at least once a week. I don't mean in that particular case, but, "Do your characters stand for—"? She just stood for herself. I've never met, so far as I know, with any prejudice from editors because I was a woman—with the one exception of my story, "Petrified Man," which was turned down by *Esquire* magazine because I was a woman. I didn't send it to them to test them, because I was too ignorant to know they didn't take stories by women. I was sending it to everybody. But, in the way of being paid what I was worth from an editor—of course, I've had an agent. So, I've never met with any prejudice. In fact, the other way. I was treated with so much consideration and kindness and politeness. I think in the publishing world, at least most of the time that I can think of, most people who are interested in the books—editors and publishers and so on—are also courteous people. They would treat each other just the way you and I would expect to be treated in a civilized room of people. I've also had jobs with salaries, and I know I've gotten this money that the man doing the same work—and I don't like that and nobody in their right mind would want or like that. I think in some of the movements women are making fools of themselves, and I'm sorry for that, because it's cast a wry sad light on the real facts of the matter.

MvN: In some ways, I think so too, but they are doing something for us all, and I believe it's necessary, and think it's something we can be thankful for—for the ones who are out there, in the streets, so to speak.

Welty: I suppose so. I hate the grotesque quality of it. And you see, if you are a woman and making your living as I am in the world, where you're on the list of everybody that sends out questionnaires—I wish you could see some of the things that you get asked and that you're asked to do. I was asked to sign something saying, "I too have had an abortion and would like to establish something." They sent a note, "Even if you haven't had an abortion, we think you owe it to the movement to sign this."

MvN: To lie?

Welty: Yes. A lot of it is done in this kind of show biz kind of way, you know. "Just come on out, be all out for this. Say "Sure I've had an abortion!" Well, all of that is the most boring thing in the world. Also, I think it's the most fantastic course of events, and I don't believe in encouraging that kind of thing. I have answered some questionnaires to some extent, what I can answer factually, and something I know about, but I believe at least half the questions are nobody's business.

MvN: I didn't know they were doing things just like that.

Welty: Oh, they are, I can tell you. And, like you, I think it should be done, but if it's making comedians of all of us, I don't know that it's worth it. It can be done another way.

A Conversation with Eudora Welty

Tom Royals and John Little / Summer 1978

From *Bloodroot* [Grand Forks, ND], No. 6 (Spring 1979), 2–12. Reprinted by permission.

Eudora Welty was born in Jackson, Mississippi in 1909. After studying at Mississippi State College for Women, the University of Wisconsin, and Columbia University, she returned to Jackson where she worked as society editor of the *Commercial Appeal* and later worked for the WPA. This travel provided the photographs later published in *One Time, One Place* and was the source of many of the stories in her first book, *A Curtain of Green,* which appeared in 1941. Of the seventeen stories included in the volume, eleven are frequently anthologized, and four, "Petrified Man," "Why I live at the P.O.," "Powerhouse," and "A Worn Path," have become classics. Her fourteen books of photographs, stories, essays, and novels have won many awards, including four O'Henry's, The William Dean Howells Medal of the Academy of Art and Letters, and the 1975 Pulitzer Prize for *The Optimist's Daughter.* In 1964–65 she taught a creative writing class at Millsaps College. Two of her students from that class did this interview in her home during the summer of 1978. Tom Royals is presently a lawyer in Jackson, and John Little teaches writing at the University of North Dakota.

Tom: What do you think about the concept of what we're trying to do here, that is to say, to interview a writer and try to arrive at something worthwhile through the medium?

Eudora: I don't rightly know. I've always been tenacious in my feeling that we don't need to know a writer's life in order to understand his work and I have really felt very opposed to a lot of biographies that have been written these days, of which the reviewers say they're not any good unless they reveal all sorts of other things about the writer. I know you're not talking about that kind of thing, but it's brought out my inherent feeling that it's good to know something about a writer's background, but only what pertains. I'm willing to tell you anything I can if I think it has that sort of value. You asked me what I thought the value was, and I'm just not sure.

Tom: Not sure as to whether knowledge of the writer has a value? The works may stand on their own. Is that what you mean?

Eudora: Well, take somebody like Chekhov. It's important to know that he was the grandson of a serf, that he was a doctor, that he had tuberculosis, and that his wife was an actress. All these things matter in understanding his work. But there are a lot of other things, as you know, that don't matter.

Tom: The idea of interviewing writers is fairly recent, isn't it?

Eudora: I don't know. I think mostly in the past they relied on letters, because, you know, people were great letter writers, and they wrote seriously and fully to their friends, relatives, and so on, so there was a written record of many things about people's lives that just doesn't exist now. Nobody writes letters anymore.

John: But do you think it helps to know about your family life to interpret *The Optimist's Daughter?*

Eudora: No, I don't think it's necessary in the least. I think the key fact in my case—I can only speak for myself—is that I have to write out of emotional experience, which is not necessarily out of factual experience. What I do is translate something that's happened to me into dramatic terms. And they don't coincide; well, they almost never coincide. But I couldn't write about any important emotional thing if I hadn't experienced it; that wouldn't even be honest. You have to understand the feelings, and of course, I've got my feelings out of my own experience, but the experience itself is altered, transmuted, made to convey the story. For instance, in *Optimist's Daughter,* I write about the death of a middle-aged woman's elderly father. My own father died at the age of 52 of leukemia. That was entirely different from what happens to the judge; I made him up from whole cloth. But my mother did have operations on her eyes, though not his operation, and my mother did die within my recent experience. So, you can see what happened, it's a transposition, but a complete change, using feelings I understood about the daughter and her parental experience.

John: You can see things in the novel like the recipe, and I know about your mother's use of recipes from reading other background stuff, but neither of us probably knows that this kind of knowledge is essential to interpret the novel.

Eudora: I don't think it is. But as a writer who tried to be convincing and honest and detailed, I don't hesitate to pluck detail from everywhere; but real observed detail doesn't mean that the source of it in life has any existence in the imaginary world of my book.

Tom: Flannery O'Connor. I've heard people say one needs to know about her Catholic religion to interpret her works.

Eudora: I may have said that too, because I know when I did learn something about that, a whole lot of her work opened up for me, and I wish that I had had that benefit in the beginning.

John: When did you learn about her Catholicism?

Eudora: Well, I knew she was a Catholic, but I heard her give a lecture at, I think it was Converse College, called "The Catholic Writer," in which she dealt with that relationship directly and it was a revelation to most of the young students and to me too.

Tom: Does it open up new views into O'Connor's works?

Eudora: Yes, more specific at the time than I can think back to now. But the whole idea of salvation and . . .

John: grace . . .

Eudora: Yes, grace and redemption and all of that are so much more deeply rooted in her fiction, enhancing her stories more than I had realized because I didn't know much about the church itself.

Tom: Which of her stories did we study in your class, Eudora?

Eudora: We read several—"A Good Man is Hard to Find."

Tom: That's the one. I read that and thought it was a tremendous story and knew nothing about her Catholicism, or . . .

Eudora: Me too, Tom. That's exactly how I read it. And it is a tremendous story.

Tom: What else would I have gotten out of it if I'd known about the Catholic aspects?

Eudora: Don't ask me that, because I can't be specific enough. But we should go back to the scene with the old lady and the criminal and their confrontation, to some kind of state of grace that is achieved, to be aware of the difference that conviction made in a violent story.

John: We read "The River," the story with the Reverend Bevel Summers and the baptism in it, and we talked about the name Bevel.

Eudora: Yes, we did. I don't know whether I said that or whether I knew it then. I didn't realize it but Bevel is a common name over in Georgia and so she got it perfectly legitimately. It wasn't just a symbol thrown in. It was complete with antecedents. She would be the first to underscore that!

Tom: You said you didn't think it was absolutely necessary to know a writer's background to find out what they're all about. Do you think Flannery O'Connor was an exception to the rule?

Eudora: No, I don't really. I expect a lot of people simply know more about Catholicism than I happen to, but I shouldn't say "it's a rule" that you don't need to know about the writer's life. What I said about Chekhov would apply. I do think that we need to know general things, somebody's century, and where they come from and what kind of people; those general things, I think do belong. They pertain.

Tom: What profession they are, maybe, and that sort of thing.

Eudora: It's important if it's illuminating to a writer's work. I didn't mean writers should be completely anonymous.

John: But do you think it's helpful if the reader knows, for example, that "Why I Live at the P.O." grew out of your seeing a woman at a post office with an ironing board?

Eudora: No, I don't think that's any help at all.

John: It's important, I think, to other writers if they learn more about the process of creativity, how stories evolve, how stories are born.

Eudora: But that's a good example of how something like that could be said that's a fact but nothing like the truth, the real truth. I did see a woman like this, but what the story grew out of was something much more than that. I mean, it was a lifelong listening to talk on my own block where I grew up as a child, and that was in my head to write out of all the time. The sight of the lady ironing was the striking of the match that set if off, but I wouldn't have written a story just about seeing somebody with an ironing board in the post office. It's nearly always too simplifying to say that any story, however slight, comes from one thing.

John: Sure. It's like, you hear it said that the germ which produced *Anna Karenina* came from an obituary that Tolstoy saw in the paper about a society woman who committed suicide. It's interesting to know about the spark in understanding how a story gets started or the impulse that triggers it in terms of understanding, I guess, the process or craft. But it doesn't help you to interpret or understand the story itself to know where the writer got the idea.

Eudora: I think most stories and especially novels have long fuses that run way back, you know, so long that you don't even know the origin, probably. It started so long ago out of something so deep in you. Something sets it off. But you can't say that from that you can certainly see right off what made the story, because you have lived with it, of course, in the meantime.

John: Did you ever tell a real story or an incident, and from the verbalization of that, realize you've got a story?

Eudora: Never. In fact, that isn't the way I work. It reminds me of what I've heard of the author James Stephens in Ireland, though. He was like so many of the Irish, they were great talkers, and they met night after night and talked. And people who knew him said he talked all of his stories away, because he told them all and that was it. Of course, he wrote a lot, too, in spite of the talk. But stories don't exist to me in those two elements, sound and penmanship. Not at all.

John: You mean you make an effort not to tell about something you are working on?

Eudora: No. It just never occurred to me. You know, it also reminds me of what a club woman asked me to do once: "Would you just come and tell us one of your stories in your own words?"

Tom: That's fantastic.

Eudora: Honestly.

Tom: Speaking of telling stories, I think that's the difference between a writer and a story teller. A writer writes them. A story teller tells them. I don't see the same thing occurring among writers I know. Jim Whitehead tells stories but mostly he listens and writes.

Eudora: Well it's two different gifts.

Tom: Right.

Eudora: And I think, John, this is not to say that when you're writing dialogue stories, you don't hear them in your head, which I do, and I think most writers do; they can be tested. But when you're writing a story, you're constructing something. You really are making something using dialogue, and using what the ear tells you to help you out. When you're telling a story, it's just different. It's just different.

Tom: Did you ever ask anybody to read drafts of your stories?

Eudora: I couldn't work that way, Tom. I have to get a thing as well made as I can do it before I let anyone see it.

Tom: And then that is the publisher.

Eudora: Yes—or editor. I like my friends to see them, and I have shown things to friends, but they've been completed sections of something, for instance in *Losing Battles.*

Tom: Didn't you ever do that? Most writers, when they're beginning, go and ask teachers or somebody for suggestions.

Eudora: I never have. Perhaps it's shyness. Wanting to get something right and not trusting myself until I get it as well as I can, and probably pride. I don't want anyone to see it if it's not the best I can do.

Tom: Do you feel like the magic of it might be taken away or the spirit let out or something like that?

Eudora: I don't know . . . I don't mean to sound . . . I think I am superstitious, not pretentious. I am superstitious that something would go—its possibilities would go—if you . . . told it before you wrote it. It would take off the bloom before you ever got to write it down. For me. Different people work different ways.

John: I guess it varies among writers. Do you remember telling us about one of your earlier stories that you'd sent to the *Southern Review?* When they rejected it, you burned it and then they wrote back and accepted it. Then you had to sit down and rewrite it from memory?

Eudora: That was "Petrified Man."

Tom: It was?

Eudora: Yes, I had sent it all over to every magazine in the U.S.A., I guess, and everybody had sent it back. The *Southern Review* liked it but had faults to find which were certainly legitimate. You know it was a very wild kind of story. They had published me pretty regularly, but they said they didn't think this one was quite right and sent it back. So after that, I burned it up. Then the *Southern Review* wrote and said "We would like to see it again," and so I did write that over from memory. But that was a "by ear" story.

Tom: A what?

Eudora: By ear. I could just listen to it, and, click, could play it back as if it were on a tape. You couldn't do an interior story that way, at least I couldn't.

John: Do you feel that when you played it back you got everything exactly as you had it the first time?

Eudora: As far as I know. It was pretty easy to do. I could probably write that again from scratch if I burned it up because that kind of thing is just like hearing a song—once heard—you could sing it again.

Tom: How much of your work do you get from current events?

Eudora: I should say I get more general information than particular information. Things stay in my head a long time, maybe years, before I use them, and by the time they would ever surface in one of my stories in some general way, the news story might be old hat, politically.

John: Are you ever bothered by your fame in Jackson, or is it usually the telephone and strangers that bother you?

Eudora: Jackson is very understanding of me. I'm very proud of it—my relationship with my hometown. Oddly enough, it's since the recent television interviews that came out this year on public television that I have had an absolute inundation of letters and manuscripts and people wanting interviews. I must have about ten of those requests a week, and I'm so behind in correspondence as a result of that. These letters have been very—many of the letters have been just plain—they don't ask or want anything. An entirely different audience from my book audience. Although it is pleasing to me, I must be hundreds of letters behind with answering.

John: I want to follow up on something you said at the March 1978 writers' conference in North Dakota. You said during a panel discussion that you didn't think your stories had the ability to change society. What sort of response would you expect a Southern white person to get from your writing? What kind of understanding would you shoot for?

Eudora: Well, for any reader I always hope that my story justifies itself as a revelation of character, and I would hope for recognition of the common humanity there. I would hope that readers might look in there and see themselves, as I was trying to look in there and see the Southern character. I write of my fellow Southerners out of a conviction that I know what they are like inside, as well as outside. They're my credentials.

John: Do you think that is true for both your stories, "The Demonstrators" and "Where is the Voice Coming From?"

Eudora: Well, for any story, I hope, and in "Where is the Voice Coming From?" about the murder of Medgar Evers—I was definitely hoping to say, "This is what I think these characters are like on the inside. This is what is going through the mind of that murderer," and I would hope that story could be recognized as such by the readers.

John: All right. The readers should recognize that they have inside themselves something like the murderer in "Where is the Voice Coming From?" had inside himself?

Eudora: Well, not literally—but I felt able to suggest they might have—in those bad times in particular. The different members of the human race are not very different potentially, you know—I mean we're all able to recognize the elements of good and evil in human behavior—we comprehend good and evil, we're familiar with violence in our world. And that particular element of evil was running all through the South at that time. And I feel that anybody who read that story would recognize things they had seen or heard or might even have said, in some version, or imagined or feared themselves.

John: When "The Demonstrators" came out, you said it was not primarily a civil rights story. Would you comment on that?

Eudora: Well, all of it was a reflection of society at the time it happened. Every story in effect does that. And I was trying for it in both those stories and in several others that I have underway here in the house that will be in my next book. They all reflect the way we were deeply troubled in that society and within ourselves at what was going on in the sixties. They reflect the effect of change sweeping all over the South—of course, over the rest of the country too, but I was writing about where I was living and the complexity of those changes. I think a lot of my work then suggested that it's not just a matter of cut and dried right and wrong—"We're right—You're wrong," "We're black, you're white." You know, I wanted to show the complexity of it all.

John: OK, let me ask you a technical question. There is a great deal of light imagery in "The Demonstrators." There is moonlight, electric lights, sockets left out of bulbs on the theatre sign that spells "Broadway." There are also lots of shadows. Was this imagery designed to show the obscurity and confusion that people see in things?

Eudora: I think it was, John. I never had looked at it in that calculated way, but I saw it like that, was guided by my imaginary scene. I go by that, as a rule. In a story I'm writing now, I'm using light to suggest the shadowy nature of what we know and what we can see and observe. I try in all stories to use the whole physical world to assist me. I think I probably do that instinctively.

John: OK. That is something I noticed in "The Demonstrators."

Eudora: It's odd that I'm doing the same thing now in what I'm writing but very consciously as opposed to unconsciously in "The Demonstrators."

John: What are you writing on now?

Eudora: I can't talk about that for the same reason I've already told you. I can't discuss things in progress.

John: Yeah. Sure. With "The Demonstrators," there was Eva Duckett, the Fairbrothers, Alonzo Duckett and Horatio Duckett. One owns a newspaper, one is a preacher, and one is married to the mill owner. Are they sisters and brothers? Are they of the same family?

Eudora: Sure. Sure they would be. Because in a small town like that you know how it is.

John: Uh huh. Are you making a point with that?

Eudora: Yes. I was. I was absolutely.

John: What exactly is that point?

Eudora: Well, it was an observation of the way a small town society in the South is often in the control or the grip, whether benevolent or malevolent, of the solid, powerful family. It makes it all the harder for any change to penetrate a town like that. Some may be good people and some not so good, and they may be in themselves helpless to bring about change. They may be victims too.

John: At the end of "The Demonstrators," Dr. Strickland says to Eva Duckett, "If I had what Herman has, I'd go out in the backyard and shoot myself." Is Dr. Strickland showing a more compassionate, human side than what is usually visible in a powerful person?

Eudora: He is showing the vulnerability of all of them.

John: And with Marcia Pope, are you saying that she may be the only one who has the strength to come through it all?

Eudora: Well, she—I meant she was tenacious to the kinds of things in her teaching and her understanding in a removed, elderly way that was maybe not as affected as the day to day things. She was trying to hold on, to keep the principles. I guess that's what I intended to say about Marcia Pope. She remained impervious.

Tom: It comes off, and I wonder if you did a technical thing that made it come off that well. The first and last paragraphs of the story deal with Marcia Pope. So the action was bracketed by Marcia Pope. How much thought did you give to that technique?

Eudora: Well, that's important to me, Tom. I like the form of something like that. That is a loose form but yet I feel that it has its own strictness.

Tom: I agree.

Eudora: I've sort of developed new forms for my more recent stories. They're not nearly as compact in one way as they used to be, but they're more compact in another. That is, they have density of another kind than the plot iself. I want there to be a "felt" form running through that the reader will get. You know, it's like what you said about Miss Marcia Pope, a "felt" connection between things that has its own intensity, its own development.

Tom: I think your compactness and density come from the economy of your prose. You just don't waste words.

Eudora: Thank you.

Tom: In North Dakota when I introduced you at the writers' conference, I said that you were honest in your writing and also an honest person. I might add to that "cautious." Maybe caution has to do with honesty. I've learned here this morning that you're getting ready to publish a new book containing several stories about the sixties. Do you think that you're just now publishing a book about the sixties because of your caution and your desire to be honest—the desire to give such difficult and complete material plenty of time to mature in your mind?

Eudora: That might be. Time is an important ingredient in understanding a situation. But the practical reason why I haven't produced more stories of any kind is that they've turned twice into novels. *Losing Battles* was to have been a story. (They weren't all to have been about the sixties.) *The Optimist's Daughter* turned into a novel. Now I still have some others that I'm working on and I'm praying that they won't turn into novels.

John: Before we leave "The Demonstrators," I want to know what the term "I bid that" means in the story. Twosie, the sister, says to Dr. Strickland, who is about to remove the necklace from the fatally wounded woman, "I bid that." Is bid a verb?

Tom: B-I-D. As in "I bid that."

John: I made that? Is that what it means?

Eudora: No, no, no. She bids to have it.

Tom: I put in a bid for that? Would that be closer?

Eudora: Yes, I bid that. That is to say, I want it to be mine.

John: Wow, she's anticipating the death and wants the necklace.

Eudora: Oh, yes. She wants it.

John: For her own, I see.

Eudora: She wants to get her name on it. You may not have heard that before. That was an expression when I was a child. You know, somebody would bring back a stack of sandwiches; "I bid the ham."

Tom: You say so much so fast, and I think you're pretty literal about it in your fiction.

Eudora: Well, I try to be.

Tom: We need to talk about "The Demonstrators" some more. Did anybody ever ask you who the demonstrators are in that story?

Eudora: I can't remember that I've been asked that.

Tom: When John told me he was teaching the story, I hadn't read it yet. I said "What's it all about?" He said, "The Demonstrators." And I asked, "Who are the demonstrators in the story?" and he said "That's a darn good question."

Eudora: It is a good question, though I think every character in it is a demonstrator. In fact, I wanted to suggest that. Even the birds at the end when they—

Tom: Clothes on the clothesline even?

Eudora: Yes, everything is to show. Everything, everybody's showing something.

Tom: It's a visual story?

Eudora: A visual story. It is a visual story.

Tom: And that's where the demonstrators come in.

Eudora: Well, I have some real, literal demonstrators who came in off-stage. But also, everybody was showing something to anybody, including the victim . . . those birds at the end, the flickers that showed the red seal on the back of their heads. Everything was showing themselves. Everybody was showing themselves.

Tom: You mentioned that the literal demonstrators were off-stage.

Eudora: They were.

Tom: You write about them in the newspaper, and the guy who . . .

John: And Dr. Strickland sees this picture about a guy burning his draft card, and the front pages of the newspaper . . .

Tom: Yeah. But they're really giving the energy to the story. I thought the story might be about the effect the demonstrators have had on that town.

Eudora: Well, it was in a way, I think. But also, the demonstrators, who falsified their position, soon exemplified what already existed there. The society.

Tom: You know, I've heard that great tennis players and great baseball players have 20-20 vision, or 20-10 vision and that things really look slower to them than they do to people without really good eyesight. I've begun to think that your vision is probably like that of a great athlete. Maybe you see the world more slowly and in more detail than many people do. How is your eyesight?

Eudora: That's very generous of you to say that. I thought I'd just seen it longer than most people by now. I don't know. I have got a visual mind. Most people do have, I think. I observe closely because I'm interested. I want to see, but I don't think I have any special gift. I remember reading that Goya had trained himself as an artist to see action, and when he drew a falling horse everyone said the figure was completely grotesque, but that was before the invention of photography, which proved that Goya's eyes saw everything absolutely right, the way a falling horse looked in mid air. Isn't that extraordinary?

Tom: That is.

John: Well, when you read a story like "Petrified Man," you know you must have awful good ears. Would essential ingredients of a writer be good ears and good eyes?

Eudora: I believe that. I think that they're the tools of your trade.

They're not only the tools of your trade; they're probably what made you a writer to begin with, if you did like to look and to listen. You can't tell which came first. At least in my case. I think everything begins with a given, you know, like a proposition to prove. You set out with a given and then you follow that through, and there are all kinds of givens you can start with, that we give ourselves to begin with.

John: Is that like in the form of an idea? In the form of a theme?

Eudora: Sure. Sure, and intention and the whole germ—no, not the germ of a story—the nucleus, whatever one starts from. The whole beginning of a story, which unfolds in it.

John: OK. You don't start with an incident or character. They're included, but you start with an idea?

Eudora: There has to be an idea. What is alive in it is this idea. But what gives me the idea is always people. In general, human life gives me the idea; the character, the situation.

John: How articulate, how fixed is that idea when you start? Is it something that happens as the story develops?

Eudora: No, I think it's the very heart of it, this idea.

John: And that's there to begin with.

Eudora: It's alive in the story.

John: Can you say the theme?

Eudora: It develops. Well, I never know what any of these different terms mean. They're all in the story in embryo form, I guess you could call it, before you ever begin writing. Of course, they develop as you go, but it's all toward the fulfillment of the story's whole that you had to begin with. Working without that, I think your characters would be rattling around in a vacuum. With me.

Tom: What we're talking about mostly is you start with the character.

Eudora: I just mean the way ideas come to me is through people from the living world, not from the abstract, but from the living world. I don't say, "I'm going to sit down and write a story about Greed." But if I'd grown up with somebody that I thought was a terribly greedy old man, and had come to see what that does to a human being, then I might write a story to show what it does to a human being, but I'm not making up an abstract character to illustrate a moral judgment. That wouldn't interest me in the least. Neither do I think I could make it come alive.

Tom: What kind of emotional distance and separation do you feel you have to keep from your work?

Eudora: I don't know, Tom. I'm sure there's been a variation of those distances in my work, depending on the story and depending on what I'm trying to do. Some subjects I'm much closer to personally than others. I think the closer you are, the more difficult the work is. I'm sure it depends on the story in my case.

Tom: I've read books or stories by people who were too emotionally involved. That seems to show . . . but I'm not talking about passion or having creativity or energy.

Eudora: Well, getting too close is the easiest thing in the world to have happen, you know, and that is the danger. When it interferes with your impersonality. You have to show—impersonality is not the word.

Tom: Objectivity?

Eudora: Objectivity. That's exactly it. You can't let anything interfere with that.

Tom: I think you do a good job of letting those characters be their own people. You don't even impose your own political beliefs on them.

Eudora: I try not to.

Tom: In "Where is the Voice Coming From?" was it difficult for you to create that character and not feel some contempt for him because he was a murderer?

Eudora: Oh, yes, sure. In fact I did feel it, but I was trying to. Since I wrote it on the night it happened, I was terribly emotionally involved in the writing, but I think that gave me a kind of steely feeling about it, you know, the need for understanding a murderer, which I couldn't have done maybe if I'd thought it over for a period of time. In retrospect, I would have lost my daring, picked the story up with tongs or something.

Tom: So, it was a kind of anger, almost anger, you steeled yourself . . .

Eudora: It was, it was . . .

Tom: . . . not to get soppy about the situation.

Eudora: I made myself do it.

Tom: I don't believe that could be done by a lesser writer.

Eudora: Well I don't know if it was done by this writer or not.

Tom: I think it was very successful.

Eudora: Thank you. It was hard to do and I was still . . . I stayed in the same mood for a long time afterwards as if I really hadn't finished the story, you know, I should have done more with it. Too late. It was pushing—I was writing *Losing Battles* at the time, it just pushed right through it.

John: How many stories have you written in one sitting? I remember your saying "Powerhouse" was done in one sitting.

Eudora: I did. Almost never have I done anything else in one sitting.

John: This one and "Powerhouse" and . . .

Eudora: And both of those were completely outside my usual orbit. In both cases I was writing about something that I couldn't personally have known too much about.

John: The amazing thing about "Powerhouse" is that it seems that you did know exactly what you were writing about.

Eudora: I know it. I knew about my feelings. Well, I knew it, sure I knew that man's music from way back, but not technically. Sure, I knew it. And it was the experience of seeing the man alive . . .

Tom: The man you are referring to is the jazz musician, Fats Waller, right?

Eudora: Sure.

Tom: You know, we were talking about believability of characters. I think the jazz musician in "Powerhouse" was a little hard to believe in everything he said. I never knew for sure whether he was putting us on or not.

Eudora: Yes, well, I tried to make that a little ambiguous that way, I intended it to show he was really improvising the whole thing. I meant it to be that way.

John: Which is what the story is about. And all his band members don't even know he is improvising the whole thing, right?

Eudora: Yes. That's right.

Tom: The more you read that story, the more you do realize it is about improvising. I went into it knowing it was about improvising, but I still kept asking, "Is that true?" And then I'd remember that this is a story about improvising.

Eudora: Yes, but all the same I wanted the improvising to be kind of mysterious. Powerhouse is an artist. He improvises, they fall in with it—I think it is mysterious. Another consequence is, Tom, I was not in a position to revise that story, because how could I do it? You know, I didn't know enough to have started it to begin with.

Tom: Well, I don't think . . .

Eudora: So I never did. I knew that it was either that or nothing. So that was it. It could have been helped as a story but not by the author.

John: One last question. Are there any rules beginning writers should follow?

Eudora: No. God knows writing is the most independent and individual thing you can do.

A Conversation with Eudora Welty

Joanna Maclay / 22 June 1980

From *Literature in Performance*, 1 (April 1982), 68–82. Reprinted by permission.

Jackson, Mississippi, in June is hot, very hot. But in the living room of Eudora Welty's home—a two-story brown brick house built by her father in the 1920s—a cool breeze manages to drift through the windows and dispel the heat as we sit there in a pair of chairs that seem designed expressly for persons who like to sit comfortably for hours on end and read or talk. Miss Welty is just recently returned from Washington, D.C., where she was presented with the Presidential Medal of Freedom. The week before I arrived, she had been reading page proofs of her complete stories. [*The Collected Stories of Eudora Welty* was published by Harcourt Brace Jovanovich in October, 1980.] However, it is neither awards nor proofreading that we talk about just now, as we keep ourselves cool with tall glasses of ice water.

Maclay: Throughout your career, you've entertained many audiences with readings from your own works. Do you have any favorite stories that you enjoy reading aloud publicly?

Welty: Well, purely for reasons that help me, I want to read something with lots of conversation and plenty of action, which eliminates many of my stories to begin with. When I read for an audience, I wouldn't choose those very quiet stories that are interior or are more meditative, more contemplative. So I take stories that have something in them that I think would keep an audience interested.

JM: Do you find that you read stories that have more comedy in them, then?

EW: Yes, and I think that's because I usually use the form of dialogue when I want to write a comic story. So it works out that way. Also, it's nice to hear the laughter of people. I must say, that goes to my head and makes me feel very fine. You feel that your audience is really listening to you. And that kind of experience encouraged me, because I hadn't ever thought of myself as a "reader" of my stories out loud, until I was just sort of talked into it once. Then I found I enjoyed it so much. I like the give and take of audiences. But I still don't think of my stories as being spoken when I'm writing them. I think of them as on the page, because as a reader I think in terms of the word and working with the word as I see it written. On the other hand, I never wrote a word that I didn't hear as I read.

JS: Do you mean you sound out a story when you write it?

EW: I just *hear* it when I'm writing it. It comes to me that way. In everything I read. I hear the voice of I know not Who. Not my voice. I hear everything being read to me as I read it off the page. I used to think all people read that way; but I gather this is not so. But I have learned one important thing from reading aloud: it's a marvelous acid test for right or wrong. You hear every flaw come back to you. You learn things about where to cut, where you've said something more than once. Something may not look unnecessary or redundant on paper; but when you speak it, you know.

JM: Is it this kind of experience with reading out loud that leads you, for example, to cut out parts of "Petrified Man" when you read it aloud?

EW: Yes, I do cut out some of that story when I read it. That was a very early story and I didn't know then the benefits of close revision and cutting. I wasn't in the habit of going back and checking about things like repetitions. I hadn't learned then how really strict a form dialogue is. As you know, and as I am proving with every word I say, we don't make very strict sense in conversation, because so much is done with gesture and with mutual understanding between the two people talking. Put on a page, that's gone. And I hadn't learned that sort of thing.

JM: Have you ever had any occasion to encourage novice writers to read their stories aloud?

EW: Well once, after I had begun reading my own work aloud and had found what I had learned from that, I did a writing workshop here in Jackson at Millsaps College. That year was my first experience with such. I knew nothing about it and we had to make up our own rules. I said that I did not believe you could teach writing, but I thought that in the workshop we could find out things for ourselves by writing and bringing our stories to the class and reading them aloud. We would work with specific pieces, not with generalities about writing. So we did that, and I made each writer read his own work. They would say, "I wanted to let so-and-so read mine," or "You read it"; and I said, "No, part of the responsibility goes away if you don't read your own. You're the one who wrote this and you're answerable to yourself. You're the one who teaches yourself. When you hear your own voice saying it, you learn."

JM: Do you now ever read a story of yours aloud while you're in the process of writing it?

EW: I would be too self-conscious to do that, because while I'm writing a story it's all so interior to me, regardless of whether or not it's in conversation, that I'm still too deep in it. I think you would have to have finished writing it and have a complete story, and then you could try reading it out loud.

JM: I gather then that you never write a story with an eye to its being performed, as the playwright does?

EW: No, I don't. I have a completely different end in view.

JM: Well, have you ever thought of writing for the theatre?

EW: Oohh! It would be my dream. I realize now how much I would have to learn. In fact, I found out by trying it for myself. I thought, "I love dialogue and I've worked hard on it in my stories, and I think I've gotten to a certain degree of competence in that." But I found that that did not apply when it comes to writing for the theatre. Of course, any person who has ever performed knows how little that really applies.

JM: I asked that question because many of your stories are, for lack of a better phrase, highly theatrical.

EW: Well you proved that in your own performance of "Why I Live at the P.O." and "Petrified Man." But then you had the talent of performing and your physical and personal presence to give it. You also had other people, all the theatrical elements. You concealed my weaknesses with that performance. And you also did it as a reading of that story. You weren't trying it out as something written as a play for a playgoing audience. And the difference between writing a story and writing a play would require a different procedure, a different end in view, different everything. But I love the challenge of writing drama, and I would adore to because I love the theatre.

JM: There are obviously certain similarities you as a narrative

writer have to a playwright. For example, you both must be concerned vitally with dialogue.

EW: Certainly.

JM: Yet as a story writer, and particularly as a novelist, you don't
have time constraints the playwright has.

EW: And also, things that a performance can give by acting have
to be conveyed in a novel in many other ways. The short cut which a
play can do and convey in silence or by action still has to be conveyed in a novel. But the novel must use other means. Also, you
don't employ the feeling of urgency in writing a scene in a novel that
you would when writing a drama. The urgency should be there in a
novel, but it is an urgency of its own kind, not something that should
happen, be made overt, in a certain number of minutes. When the
point has to be conveyed in a drama, not a word can be wasted, and
I think it would be a marvelous discipline for a novelist. When I wrote
Losing Battles, I was also trying to challenge myself to see if I could
try to express everything in dialogue and action and not enter inside
anybody's mind. And I never did go inside anybody's mind until the
last chapter, when I went inside the little boy's mind—I couldn't resist
that. I wanted everything to be brought to the outside and presented
openly, in action. That impulse determined the setting, the kind of
people who would be in the story, the sort of occasion it would be. I
wanted to see if I could meet this sort of challenge, and it captivated
me to try it. I think that's why I wrote so much that I never put in the
finished novel, because I just couldn't stop. It just proliferated into
scene after scene, in which I would try to do something five or six
different ways and then pick the one I wanted. It was so much fun.
But that didn't teach me to write a play. It just taught me to write a
novel in dialogue. Of course, it's true that we're all (novelists and
playwrights) dealing with human relationships and the dramas that
arise from that; but I don't think you could write the first line alike in
a novel and in a play. From the start, from the very beginning, they
start out on two different roads. And that's something I had to learn.

JM: Would you ever consider rewriting any of your stories as
plays?

EW: From the writing point of view, I wouldn't be interested in
rewriting anything I've written as a story into a play. I'd want to start
from scratch. I would have to. Once I've done something as a story,

to me those people who make the story are enclosed in that world and you can't take them out.

JM: You've said that you believe that writing short stories comes out of a lyric impulse.

EW: I feel that, yes.

JM: Is this different in some way from the story-telling impulse?

EW: It may not be. I love the told story, and I can see how certain stories and novels are descended from it. But that is, in a way, lyrical. The tale certainly appeals to the emotions that everyone feels—a sort of community of emotions—through the senses, through the ears and the voice. And I think a short story does the same thing. Often, also, the old tales dealt with a single strand of experience, just as a short story does. In the same way as lyric poetry does, it follows its own path through a certain space and time, and is a whole in itself.

JM: Do you think that's somehow different from the dramatic impulse?

EW: I don't think so; I think it's connected up with it.

JM: Then do you think there is something within a particular artist that propels him or her to move in one direction primarily as his or her natural medium, for whom there is a natural impulse toward the lyric or the dramatic?

EW: I can only answer for myself. Of course we all know of people who can write in any medium. But I know my own limitations. I think I'm a short story writer naturally. I know I could never write a poem, and I never intended to write a novel. Every single one of my novels came about accidentally. That is, I thought I was writing a long story. When the scope was revealed to me and the story revealed itself as something that needed developing as I went along, then I had to discard that and go back and begin over with the long length and scope in my mind. Every time I wrote anything long, I never dreamed it was going to be a novel. That includes the longest one, *Losing Battles*. And most of my novels are pretty short, like *The Optimist's Daughter*. I consider those as long stories, because they almost never relax the tension I tried to start—which is the way a story goes.

JM: That's very interesting, because stories such as *The Ponder Heart, The Robber Bridegroom,* and *The Optimist's Daughter* seem to have a similar rhythm that's different from the rhythm of *Losing Battles.*

EW: *Losing Battles* is episodic.

JM: Yes, and it has valleys of rest, if that makes any sense.

EW: It does, it makes all the sense to me, because that's how I learned the difference between writing a novel and writing a short story. You can't write a novel like *Losing Battles* and never have a slack. It's not good to change points of view in a story. You need to change scenes and so on, for variety; but you shouldn't relax that single hold either in the mind of the writer or the mind of the reader. And of course in a novel, I had to make myself write that way.

JM: Well, the intensity level is quite different in the two kinds of novels as well. When I pick up a novel like *The Optimist's Daughter,* I feel I shouldn't put it down until I've finished it.

EW: Good. That's the way it was written.

JM: But when I go back to *Losing Battles,* I don't feel that way. I can read that novel more leisurely. I guess that's another thing that makes me sense different rhythms in the works.

EW: It is. And, as I say, I didn't change my conception of *The Optimist's Daughter.* To me, it's still in form a long story, though it undertakes the scope of a novel. But I did not change that feeling of tension and of everything magnetized around the one situation. I couldn't have put it into analytical terms when I was working on it, but that was my feeling. I like to work on a thing that is a whole, that I can feel the wholeness in every piece as I go. I think that's essentially a quality of a short story.

JM: You've seen some of your stories performed publicly. I'd be interested in hearing some of your responses to some of the readings or productions that you've seen of your stories. How about your reaction to one of the earliest adaptations, the New York production of *The Ponder Heart?*

EW: Well, the adapters of *The Ponder Heart* (on Broadway, back in the fifties) confounded me in two ways when they did the play. One was a necessity, because the story was written in the first person. The story I had written was Edna Earle's feeling about what happened, all from her point of view. When it was rewritten as a play, it was no longer her story; she became another character in the play and was reduced to second or third place. That's what it had to be, but it was confounding to me. The second thing that confounded me was hearing lines from other characters out of my short stories brought into the dialogue of the play. And I would think, "How did that get in here?" because that line belonged to a character in a short story written in *A Curtain of Green*. It made me feel almost dizzy to hear that, because those lines did not exist for me except as spoken by a certain person in a situation of her own. The performances by the actors, however, made that show for me. Una Merkle as Edna Earle and David Wayne as Uncle Daniel were so sensitive and understanding. The whole cast was supportive.

JM: Moving from professional to amateur productions, you saw the adaptations of "Why I Live at the P.O." and "Petrified Man" at the University of Illinois a year ago. I was wondering if there were any particular frustrations you felt in watching these or other productions of your stories. Or if the performances made you aware of anything that you may not have seen in the silent reading. For example, after our production you said you had wondered if the dinner table scene where Uncle Rondo explodes and spills all the ketchup would work, because it moves so fast in the story. And you said, "It did work." Does anything like this ever happen, where you say, that *can* work theatrically?

EW: No, but I'll tell you the thing that amazed me about "Why I Live at the P.O." Of course I knew you and I trusted you and what you were going to do. But I had a feeling of alarm at the prospect of seeing for the first time the other characters in it. It had been read before as a straight monologue with the existence of the other characters being entirely Sister's representation of them. And here I was, knowing I was going to be seeing other human beings as those other characters. I had never seen them either, you see. I was really galvanized when it began, because I thought, "I just can't imagine what it's going to be like to *see* Stella Rondo come out. And Shirley-T! and Mama!" Well, anyway, I thought you had just re-imagined it the way I had imagined it when I was writing, and they seemed to me very close kin to what I had thought of. And I mentioned that about Uncle Rondo and the ketchup because of my experience with *The Ponder Heart*. My big scene in that little novel occurs when Uncle Daniel tries to give away all of his money in the courtroom, and it was eliminated from the stage production. When I asked about it and said, "I thought that was the only scene in the novel that would be dramatic," I was told, "Honey, don't you know you can't show money on stage. It means only one thing—bribery." And David Wayne, bless his dear heart, could never make anyone believe that he was bribing anyone. It came out of him—his goodness and sweetness. However, it was done in Jackson by New Stage Theatre and Frank Hains, who directed it, rewrote the play. (I don't mean we didn't pay our royalties; we did.) It was rewritten from the point of view of Edna Earle, who again told her tale to her captive audience, as in the book, with vignettes of action as she went along. The adapter said, "I know it would not go down as a well written play. But it works." And it did, beautifully.

JM: So this staging of *The Ponder Heart* in Jackson was more like the staging of "Why I Live at the P.O." that we did at Illinois?

EW: It *was* like that, almost exactly, because it was another "I" story wherein sometimes things were told and sometimes things were happening. And it was done in front of an all-purpose set, just as you had done, where spaces and stage props did double duty.

JM: Did you see the New York production of *The Robber Bride-groom?*

EW: I saw it in many shapes and forms. I was glad I had had the experience of *The Ponder Heart,* which again taught me something fundamental which I should have learned: a play that's adapted from a story can only use that material as a springboard and then go on and be its own kind of thing; it can't try to stick meticulously to what the author had written, especially in totally different terms, as was the case in *The Robber Bridegroom.* So when someone wanted to do a folk musical of *The Robber Bridegroom,* I knew it was bound to be different from what I had done in my satirical fantasy. But I think it did its own thing in its own way. It was so robust, so youthful, so vigorous. Yet it eliminated many of the approaches and strands of real history that I'd put in the novel; I made free with all kinds of Mississippi history, story-telling traditions, fairy tales, myths. And of course the musical ignored everything but its own thing. That was proper. And I enjoyed it very much. I saw it with two or three companies in New York. Also, it was done within the last month or so locally by our same group, New Stage Theatre, in Jackson, and the production was marvelous. (That's not chauvinism!) It was really terribly good, and it was rather adapted to the local scene. Of course they used the script and the songs. I think the music is beautiful, and the dance, the staging—well, the whole thing is so imaginative. All the business of making the sets out of human beings and props in a barn is so poetic.

JM: Did you have any dealings with the director or adapter about the show, prior to its appearance in the theatre?

EW: No, we talked about things, but I would never have a single thing to say about a production. I don't even want to see it until it's ready. Putting on the production is their job.

JM: Then you had no control over or supervision of the production?

EW: None. They didn't ask for it and I didn't offer it. It was understood that that was theirs. I can't think of anything worse than having Author tripping in and saying, "But I don't think. . . ."

JM: Do you receive many requests from universities or people in professional theatre to adapt your stories or novels?

EW: I'm not sure from whom they come; but they're usually from individuals, and not from universities. And many of them are young people just beginning who want something to work on. Some sound promising and some sound death-defying to the author. I'm interested that people want to use my work, but I don't feel like giving carte blanche because I feel a certain protectiveness toward my characters. I don't want to see them distorted for a purpose that is not mine. And sometimes this happens. I've had several things like that.

JM: I'd like to know how you feel about the responsibility of a performer to receive permission to perform one of your stories.

EW: Well, after all, it's just a matter of what is legal. It's something about which I'm not informed enough to act on my own, so I have my agent and his lawyer do it for me, just to be sure everything is in order. Just a matter of housekeeping. Permission is necessary, not only to protect both the writer and the adapter, but also to protect the work from having a mark against it for future performance. In case a legitimate approach is made by a professional, he won't touch your material if it has been performed previous to that. Even though

the performance was done without the author's knowledge or permission, the material is jeopardized. I don't think anything like this is
ever done with deliberate intent to deceive. I think it's just innocent
or careless. But for every reason, it needs to be guarded against.

JM: I've heard you say that you're interested in the translation
process from one medium to another, particularly from the printed
page to some other form. Could we talk a little about the degree of
latitude you think a director or adapter or actor can have in translating one of your stories to the stage? That is, how far can one stray
from the literal text and still come up with a performance or showing
of that story that somehow embodies or faithfully represents it?

EW: Well, I'll tell you what I would want. Something that really is
true to the *spirit* of the story. I think often that would mean that you
couldn't be literally true to it, because everything can't translate. And,
in addition to being true to the spirit of the story, the production has
to be alive itself. And to see to that, it might have to use other means
from those the story has used. I can certainly understand and agree
to that. But if the end in view were the same, if the truth to character
were kept, and if the truth to relationships were kept, I would want
those things to be very faithfully regarded. That's the whole basis for
the story. And if that were made to be nonexistent, I wouldn't want
that treatment no matter how literally true it was. I think of that inner
core as a sort of magnet to which the details—the true ones—would
cling and the others would fall away. And when things adhere with a
genuine reason to adhere, that's fine—even if it's different from
what's in the story. I would never attempt to tell a playwright how to
do something of mine, any more than I'd want a playwright to tell me
how to write a story. I recognize the difference in the two procedures,
and a professional person is a professional person. But if an adaptation of one of my stories didn't come off, I'd like simply to say, "I
don't want you to produce this." If it's going to be my work, with my
name attached, I'd want it to be what I want it to be. I'll give you an
example of something not keeping to the spirit of the original story.
This was a production in New York that was done at a small off-
Broadway theatre. It was called something like "The Stories of Eudora Welty." They had decided to present all my characters
simultaneously in a sort of general carrying-on in which all the

characters from one story mingled freely with characters from other stories. And the casting was done without any regard to age, sex, or color, so that no one looked like the person who was in the original story. It was done this way on purpose, to show that anyone can be anyone. For instance, an old white man might be played by a small black boy. The lines were the same, but that was all that was the same. Everything else was like a big whirlpool of different people going round and round. There was no identity left. Well, I was so mystified. They had some marvelous people acting the parts, but the idea was to no purpose.

JM: Do you see your characters when you're creating them?

EW: Oh yes, I do.

JM: Then if you saw a production in which a character didn't look the way you had imagined him or her, would you be disturbed?

EW: Yes, but that might work if they stayed in the context of the story, and the inner truth of the character came through. So much is done by the gift of acting. I mean, appearances can be overcome. Actors have to work from the inside, the same as the writer works from the inside. And if they work from the inside, then the outside will be acceptable, I think. Don't you? If you're watching or listening to a performance given in the same spirit in which you wrote the story, all of that is transcended. I can see that there has to be some physical congeniality between the actor and the character. For example, in the case of a character who has to convey strength, you would want an actor with a certain resonance of voice. You couldn't cast a little piping tenor.

You know, I liked sitting in on the casting of *The Robber Bridegroom* musical in Jackson, because I was glad to see how those things work. It was especially interesting because so much depended on *three* different conceptions of the characters—those of the director, the music director, and the choreographer. Of course there had to be compromises; but I think that maybe the way people move must come almost in the forefront of many casting decisions. It is funny that you asked the question, because I do know what people look like when I think of them in my stories. Different authors know different things about their characters. Katherine Anne Porter knows their names immediately. I can think of their names only if I work awfully hard on it. It's like trying to remember the name of somebody you've met. It has to be just right, and getting the right name is the hardest thing I do. But Katherine Anne says, "Why, I know the name instantly when I think of the character." Some people know some things and some people know other things. I know the character's name when I get it.

JM: Like many Southern writers, growing up and living in a culture where storytelling is a highly prized social activity, you yourself must have heard stories all your life, sitting around with people telling stories. I would assume that this would affect the way you write and the kinds of things you hear. You've said about your characters, for example, "I hear them. I know what they sound like."

EW: Yes, I do know what they sound like. I'm almost certainly not writing something I've actually heard; I'm not writing *true* stories. But I know just how a story about such people would sound. It's an invaluable ingredient in a writer's make-up. Don't you agree? You know what that means in your work, too.

JM: I surely do.

EW: In the South so many things are going on simultaneously, and many stories are being told at the same time. Sometimes two different people are telling the same story in two different parts of the room. That's challenging!

JM: So you're obviously well aware of the importance of your Southern background in your rendering of "talk," but do you know what allows you to make a character's speech simultaneously authentic *and* artful?

EW: Early on, I hadn't learned that speech has to be absolutely authentic and of the character, but it also has to further the story. Dialogue has to show not only something about the speaker that is its own revelation, but also maybe something about the speaker that he doesn't know but the other character does know. You've got to show a two-way revelation between speaker and listener, which is the fascination of writing dialogue. Dialogue is action. But I only learned that through working at it. I didn't know it when I was writing those early stories like "Petrified Man," and that's one of the reasons they're too long. I just let them run on because that's the way they talk in beauty parlors. I made up the story as I went, just the way I think they make up their conversations. I got the way they talked, but I should have gotten other things as well. Between "Petrified Man" and *Losing Bat-*

tles, I learned something about what dialogue is.

JM: Well, the dialogue in *Losing Battles* is certainly far more purposeful and economical.

EW: It is. The novel may be too long, but I was highly conscious of what I was trying to do in that novel. I'm not talking about succeeding; I'm simply talking about different objects in view. I think a lot of that is conveyed to an author through his reading. I've learned a lot by reading Faulkner; he showed me so much about speech rhythms, in which he is faultless. And I've learned a great deal from Chekov, in whose stories you find it all in only a *suggestion* of a conversation. Maybe one line or two is enough. It does everything. If only I could just correct everything by him! He's just a wonder. Imagine what his stories must be like in the original!

JM: I seem to remember that you said during your PBS interview with Dick Cavett that Faulkner had taught you by his own practice that a writer did not have to represent a dialect orthographically in order to create the sound of the dialect of a character's speech, that a writer does better to suggest dialect and background with key words or phrases or various kinds of syntax that would clue the reader to the whole sound or the whole kind of speaking. Am I representing you correctly?

EW: Sure you are. It's not a matter of dropping g's and all that sort of thing, trying to spell words the way they are pronounced. This is only distracting to the eye. What I learned from Faulkner about speech was more important than any of those other things—it's that our rhythms in the South are different. Don't you agree? The times we breathe in a sentence or don't breathe—they come in different places. Our phrasings and rhythms show how we think.

JM: That's true; and also, if you're a Southern reader, you can pick out, from a character's rhythms, his particular roots within the South.

EW: You certainly can. That's another thing Faulkner showed. You knew exactly what beat this character lived on, where he'd been to school—if he'd been to school. You certainly knew whether he was a Snopes or a Compson; but there was so much more you knew, so many, many little gradations. You could tell anything— whether he voted or not, his race, religion, whether he was a Baptist or a Presbyterian. Anyway, that was his great artistry and I think he was absolutely flawless. It's like somebody who has true pitch.

JM: I assume that you assume that if you've done it right the reader will be able to fill out the dialect and total rhythmic sound of a character's speech.

EW: Yes, that's certainly your whole hope when you're writing. But if you've made a mistake or a slip, then you've given the wrong clue. You know, I had not been around much in Mississippi when I wrote those early stories. I didn't even know the difference between North Mississippi and South Mississippi. Can you imagine not knowing that? Just like every state, every section is quite different. Every county is different, or used to be. This may not be true any more, with people moving around so much. But I think you can still at least tell origins. It comes from living in the midst of it and listening with your ears open. You could never learn that from reading.

JM: When you read your stories publicly, you clearly fill out your characters' speech. When you read "Petrified Man" and "Where is the Voice Coming From?" I hear very different origins in those characters.

EW: I can hear them that differently in my head.

JM: This awareness of the connections between speech and region must surely be tied up with your notions about the sense of place in fiction. Since you have such a strong sense of place in your stories (as do, someone said, your happiest characters; as your saddest characters seem not to), do you find that having such a strong sense of place allows you to ground your characters strongly in place at the same time you transcend it?

EW: It's what I would hope to do. I have a feeling that the two things are connected. If you do ground the characters authentically, then they have a place from which to take off and do what you need them to do dramatically. Their meaning must always bear on and be defined by what they came out of. I think every generality in the world must come out of the particular. Since that's the way my imagination works, I can't imagine working with any other premise.

JM: You write in a number of places of that special pleasure that comes in fiction when the writer and the reader meet through the story. And since you obviously don't write in a vacuum, since you are aware of this potential for communication between writer and reader through the story, do you make any kinds of assumptions about this reader? I'm not asking if you have some person in mind for whom you're writing, but if you make any kinds of assumptions about the reader with whom you wish to communicate. How does your notion of the potential reader affect what you feel you must do to make your meaning clear?

EW: I don't know. Maybe I'm assuming a reader who is the same kind of reader I am. (I don't mean I'm writing to myself; that sounds like vanity—would be.) I'm assuming a reader who has the same hopes, wishes, groundwork as I have, I suppose. I never have really thought of it like that before. One wonderful sequence of sentences from Henry Green is the most perfect expression of it that I can imagine: "Prose is not to be read aloud but to oneself alone at night, and it is not quick as poetry, but rather a gathering web of insinuations which go further than names however shared can ever go. Prose should be a long intimacy between strangers with no direct appeal to what both have known. It should slowly appeal to feelings unexpressed, it should in the end draw tears out of the stone."

JM: We were talking earlier about reading aloud and performing. Do you think there are any of your stories that couldn't or shouldn't be performed?

EW: Oh yes, I do. That is, by me, because I'm not a performer. But as an amateur reader, I wouldn't try anything that had no dialogue or no action, because I need every assistance I can get. And I think a story that's totally interior would just sort of lull someone listening to it into a state of not really knowing what was being said.

JM: A story like "A Still Moment," for example?

EW: I was thinking exactly of that story, because I've just been reading proof on all my stories, and I remember thinking that might be the story that did what I wanted to more than any other story. But I would never read it aloud. It is totally interior. Nothing is ever spoken. Well, Lorenzo Dow, the preacher, shouts things from his horse; but that's what he's thinking, in the way he preached. I don't believe that story could be conveyed off the page. What do you think?

JM: I would think, yes. Yes, it could.

EW: But how would you differentiate among all the different people? And how would you deal with the fact that these are all real, actual people? I mean, there are all these things that, once you've made them physical, you've got something else on your hands, haven't you? I mean, how do you know how the bandit Murrell spoke, or how Audubon spoke? And how differently did they speak? And I don't know. It would be interesting to know what you would do with it. But it would never occur to me in my wildest dreams that I could ever read it aloud. In fact, I couldn't.

JM: You mentioned that some of your stories might be easier to perform or read because they were written in the first person. It seems that very few of your stories are written in the first person.

EW: I'd never thought about how many.

JM: Well, there's "Why I Live at the P.O.," *The Ponder Heart,* "Where is the Voice Coming From?" "A Memory," "Circe," the two in *The Golden Apples.* And I'm hard pressed to come up with more examples.

EW: I suppose not. Some of the other stories might as well be in the first person. I don't mean by this that they're autobiographical, because they aren't. But when I say "she" or "he," I'm still as much in that character's mind as I would be if she or he were saying it.

JM: Do you know why so few of your stories are in the first person? Do you prefer the privileges that are afforded to a third person or an omniscient narrator?

EW: I choose a narrator for a purpose that is one with my original idea. I know who is speaking and why; I know who is telling this story from the beginning. For example, my whole point in writing "Where is the Voice Coming From?" was to convey an obsessed person and to write the story from the inside—something I didn't think anybody away from the South would have known. I wrote that story for the reason of the first person. So the question of who's talking is implicit in the idea of the story.

JM: Of course my question may come out of a performer's point of view, too, because the first person stories seem more accessible or readily available for performance. The narrators seem more dramatically embodied.

EW: And want to *tell* you, *want* to talk.

JM: Surely. It seems to me that one of the more difficult and challenging forms to adapt to the stage is that Jamesian narrative where a third person narrator tells the story and gives you a prolonged inside view of the major character. This form seems particularly challenging to adapt if the central intelligence is a character who's not given to

speaking his or her inner thoughts and feelings publicly. Laurel in
The Optimist's Daughter, for example, is someone whose interior life
is very rich, but she's a woman of few words.

EW: That's true. On the other hand in that early story, "A Memory," that girl is not speaking that story out loud, I think. It's in the
first person, but I think it's like a soliloquy or a meditation. She would
not tell this to anyone. She's not telling people something like "Why I
Live at the P.O." But there is a difference in first persons. Edna Earle
has captured an audience in *The Ponder Heart,* and that's her
character. I mean, she's got to tell you this story.

JM: Do you think a story like *The Optimist's Daughter* could be
adapted to the stage?

EW: My instant reaction is, "No." I've had several propositions;
people have wanted to do it, but I feel dubious. I would have to see
what an adaptation could be. That novel does have a certain number
of scenes and a variety of characters speaking in a group. But it
doesn't have any overt action that is grippingly dramatic. There are
just people sitting around talking. The real action is still interior.

JM: Because the focus of the novel is on Laurel and what she's
going through internally.

EW: Yes, it's all interior. And the things that are said are coming in
to bear on her own interior activity. How could it be performed as
visible action and significant action in itself? You might be able to
overcome these problems, but I'm not sure.

JM: Ruth Vande Kieft, who edited the most readily available
volume of your stories (at this time), argues in the prefaces to *Thirteen Stories* that the stories in that volume all deal with what she calls
your "major theme"—love and separation. Do you think that's an
adequate or accurate assessment?

EW: I don't know. I don't really mind people saying what my
stories are "about." I just suppose I never do think of them in terms
like that, abstract terms. I think my stories certainly concern the effort
to reach love or achieve communication, whether it's satisfied or not.
I don't know. I think so specifically about such-and-such situation,
such-and-such human condition. Let the story arise of itself. Let it
speak for itself. Let it reveal itself as it goes along.

JM: Haven't you said that the form also forces itself on the story?

EW: I think it arises out of the situation you're writing about. The situation sort of dictates the form of the story. You certainly have your idea of the whole in mind, and that whole stays the same, regardless of how it's worked out. But how it's worked out depends a lot on what happens in the story, what it tells you. I think you learn from every story both what you can do with it and what is there to be done. It would be too bad if form was all cut and dried.

JM: So once the story begins, once you and the story begin together, there is a kind of dialogue between you and the story. You're talking to it and it's talking back to you.

EW: Absolutely right. Which is the joy of writing.

JM: Now that you've just finished reading proof on all of your stories, do you find that you have a favorite?

EW: You know, I would always have had to answer that my favorite was whatever I was working on at the time, because that's the only story I'm thinking about. It absorbs you. But just having read over six hundred and twenty pages of my work, I think the story I wrote called "A Still Moment" might qualify for that. It struck me as having had a very happy fulfillment of what it set out to do. It seemed better than I had thought; it made up for some of the ones that were worse than I had thought. But as far as purely personal pleasure is concerned, I think "June Recital" gave me more of that. Things I had forgotten about since I wrote it—little details of childhood life and taking music and recitals—all came back. I think I had it down pretty well. I was just at the right point to do it, I guess. It was a very felicitous moment. I loved writing it at the time, and I still like it. "June Recital" is pretty long, but I was starting in on the kind of story I like—something that goes between sixty and ninety pages.

JM: I heard you say once that *The Golden Apples* had been written with the most love.

EW: I think it was. I liked the sort of freedom out of which I wrote that whole book—being able to give everything, unhesitatingly, to what I was trying to say, and not being held back by any kind of fear that I might not be conveying what I meant. I didn't over-revise anything. But again, I felt that there was one story in there that I wasn't sure belonged in it—the San Francisco story, "Music From Spain." It had its legitimate place as the story about the one person who had left Morgana. But I wasn't sure. I thought it was all right as a story; I just wasn't sure if its proportion was correct or its placing was correct in the context of *The Golden Apples.*

JM: What are you working on now?

EW: I'm kind of superstitious about talking about something like that. Because how do I know what it may turn out to be? I have got some work underway, though.

JM: One final burning question that seems to be on the mind of every one of your readers: Is Phoenix Jackson's grandson dead yet?

EW: Ain't dead yet and ain't gonna die! Gonna live on!

Looking into the Past: Davis School

Christine Wilson / 7 October 1980

Interviewers: Sarah Beardsley, David Carr, Amy Bercaw, Sherry Gladney, Kimani Jones, Geoffrey Wilson, Beth Canizaro, Austin Wilson

From *Looking into the Past: Davis School,* an oral history proj-ect of the Alternative School, Jackson, MS, coordinated by Christine Wilson. Project partially funded by the Mississippi Committee for the Humanities (1981 MCH grant publication). Reprinted by permission.

Student: When did you attend Davis School?

Welty: From the time I was five years old—which was around the time of World War I, I guess—and I went through seventh grade there. What do I do with this? (microphone) I can hold it, like at the dentist's office, the thing you spit in.

Student: What time did school start in the morning and get out?

Welty: I believe it started about 8:30. I lived right across the street and I could get there at the last minute. I suppose it let out about 2:30 in the afternoon. Everybody really had to be on time, on ac-count of that principal we had, who rang a big brass bell when it was time to come in. You could hear it for blocks. Everybody lined up on the outside and marched in while somebody played the piano.

Student: Do you know what happened to that bell, by chance?

Welty: I don't know. I always wondered if it was buried with Miss Duling. It would be something that should have been kept. Some-body who might know is Katherine Lefoldt. She took the role of Miss Duling in a re-creation of Davis School and she rang a bell.

Student: Did you enjoy school?

Welty: Yeah. I liked it. We worked hard, we took it pretty seri-ously. One of the things that made me like it was that, Jackson being small, you knew everybody in your room and you went clear through the seven grades with them. So they were old and trusted friends long before you graduated from Davis School. And then we all went down in a body to the one high school in Jackson—Central

High. We all knew each other very well. Nobody came and went the way they do when people move around a lot.

Student: Was there anything you didn't enjoy about school?

Welty: I hated exams, but who doesn't?

Student: What did you wear to school?

Welty: Well, in the winter we wore union suits. It seems to me it was cold there. Most places were heated by fires and fireplaces. There was no central heating much. Everyone dressed very warmly in the winter. I believe it was George Stephenson, here in Jackson, the rector and Greek scholar—he was in my class at school—he recollected there were no electric lights there. They didn't figure we'd need them. We were only there in the daytime. And on rainy days when you couldn't see at your desk, the teacher went and stood at the window and read to us—it was heavenly. She read from *King of the Golden River* and things like that.

Canizaro: You said there was no central heating in the buildings?

Welty: I don't know—there must have been. There must have been radiators. You know, children don't notice whether it's hot or cold. But I remember when sometimes—we had such rare snows in those days—really about two in Jackson before I was sixteen years old—when it did snow, of course, there was great excitement and we always had a holiday. If we were trapped in school, mothers would arrive with the union suits. They would come down, and the children would be summoned—it was so shaming. My mother never did me that way.

Canizaro: Do you people know what union suits are?

Austin Wilson: I don't think they know.

Welty: They're what's called now . . .

Canizaro: Thermal underwear.

Welty: They were long cotton underwear. They were all in one piece, like pajamas. They sell them all the time now, but they're very costly and smart to wear. You have to get them from L.L. Bean. But when you put them on before the fire, you had to fold them over and put your stocking on on top of them—that was an art. And then lace your shoes up. Course they were high-tops, for cold weather.

One time the teacher opened the window and put her cape outside and collected snow crystals and she went up and down the aisles and showed everybody her snow crystals lying on the black cape. It was exciting. We were always aware of the world in those days. There were open windows in the summer. You knew what was going on. You weren't shut away.

Canizaro: Were there a lot of children in that neighborhood?

Welty: The ones from State and North and Jefferson came the back way—you shouldn't have—they walked through people's gardens. Everybody walked to school. They lived close enough.

Austin Wilson: What would Miss Duling have thought of girls wearing trousers to school?

Welty: I don't know, because . . . she was stern, but she was so reasonable and practical. She did a lot of shortcuts—no foolishness. She would probably say "good idea." Who knows? She took stock of what she thought would be the sensible thing to do.

The best thing I can remember Miss Duling doing was . . . she believed in learning, really learning. You weren't in competition with others, but you were learning against perfection—you know, trying to get it right. And she believed in learning to spell and do arithmetic, right from the start. She would come into your school room and tell your teacher, calling her by her first name, "Sit down, Lizzie. Children, go to the board." And then she would teach a lesson, with made-up examples of arithmetic or give a spelling test to see how we were doing. Just keeping in touch.

So once she decided everybody should learn to spell, that it was a great awful thing, that people couldn't spell, even grown people, and she had the fourth grade at Davis School go down and have a spelling match with the Mississippi Legislature. You can guess who won.

Canizaro: That's wonderful.

Welty: I mean, she was in touch.

Canizaro: The interesting thing about that is that this year teachers and I have talked about spelling. Things don't change. (To children): Would you like to go down and have a spelling match with the legislators?

Welty: I bet you'd win.

Austin Wilson: That doesn't change either.

Student: What was lunch like?

Welty: You took your lunch from home. Delicious homemade sandwiches. Of course, what you did was swap sandwiches. You never ate your own. The other child's lunch was always more alluring. Something your mother worked very hard to make nourishing you gave away for somebody else's. And you brought a thermos of hot chocolate in the wintertime. And when it rained you ate in the basement. Otherwise you sat outside, like a picnic, under the shade trees.

Student: What kind of P.E. equipment did you have outside? Did you have monkey bars?

Welty: I guess there were some swings. That was about all. We mostly jumped rope, you know, things you brought from home. And we played jacks. Mostly jumping rope is what I remember.

Austin Wilson: Do you remember any of the jump rope chants? rhymes?

Welty: Yeah. Salt-pepper-vinegar-mustard-hot!

The boys and girls remained separated throughout life to the seventh grade because Miss Duling thought, as Nash Burger said, "She thought the sexes were different. As indeed they are." The girls played on *their* side and the boys played on *their* side.

Canizaro: Do you remember which was which?

Welty: The boys were on the right-hand side. It was more suited to a baseball diamond because there weren't as many shade trees. The girls were on the left.

Student: What did the school look like when you were there?

Welty: (shows snapshot) This is what it looked like, but it was brand new and there was nothing planted around there. There was a green hedge along the front—a long, green hedge. Shade trees in the yard. It was sort of a soft yellow clay-looking brick. Two stories high, with two big halls upstairs and down.

Student: Do you know why they tore it down?

Welty: I have no idea.

(identifies pictures of teachers) Mrs. McWillie was there when I came and was there, lord knows how many years. I never had her, but everybody knew her. (identifies Miss Duling)

Miss Duling was from Kentucky and came down here as a mission. She was really coming down here because she was needed. She could've got better jobs somewhere else. But she thought she'd like to take charge of that school. Everybody in Jackson for generations knew Miss Duling. She could call the mayor and everybody by their first name and tell them what to do, when they were middle-aged—she'd seen them through from the first grade.

Canizaro: She sounds like a marvelous person.

Welty: Everybody was terrified of her. She was supposed to have kept a whipping machine in her office, which was entirely a myth, but we all believed it. I think it was probably an adding machine or something—under a cover. Or maybe it was even a dress model. I think sometimes she sewed. There was *something* covered up in there. And she did give the whippings. If somebody was really bad, they'd have to go and she'd give them a few disciplinary whacks or maybe it was more than a few, I don't know.

(identifies picture of school building) It was a nice, solid building, very gracious looking. A good place to play—you could jump from one banister to another.

(Children discuss having gone to the Welty birthplace home, Congress Street, immediately before interview.)

Welty: It doesn't look at all like it used to. We left it in the twenties. People have lived in it and remodeled it and made it into rooming houses and I don't know what all, so that some of it is there. Things like the sleeping porch are gone, made into an apartment. There was a great big kitchen there and it's now just a little. . . . That's just naturally what happened. That's what they needed it for.

Student: Were you an only child?

Welty: No, I had two younger brothers. I was the oldest.

Student: Did they go to Davis School?

Welty: Oh yes.

Austin Wilson: Did you look after them at school? Were y'all that close together?

Welty: We were about three years apart each. We were there at the same time. By the time my youngest came along, we were probably out here and he went to Power. I don't believe he ever began at Davis School. The middle child and myself were the ones that went there. Power used to be down here at the corner of State Street and Pinehurst.

Austin Wilson: I didn't know that.

Welty: That was made into a parking lot for the Presbyterian Church.

Student: They still have that plaque of when they made the school [Davis].

Welty: Oh, really?

Austin Wilson: Cornerstone.

Student: Did you stay in your home classroom all day?

Welty: You were in the same one all the time. The only time we were all together, the student body, was at recess or on rainy days. And then we marched up and down the long halls upstairs where somebody played "Dorothy: An Old Country Dance." And then we had wand drills there on rainy days. Everyone had, you know, like signal sticks—like fencing—we went through. We had people like Miss Eyrich, who came every Thursday to teach physical training. A teacher came Friday to teach art. Miss Johnson came on Monday—she went from room to room—to teach singing. So we had instruction from the outside. Miss Eyrich was very fearsome. She'd walk up and down the aisles and we all had to put out our hands and she'd look and see if we'd bitten any nails. I didn't.

Canizaro: So everyone came in as the piano played, and went to their classrooms each morning.

Welty: Yeah. Went to your room.

Student: Mr. Charles Galloway said if you put your foot out in the aisle Miss Duling would come and step on you. Is that true?

Welty: I wouldn't be surprised. Anyone who put their feet in front of Miss Duling deserved what they got. I don't think people should put their feet in the aisles anyway—even if she weren't there.

We all had inkwells in our desks. And we wrote with ink, dipping the pen to write writing lessons with. We also studied writing—the Palmer method, I think that's what it was called. We wrote our exams with pencil so we could erase.

Student: Who was your favorite teacher?

Welty: I don't know. I used to really love all my teachers. The one I remember best of course was the one I had as I grew older, and I had the same teacher for both the sixth and seventh grade, who is now Mrs. Percy Clifton, in Jackson. She was then Miss Mabel Gayden. She was Gayden Ward's aunt. She's still alive. She said, "Little did I know when you were going to school you were going to turn out to be a *(clicks tongue)* writer." She was a good teacher.

Student: Did you celebrate Christmas at school?

Welty: Yes. We did things like—we didn't have parties so much as we decorated and made booklets to take to your mother, you know, about things. We had Valentines given out and everybody got a Valentine. We made Valentines. We put Halloween cutouts in the window—daffodils for spring—I'm sure the same thing goes on at your school.

Student: Do you remember what room you were in?

Welty: Yes. I remember where they were. I don't remember the numbers. The little children were on the first floor. And when you got to, I believe the fourth grade, you went upstairs. We had seven grades in grammar school and four in high school—that just made eleven. And they added the twelfth grade on the year I graduated.

Student: How did you feel about living so close to school?

Welty: Well, it was handy in a way. You could always go over there and play in the afternoon in the school yard. When I was sick in bed, like with the measles or something, it was fun lying in bed and looking out the window and watching the others going to school.

Chrissy Wilson: You had nice windows to look out. That's a nice room.

Welty: That upstairs room—it was really my parents' bedroom. I moved in there when I was sick. I lived in the little one—the one in the little tower—sort of like the sitting room.

Student: Did you make up your own creative writing or did your teacher give you ideas?

Welty: It was never heard of when I went to school—creative writing. I went through college and never took a course in it. We had plenty of things to write, which I guess was what you'd call that—and we had book reports. It was mostly exercise—learning to write clearly, to write good sentences that were grammatically correct. It was good background. We had plenty of homework to do. I guess the only thing kin to creative writing was the first theme you had to write when you went back to school, "How did you spend your summer?" That was always creative writing—it never was true.

Student: I read in your essay that Miss Duling lived across the street from you. Did that ever bother you?

Welty: Oh, I was scared. It wasn't directly across—safely removed about three or four houses down across the street—wasn't directly across. But still, whenever I went anywhere toward town, I had to pass that house.

Student: To the grocery store . . .

Welty: I was scared of her, really scared of her, because she was like something almost supernatural. She was so all-powerful. My mother was crazy about Miss Duling. She made us learn. And she really was a delightful person after I got to know her a little, but just on a human basis, I realized what a really great person she was.

Chrissy Wilson: We were amazed to learn that teachers in the Jackson Public School system could not marry. That's what Mr. Galloway said, that if they married they had to leave the school system.

Welty: The Jackson Public Schools didn't think anyone could be a public school teacher and be married and raise a family. I think that was the plan just about everywhere. Miss Duling, she gave up the other kind of life for the school because she must have been radiantly attractive as a young woman. She was really beautiful and she was so lively and spirited. I bet she had a lot of proposals, especially back in Kentucky. People'd be scared to propose if they knew her, maybe. I don't know—I had the feeling it was a real calling she felt to do what she did.

Student: Why didn't you become a photographer?

Welty: Because what I wanted to do all the time is be a writer. I did photographs in connection with the job I had. I was supporting myself with a job so I could write in my free time. Photography was part of the job. It was publicity and journalism. I took those pictures for myself because I was interested at the time. I liked it, but that was not my end in view. I wanted to be a writer. I like using words. But it taught me a lot—photography.

Student: Were you interested in being a writer when you were in school?

Welty: Interested in being a writer? I always did write little things. I loved reading. I read all the time—in and out of school. I went to the library a lot. I loved stories, right from the beginning. I was always drawn toward fiction, whether it was children's fiction or any other kind.

Student: Were there favorite books you had as a child?

Welty: Oh, I don't know. I liked Mark Twain a lot. We had those at home and I enjoyed reading all those. And of course I liked myths.

(Tape recorder shuts off.)

I think I should quit. I've used up all the tape. I love the subject of Davis School.

Canizaro: This has been wonderful.

Student: Was there ever much traffic on the street you had to cross to school?

Welty: Well, you see Jackson was only about 30,000 people, with the main traffic on North State and West streets. They were paved. The others had—not exactly a kind of gravel. I don't know what it was. But I remember when the fire engines were called out. They would race up West Street with horses and the steamer was steaming. You could see the sparks fly out from the hooves of the horses galloping to the fire. None of them ever came up our street, because it was all residential.

Chrissy Wilson: Before we go, are there any special anecdotes from your school days that the children would appreciate? Did you ever get in trouble?

Welty: Well, we were pretty well disciplined. The only bad thing anybody ever did there was throwing spitballs.

Canizaro: We brought along a school contract—all the things we try to do to make it a good place to work.

Student: And we'd like for you to have a copy of our flood book.

Welty: I'd love to read this. I'm delighted to have this. This is beautiful. We never did anything fine on this order.

Canizaro: I've learned so much about Miss Duling and Davis School.

Welty: There are others who can tell you better. Call George Stephenson. He's a big source.

Struggling against the Plaid:
An Interview with Eudora Welty

Jo Brans / November 1980

From *Southwest Review*, 66 (Summer 1981), 255–66. Reprinted by permission.

Eudora Welty is the author of five collections of short stories, a book of photographs, a volume of essays, and five novels. For her novel *The Ponder Heart* she received the American Academy of Arts and Letters Howells Medal in 1955, and for *The Optimist's Daughter* she was awarded the 1973 Pulitzer Prize. Among the most honored of American writers, she has also received the National Institute of Arts and Letters Gold Medal for the Novel, the Presidential Medal of Freedom, and in 1979 the National Medal for Literature for lifetime achievement.

Jo Brans is a member of the English faculty at Southern Methodist University. Brans interviewed Eudora Welty when she visited Dallas in November 1980 to speak at SMU's sixth annual literary festival.

Brans: One thing that especially impressed me in the conversation yesterday was that you said you wrote because you loved language and you love using language. I know you are a photographer, and you've painted too.

Welty: Well, I was never a true or serious painter, just a childhood painter.

Brans: How does writing compare in your mind with those other art forms?

Welty: Oh, it's in the front. The others are just playthings. I didn't have any talent for photographs. I was strictly amateurish. I think the book I did [*One Time, One Place*] has a value in being a record, just because it was taken in the 1930s. And I was in the position of being perfectly accepted wherever I went, and everything was unselfconscious on the part of both the people and myself. There was no posing, and neither was there any pulling back or anything like that.

Our relationship was perfectly free and open, so that I was able to get photographs of things really as they were. I think today it has a sort of historical value, which has nothing to do with any kind of professional expertise in taking pictures, which I knew I didn't have. But I am a professional writer. That is my work and my life, and I take it extremely seriously. It isn't just the love of language, or love of the written word, though that is certainly foremost, but the wish to use this language and written word in order to make something, which is what writing is. It's a tool. It's the tool, not the end result. So I guess that would be how you could describe what I'm trying to do.

Brans: To create a reality with words. Why is dialogue, spoken language, so important to you—say in *Losing Battles?*

Welty: I tried to see if I could do a whole novel completely without going inside the minds of my characters, which is the way I do in most of my writing. I didn't tell how anyone thought—I tried to show it by speech and action. I was deliberately trying to see if I could convey the same thing by speech and outward appearance, as I used to do by going inside people's minds.

Brans: It seems to me that in your writing you're hardly ever autobiographical. I've heard you say that you're working out of your feelings, but not your own experiences. Are there any stories that are autobiographical?

Welty: I don't deliberately avoid being autobiographical; it's just that when I'm writing a story I have to invent the things that best show my feelings about my own experience or about life, and I think most of us wouldn't be able to take our own experience and make a dramatic situation out of that without some aid. And I do much better with invented characters who can better carry out, act out, my feelings. I don't think you can describe emotion you have not felt. You know, you have to know what it's like—what it is to feel a certain thing—or your description or your use of these emotions will be artificial and shallow. So I certainly understand what my characters are feeling, but I try to show it in a way that is interesting dramatically.

And I don't lead a very dramatic life myself, outwardly. So it's not that I'm concealing myself, it's just that I'm using whatever—a lot of the details come out of my own life, things that I've observed. There was a scene in my novel, *The Optimist's Daughter,* about a three-

year-old child in West Virginia, a whole section in there that I suppose you could call autobiographical, but actually it was my own
memories of being at my grandmother's, on the farm, and all the
things that the child felt—the rivers and the mountains and all those
things. Nothing like that could be made up, you see. If you've never
been in the mountains you wouldn't know how to say what it was
like to be in the mountains. But it was not me as the character. It was
my feelings, my memories, my experiences, but it was that character
that was feeling them, not me. The character was not me. So, that's
an example.

Brans: You sort of projected your feelings into this creation.

Welty: Yes, and use them to describe this character. I didn't use
all that I had, I used just what would help me to explain the character.

Brans: How do those characters come to your mind? Do they just
spring full-blown into your mind? Or do you work them out. . .?

Welty: Well, it's just part of the whole process of making a story. I
mean, they are all one with the plot and the atmosphere of the story
and the weather and the location. They don't exist apart from the
story—they're not even in the world outside the story. You can't take
a character out of this story and put it into another.

Brans: It doesn't work?

Welty: Well, they wouldn't live. So the characters are all integral
parts of the story in which they occur. Of course you use many
sources to make a character—occupation, memory, knowledge,
dreams, newspaper articles, many things. You may get little bits here
and little bits there, because the character is a sort of magnet and
attracts different kinds of observations. Not just any, you know; it's
just what applies to the character. So how can you tell where they
come from, any more than you can tell where anything comes
from—where a tune comes from to a composer.

Brans: Do you have any set pattern of working? That is, do the
characters occur to you first, or a trick of plot, or some idea that you
want to express? Is there any particular order that seems to be the
same?

Welty: It's different with every story. It just depends. Sometimes
the story begins with the idea of a character and then you invent a
plot which will bring this out. Take that one story that's used lots of

times in schools called "The Worn Path." That character called up the story. Such a person as that would take a trip like this to do something. That's a good simple case.

Brans: What I love about "A Worn Path" is not so much the endurance of the walker as the windmill or whatever you call it at the end. For me that was the beauty of the story, that all of a sudden old Phoenix does move above the . . . just the endurance . . .

Welty: I love that, too.

Brans: And walking all the way back down the path with the windmill. I have a clear picture of that. It made the trip into town worth the coming.

Welty: Absolutely.

Brans: In one of your essays you talk about Faulkner, and you say that Faulkner has this sense of blood guilt about the Indians and then about the blacks. In your own work you don't have that.

Welty: Well, it's not my theme. You know his work encompassed so much and so many books and so many generations and so much history, that that was an integral part of it. I don't write historically or anything. Most of the things that I write about can be translated into personal relationships. I've never gone into such things as guilt over the Indians or—it just hasn't been my subject. My stories, I think, reflect the racial relationships—guilt is just one aspect of that. Certainly I think any writer is aware of the complicated relationship between the races. It comes out in so many even domestic situations.

Brans: Very few of your stories deal directly with blacks, though. And those that do, I've wondered if the blackness is a necessary part of the character. For example, old Phoenix. Why is she black?

Welty: It's not a deliberate thing, like, "I am now going to write about the black race." I write about all people. I think my characters are about half and half black and white.

Brans: Really?

Welty: I would guess. Considering the novels and everything. I think it's the same challenge to a writer. It doesn't matter about color of skin or their age or anything else. Then again, I never have thought about "The Worn Path" as being anything but what it was; but one thing may be that when I wrote that story, what started me writing it was the sight of a figure like Phoenix Jackson. I never got close to her, just saw her crossing a distant field early one afternoon in the fall. Just her figure. I couldn't see her up close, but you could tell it was an old woman going somewhere, and I thought, she is bent on an errand. And I know it isn't for herself. It was just the look of her figure.

Brans: It's not true, then, what I read—that you were the lady old Phoenix asked to tie her shoe.

Welty: Oh, no. I was out with a painter who was painting his landscape and so we were sitting under a tree. I was reading, and I watched her cross the landscape in the half-distance, and when I got home I wrote that story that she had made me think of. She was a black woman. But then I suppose it would be more likely to be a black woman who would be in such desperate need and live so remotely away from help and who would have so far to go. I don't think that story would be the same story with a white person. The white person could have the same character, of course, and do the same thing, but it wouldn't have the same urgency about it.

Brans: Well, old Phoenix does fox white people. You know, she takes the nickel from the hunter, then asks the lady to tie her shoe.

Welty: It wasn't because they were white, though. Those are two different things altogether. It was the desperate need for the money and for the child that she needed that nickel—she knew it was a sin, too. But asking the lady to tie her shoe—she knew who would be nice to her. She picked a nice person, because she was a nice person, and she picked one. Those are two entirely different motives, taking the nickel from this really nasty white man and asking a favor of a nice lady. She knew in both cases.

Brans: She had a wonderful graciousness.

Welty: She knew how to treat both.

Brans: One of my students went to your reading Sunday night, and she came in with a paper on it. She had misunderstood the title of the story called "Livvie," and she referred to it as "Living," which showed she understood the story anyway.

Welty: That's very cute. I'm glad to hear that.

Brans: A misprision, I guess, but a nice one. What I'm saying is, I know sometimes I fix interpretations on the things I've read.

Welty: Well, I do too. We all do that. And I don't feel a thing bad about it, because a story writer hopes to suggest all kinds of possibilities. Even though it may not have been in the writer's mind, if something in the story suggests it, I think it's legitimate. You know, it doesn't have to be exact. The only way I think to err is to be completely out of tone or out of the scope of the story or its intention. No, it doesn't bother me one bit if someone interprets something in a different way, if I think the story can just as well suggest that as not, because you try to make it full of suggestions, not just one.

Brans: As a teacher I'm very sensitive to this whole question, because students frequently say, at the end of the discussion of the story where you really are trying to get at all the things that make the story possible, "Now do you think that Eudora Welty really intended all of that?" And of course there's no defense for a teacher, and all I can say is "How do I know?"

Welty: That's all we say when we read anybody's work.

Brans: How can I know what she intended? But if we find it here in the story, the story belongs to us when we're reading it.

Welty: Exactly. The only thing that I know bogs a lot of students down, because I get letters all the time, is in the case of that dread subject, symbols. You know, if they get to thinking, this equals this and this equals that, the whole story is destroyed. Symbols are important, I think, but only if they're organic—you know, occur in the course of the story, are not dragged in to equal something.

Brans: No, no. It takes all the life out to do that.

Welty: Of course. And symbols aren't equivalents.

Brans: —not algebraic equations!

Welty: I know it. But, you know, some students get the idea, and it's very troubling to them. And what I hate about it is it might discourage them from ever enjoying reading stories, if they think they're supposed to make an algebraic interpretation, as you said.

Brans: In connection with "Livvie," let me ask you something that's really off the wall, probably: was there any thought in your mind at all of reflecting Faulkner's As I Lay Dying? Just the name of the character Cash, and then the fact that Livvie . . .

Welty: No, that was a coincidence. No indeed—I mean, I wouldn't—you're not aware of any other person's work when you write your own. At the time I wrote that story I didn't know about Faulkner's Cash. When did he write As I Lay Dying?

Brans: I think about 1930.

Welty: You know, Faulkner was out of print when I was growing up.

Brans: For a long time, right.

Welty: It was about 1940.

Brans: When Malcolm Cowley did *The Portable Faulkner.*

Welty: Everything I have of Faulkner's I've bought through searching in secondhand bookstores in order to read them. He wasn't in the libraries. He wasn't to be had—at least in Mississippi. I don't think he was to be had anywhere. He was out of print, for a long time.

Brans: That's right. I had forgotten that. That's important.

Welty: Well, I guess I hadn't read him until I had been writing for some time. But, at any rate, the presence of Faulkner's writing in Mississippi—I was glad he was there, and I loved his work, but he wasn't hovering over my work. Because when you're writing, you're just thinking about your story, not how would Faulkner do it, how would Chekhov do it, how would Katherine Anne Porter do it?

Brans: I wasn't really asking you that. I know that's not true.

Welty: Well, a lot of people do wonder, just because he lived there, and of course it is a formidable thing.

Brans: His shadow.

Welty: I wish that he could have helped me.

Brans: What I was thinking was just that sometimes I feel that you've taken some of the same themes. I suppose that was inevitable.

Welty: Because we get them out of the same well.

Brans: But that, in your mind, is more or less unconscious. And you give them a comic twist. In *Losing Battles,* for example, all the Beecham kin decide at one point that Gloria might be a Beecham, and that her father might be one of the Beecham brothers, and they seem to be delighted with the whole idea.

Welty: Yes, they're thrilled. That makes her okay.

Brans: Right. Even though by Mississippi law at the time that would make the marriage incest. But that's kind of a Faulknerian— I'm thinking of *The Sound and the Fury,* where Quentin says he'd rather have slept with his sister Caddy himself than have an outsider—incest would be better. I always think of Faulkner in connection with that idea, because I got my first gasp of shock from him.

Welty: Well, I didn't mean anything serious and tragic at all. I just meant it to show what the Beechams were like. That is, to be a Beecham made everything all right. That was what I was showing.

Brans: You have commented that Faulkner's comedy may have more of the South—more of the real life of the South in it than his tragedy.

Welty: I think it has everything.

Brans: And it seems to me that your writing is basically comic. There is almost always that sense of harmony and reconciliation at the end.

Welty: Yes, I think it's a part of tragic things. It intrudes, as it does in life, in even the most tragic situations. Not comedy—I would say humor does. Yes, I like writing comedy. It's very difficult and it's much harder, because one false step—and I've made many of them. . . . That's why I have to work very hard on the comic theme, because it's so much more difficult to do. One false step and the whole thing comes down in a wreck around you.

Brans: When I think of comedy, I don't so much think always of humor, as I think of the something at the end that suggests that the world will continue—that life will continue. A kind of optimism for the species. You always suggest this, usually with a synthesis of opposing elements. I love that line in *Losing Battles*—in Miss Julia's letter— "The side that loses gets to the truth first."

Welty: Oh, yes, that's when she was in her desperate state.

Brans: Had she thought of herself at that point as having lost?

Welty: Oh, I'm sure. She did.

Brans: She did lose?

Welty: Well, look at all the people around her. All her class, all the people she'd taught, they didn't know a thing, except the thing that mattered most to them, which I think is most valuable—that is, their love for one another and dependence upon one another, and their family, and their pride, and all of that. But nothing Miss Julia had tried to teach them had ever taken root. Nothing.

Brans: In your mind is she like Miss Eckhart in *The Golden Apples?*

Welty: She filled a function in the story perhaps that would be kind of similar, in that she was a person unlike the world in which she lived, trying to teach and help somebody. But Miss Eckhart was a very mysterious character. Julia Mortimer was much more straightforward and dedicated and thinking of the people as somebody she wanted to help. Miss Eckhart was a very strange person.

Brans: I hope you know that in some ways these questions are meant to serve as checks for me if I need checks in reading your books, and apparently I do. I thought I saw this pattern in several of your things—Miss Eckhart, Julia Mortimer, those characters in the same mold. That is, they represent a discipline. Could I ask you what your sense is of the differences between male and female characters in your stories? I keep thinking about that line from "Livvie" that I mentioned yesterday, "I'd rather a man be anything than a woman be mean." And also, in *Delta Wedding,* say, the women are obviously making demands on the men.

Welty: Well, men and women are different. I don't mean they're not equally important. But they're different. That's the wonderful thing about life. No, in those different stories I'm not writing about them as men versus women. In the Delta it's very much of a matriarchy, especially in those years in the twenties that I was writing about, and really ever since the Civil War when the men were all gone and the women began to take over everything. You know, they really did. I've met families up there where the women just ruled the roost, and I've made that happen in the book because I thought, that's the way it was in those days in the South. I've never lived in the Delta, and I was too young to have known what was going on in anything in the twenties, but I know that that's a fact. Indeed it's true of many sections of that country after the Civil War changed the pattern of life there. So I've just had that taken for granted—it was part of the story. That was something the men were up against. I think that in many of my stories I do have a force, like Miss Julia Mortimer or Miss Eckhart, but those two are so poles apart in their characters that I can't see much connection.

Brans: There's a real passion in Miss Eckhart.

Welty: There certainly is. Well, it's a passion for getting some people out of their element. She herself was trapped, you know, with her terrible old mother. And then no telling what kind of strange Germanic background, which I didn't know anything about and could only indicate. I mean we don't know—they had tantrums in that house, and flaming quarrels.

Brans: Well, there's that one quarrel that surfaces when the girls are there. She hits her mother, doesn't she, or—?

Welty: Or something. I think her mother hits her. But anyway, I wanted to indicate that they were passionate people. And Miss Julia was passionate too. Most of my good characters are. Virgie Rainey had it too, and Miss Eckhart saw it, that Virgie had that power to feel and project her feelings, and she wanted her to realize all of this.

Brans: Do you think Virgie does?

Welty: I think at the end of the story she is saying good-bye to the life there in Morgana. I think she's got it in her to do something else.

Brans: Remember that line about Virgie's sewing? Virgie is cutting out a plaid dress, trying to match up the rows, and Miss Katie says, "There's nothing Virgie Rainey likes like struggling against a good hard plaid." I'm thinking of the struggle in *Losing Battles* too—Jack and Gloria, who in a way have come from separate worlds. Although Gloria resists it, she's very much the child of Miss Julia Mortimer. She was brought up to be the teacher. And Jack is very much the hope and promise of the Renfro clan, and yet I felt reading the book that even though they've been apart most of the time they've been married, they've already impressed their worlds on each other. Is that what you intended?

Welty: Yes, indeed. I certainly did. That's exactly correct. And why Gloria—I think every instinct in her wants them to go and live to themselves, as they put it there.

Brans: Yes, in that little house.

Welty: It's going to be mighty hard to do. But she knows where she stands all right, and she's not intimidated at all. And Jack, of course, is just oblivious to the fact that there could be anything wrong with his staying there and having the best of both.

Brans: He wants her to love Granny. Granny is just so unlovable.

Welty: Granny doesn't want to. "She didn't say anything, she nodded. She would love you."

Brans: I thought Granny was just as mean as she could be.

Welty: Well, she's living in her own world, too.

Brans: And she wants to be a hundred instead of ninety.

Welty: She thinks she is a hundred.

Brans: But the most amazing thing is that Jack is willing to love Miss Julia Mortimer.

Welty: Yes. He's willing to.

Brans: Nobody else in his family is.

Welty: No. He is. I really love Jack.

Brans: When I asked you in the panel yesterday which of your characters you thought spoke for you, I kind of expected you to say Jack.

Welty: Oh, I was thinking about stories yesterday, I wasn't thinking about the novel. Well, Jack is really the reason I went on and made a novel out of this. Because when I first began it, it was a short story which was to end when Jack came home. The story was about why he happened to go to the pen. All that crazy story about the fight. And he was to come home and wonder why they thought anything was wrong. You know: "What's happened?" Well, as soon as he walks in the door I think, "No, I want to go on with him." I had to start all over and write a novel. Yes, he's willing to love Miss Julia. In fact, he says in there, "I love her. I feel like I love her. I've heard her story." I think that's very direct and penetrating: because he's heard her story, he knows what's happened to her.

Brans: And she has a reality for him even though he "never laid eyes on her."

Welty: And the people who have gone to school to her didn't really see her. Jack is really a good person, even though he is all the other things.

Brans: I don't see anything bad in Jack.

Welty: No, except that he allows himself to be used by everybody.

Brans: But that comes out of his goodness.

Welty: It comes out of his goodness and it's so typical also, I think, of just such situations. Haven't you known people like this? We all have. Yes, I really like Jack. He's a much better person than Gloria.

Brans: Well, she's a little have-not. Don't you see her in that way? A have-not, so that she's clutching.

Welty: An orphan.

Brans: And that's what Miss Julia represents too. But when Jack says, "I've heard her story," he's really—

Welty: They're all living on stories. They tell each other the stories of everybody. And he heard her story. They were blinded to her by having gone to school to her. They just took her as their bane. They're struggling against her. But he heard her story.

Brans: Now Virgie Rainey—she struggles against herself. Isn't Virgie essentially a wanderer, who really wants to wander, but for years she makes herself stay there in Morgana?

Welty: I guess so. I use that term rather loosely because it also means planets, and I have got a number of characters that I try to suggest can move outside this tiny little town in the Delta, though it's not a cut-and-dried kind of thing. It's not A, B, C, D. But I wanted to suggest it.

Brans: They could make it in a larger world.

Welty: Yes. That there was a larger world. Whether they could make it or be broken like Eugene MacLain is something else. They know something else is out there. It's just an awareness of the spaciousness and mystery of—really, of living, and that was just a kind of symbol of it, a disguise. I do feel that there are very mysterious things in life, and I would like just to suggest their presence—an awareness of them.

Brans: Is the sense of mystery and magic related to your use of mythology?

Welty: I think it is. Exactly, that's what it is. Because I use anything I can to suggest it.

Brans: And myths then seem to suggest something timeless?

Welty: Yes, or something . . .

Brans: Perpetually reborn or re-created?

Welty: I think so. Something perhaps bigger than ordinary life allows people to be sometimes. I find it hard to express things in any terms other than the story. I really do. Some people can, but I can't. I never think that way. I only think in terms of the story. Of this story.

Creators on Creating: Eudora Welty

Scot Haller / April 1981

From *Saturday Review*, June 1981, 42–46. © 1981 by Saturday Review Magazine Co. Reprinted by permission.

With a career encompassing nearly four dozen short stories, five novels, a Pulitzer Prize for *The Optimist's Daughter*, and 40 years of tale-telling, Eudora Welty has indeed earned the title bestowed by one critic: "the Jane Austen of the South." Whether describing mishaps at the altar *(Delta Wedding)* or mayhem at a family reunion *(Losing Battles)*, Welty fashions a delicate balance between acerbic comment and empathetic examination. As evidenced by her recent best seller, *The Collected Stories of Eudora Welty*, she is as venturesome in approach as was her mentor Katherine Anne Porter, and more forgiving of Mississippi folk than was her friend William Faulkner.

The author of such antic, ironic yarns as "Why I Live at the P.O." and "Old Mr. Marblehall" is a low-keyed, gracious, good-natured lady who could moonlight as a professional grandmother. Her Southern drawl renders even the most matter-of-fact remark melodic. Her blue eyes are enormous, as if grown large from the tireless effort of astutely observing the world around her. In this case, that world is primarily Jackson, Mississippi, where she was born, raised, and still resides—in the same family house of her girlhood.

A vigorous proponent and practitioner of the short story, Welty predicts the hell-or-high-water survival of this endangered species. "It's such a natural way for the human imagination to express itself. I can't believe a little television is going to kill that." These conversations took place during a visit to New York City, in the days just before the writer's 72nd birthday.

SR: Have you always favored the short story over the novel?

Welty: I'm quite certain that by nature I'm a short-story writer rather than a novelist. I think in terms of a single impulse, and I think of a short story as being a lyric impulse, something that begins and carries through and ends all in the same curve. Even though it may not be that in the working out. The novel, of course, from its inception is a different form of energy and direction and destination. So, if I discover by mistake what I think is a short story is really going to be a novel—which is the only way I've ever written a novel—I have to scrap the story and go back and begin again with that totally different timing.

SR: You've never consciously set out to write a novel?

Welty: No, I'm not a very good novelist. In fact, I don't really know very much about it. I have to work it out as I go. I like to write scenes and I think of a novel in scenes, which is sort of like a short story. But for a novel, the scenes have to mount and have a continuity and momentum. So that's the work.

SR: When you're working on a story and you realize that it should be a novel, that it should be *Losing Battles,* is that a good feeling or a bad feeling?

Welty: Oh, it's a sinking feeling. But I wouldn't do it if it didn't tempt me madly. *Losing Battles* is a good case because I thought it was going to be a story of 45 or 50 pages, consisting of a family at a reunion, talking about the return from the penitentiary of a father. The whole story was to be their view of what he had done, and it was to end with his bursting upon this scene asking them what was the matter. But as soon as he appeared, I just was crazy about him and I had to go on and have him in the scene. So I kept doing it. *Losing Battles* gave me such a hell of a time.

SR: When you start writing a short story, do you always know what the end will be?

Welty: Yes. I think the end is implicit in the beginning. It must be. If that isn't there in the beginning, you don't know what you're working toward. You should have a sense of a story's shape and form and its destination, all of which is like a flower inside a seed.

SR: Is revision pleasure or pain for you?

Welty: A pleasure. I do an awful lot of it. It's strange how in revision you find some little unconsidered thing which is so essential that you not only keep it in but give it preeminence when you revise. Sometimes in the dead of night, it will come to me. Well, that's what I should do, that's what I'm working toward! It was there all the time.

SR: And then do you get up in the dead of night and work, or do you wait until morning?

Welty: I usually make a note right away: "Move something." Just a word. When I get back to the story in the morning I just write.

As I go along, I usually destroy drafts of stories. Unless I realize it's going to be a novel and then I cautiously keep—overcautiously keep—everything because I'm too dumb to know whether I'm going to need it or not. But in a short story, I like to tear up as I go. I can correct better then and not have such an intimate feeling about the story. Some piece of stubbornness in the back of your mind always wants you to leave in some pet thing, but you really ought to take it out.

SR: Have you discovered any perils in revision?

Welty: There's something you don't want to lose, which is the freshness and spontaneity of the original burst forward. You don't want to lose it, even if it means for flaws of one kind or another. You can correct with gentle revision, but leave the sense of that headlong feeling of a short story. I don't really write as headlong as I would like.

SR: Does the Southern climate play any part in your writing?

Welty: I find it easier to write in the dead of summer when it's hot as blazes, and nobody stirs very much. It's much calmer and more quiet in Mississippi. I like to write in the summer. In fact, I associate it with typing and sweating, because it's hard work to type, even if you're in an air-conditioned room. I associate happiness and getting something right with hot summer.

SR: What shape does your writing routine take?

Welty: Well, I'm a morning person. The earlier I can begin, the better. I wake up knowing what I want to write—when I'm in progress with a story. So I wake up ready to go, and I try to use that morning energy and freshness. I used to keep it up practically all day; I can't do that anymore. I get tired and miss things and have to do it over.

I have a stenographer notebook, one of those things you can carry around. And I usually make notes, all kinds of notes, in this book toward a first draft. Then I type out my first draft. I like the objectivity of a clean sheet of paper. To judge if a scene or page is any good at all, I have to type it first. And then I keep working on the typewriter, but I correct all the time in pencil. It's too long and too slow to write anything in pencil when you want that first rush of feeling. And my last draft, I like to type all at once, which gives me a sense of the thing as a whole.

SR: But you only write when you feel moved to do so?

Welty: I just work whenever I have something to write. A work of fiction creates its own rules in the writing. Each story is a different challenge, a different opportunity to do something. It has a life of its own and I think you should honor that. You know, when you're writing a story, it seems to be with you at all times. You think about it all the time, whether you're working on it or not. And your ears are magnets that hear things pertinent to the story and they don't quite hear the other things.

SR: Why did you turn to writing?

Welty: Oh, I think I became a writer because I love stories. And I just decided I wanted to write some. I never had any idea that I could be a professional writer. I'm now realizing, maybe the reason I first sent stories out to magazines was that I was too shy to show them to anybody I knew. When I began to write stories, I could not have let my family or my friends see them. I thought, well, I'll send these to an abstract reader. And so I sent them out systematically to the editors of magazines, just to see what they would say. That kept it on an objective basis. And I was not surprised to receive rejection slips, and I was thrilled if there was a note that said: "Try us again."

SR: Why couldn't you show your friends and family the stories?

Welty: I was just too *shy*. I'm a shy person anyway. I still am.

SR: What intrigued you about writing then?

Welty: I'm not sure how soon I could have put any of this into words, but I think I was trying to write about the intensity of the spirit. And since I'm a visual-minded person, I think I often did it—maybe overdid it—through description. Also, I like funny things and I've always enjoyed listening to people's conversations. And it was a great discovery to find out that I could work with that. I soon realized that it was much more than just transcribing what you hear. You have to shape and form to make it function in a story. That's hard, isn't it? And I love to do it.

SR: Do you believe that the South perhaps has a monopoly on the best stories and the conversation to overhear?

Welty: Yes, I do. I don't think that there's any doubt that you grow up being aware of being amused and delighted and impressed by things that are told. And also I think—this is probably no longer true in the South or anywhere—in the days when no one moved around very much and you and everybody else in town lived in the same place for a long time, you followed the generations. You had a wonderful sense of the continuity of life. And I think that's terribly important. It gives you a narrative sense without knowing it. Cause and effect. And the surprises of life and the unpredictability of life. I do think that's important. It has been to me.

SR: You've spent most of your life in the same house in Mississippi. You don't believe then that a writer must go and seek out experiences for inspiration, as did Hemingway and his crowd?

Welty: No, it's always at hand. I've always had the feeling that—whatever people's experiences are—their emotions are universal. And so you can put yourself in any imagined character's shoes or lay your story anywhere and you're still writing in the common language. It doesn't too much matter where you are. To me. It's funny because the critics did say that everything that I wrote was laid in the South and it was bad to be so parochial. Then when I wrote a book of stories laid in Europe, written from the point of view of a traveler [*The Bride of the Innisfallen and Other Stories*], the critics complained: "She should stick to where she knows best."

SR: Flannery O'Connor once suggested that anyone who has survived childhood knows enough about life to write for the rest of his days.

Welty: I'm sure that's true. Especially in Flannery's case. I don't live such an eventful life on the outside, and it wouldn't translate very well into an exciting narrative. It's all on the inside. I have a good imagination. I can imagine a lot better than I can remember.

SR: Since you work only when you feel compelled, how do you spend the rest of your time?

Welty: Well, there's a lot of things to do at home. I'm interested in the stage. We have a group there and I have a family there and I love to read, of course. Every night and a lot of the time in the daytime, I read for pleasure.

In fact, the only advice I give young writers is something that is alarmingly new to some of them; that is to read. It never occurs to them. I say, "If you love to write, how can you miss what has been written? How can you do without that great pleasure and wonder of what other people have written?"

I know one of the things that has influenced me is my childhood reading of myths and fairy tales. I had these books at home, and I just read them as soon as I learned to read, you know, and loved them. I suppose they answer the same need, really, that lyrical impulse.

I was crazy about all the bloody Grimm ones, like the Goose Girl and all those things about the seven brothers going out and one being changed into a swan. They're perfect short stories, worn down through the centuries by air and smoothed over to perfection.

SR: Are you conscious of myths and fairy tales in your short stories?

Welty: Yes. I wrote one book that does draw freely on myths—all kinds of myths, Greek, Norwegian, anything—just because I feel they do permeate life and endure in our imagination. So, I drew on that, without having to think, really. It was not an artificial kind of thing. I've suffered a bit from people finding one-to-one symbolism in it.

SR: Which book was that?

Welty: It was called *The Golden Apples* and the golden apples themselves are in many myths, not just one. I used them in several different senses. That was fun to write, but in those days it never occurred to me that people would seize on these things and press to explain why I did this and that. You know, maybe I would have thought twice. I would have gone on writing it, but I might not have been so free.

SR: Do you read reviews of your work nowadays?

Welty: When a book comes out, I'm very anxious to know if people like it. I do read the reviews. What I don't too often read are critical articles about old work of mine. Many are valuable to me but some are perturbing, and some of them I don't even get a handle on.

SR: Since you also write criticism, can you tell us how a critic can be helpful to a writer?

Welty: I don't think I really am a critic. I like to respond to a work and to do so with a full heart, but I'm not a *learned* person and don't know the histories of things. I could not write a critical evaluation of anything. I just review the things that I respond to. I'm a reviewer, if anything; I'm not a critic.

SR: You clearly derive more pleasure from the act of writing than do a good many authors.

Welty: I love writing! I love it.

SR: Is there anything about the experience of writing you don't like?

Welty: Just the sheer drudgery. I never used to mind all the typing I did. But now I resent the time it takes from really writing. All that typing has nothing to do with the act of writing. It's just your being your own secretary. But I really enjoy everything, even proofreading.

SR: Was there ever a time when writing wasn't a pleasure?

Welty: Oh, I've often found it difficult, but I think the difficulties are pleasures. You know, I really like something hard to do in the way of words. That's part of the pleasure. In fact, I wouldn't be very interested in writing a story that didn't pose something that had to be solved.

SR: Which among your stories are your favorites?

Welty: I think the ones that were the hardest to do. I love a story I wrote. I realized it when I was reading the proofs on *The Collected Stories,* at which time I read them all through for the first time in years. I liked the one called . . . it's the one about the three figures meeting in the woods, about Lorenzo Dow, John James Audubon, and Murrell the Bandit, back in 1798. I'll think of the title in a minute. "A Still Moment." "A Still Moment" I think is the name of it. I imagined them meeting in the wilderness, because they all were in that part of the world at that time, three visions of life that meet. It was a complicated story and was entirely imaginary, but those people were all alive at one time. And it gave me a great deal of pleasure to write it. It's not my usual story.

SR: What did it feel like to read your collected stories?

Welty: It was extraordinary because, as I say, I'm not in the habit of reading my own work. So I was surprised a lot of times. I had forgotten until I reached each story. It was just like going on a train into a landscape that you're familiar with. You forget what's ahead and then as you see it, everything unfolds. It was a very strange feeling—almost like another person and yet terribly much like yourself.

SR: Have you been surprised to find your book on the best-seller list?

Welty: I'm absolutely astonished! I've never had this kind of thing happen. I'm really very thrilled about it. I'd be a fool if I weren't. I can't imagine how it happened. Sometimes the books have done well for a few weeks. But, you know, I'm not one of the *sellers*. I make a respectable living, but I have to do many things to guarantee that. That's the reason I do college visits and book reviews. I like it that way.

SR: Can you tell us about your work-in-progress?

Welty: I'd rather not. I have a superstition that you can talk it away.

SR: Is it a novel?

Welty: Well, I *hope* not. It's a great big envelope full of stuff that looks as if it might be a novel. But I don't want it to be. I don't think it deserves to be. I'm going to see if I can't shape it back the way I thought it was going. When I get home, I'm going to whack at it.

Eudora Welty

John Griffin Jones / 13 May 1981

From *Mississippi Writers Talking*, I (Jackson: University Press of Mississippi, 1982), 3–35. © 1982 by the University Press of Mississippi. Reprinted by permission.

We met at her home on a warm afternoon in mid-May. She still air-conditions only a few rooms in her house, so we kept an oscillating fan running at our feet as we talked. Scattered about the table surfaces in her living room was a variety of new books by some of her favorite female writers: *The Stories of Elizabeth Spencer, The Collected Stories of Elizabeth Bowen*, the former with a foreword by Miss Welty, an older copy of Virginia Woolf's *To the Lighthouse*, and, stacked in the corner of a work table behind me, a few copies of *The Collected Stories of Eudora Welty*. It seemed the right company for her. I hope the interview shows that at times she grew excited over the things we were discussing, assaulting the subject with wide-eyed interest, all the while swearing she didn't make any sense when she talked.

Welty: I once did a whole interview in New York for the *Paris Review*.

Jones: Sure. I read that.

Welty: Well, yes, but what happened was that none of it took. When the lady got home there was nothing.

Jones: I've done that.

Welty: And we had to do it again. That was awful, because she asked me the same questions and nothing was fresh anymore. I can answer spontaneously a lot better than I can if I think ahead. She asked me the same things.

Jones: Oh, no. You must have been good the first time.

Welty: Oh, it just wasn't very good.

Jones: It was.

Welty: A lot of it had to be written, you know. That's the hardest part about doing an interview because it turns out you have to write it too. I do. Now, this, though, is for oral records. It's done for . . .

316

Jones: For the state. I needed to explain this to you. As you did with Charlotte in the early '70s, you will see a copy of the transcript of our talk before we put it in the collection.

Welty: That's what's going to be hard. I swear I don't make any sense.

Jones: You do.

Welty: Charlotte and I, neither one of us made any sense on that one.

Jones: I like them. I read through all of them.

Welty: They really were silly.

Jones: No, they were fun to read because you all get along, and your conversation shows that.

Welty: Oh, yes. We thought it was a lot of fun.

Jones: Yes, ma'am. Let me say a few things. This is John Jones with the Mississippi Department of Archives and History. I'm on 1119 Pinehurst Street in Jackson, Mississippi, about to interview Miss Eudora Welty. This is my first time to interview Miss Welty, it's about the fifth or sixth tape you've done with the Department of Archives and History, and it's about the 170th time you've been interviewed. I didn't want to repeat any of the information that Charlotte was able to get from you. I just wanted to ask you some general questions about your career, your writing, your art.

Welty: Anything you want to. I haven't got a very good memory about dates, but that's all right.

Jones: Fine.

Welty: We can check up on that later.

Jones: Yes, because you will be getting a transcript of this later.

Welty: Oh, yes.

Jones: Let me ask you this first: In talking with these Mississippi writers as I've done it's interesting to find out when they first got the impulse to sit down and write; when the creative impulse first took control of their lives. Do you remember when that happened to you?

Welty: No, I don't. I couldn't put my finger on it. I think in my case I almost couldn't notice the transition between loving to read and loving to write, because I've always been a reader. I love stories. Actually I can't remember when I felt, "Now I'm going to write something." It seemed to be sort of a natural overflow. Maybe I always wanted to write. How do I know? But I had no revelation that that was what I wanted to do. I'm glad, because I would have been rather startled if I had taken it too—if I had felt a responsibility or something of "being a writer." I'm glad it didn't happen too soon. It would have stopped me.

Jones: Yes, that's a point I've heard made before. It seems like it would be intensely intimidating for a young person who, after reading the best of American literature, might think that that's what they wanted to do with their life.

Welty: Yes.

Jones: So it's really a gradual process?

Welty: I think so. What always remained with me was the love of the story, whether I was reading or writing it. I didn't have any self-consciousness about the writing, which I think I would have if I'd felt a stern command to go and write. I don't know that anyone does have that. It was so natural for me to want to do it. In fact, at one point Katherine Anne Porter, who was always kind and helpful to me from the beginning when my stories first appeared in *Southern Review,* had invited me to Yaddo, a colony up in New York State near Saratoga, where artists of various kinds had studios to themselves and were given privacy and time to work and so on. It was just everything you dream of as a writer. But at that time I didn't dream of it because I seemed to write in connection with everything else I did too. When I was put into this silent studio with a sign on the door saying "Silence. Writer at Work," I was so self-conscious I could not write anything. I think that's the way I would've felt if I felt I'd had a calling to do it. It was much better to just take it as part of life. I never have felt a divorce between my life and work, except the act itself, of course, which is something done in solitude and with much thinking. But I never have felt cut off by my work. I never have felt isolated and the things people always say, you know, like, "Isn't it a very lonely life?" I think I must have been very blessed that I didn't have a feeling of self-consciousness, of being picked out to be a writer.

Jones: So what did make you sit down to write that first story?

Welty: "Death of a Traveling Salesman"?

Jones: Yes, ma'am.

Welty: I know why I wrote that story. This was in the Depression. A friend of our family traveled for the Mississippi Highway Department. He went into the remote parts of Mississippi, and bought up property for the right-of-way for them. He went into the most far-flung places. When he came back one day he said he'd been up there somewhere, and he told a tale. It had nothing to do with "Death of a Traveling Salesman," but he quoted this man saying they didn't have any fire and he had to go to Mr. Somebody's house and "borry some fire." Well, those words just hit me. They were electrical. You could just see a whole situation from that. It was just so far back in time, and so remote. It made me think of something very far away and elementary about life; elemental, whichever it is. So I wrote that story then, you know, just from hearing that remark. I was working toward "I had to go borry some fire," and the story sort of grew from that. I think all my stories have grown from something in life and not from other sources like a book, no literary sources. They never remain in a story as themselves. They are transformed and made into something else, but they come out of real life.

Jones: Yes. And from "Death of a Traveling Salesman" through *The Optimist's Daughter* certainly your place has not changed, but your theme is something it seems to me you've been developing from the start.

Welty: I'm glad you think so. I think I must have. I'm sure I have.

Jones: I wanted to ask if early you saw a void that you could fill through your writing from the very first.

Welty: I don't quite know what you mean by "a void."

Jones: That there was a void in Mississippi literature even, and . . .

Welty: Oh, no. I don't think about anything else, other people, me, when I am writing; just the story. I don't have those feelings of ambition, either. There's no time to because you're thinking about the work. Of course I love to do things well, and when I feel like I've done something as well as I can I am pleased about it. But at the time I'm working I don't know whether it's good or bad. I just want to do the best I can for that story. Each story is like a new challenge or a new adventure, and I don't find help anywhere, or look for it any-where, except inside.

Jones: So there was never a long-range plan to develop these stories toward something, some theme?

Welty: Oh, no. I think that would've paralyzed me too. No, the thing at hand is the one. I see now how that refers to that question you asked me, but I didn't have an overall idea about working toward something. I think such things evolve of themselves out of the work. It sort of teaches you as you go. You learn what you're writing about, in one sense, through the work. Of course you know what you want to do, your destination and your direction in a story, but you also learn a whole lot of things about that destination and direction through the work. That's why you like it.

Jones: I know you have said that your WPA experience planted in you the germ that grew into your becoming a writer. I know your father was from Ohio and was president of Lamar Life Insurance Company. Your mother was from West Virginia. Your father being a banker/businessman, what did he think of the New Deal and Franklin Roosevelt, and your work with the WPA?

Welty: Oh, poor man, he died before then. He died in 1931, shortly after the bank failures and everything.

Jones: Oh, that's right.

Welty: So he never knew any of that. He was not always a businessman. He was born on a farm in Ohio. He was a country school teacher. He lived in the country and came from country people. When he decided to marry my mother, another schoolteacher, they decided to make a new life for themselves in a different part of the world, and they selected Jackson. He came down here and got a job with what later turned out to be the Lamar Life. It was, you know, a lowly job—bookkeeper, I think. Would he have been about your age? I think so. He just worked his way up. He always stayed with that company. He loved it. He was a businessman. But he was for me being a writer, but he said, wisely, that I needed to be able to support myself some other way, because you can hardly sell stories and earn a living that way. I'd never thought about that one way or the other. It was, of course, true. So that's what I did.

Jones: Good advice.

Welty: It was good advice. But he never knew that I became a writer and I don't know what he would've thought about what I did.

Jones: I know in reading the criticism of your work much ado is made of the fact that your mother and father weren't from the Deep South, but I've never heard you comment on it. I was wondering if the fact that they were from the North and upper South made your perceptions of southern life that much more acute.

Welty: It could have been, but you see, although my mother came from West Virginia, was born there, she was from Virginia stock on both sides. She considered herself a Southerner of the first water. I think something to do with the Civil War and anti-slavery was why they moved to West Virginia. They set their slaves free—at least on one side; I don't know about the other—and went to West Virginia where there was no slavery. They were Methodist preachers, the men; one was a Baptist preacher. They went over there out of a sense of bringing up their family in West Virginia. My mother was a Southerner and a Democrat. My father was a Yankee and a Republican. They were very different in everything. At that time there weren't very many Republicans in Mississippi. I was very worried about that. I think there were maybe two in Jackson that I knew of.

Jones: Hiding.

Welty: I don't know. So my parents used to have good political discussions at the table all the time. It was interesting to grow up learning there were two sides to everything. It made you think.

Jones: That's interesting. So your mother was indeed a Southerner, and you had that kind of heritage too.

Welty: Yes.

Jones: "Death of a Traveling Salesman" came out in 1936.

Welty: Yes.

Jones: Even then in Mississippi there was an established literary tradition. I was wondering if that meant anything to you when you began writing? Had you at that time read Mr. Faulkner and other Mississippi writers?

Welty: I hadn't read Faulkner then for the reason that you almost couldn't find any books of his. I tried to. They weren't in the library. You know, he was almost out of print until Malcolm Cowley brought out the *Portable*. I used to buy his books second hand in New Orleans and places, and I read them as I could find them. But I didn't connect myself to any kind of tradition or to any other writer. It never occurred to me that my work—I didn't know what it would be— would be taken seriously enough to "place." I was just reading his books because I loved to read them, and not that I could emulate— indeed I never did emulate. Of course as time went on, Faulkner became much more accessible and much more widely appreciated in his home state, which took some doing.

Jones: Which occurred after Stockholm, in the '50s?

Welty: Yes, but he got back in print before that. That's when Fred Sullens on the *Jackson Daily News* used to lash out at him. I believe he once included me in the "Garbage Can School of Literature." I don't recall why. He could never have read anything. But he thought we all could be lumped together. He put a whole bunch in there. Faulkner had that to contend with. He got to be well known, but not accepted by any means.

Jones: Did you meet and talk with him ever? Do you remember your first meeting with him?

Welty: Yes, I surely do. I went to Oxford with a friend who'd gone to Ole Miss, and I stayed with an old friend of his, Miss Ella Somerville. You probably know who she is.

Jones: Yes. Charlotte and I have talked about her.

Welty: Yes. She was a marvelous lady, and a contemporary and friend of Faulkner's. She gave a small dinner party, and they were invited along with Bob Farley and all these other friends of Faulkner's. So I met him under those wonderful auspices of Miss Ella's home at her table when the conversation was among all old friends and I was the new person. So that was the most natural way to meet anyone. I never got to know him well.

Jones: What year was that first meeting?

Welty: I don't know. I believe it was in the '40s. But William Faulkner and I never had a conversation about writing, of course. He did invite me to come out to the house, and I did. We had a nice time, told tales. He never brought up writing, and you know I wouldn't have done it. But we never had any kind of literary—no ties between us at all. But one time, William Faulkner, when he was in Hollywood, wrote me a letter, and I misplaced it, couldn't find it high or low. I looked for it over many years. Well, I've just found out what happened to it. I had sent it—bragging!—to a friend in Oxford to read—one of the group who knew William Faulkner—not Miss Ella. There it remained forgotten among her letters until last year when one of her relations found it, the letter from Faulkner, and put it with the letter that it was enclosed in, and sold it to the University of Virginia for what they say was a horrendous sum. I heard about it from the University of Virginia. They wrote and said, "You'll be interested to know that we have this letter." I wrote back and said, "So that's where it is! Doesn't it belong to me?" They said, "Unfortunately, it belongs to the Commonwealth of Virginia." I thought that was awful, and I wrote her an indignant letter. It wasn't her fault, but I just didn't think that should be true. I said, "Would you at least send me a Xerox copy so I can read it again?" She did. But don't you think that's funny?

Jones: Yes, I sure do.

Welty: See, I'd just published my little book *The Robber Bridegroom,* and he said he thought it was good, and "Is there anything I can do for you in Hollywood?" Wasn't that wonderful?

Jones: Yes.

Welty: And I couldn't find it! That was the nearest we ever came to talking about anybody's work, his or mine.

Jones: What do you think he meant by "Is there anything I can do for you?"

Welty: I think in Hollywood, probably. Wouldn't you? He said "I will be here until . . ." whatever it was.

Jones: Yes. We'll leave Mr. Faulkner for a minute. The other great literary strain in Mississippi at that time came from the Percy family in Greenville. I don't know if you were aware of this, but I've done a number of interviews with people who knew Will Percy.

Welty: Oh, how wonderful. I'd love to hear them.

Jones: It's a fascinating family.

Welty: Absolutely! I agree with you, from the ones I know now.

Jones: Yes, ma'am. And I know you said in your address at the inaugural ceremonies for the governor that at one time in your memory Greenville was a town of 20,000 people, and had seventeen published authors.

Welty: Those figures may not be exactly accurate.

Jones: They're close. I was wondering if you ever got to know Will Percy.

Welty: No. In those days I don't think young people went anywhere and met someone the way they do now, the way that students do. I wish I could've met him, but I never did. I read him. In the mid '40s I did get to know Hodding Carter, that is young Hodding's father, and Ben Wasson, and all those people who did know him, and Shelby Foote. All of them did know Mr. Will Percy. David Cohn. He seemed a very real presence to me, a bulwark up there. But it is a marvelous family. What a good thing you've done.

Jones: It's been fun.

Welty: I'm sure.

Jones: But there's something remarkable about the fact that in that small place there could've been Walker Percy, Shelby Foote, Ellen Douglas . . .

Welty: Yes, I met her too at the same time. That was before she began to write, I think.

Jones: Yes. Early in your career, who influenced you among the female writers across America? Were there any great influences?

Welty: I don't know, John. I never can put my finger on these things for sure. Of course I was influenced. I love to read, and I adore what I read. You know that it's worked on me, but not in any specific way I can think of, not in any immediate ways when I work. I can just do some detective work after the fact. I must have learned this or that from this or that person, but not consciously.

Jones: No big book that changed your life?

Welty: I suppose Chekhov would come closest to it, and also Katherine Mansfield, and Virginia Woolf. Of course, those people are not Americans. Willa Cather, did, but I was kind of slow finding her. I wish I had had the sense to read her sooner. One time I just sat down and read it all through. That's what I love to do: from start to finish. Let me think. Fairy tales and myths in my childhood reading had a profound effect on me. That was not always indirect; sometimes it was direct. In those stories called *The Golden Apples* I just made free with them—and *The Robber Bridegroom*. And the Bible, because I love to read the Old Testament. The Old Testament has the best stories. The King James Version stays with you forever, rings and rings in your ears. Oh, *Don Quixote*. That feeling of discovery you get with such a novel is the most marvelous thing. A door has been opened. I've just now been trying to write about Virginia Woolf's novel *To the Lighthouse*. Harcourt Brace is getting out a new edition of three of her novels, and they're having a living woman writer to write a little foreword for each; just sort of what it means to you. So I'm doing the one that meant the most to me which was *To the Lighthouse*. I've been trying to describe that feeling you get when you come upon something. I came upon it absolutely cold and it just knocked me out. I've read it lots of times since, but I read it again in order to write this piece, and it did the same thing. So I know, even though I couldn't show in my work, heavens, the sense of what she has done certainly influenced me as an artist. Mark Twain and Ring Lardner I loved. I read them when I was growing up.

Jones: That's a good list.

Welty: I suppose it must show how varied a writer's loves can be, and what a great circumference the reading covers.

Jones: Yes.

Welty: I've had people say to me, "Do you ever read anyone else's work?" That has always just amazed me. People would ask me down at the library, "What are *you* doing at the library? Are you interested in other peoples' work?" I just think that's amazing!

Jones: When you published *A Curtain of Green* in 1941 the critics, reviewers, said, "Here's the spontaneous work of a born writer." Two questions about that: Is writing for you spontaneous? And, of course, is there such a thing as a born writer?

Welty: Who knows about the born writer? I couldn't answer that. It would be terrible if you were either a born writer or not, and that it all depended on that. It would be kind of like, "Are you saved?"

Jones: Elected. Right.

Welty: I don't know about that, but as far as spontaneous goes I can answer that exactly. That first book of stories really was spontaneous. They were almost never revised. They would've been the better for it. It never occurred to me. I thought you sat down and wrote a story sort of the way you read—you know, you just sit down and write it. That was how they were left. They did have a certain quality of the spontaneous that, I suppose, I have lost over the years because I now know there are dozens of ways you can do everything, especially since the longer you write the more possibilities occur to you. As long as you are writing a story, its possibilities are endless. So, I don't know. I think they have gained, I hope they have gained something by being carefully revised. I do a lot of editing. They might have lost some of the spontaneity. I still write the first draft spontaneously. I hope I have enough sense, I don't always, to keep the true thing in there; the one that hits it on the head; that's really it. I hope I have enough sense to know it and not tamper with it. It may not be perfect, but it has got something that shouldn't be altered.

Jones: Following *A Curtain of Green* came *The Robber Bridegroom* the very next year, then *The Wide Net,* and then *Delta Wedding* in, I believe, '46.

Welty: I think so. I wrote it during World War II, so it must have come out soon after that.

Jones: That was my question. That was a period of incredible output for you, during the war.

Welty: That's not exactly as it seems, because it took me so long to get published. When I got out *A Curtain of Green* I already had most of the stories in *The Wide Net* on the way, anyway. I'd been trying for quite a long time to get them published. So, although they all came out just about the same time, I'd been sending them around for years. I caught up with myself with *The Wide Net.* I think I could have published *The Wide Net* almost at once after *A Curtain of Green,* but the publishers were hoping I'd write something long in between. *The Robber Bridegroom* is really just a little tale. It was the publication that made it seem like a short novel, not the writer. I did write fast and quite a lot.

Jones: It's such an achievement! Do you remember when your period of greatest productivity was? Was it following *A Curtain of Green,* during the war?

Welty: I don't know. That's when I was doing *Delta Wedding.* Also, most of these times I had a job too and I was working on nonfiction bits and pieces and things like that. I think the time when I went through the most intense, sustained writing was when I did the collection called *The Golden Apples.* These stories were revealing themselves as interrelated. I wasn't quite sure in what way. That came a little later to me. Halfway through I realized the big connection there, the deep connections. But I was writing without stop, going from one story to the other, a sustained burst. It was writing something as long as a novel but as stories. Also I was very happy writing that book. I loved working on those stories. I love that period.

Jones: Yes. That's my personal favorite.

Welty: Is it really?

Jones: Yes, *The Golden Apples.*

Welty: Oh, I'm glad.

Jones: Yes, ma'am. It may be the best thing I've ever read. Honestly.

Welty: I'm terribly glad you like that. I don't find many people are familiar with it.

Jones: There's not a better story than "June Recital" anywhere.

Welty: Oh, thank you.

Jones: We'll talk about *The Golden Apples* some more in a minute. Also during the Second World War you were writing first as Eudora Welty and then, under the pseudonym Michael Ravenna, reviews of front line World War II action . . .

Welty: I wrote some reviews and signed them that, but they weren't front line war things. That was a mischievous figment of imagination on the part of Nash Burger of Jackson, Mississippi. I think they were mostly about art the soldiers drew in the war and things like that. It was because I was working on the *New York Times Book Review* at that time, and they didn't like the staff to sign reviews because we were supposed to get other people to do the reviews. When we couldn't we would do them and sign them.

Jones: I don't think that detracts from my point, which is—I hope you don't take any offense at this . . .

Welty: No, of course not.

Jones: But here you were, a lady from Jackson, Mississippi; obviously there wasn't a whole lot about war that you knew about firsthand. And in your early stories, in a story like "Powerhouse," how a woman from Jackson, Mississippi, a white woman, could have known and put down on paper the life and words of a musician, and a black musician at that, like Powerhouse, is an amazing achievement in anyone's eyes. Can you tell me something, maybe by illustrating the story "Powerhouse," that could hint at the answer?

Welty: Well, I can tell you as well as anyone could about "Powerhouse." I know exactly how that came about. I loved the music of Fats Waller and had all his records. He played here in Jackson at a program sort of like the one, well, just like the one I described. I went and watched him, and I was just captivated by his presence, in addition to the music, which I already knew and was familiar with. As you know, I'm not a musician like your father [Howard Jones].

Jones: But you knew the lingo, and the lingo of a black musician.

Welty: Oh, I was listening to them. I was one of those people who were just hanging around listening. Of course, what I was trying to do was to express something about the music in the story. I wanted to express what I thought of as improvisation, which I was watching them do, by making him improvise this crazy story, which I just made up as I went. Nothing like that, of course, happened. I didn't hear anything like that. But I made it up to illustrate the feeling I got a sense of among the musicians; how they talked to each other. There was this sort of inner core of musicians, and this outer core. I have no idea what they did at intermission. Everything I wrote is made up except the program itself and the impression it made on me, both hearing and seeing it. I had no idea I was going to write anything when I went to that. I would've thought, rightly, "You don't know anything." It's true, I didn't. But I was so excited by the evening that I wrote it, after I got home. And the next day when I woke up I said, "How could I have had the nerve to do something like that?" But I did have the sense to know that there was no use in me trying to correct or revise or anything. It was that or nothing, because it had to be written at that moment, or not at all. I could not have gone back over it and tried to shape it or do something constructive like that. You know, I just left it. But that was a one time thing. I couldn't write another story like "Powerhouse." I don't see how I wrote that one. It was just the music, that's what did it. But that's valid!

Jones: Yes'm.

Welty: I don't see why not.

Jones: Also, as people all over the world have pointed out, you knew and got down the language of everyone who speaks through your stories. In that vein I was wondering if you could tell me to what extent your experience was translated in the stories and to what extent your fiction is written to make up for what your experience lacks, what is missing in your experience? I guess another way to ask it, and this is maybe highfalutin, but does life give literature meaning for the artist, or does literature give your life meaning? You understand what I'm asking?

Welty: Up until the last I thought I did. Does life give literature meaning or does literature give life meaning. Is there a choice? It's such an intimate relationship. I don't really separate them. The life blood of one is in the other. I don't know. Your question began with the way people talk. It's one of the things that has always absorbed me because I love to listen to people talk. Cut that off and let me get some water.

Jones: I've choked you. I'm sorry.

Welty: No. I'll be back.

Jones: Yes, ma'am.

(Break)

Jones: Let me reiterate that question.

Welty: Okay.

Jones: I was asking to what extent does your fiction come out of your life's experiences, and to what extent is your fiction written to sort of make up for the missed experiences in life?

Welty: I can answer that. You can't write about any feeling or emotion that you've not experienced. But I don't like to write auto-biographically. What I like to do is invent the characters, situation, action that dramatizes it, which will act out my emotions. I know how these invented people feel, or I couldn't write it; but I give them other, comparable reasons to feel that way. I don't think you could even begin to make up grief, or love, or something. I'm always alert to anything going on in life that gives me a clue or gives me a starting point on a dramatic situation, that would let this emotion unfold in a way that I can handle it on paper. When some clue comes along you realize it. Maybe it's a news item in the paper or an overheard re-mark, or the experience of someone that you know about. And then all of this accumulation of your own experience of feeling finds a way to be communicated in a better way than your own life does it, more dramatically, anyway. So to simplify it, that's what my own writing process is. There's no way of knowing what others' is. So I often write about some things it would seem to you I wouldn't know about, but I know about them deeply in my own experience, of my own perceiving, or I would not want to write about them. Well, I've never murdered anybody. I have murders in my stories. But I can certainly feel and understand anger. And so on.

Jones: That's a wonderful answer.

Welty: To show you my reservations about not writing about what I don't know: I wrote one book of stories all laid in Europe, but I had to write every one of them from the point of view of the traveler or the outsider.

Jones: *The Bride of the Innisfallen.*

Welty: I don't know how Italians or Irish—I don't know enough. All I know is the overheard, the observed. I don't know firsthand. The point of entry is what you're looking for, then you can go ahead. All the rest is simply general human nature in which we all share.

Jones: I believe you call it the point in which people reveal themselves.

Welty: Well, in this sense I just mean the point you can get in. When I wrote that novel *Delta Wedding*—I don't know much about the Delta, which I probably don't need to tell you. So I made my person a little girl nine years old.

Jones: Sure. Laura.

Welty: She knew just about what I knew. In that way I could venture as far as I liked. I could tell my story, but I wasn't telling it as an old hand at the Delta. I didn't know it, except how to get there from here.

Jones: In this sense, let me ask you something about your use of humor. Walker Percy said that there is something in the modern consciousness so that there is communication from writer to reader which is greatly facilitated by humor.

Welty: Yes. That's interesting.

Jones: In your work, especially as seen in "Petrified Man," "Why I Live at the P.O." and *The Ponder Heart,* humor is used extensively. Even though you have ridiculous events and characters in many ways, you never tell it ridiculously. I was wondering if you could talk about your use of humor, its function in your work.

Welty: I don't know. I think it's one of the hardest subjects in the world to speak about. Don't you? In a way it may be a way of entry, too, through humor. It's a way to try, risk something, a way to get around something to make it endurable, to live with it or to shrug it off. And then it's inherent in a whole lot of living, I think. I think it's just there. It's there! If you can show it and make it a process of revealing, that would be its justification; not for its own sake but to show something. People show an awful lot of things through humor, both conscious and unconscious. Don't you think so?

Jones: Yes, ma'am.

Welty: I think it can also take form as something Southern. We've always appreciated humor and humorous things. We've also contributed to the humorous.

Jones: Certainly you have. Is it a different frame of mind that you're in when you sit down to write something like "Why I Live at the P. O.?"

Welty: Those are early stories. I don't know why I wrote them except to show how people talked. I love to write dialogue but it's very hard to prune it and make it sharp and make it advance the plot and reveal the characters—both characters—the one listening and the one talking. You can use it to do all kinds of things. I like to do it because it's hard, I guess. I really like it. I laugh when I write those things.

Jones: I loved *The Ponder Heart,* and I was interested to see that Miss Capers played Edna Earle in the production . . .

Welty: At the Little Theatre, yes.

Jones: I asked her about it but she didn't feel like talking about it very much.

Welty: She was very funny; she was Charlotte, of course, and it worked out really well. It was the earliest production I had seen, except for the original one on Broadway.

Jones: *The Golden Apples* came out in 1949. I read it for the first time in preparation for this interview and found it to be my favorite of what you've written. It was so good and complete I couldn't think of a good question to ask you about it other than to just ask you to comment on it a bit more, and maybe tell me something about the idea behind it and what interested you about the golden apples myth?

Welty: Well, you know, now I think I'd think twice before I threw around myths and everything so freely. I'm glad I did then because I just used them as freely as I would the salt and pepper. They were part of my life, like poetry, and I would take something from Yeats here and something from a myth there. I had no *system* about it. But people write papers on these things and they just make things up. I got one in the mail last night.

Jones: A dissertation?

Welty: It's the beginning of one. Somebody out in California has written it. You don't want to hear about that. What those people do is not treat your work as fiction; in fact they don't seem to know the difference between fiction and anthropology and mythology . . .

Jones: Sociology.

Welty: They are making your work fit in with their scheme—*their* myth. "Well, if Virgie was . . ." I forget who Virgie was supposed to be, ". . . and the boy Loch is really Perseus, then Easter is, or should have been, the Medusa." Well, equivalents like that are all apart from my intention. I used them in the way I think life does. Life recalls them. These likenesses occur to you when you are living your life. They are plucked out of here and there because they seem to apply. I wanted to show mainly in that collection something about illusion in our lives—I made a little town where everybody was living in a sort of dream world, and I called it Morgana.

Jones: Sure.

Welty: The name is sort of like the Fata Morgana, or sea mirage, but it worked in with the Delta, where people often named a town after a family and just added an a: Morgan-a. It seemed right. Everybody was sort of trapped in their own dream world there, or were apprehensive of leaving, of getting outside of it; all but Virgie who really was and is a courageous and fine person.

Jones: Talented.

Welty: I love Virgie.

Jones: I do too.

Welty: I did not realize until I'd written half of these stories that all these people really did live in Morgana. So I was just showing different phases of it, different aspects. They were all under the same compulsion. I realized that the stories were connected. It was a marvelous moment with me when I realized that a story I'd written really was about a character from an earlier story. My subconscious mind, I guess, had been working on the same lines all the time. Everything slid into place like a jigsaw puzzle. It all worked out. I loved it because I felt that I could get deeper into all the people through using a number of stories and different times in their lives than I could hope to do using one story.

Jones: Did "Music from Spain" come in the same creative burst?

Welty: Yes. It came in last. I wanted to show somebody from Morgana who'd gone outside the local circle; and yet he was no better outside than he would've been inside. It was such a strange story. I wrote it, as you can tell, in San Francisco. It's kind of a love letter to San Francisco on the side. But I never knew for certain if I should include that with the other stories or not. What did you think? Did you feel it was dragged in?

Jones: No'm, I didn't. I wanted to find out what happened to the other brother of Miss Snowdie's two twins.

Welty: Well, I think I had been wondering too as I went along, and then when I was in San Francisco I thought, "Here he is."

Jones: "I found him!"

Welty: Yes.

Jones: I knew that it had been in the Levee Press edition.

Welty: They printed it before *The Golden Apples* came out. It was already part of the book.

Jones: You did not write it expressly for the Levee Press?

Welty: No. It was just something I had that had not been printed.

Jones: Right. What about Virgie Rainey? Your eyes seemed to light up when you talked about her. Is she one of your favorites? Is she somewhat closer to your own condition?

Welty: No, I don't think so. I suppose vaguely we would connect somewhere, like the feeling of independence, and of wanting to do something about your life for yourself. But I gave her a musical talent about which I know nothing. Certainly I had a music teacher who rapped me with a fly swatter, but I didn't know too much about music. I heard it all the time because Belhaven at that time had open windows, and all those pieces in there came straight across the street from Belhaven. I just put them in my story. I wanted to give her the outlet of some art. I felt that need about myself, and I felt that independence. But that's such generalities. I guess I felt a part of everybody in the book, every one of them. You have to if you're going to be a writer.

Jones: The Big Black River.

Welty: Yes, the Big Black, Vicksburg.

Jones: What about the dangers at that time of creating another mythical county in Mississippi? Were you intimidated by the county to the north?

Welty: Oh, no, because mine's just on no scale. It was just something that served. Faulkner created an entire world; all the history of Mississippi and the Indians and everything. Mine was just an appropriate location I wanted to mean something for that set of stories.

Jones: You weren't scared of the inevitable comparison?

Welty: It never occurred to me. There isn't any comparison. You know. Every writer has to create his stage, the set. The setting is fundamental to a story.

Jones: Yes. Let me ask you something that may be a little too general but I think is to the point in terms of your work. From Virgie to Laurel McKelva, there seems to be something you are saying about the importance and significance of memory, of holding on to memory. Walker Percy calls it living in some authentic relation to the chief events of one's life. This seems so important for the characters in your work.

Welty: Yes.

Jones: I was reading an interesting review of a children's book by a man named Maurice Sendak.

Welty: Oh, yes, I've got it. I've got that book!

Jones: I haven't read the book, or seen it.

Welty: I'll show it to you.

Jones: In the review Sendak is quoted as saying that writing this book has made him a happy man, has put him in touch with a memory that he had but wasn't aware of, which released for him all kinds of possibilities.

Welty: Yes, yes.

Jones: Do you think that there is in a person's memory something that can make him happy?

Welty: Oh, yes. I certainly do. To me memory is terribly important, a source and a force, too. If you've ever tried to go back and recall *all* of something—you may not be old enough yet—but you do realize that there're things back there you had no idea were still there. The more you try to remember, the more comes up. It's like Thomas Mann said in *Joseph and His Brethren,* the past is a well. It's wonderful to think of, that it's all there, all your experience, down deep in your memory. Writing does the same thing, it brings your past to the surface. I don't often put really straight autobiographical things in my work, but when I wrote *The Optimist's Daughter,* all that part about West Virginia was true. That all came back to me when I started thinking about it. I had remembered it in general, but not as much as came back. The fact of learning what it is you remember is instructive. How do you store this up? Why? I think any writer has more to thank memory for than most anything. I don't mean writing about the past. What you remember can apply just as well to something you are writing today. You learned it through something in your memory, but you use it for anything that you might wish. You might be writing about the future. I hadn't realized—I know what you are thinking about now: that last story in *The Golden Apples,* where Virgie is remembering everything.

Jones: Yes.

Welty: I realized that myself when I was doing proofreading. I'd forgotten what I did at the end of that book, you know, in precise detail. I remember what I was trying to do, but not what I had done. I hadn't connected that with Laurel McKelva, but there certainly is a connection.

Jones: Oh, yes.

Welty: I'm grateful to you for thinking of it. I never do connect any book with any other book, and when someone is able to point out a connection I'm fascinated. It's something else that your mind has done that you're not aware of. One may have led to the other. Virgie and Laurel were such different people, backgrounds and everything, but they were doing the same thing. I'm glad you told me that.

Jones: And Laurel finds the breadboard her dead husband made for her mother, and in releasing the breadboard, by letting it stay in the house with Fay, she is making a commitment through memory to her future, she is able to live on without being drowned by memory.

Welty: Yes, yes.

Jones: That's one of the most fascinating things in your work to me.

Welty: Well, it fascinates me in itself, the process of memory. Also, it seems to have its own timers, and it comes to you at very strange times. You know, you can wake up in the morning and it will present you with something; the way it used to work your math problems. You wake up the next morning and it would be worked. Your memory puts that together too, even though it doesn't know any math.

Jones: And with characters like Wanda Fay McKelva, and Bonnie Dee Peacock in *The Ponder Heart* people who live without memory, is that their greatest affliction? I don't even know how to ask that.

Welty: I think you ask it well, and I agree. I think it is one of their greatest afflictions. If they had memory it would've taught them something about the present. They have nothing to draw on. They don't understand their own experience. And they would have to understand it in order to have it in their memory. Their memory hasn't received it because it hasn't meant anything. That is putting it in blatant words. It certainly isn't simple like that.

Jones: Also one of the things you are indicting in your work is noncommunication between people. I remember one of the interesting things you said about Tennessee Williams's characters was that they never break through the "sound barrier of communication." Is non-communication the real enemy in human understanding in our modern world?

Welty: I suppose so. That is at least the effect. I don't know the cause of it. It might be different. The *effect* might be non-communication. I was thinking about the plays of Chekhov. You know, the characters sit around, and none of them are really talking to one another, they are just talking like this; yet they possibly love each other, they feel their private emotions. They don't really talk to each other, and Chekhov uses that dramatically to show the human predicament. It does. It does show it.

Jones: Like the ladies talking in the back yard of the McKelva house in *The Optimist's Daughter* denigrating Fay, and Laurel won't listen to them and goes back in the house.

Welty: Yes.

Jones: Yes. That's interesting. Creating as you have this world of characters—I hope this isn't too personal to ask you—this vast world of totally alive people, have they taken the place of anything so that you don't need as many personal connections in your own life?

Welty: No, no, they couldn't do that. They came from me. I mean, my feelings of affection and admiration and all that couldn't go to somebody I've made up.

Jones: Sure. I hadn't thought of it that way.

Welty: You know what I mean. No, they don't take the place of real human beings. I love my characters, but as characters. They don't live in this house. They're real to me, but they're in my mind, not in the world. I like people in the world.

Jones: Yes, ma'am. I don't have too many more questions. I appreciate your patience. I've also done an oral history of the civil rights movement in Mississippi.

Welty: Oh, yes.

Jones: I've talked with a number of people, black and white, involved in those times. You have an interesting quote in your essay "Must the Novelist Crusade?" which I thought answered most all questions I might ask you in this area. But you do say, "Entering the hearts and minds of our own people is no harder now than it ever was, I suppose." You wrote this in '65. "Entering the hearts and minds of our own people . . ." which is, as you say, what the novelist is trying to do, "is no harder now than it ever was, I suppose." I heard William Styron speaking at a literary symposium at Millsaps with Willie Morris and Governor Winter, and he said people are no more fragmented now than they've ever been. One thing I did want to ask you is has this great turnabout that happened in Mississippi in the 1960s, this new direction in terms of race relations which occurred, has this changed the hearts and minds of the people?

Welty: That's a thoughtful question. I think I was mistaken in what you read about it being no harder than it ever was. I was sincere as far as I knew, but I didn't know enough. It was harder. I think more effort had to be made, and that it was made, you know, as time went on. We had to learn to do it. I was thinking of the people whose hearts were in the right place, but that wasn't enough. It took more learning. I think we've been through an experience which was more profound than we'd guessed; both black and white. Now we are both more open in a way that—well, I had not experienced it because it had never happened. Now, seeing how much more there was to communication than the wish, and the desire, and the heart, I feel I have more to learn now than I had to learn then.

Jones: Yes. In talking about the effect of the civil rights movement, here's an argument or a point I'm sure you've heard made 100 times: That one of the factors which contributed to the fact that there were so many writers from Mississippi was the treatment of the black man, that sense of guilt.

Welty: Yes.

Jones: Now that that's removed—certainly it is for my generation—is that going to have an effect on Mississippi being a spawning ground for writers?

Welty: Well, I think all writers have to reflect their own times, you know, whatever they are. Everything changes in time. No writer could write about today in the same way that he might have written back in the '50s, or the '60s, or in ways the '70s, because everything is different. I don't mean that he would change his sensibilities or his understanding. That remains the constant, his openness to what he's trying to write about. The subject itself would be very different. The problem is not the same now. The writer would be the same, I think. I don't know if he would have an identity as "a writer of Mississippi." I don't see why not. But whatever it is, he's got to write about life as he knows it, or else it won't be worth doing, and he won't be fulfilling his role, or obligation, as an artist. You've got to write about what you see. Whatever comes next, you've got to handle it. Do you agree?

Jones: Yes, ma'am. I do. I suppose the crux of the question was is there something basic, deep-down, that has changed in the Mississippi character that you see?

Welty: I feel at least for now, I don't know how long it will last, that the Southerner, the Mississippian, has got a character that does stem from his sense of place and of the significance of history and so on. That hasn't changed. I don't mean he's living in the past. I'm not talking about that. It's just a sense of continuity that has always characterized us, I think; a knowledge of family stories, that sense of generations and continuity. That gives us an identity. I think that's still there. I don't think there would be any point in trying to eradicate that.

Jones: I've saved a couple of hard ones for the end. In your great essay "Place in Fiction" you say in talking about the novelist and his duty that "the measure of this representation of life corresponds most tellingly with the novel's life expectancy." Do you remember that in its context?

Welty: Yes.

Jones: "Whenever its world of outside appearance grows dim and false to the eye, the novel has expired." Do you think that the outside world has grown dim in any of your work?

Welty: I hope not, but it's not for me to say about my own work—that would probably always remain clear to me. I still hold with that idea: this was a remark the essay made about the writer's craft. I was referring to the *novel's* outside world, the world of appearances, in which the fiction takes place—not the actual outside world. The novel's outside world, if well enough created, does live on, when you look at the world of Jane Austen, Flaubert, Turgenev, Tolstoy, Proust! They're indelible. *War and Peace* is not only real to today's reader, it will outlast him too.

Jones: What about this argument I've heard expressed: "The world that Miss Welty is writing about in her work up through *Losing Battles* is dead for the most part; at least it's dead as an inspiration for novelists." Do you think that's accurate? I don't think it's fair.

Welty: Meaning the society is dead?

Jones: Yes, and even the interpersonal relationships.

Welty: Oh, no, I don't agree with that. I can't agree with that. The last things that will ever change are personal relationships. Society changes, of course, but human beings never have. I've heard people say that there's no such thing anymore as the family unit—well, I don't agree there either. We know it's still strong in the South. That's just rooted in our character, for the time being anyway. I think those things persist. Physical aspects could change in the society, but not the human qualities—belonging to Southerners and everybody.

Jones: You have also said that you think writers write on the same subject all their lives. Do you still think that that's true?

Welty: I don't know how specifically I meant that. I suspect I meant it in the most general sense. For instance, personal relationships will probably always be my subject, no matter how circumstances alter. That is what interests me and instructs me.

Jones: One final one: From the mid '60s when Frank Hains identified you as Mississippi's foremost literary figure and Jackson's most illustrious citizen until this minute you've been praised and received the kind of total adulation that very few heroes, much less artists, receive in their lifetime. I don't mean to embarrass you. Is that too strong?

Welty: I'm so overwhelmed and thrilled by all of this. It's much more, of course, than I ever deserve. Mississippi has been so good to me. In fact, elsewhere too. I have been truly lucky all my life, not only in my family and my friends but the people who turned out to be my editors and agents and almost everyone I've ever been connected with professionally. Somehow it has come my way that they have been just the very best and the most sympathetic. It's incredible.

Jones: It's because you're worthy and you've earned it.

Welty: No, I do work hard, and I like to do a good job, but you could do that all your life and nobody might ever bat an eye. You know that's true. It takes a lot of luck and I don't know what combinations of luck for something like that, a book's success, to happen. I know the chances. I'm grateful. It has helped me so much in all my work to think that at the other end there are people who are interested. That has meant so much to me, to have editors understand what I'm doing. There have been plenty of writers who've never had anything like that happen.

Jones: You tend to be a little bit better than most.

Welty: You can't tell. You can't tell. I still have a feeling—my agent Diarmuid Russell used to say when he was having such a hard time selling my stories, he said, "I believe anything that is a piece of good work is going to surface. It won't go forever unpublished." He said he'd believed that all his life. Well, of course that gave me courage. It may be true. I don't know. I hope so!

Jones: What has the creative life that you've led—has it cost you anything, in personal terms?

Welty: Well, I suppose so. It has given me more than it has cost me. Well, of course I work very hard. I don't count that as a cost. I love writing. I don't count that as a minus, I count that as a plus. But what has cost me is buying the time to work in by other means, you know, like lecturing or writing assignments and book reviews and so on. That's something I'm doing instead of fiction. I sometimes think I will never see the end, you know, that I can never stop. I've been working for the last couple of years to buy some time. Now for the present I don't need to because my book has made some money, but I didn't know it was going to. You know. Earning a living is a very big question mark when you are a writer. You don't know how, when, where, or if. It's just part of it, and you try to allow for it by doing things that are cash down on the barrelhead. And that has cost me in work of a different kind, travel and wear and tear. I like young people, and we get along, or seem to. I enjoy it, but it drains me. I don't always have enough energy left over to do my writing. But that's not a complaint. I'm just trying to answer your question. My writing life has given me so very much more than it cost.

Jones: It is not equal to what you've given us. I say that seriously.

Welty: I really love to work, to write, and when—it's my own fault—I don't manage the privacy or that time, it upsets me. I get so behind. I mean, look at that table. Every table in my house is like that. This one was just like that until just before you came. I thought you were going to put your thing up here. My conscience hurts me, you know, guilt, unanswered mail. But I'm going to deal with it. I have to.

Jones: Today one of the staff members at the Archives was taking a group of high school seniors around the building, and she took them up onto the mezzanine and showed them the Chinese translation of *A Curtain of Green* and said, "Here's a book written by Eudora Welty in Chinese," and one of the girls piped up and said, "I didn't know Miss Welty could write in Chinese!"

Welty: That's what I feel when I see them. I feel so proud. To think I could do that!

Jones: Write in all those languages.

Welty: I know it. That's wonderful.

Jones: Well. Let me tell you how much I appreciate your doing this.

Welty: No, I enjoyed it. I'm glad we got to talk.

Jones: Yes, ma'am, I am too.

Welty: I must say I thought all your questions were thoughtful and serious and sympathetic.

Jones: I'm just glad I got the opportunity to meet you and talk with you.

Eudora Welty's South Disdains Air Conditioning

Raad Cawthon / 1982

From *The Clarion-Ledger Jackson Daily News* [Jackson, MS], 12 Sept. 1982, sec. E, 1. © 1982 by The Clarion-Ledger Jackson Daily News. Reprinted by permission.

Eudora Welty's house has a feel about it of an earlier time.

The source of that easy feel is difficult to place. Maybe the gentle light brings it in as it filters into the large rooms through open, wide windows. Or perhaps it wafts in on the un-air conditioned breeze, cool for September, which stirs the draperies.

The breeze has the mild chill of those first days, between the dog days and Indian summer, when you know the season is changing and another year is dying. It is a time of year Miss Welty loves.

"I love to be in touch with the seasons," she says, gazing at the oak which shades her front windows. "People simply cannot understand that I don't air condition, but this is so lovely. The other day between the time I was fixing to go to the Jitney and the time I left I counted six pairs of robins on the lawn. I said to myself, 'The season is changing.' "

Eudora Welty, the 73-year-old literary treasure of the state of Mississippi, is about as Southern as you can get. Her fiction, heavily flavored with Southern scenes and personalities, has brought her every major literary award this country can offer, including a Pulitzer Prize. The people who fill her numerous short stories and five novels populate a portrait of the South as accurate and indelible as any since William Faulkner's.

And Eudora Welty's voice is as Southern as the Delta is flat. It's bright, pleasant and precise. It sounds like pear honey tastes.

Born on North Congress Street in Jackson on April 13, 1909, Miss Welty was raised here. Her father, a business executive with Lamar Life Insurance Co., chose Jackson to move to from Ohio. Her mother, a West Virginia native, was a teacher.

The house where she was born still stands. It is the pretty two-story

one on the west of Congress Street which was recently renovated as
an architect's office.

During her childhood Miss Welty's father, the son of a farmer, decided to move to the country. He chose a lot across from Belhaven
College and built a sturdy burgher's house of stucco and brick. Miss
Welty, who has never married, still lives there, working at a desk in
front of her upstairs bedroom windows, shopping at a nearby grocery, supporting the local arts scene, puttering in her yard and always
writing.

"My friends are very protective of me," she says.

At other times Miss Welty has termed herself "locally underfoot."

The house is large and comfortable but still modest. Easy chairs
dot the living room and books, mostly English novels right now, are
stacked on a table beside one of them. A large portrait of Miss Welty,
dressed in yellow, is framed on an easel in the dining room door. The
overall atmosphere is of genteel ease.

Ever since they began taking notice of her, critics have written
about Miss Welty's remarkable "ear," her uncanny ability to put onto
paper the way people actually speak. It is a gift which few writers
have. And Miss Welty's virtuosity with it is matched by only one
other, the late Flannery O'Connor.

"When I was young, maybe 4 or 5 years old, my family would go
driving on Sunday afternoon. My mother told me I used to get up in
the backseat and sit between her and one of her friends. I would get
myself all fixed and then say, 'OK, start talking.' I suppose I learned a
lot about dialogue that way."

Miss Welty looks out the windows and smiles. Her white hair is cut
short and curls around the top of her ears. With blue eyes and an
animated smile she has in person a look which is softer, more at ease
than any photograph of her I have ever seen. Indeed, she does not
like cameras and is uncomfortable in front of one.

But in conversation Miss Welty relaxes. Her eyes sparkle. Caught
up on a thought, she sits deep in her chair and drapes a long arm
above her head. Even though her fame reaches far beyond the parochial confines of Mississippi it is obvious Miss Welty has given much
thought to the literary richness of the South where she and so many
writers took root.

"I was very fortunate to grow up here. I think anyone who grew up in the South was fortunate, particularly writers. In the South the story is an integral part of life. Stories are just told. You get a sense of narrative.

"One of the most marvelous things is hearing all these stories and getting a sense of family and continuity. It is the world of memory. Through all these stories everything that happens can be kept and repeated and maybe understood later on.

"Because of all that I feel I am a link in a chain. Somehow I am a part of all this, more than an individual."

The first two years of Miss Welty's college life were spent at the Mississippi State College for Women in Columbus. She went there from the sheltered life of a small-town Jackson and discovered diversity unlike any she had known before.

"When I went to MSCW there were a lot of girls there, four to a room. It was crowded. I remember it was my first exposure to people from across the state. The different voices! There was the difference in the way the people from the hill country spoke and those from the Delta.

"I loved it. I used to sit up at night and just listen to the voices coming down the hall. I would try to see if I could tell what part of the state the girls were from by their different voices."

It was a key link in her education as a writer.

Miss Welty took the memory of those voices with her when she left Mississippi for the University of Wisconsin and on to study business at Columbia University in New York.

After her schooling, where she learned to type "so I could be a secretary and make a living," she came back to Jackson. The Great Depression had a strangle hold on the South. About the same time Miss Welty's father died and she took a job as a photographer with the Works Progress Administration. Her project was Mississippi and she traveled it from end to end, taking pictures of its people and listening to their stories.

It was a short course in her native state.

"It showed me another side of the state and of life that I hadn't seen. I think it was good for me."

Her first book of short stories, *A Curtain of Green,* was finished shortly after her job as a WPA photographer ran out.

"I have always written. I love the story. I love to write.

"I've written everywhere, on trains and in motels. All I ask for to write is privacy. And sometimes the only way to get privacy is to leave home."

"As a matter of fact I have found the anonymity of a motel to be a good place to write."

The richness of her imagination and her sure knowledge of place takes precedence over monotonous motel decor.

So, almost wherever she is, Miss Welty spends the early morning hours writing. "The earlier the better," she says. "I have always had more ideas than I could write. I wake up now ready to go."

It is a great gift to a writer to have the love of language, the memory, and the stamina Eudora Welty obviously has. But the gifts were honed for years before she saw her work published. For anyone it must have been a time of frustration, but she never faltered.

"No, it didn't surprise me that I became a writer.

"Perhaps, if I had been more aware of how difficult it can be, I would have been more self conscious. And if I had been self conscious, I could have given up. You know, I published in some little magazine for the first six years I was writing but I didn't get any money for it.

"The editors in the big magazines were always encouraging. They would write me back and say 'We like your story but we don't think it's right for us at this time.'"

She pauses and laughs.

"Well, I guess everybody who has ever gotten a rejection slip knows what they say."

Her rejection slips could have filled a well. Perhaps it is indicative of her heart that Miss Welty, instead of dwelling on the rejection, thought of the "nice things" the editors said and kept writing.

Now she is acknowledged as one of the finest writers of our time. Magazines solicit her work and the *New York Times* asks her to review books. Her short stories have been collected and some of her novels staged as plays or opera.

And all the time she keeps working.

"I guess I am superstitious about my work. It doesn't exist in any way until it's finished. A work of fiction is a whole, it's not a piece of knitting. I never show anyone what I've done until it's finished. Never. Never. Never. If I did it would cease to be mine."

Miss Welty looks at the floor and shakes her head. It is as if she is reciting a personal, irrevocable commandment.

"The moment I mail a story away when no one has ever read it is the time when I feel the best. When I put it in the mail I'm elated. But by that night or within the next few hours I am in complete despair. I suppose part of that is being physically tired. Then, when I hear from my agent or editor and they like it I find that the story has changed its character."

She pauses.

"It's as if it's gone down the mail slot at the post office and you can't reach your arm down and get it.

"At that time it ceases to be yours anymore."

She stares across the coffee table with her bright blue eyes. Then, with a wave of her hand, Miss Welty sweeps the vision away.

"I guess that I am just a terribly emotional writer," she says.

"Whenever I get the galley proofs on anything I think, 'Oh, this is horrible. This can't have been done by me, there are too many mistakes.'

"But as I've gotten older I've learned to trust myself. I've learned to think that I've done the best I can. I know now that if I had it back again I would just ruin it.

"What I try to do is communicate from the writer's imagination to the reader's imagination. I don't write for anyone special . . . I write for the sake of the story. The story is everything. I am just the instrument."

There is a sudden stop to the conversation.

"Oh, my goodness!" Miss Welty says. She puts her right palm over her heart. "Don't write that. That sounds so self-righteous. It sounds like *I am* the instrument."

As she makes the statement Miss Welty twirls the index finger on her left hand toward the ceiling and laughs.

"I don't mean it that way at all."

What Miss Welty means is that she tells us about ourselves by refining and distilling the minute elements of our nature. Her writing does not chronicle our temporal history but instead records our mores and our many voices. Her writing is art of the highest order in that it helps us understand who we are.

Miss Welty's concern is not with the ticking of earthbound clocks but with the murmurs of the human heart.

And nowhere did she find so much to distill as in the worldof Central Mississippi.

"I'm glad I grew up in Jackson when it was small and managable. It's good for a writer to have a world where you know it all, where everything is accessible by foot or bicycle. I don't think we are like that anymore.

"I invent my characters from other people or from combining a number of people. My characters come from human beings. You can't invent emotions but you can have characters carry them out in a dramatic way."

As we talk we walk outside. As Miss Welty walks toward her side yard she laments the harsh toll the heat has taken on her camellias and azaleas. Running across the front of the house the porch turns and ends in a side porch open to the elements. She stops in its shade.

"I screened this porch with the first money I ever got from a magazine story. $42 and some cents. But (hurricane) Camille got the screen and I couldn't afford to have it replaced. They wanted something like $400 to rescreen it so I just had the old screen carried away."

The mid-day sun is bright and beginning to slant westward. Shadows are growing longer. The talk turns to current best-sellers and how some writers produce books in the same efficient, calculated way McDonald's produces hamburgers.

Miss Welty tells of reading a profile in a national magazine concerning a popular female author who sleeps in false eyelashes so she won't have to apply them before going on camera at early-morning talk shows.

"Can you imagine that?" she says. "It's frightening. I would do the worst sort of manual labor before I would live like that."

You can almost see her cringe. It is difficult to imagine Miss Welty even owning false eyelashes. She stops and shakes her head.

"When I read that I thought, 'Is this what writing is all about, sleeping in false eyelashes?'"

No, Miss Welty, we both know it's not. Besides, it would be a shame to hide those baby blues.

Index